Truth Works

Questions and Answers for Reviving Your Divine Existence

Volume One

Truth Works

Questions and Answers for

Reviving Your Divine Existence

Volume One

Sankarshan Das Adhikari

Radha Damodar Productions,
a division of
Sri Sri Radha Damodar Temple, Inc.

Austin, TX, USA

radha.damodar.productions@gmail.com
www.radhadamodar.com
10700 Jonwood Way Austin, TX 78753 USA

Ordering Information:
Quantity sales. Special discounts are available on quantity purchases by corporations, associations, and others. For details, contact the publisher at the address above.
For orders by U.S. trade bookstores and wholesalers, please contact Radha Damodar Productions above.

Published in Austin, TX, United States of America
Library of Congress Control Number: 2012909445

Publisher's Cataloging-in-Publication data

Adhikari, Sankarshan Das.
Truth works: questions and answers for reviving your divine existence, volume one / Sankarshan Das Adhikari.
p. cm.
ISBN 9780615645780
Series : Truth works : questions and answers for reviving your divine existence.
Includes bibliographical references and index.

1. Self-realization. 2. Self-actualization (Psychology). 3. Spirituality. 4. Spiritual life. 5. International Society for Krishna Consciousness. 6. Spiritual life --International Society for Krishna Consciousness. 7. Yoga. 8. Meditation.
I. Series. II. Title.
BL1285.892.A28 A34 2013
294.5/43 --dc23 2012909445

Printed by Sure Print and Design, Canada

Dedication

I beg to offer my respectful obeisances at the lotus feet of my most beloved spiritual master, His Divine Grace A.C. Bhaktivedanta Swami Prabhupada, who has so kindly delivered me from all suffering by revealing to me the topmost science of Krishna consciousness, patiently teaching me the techniques of how I can always remain in a state of pure Krishna consciousness in all times, places, and circumstances. To him I dedicate *Truth Works*, which is my humble attempt to serve his mission.

Next I beg to offer my respectful obeisances to that great swanlike devotee, His Holiness Vishnujana Swami, who so wonderfully convinced me by his amazing example, kindness, and instructions to accept Srila Prabhupada as my spiritual master.

My sincerest gratitude is offered to my beloved wife, Her Grace Srimati Vishnupriya devi dasi, who has for the better part of three decades faithfully and untiringly assisted me in my practice of Krishna consciousness and in the execution of the mission given by Srila Prabhupada to make the entire world Krishna conscious.

In the production of *Truth Works* my special thanks are due to many sincere souls. Ultimately, of course, it is Lord Sri Krishna to whom all thanks must be given because it is by His inconceivable potency that we all exist and can relish the sweet transcendental bliss of serving Him.

Acknowledgements

The author and publishers acknowledge and gratefully thank the efforts and contributions of the following individuals who were instrumental in the production of this book:

Questions:	Students of the Ultimate Self Realization Course worldwide
Initial Compilation:	Bhavani Devi Dasi (Vancouver, Canada)
	Raghunatha Das (Vancouver, Canada)
Editing & Index Compilation:	Jagannatha Das (Columbus, Ohio, USA)
Editing & Pre-Press Proofreading:	Labangalatika Devi Dasi (Durbuy, Belgium)
Photos:	Vishnupriya Devi Dasi (Austin, Texas, USA)
BBT Images:	Copyright Bhaktivedanta Book Trust International Used with permission.
Layout Design & Artwork:	Devadeva Das Adhikari (Mendoza, Argentina)
Layout Design & Artwork:	Govinda Damodara Das (Mendoza, Argentina)
Cover Illustration and Design:	Manish Thorat (Toronto, Canada)
Production Manager:	Mahabhagavat Das (Toronto, Canada)
Logo Design:	Deepak Khurana & Shyama Priya Devi Dasi (New Delhi, India)
Major Donors:	
	Rantideva Das (Memphis, Tennessee, USA)
	Padasevana Das (Pretoria, South Africa)
	Bhaktarupa Das (Chennai, India)
	Sanil Kumar TV (India / Saudi Arabia)
	Nandadulal Das (Melbourne, Australia)
	Indira Devi Dasi (Melbourne, Australia)
	Krishna Das (Melbourne, Australia)
	Balarama Das (Melbourne, Australia)
	Ankit & Bhumija Bhatt (Melbourne, Australia)

Contents

What Is Kṛṣṇa Consciousness? – Beginning Spiritual Life 1

Transmigration of the Soul – Reincarnation – Law of Karma 12

Living in the Material World 23

One Religion – World Religions – Universal Harmony 41

Nature of the Soul – Our Eternal Constitutional

Position - Kṛṣṇa, the Ultimate Lover – Free Will 64

Brahman, Paramātmā, Bhagavān – Different

Features - Different Levels of Realization 81

Demigods, Incarnations and Avatāras 89

The Cause of All Causes – The Origin of All : Kṛṣṇa

The Absolute Truth 98

The Bona Fide Spiritual Master – Instruction of Guru –

Guru Parampara / Disciplic Succession – Initiation – Transparent

Via Medium 110

Chanting the Hare Kṛṣṇa Mantra 134

Offering Food to Kṛṣṇa - Prasādam 150

Bhakti Yoga – Devotional Service – Dovetailing - Real Renunciation .. 160

Favorable Practice - Regulative Principles – Sadhana – Association of

Devotees 175

Self-Realization and a Job – Householder Life 193

Interacting with Non-Devotees 202

Surrendering to Kṛṣṇa – Transcending Karma - Cultivating Faith – Attaining a Higher Taste – Kṛṣṇa's Causeless Mercy 209
Going Back to Godhead – Attaining Perfection – Pure Devotion 223
Kṛṣṇa – The Form of Kṛṣṇa – Descriptions of the Spiritual World 228
Kṛṣṇa's Pastimes – The Spiritual Platform – Eternal Relationships 240
Dispelling Myths – Misconceptions – The Vedic Version 247
ISKCON –Śrīla Prabhupāda's Books & Mission – Spreading Kṛṣṇa Consciousness 263
About the Author 278
Know Who You Are, Be Who You Are 279
Bibliography 280
Index of Verses Quoted 281
Keyword Index 283
Guide to Sanskrit Pronunciation 314

Author's Foreword

There is absolutely no reason for anybody to ever be in anxiety again. Anxiety is an unnatural psychological condition for the living being. The only reason that anybody is ever in anxiety is due the ignorance of the science of the self, known in Sanskrit as atma-tattva. This science is not based on mental speculation or imaginative ecstasy. It is instead based on the pure, unadulterated nature of the self in his or her relationship with the Supreme Self, who is known by different names such as Krishna, Allah, Jehovah, etc. in the world's various revealed scriptures. That relationship is based on pure selfless love, free from even the slightest tinge of selfishness.

After many years of tortuous struggle in the 1960s, in the days of my youth, trying to discover the purpose of my existence and freedom from all miseries, I finally found a spiritual master of the transcendental science of the self, His Divine Grace A.C. Bhaktivedanta Swami Prabhupada, who fully revealed to all me all of the secrets of this ultimate science, which he presented as Krishna consciousness. I was indeed most fortunate to recognize this unparalleled opportunity, and thus I took full advantage of this great master's unfathomed kindness by opening my mind and heart fully to his amazingly profound, all-inclusive teachings. He patiently and lovingly guided me in how to fully reconnect myself in a loving relationship with Krishna, the Supreme Personality of Godhead, and instructed me to make the knowledge of this ultimate self-realization science fully available to the entire human society. In 2003, in pursuance of his desire, I went online with Ultimate Self-Realization Course, which has now attracted over 16,000 members in over 100 countries. My students are every day writing me many questions regarding how to awaken their dormant, enlightened consciousness and become perfect in this science.

This book series, *Truth Works*, is a collection of the most important and relevant questions along with their answers. It is an ongoing work. You have in your hands Volume One, which covers the years 2003 through 2007. If you will kindly take full advantage of the knowledge and the techniques revealed in this humble attempt to alleviate the sufferings of the human population, I assure you that you will discover all the secrets of how to live an amazing life full of bliss, enlightened with perfect knowledge, and overflowing with unlimited love for the Supreme and for all beings. You will experience a lifestyle which will propel you into an eternal ecstatic existence in an intimate loving relationship with the Supreme Self in the Transcendental Sky far, far beyond our present place of residence here in the realm of birth, death, old age, and disease.

Om Tat Sat
Sankarshan Das Adhikari
Written on 16 June 2012 at the ISKCON temple in Melbourne, Australia

Foreword

By Hari-sauri dasa

It is with great pleasure that we greet the publication of *Truth Works : Questions and Answers for Reviving Your Divine Existence.*

In the early days of ISKCON there was a publication called "A Handbook of Krishna Consciousness." It was a very useful introduction into the basic philosophy and practices of the emerging Krishna consciousness movement that succinctly gave the newcomer a valuable grounding into spiritual life. As more and more of Srila Prabhupada's books were gradually published, the Handbook was dropped, and personally I always thought that doing so left something of a lacuna. Sriman Sankarshan das Adhikari has now filled that gap by providing what is virtually a more extensive, updated and greatly expanded version of the handbook, and anyone contemplating taking up a spiritual way of life is certain to benefit greatly from it.

Sankarshan prabhu is a veteran practitioner of Krishna bhakti with over four decades of dedicated service to our beloved Founder-Acarya Srila Prabhupada. His sincere commitment to spreading the glories of Sri Caitanya Mahaprabhu is widely recognized. His enthusiasm to preach, coupled with his intelligent use of the internet and his extensive travels, has gained him an appreciative audience worldwide. His sage advice, dispensed in thousands of emails over many years and gathered here in an easy-to-read and well indexed format, is given weight by his strict personal adherence to the principles and sadhana of Krishna consciousness. He is indeed a man who practices what he preaches, and therefore his presentation is not merely words; he has deep realization that affects the hearts of his readers and illuminates their consciousness. It is therefore no surprise that he has inspired thousands of souls globally to take advantage of the philosophy of *Bhagavad-gita* and *Srimad-Bhagavatam* and make their human lives successful.

This book is a significant and natural product of a life well lived, and a life lived for the welfare of others. In producing this book Sankarshan prabhu is fulfilling one of Srila Prabhupada's most important instructions – that every one of his disciples should write and thus increase the storehouse of wisdom for the immediate and future betterment of mankind.

I encourage the reader to dive deeply into the contents of this book, for by so doing one's life will automatically be enriched.

Om Tat Sat
Hari-sauri dasa
25 March 2012

Introduction

Congratulations. You now have *Truth Works, Volume One* in your hands. Just in case you are wondering how this book came into existence, here's how it happened:

Back in September of 1965, as a freshman at Austin College in Sherman, Texas USA, I was quite perplexed to know the meaning of life. None of my professors, textbooks, dorm buddies, songwriting heroes, or extracurricular readings could give me a satisfactory answer. My parents, my minister, my best friend - all of my mentors had failed me. No one around me even seemed to think it was a question worth asking, what to speak of finding out the answer. Everyone was content to go for material success. From a material point of view I was doing fine. My grades, my academic marks, were high enough to earn me a place on the Austin College Dean's List for academically advanced students. But there was a void in my heart because I didn't know who I am and what the purpose of my existence is. After two years of liberal arts studies, my academic advisor told me that now I had to choose a major field of study for earning my degree. But in my condition, choosing a major did not make any sense. I was thinking: "How can I choose a major when I don't even know the purpose of my existence? Without this knowledge choosing a major is irrelevant. Why should I work so hard to make good grades, to get a good degree, to get a good job, to get a good car, a good house, a good wife, some good kids, and a good retirement - simply to get a good velvet-lined coffin for being buried six feet under the ground and to get some good flowers on my grave once a year until people forget about me? There's got to be more to life than this! It just couldn't be this bleak!" I just had to find the existential answers. I would never be happy until I did.

Finally, after years of excruciating struggle, my quest for ultimate knowledge paid off. I discovered a teacher, a spiritual master, who was able to spell out everything in a profoundly crystal-clear manner. That teacher was His Divine Grace A.C. Bhaktivedanta Swami Prabhupada, who accepted me as his duly initiated disciple on the 12th of August 1971.

From Srila Prabhupada I learned how to logically dissect existence itself and see what is there on the inside. He taught me the most powerful and potent meditation techniques available anywhere in the universe - techniques that give one the ability to become free from mortality and to enter into an eternal, blissful state of full knowledge, love, and deathlessness in the personal association of the Supreme Lord Himself. I was finally blessed with the understanding of who I am and what the purpose of my existence is. I was excited and enlivened to affirm that I am the eternal servant of the Supreme Lord, who has unlimited names and is described in India's ancient Vedic scriptures as Krishna, the Supreme Personality of Godhead. Seeing around me a world population in such a suffering condition, I naturally wanted to do something to try to relieve the anxiety that has swallowed practically the entire human race. And my spiritual master, Srila Prabhupada, ordered that this should be done. The entire world must be delivered from suffering. Therefore I fully dedicated my life to this purpose.

After thirty-two years of teaching this supreme knowledge - through television and radio appearances, lectures, university courses, and one-on-one consultations - I got the inspiration to launch the Ultimate Self-Realization Course (www.backtohome.com) in order to give the whole world immediate access to this knowledge. Quickly my course attracted thousands of enrollees from over 100 different countries around the globe. One feature of the course is called "Thought for the Day." Every day I send out an email broadcast to my worldwide subscribers, which includes a carefully and lovingly composed meditation as well as a sample of a question and answer from my correspondence. This daily question-and-answer has proved to be the most popular feature of my course. Selections from this never-ending stream of questions and answers are what make up this volume.

The title *Truth Works* states profoundly and succinctly that factual truth is that which delivers you from all suffering, while untruth keeps you entangled perpetually in suffering. So you can test for yourself whether this is true or not. Apply these teachings in your life seriously according to our instructions, and you will in fact achieve, in due course, a state of perfect spiritual enlightenment. It is not that I am giving you my teachings. I am simply passing on to you – purely, without addition or subtraction - what I have received from my spiritual master in an unbroken chain of disciplic succession going back to God Himself, Lord Sri Krishna, the Supreme Personality of Godhead. This knowledge is just as potent, powerful, and practical now as it was back in the ancient times when there was an ideal, paradisial earth society based on these sublime truths. May Lord Krishna bless you with all success as you try to understand and implement these teachings.

Sankarshan Das Adhikari
15 December 2012
Written en route from Mauritius to South Africa

What is Kṛṣṇa Consciousness? – Beginning Spiritual Life

What Should I Do?

What should I do?

Fully Surrender Yourself to Kṛṣṇa

I appreciate very much the sincerity of your question. You have asked the most important question that can be asked in the human form of life.

There is one Supreme Being, of Whom we are all children. The one duty we have in our lives is to fully surrender ourselves unto Him. Surrender means we should eternally and selflessly serve Him for all of eternity. Selflessly means without any thought for anything in return. All we should desire is the privilege to continue serving Him for all of eternity.

That one Supreme Being is known by different names according to the different scriptures, names such as Allah, Christ, Jehovah, Buddha, or Kṛṣṇa. In spite of His different names, He is the same Supreme Person. Of all the revealed scriptures of the world, the *Bhagavad-gītā* gives the most advanced understanding of how to surrender ourselves to God. Therefore, my first instruction to you is that you should carefully study *Bhagavad-gītā As It Is* by His Divine Grace A.C. Bhaktivedanta Swami Prabhupāda. Once you have completed your study you may consult me for your next instruction. *Bhagavad-gītā As It Is* is the world's most authoritative and popular edition of the *Bhagavad-gītā*.

Ryan's Wonderful Query for the True Source

My search has ultimately led me to you and to the study of the timeless wisdom that is Kṛṣṇa consciousness. Words fail to explain the emotion and passion I feel inside. For years now I have had an increasing sense of purpose but have not known where it was leading. I knew it was big. But as I learned more about ancient mythology and the similarities between belief systems the world over, I realized there was and is only one truth and one source to the story of man and all. It all makes so much sense.

I know my life must be gradually peeled away from this painful place of nonsense and assimilated into purity. Nothing else to me quite matters but this process. Yet I find myself in this world of dross and noise and perpetual sorrow. No one I know fully understands the extent of my need to pursue the truth. I speak and feel alienated; I do and am misunderstood. I need to be among those who know. I know I need to be taught, but haven't a clue where to go. I am skeptical due to commerciality and need to know that what I am learning is coming from a truly untainted source.

I believe that literature can do only so much; thereafter the presence of one who is spiritually advanced is required to raise the conscience further. Hence, my dream of finding a Master to serve and learning as much from him as possible. Thus my question: Where do I go?

Essence of All Vedic Knowledge Revealed

I am very happy that Kṛṣṇa has sent me such a sincere soul as you for guidance.

What we are teaching you is untainted by any form of material contamination. It is the knowledge coming from God Himself from the very beginning of the universe. It has been very carefully handed down throughout the ages from spiritual master to disciple. The proof of its purity is experienced first-hand by all those who sincerely follow these teachings.

You have very nicely realized that books are not enough - that you must learn from and serve a bona fide spiritual master. This is the conclusion of the authorized Vedic literatures. In this regard it is stated in the *Śvetāśvatara Upaniṣad:*

yasya deve parā bhaktir
yathā deve tathā gurau,
tasyaite kathitā hy arthāḥ
prakāśante mahātmanaḥ

> "If one has unflinching faith in the Supreme Lord and the spiritual master, the essence of all Vedic knowledge is revealed to him."
>
> *Śvetāśvatara Upaniṣad* 6.23

There are two ways that the spiritual master is available to you. The first way is that you can associate with him in his physical form. The second way is that you can associate with him in the form of his teachings. Of the two ways, the second is more important because in that way we can associate with the bona fide spiritual master in all times, places and circumstances. In other words, his physical form will sometimes be present and sometimes not be present. But his vibrational presence (his teachings) is always present for the sincere disciple.

My spiritual master is His Divine Grace A.C. Bhaktivedanta Swami Prabhupāda, the Founder-Ācārya of the International Society for Krishna Consciousness. He is fully available for you to take shelter of in the form of his books. Especially you must study and carefully follow *Bhagavad-gītā As It Is*.

There are many centers operated by his followers there in South Africa. In these centers you will find spiritually advanced devotees of the Lord. Why are they spiritually advanced? Because they are strictly following Prabhupāda's teachings. If you will take shelter of their association, you will quickly advance upon the pathway of Kṛṣṇa consciousness, the ultimate self-realization system. You may also take shelter of me, and I will give you all good instructions and blessings as to how you can make your life perfect. I hope that someday I can come to South Africa to meet you personally.

Why Am I Not Peaceful Now?

I've been praying to God (on my knees, with respect), and I have tried meditation, but I don't think I feel much difference from before. I wasn't really peaceful before and am still not really.

Why is that?

When I become self-realized, do you mean that I will find out who I really am, lose my conscious mind and become the spirit in this body I occupy, or will I still have my conscious mind?

I'm not really happy with my conscious mind. There are thoughts I don't want to think. How do I get rid of them, if ever?

Fill Your Mind with Good Thoughts

You haven't felt any difference in your consciousness because you do not know the proper technique for prayer and meditation. This is not surprising because practically no one in the world knows how to properly pray or meditate. When you become self-realized you will reawaken to your original eternal identity as a servant of God, and you will taste unlimited happiness at every minute. You will not lose your conscious mind, but your mind will become your best friend rather than the enemy that it is now.

The way to get rid of bad thoughts is not to try to kill your mind. Would you cut your head off to get rid of a headache? No. The way to get rid of bad thoughts is to fill your mind with good thoughts. If you will follow carefully the guidelines we are giving you in this course, we can assure you that you will quickly conquer your bad thoughts and become a profoundly happy, self-realized being.

What Is the Right Spiritual Path for Me?

I am in a process of selecting the right spiritual path for self-realization. I wish to know how I can overcome my sense of possession over someone I love too much. May I also know how to meditate peacefully?

Develop Pure Love of God

I am very happy to hear that you are seeking a spiritual path. This should not be difficult because the path is one, to develop pure love for God. All paths become perfect when they reach the point of love for God. So instead of wandering about in the spiritual wilderness, simply try to develop your love for God, and you will achieve the perfection of your dreams.

In regard to becoming free from possessiveness over those you are attached to, you have to see everyone as the property of Kṛṣṇa. This means that they are meant to be engaged for the pleasure of Kṛṣṇa, not for your pleasure. If you engage those you are attached to in the service of Kṛṣṇa, they will become fully happy and you will become fully happy. This is the perfection of loving affection.

The best meditation is to chant Hare Kṛṣṇa. You will quickly achieve the supreme peace:

Hare Kṛṣṇa, Hare Kṛṣṇa, Kṛṣṇa Kṛṣṇa, Hare Hare
Hare Rāma, Hare Rāma, Rāma Rāma, Hare Hare.

Can You Clarify for Me, Please?

What is Māyāvādi? What is ISKCON? What is Vedic knowledge?

I am having a hard time understanding the *Bhagavad-gītā* because I do not know what language some of the words are written in. I would greatly appreciate any advice you would have for me. I read about chanting from the "Thoughts for the Day," but I do not know what this is for. I am beginning to feel lost in all of the information that I have received lately.

The Right Mood for Understanding

I am so happy that Kṛṣṇa has sent you to me. You are such a sincere student who is carefully studying *Bhagavad-gītā* and trying to understand it perfectly. I can assure you that if you keep this mood, Lord Kṛṣṇa will reveal everything to you.

Māyāvādi philosophy is the conception that God is formless or impersonal.

ISKCON is a society that was founded in 1966 by His Divine Grace A.C. Bhaktivedanta Swami Prabhupāda for persons who are serious to achieve the topmost perfection of spiritual enlightenment, Kṛṣṇa consciousness. It now has over 300 branches throughout the world. I am running an ISKCON center in Austin, Texas. The course you are taking is conducted as part of ISKCON's world outreach program.

Vedic knowledge is the original spiritual knowledge that was revealed by God at the beginning of the universe.

I am committed to answering each and every question that you may have so that you can gain perfect comprehension of this topmost system of self-realization.

We will teach you to awaken the love of God that is currently lying dormant within your heart. The most effective technique for doing this is to chant the Hare Kṛṣṇa *mantra* as a regular, daily function:

Hare Kṛṣṇa, Hare Kṛṣṇa, Kṛṣṇa Kṛṣṇa, Hare Hare
Hare Rāma, Hare Rāma, Rāma Rāma, Hare Hare

Instead of feeling lost, write down a list of your questions, and I will try to answer all of your questions to your full satisfaction.

How Does One Become Self-Realized?

How does one become self-realized? I understand that we are a soul living in a human body and that we need to awaken that part, but I just don't understand what I should do to become self-realized. I'm really interested and a little lost. Please enlighten me.

Chant the Holy Names of God

The means for becoming self-realized is authoritatively given by Lord Śrī Kṛṣṇa in the *Bhagavad-gītā* as follows:

tad viddhi praṇipātena
paripraśnena sevayā
upadekṣyanti te jñānaṁ
jñāninas tattva-darśinaḥ

> "Just try to learn the truth by approaching a spiritual master. Inquire from him submissively and render service unto him. The self-realized souls can impart knowledge unto you because they have seen the truth."
>
> *Bhagavad-gītā* 4.34

The means of self-realization in this materialistic age of Kali is to constantly or as much as possible chant the holy names of God:

Hare Kṛṣṇa, Hare Kṛṣṇa, Kṛṣṇa Kṛṣṇa, Hare Hare
Hare Rāma, Hare Rāma, Rāma Rāma, Hare Hare.

Questions from a Sincere Soul

- Why is it considered necessary to take the help of a guru in becoming Kṛṣṇa conscious?
- What exactly does it mean to be Kṛṣṇa conscious? How does one follow the path to God? What must a devotee do to show their love and devotion? How do you become a true devotee of the Lord? What do you do?
- I can't read a word of Hindi or Sanskrit; is that a problem? I know the *Śrīmad-Bhāgavatam* is written in Sanskrit, with few English translations that do it justice, and many prayers and chants are in Sanskrit...

Seek Guidance of a Spiritual Master

If we want to become expert in any field, we require guidance from those who are expert in that field. Spiritual life is no exception. When we make a decision to seriously pursue the pathway of spiritual enlightenment, we naturally will seek the guidance of those who are expert in it. This is why we place ourselves under the guidance of a spiritual master.

Kṛṣṇa consciousness means to be always chanting, hearing, and remembering the Lord as much as possible 24 hours a day.

The pathway to God is to traverse the trail trodden by the previous spiritual masters. They have blazed a trail for us through the dense, dark forest of material existence.

Kṛṣṇa tells us how to show our love and devotion in the *Bhagavad-gītā* as follows:

man-manā bhava mad-bhakto
mad-yājī māṁ namaskuru
mām evaiṣyasi yuktvaivam
ātmānaṁ mat-parāyaṇaḥ

> "Engage your mind always in thinking of Me, become My devotee, offer obeisances to Me and worship Me. Being completely absorbed in Me, surely you will come to Me."
>
> *Bhagavad-gītā* 9.34

You are welcome to practice on whatever level you feel comfortable and enlivened. If you would like to become very serious for achieving complete spiritual perfection in this lifetime, here are some guidelines:

(These are the basic items of *sādhana-bhakti* to be executed by all those who are serious about being a devotee of Lord Kṛṣṇa.)

1. No illicit sex (sex other than for procreation).
2. No meat-eating (including fish and eggs).
3. No intoxication (including coffee, tea, and cigarettes).
4. No gambling.
5. Chant at least 16 rounds of Hare Kṛṣṇa mantra every day on chanting beads.
6. Only eat Kṛṣṇa *prasādam* (food which has been first offered to Lord Kṛṣṇa).
7. Regularly study authorized scriptures such as *Bhagavad-gītā* and *Śrīmad-Bhāgavatam*.
8. To solidify your connection with Kṛṣṇa, become an active participant in a community of devotees who are purely following the path of Kṛṣṇa *bhakti*.

You do not need to read Hindi or Sanskrit, as Śrīla Prabhupāda has so nicely translated this timeless wisdom into English. If you stick with Śrīla Prabhupāda's fully enlightened translations and purports, the full light of Vedic wisdom will manifest in your heart.

I Am Unsure of the Best Spiritual Path for Me

I have been unsure of the best spiritual path for me. If I am starving and you tell me that you have the best food for me, food that is worthy of my veneration as it will cure all my hunger, I feel myself excited and intrigued. But I cannot change my life and agree wholeheartedly with you until I have tasted this food.

So while I feel drawn to Kṛṣṇa consciousness and many of the teachings make sense to me, I cannot say from this day forth I will follow this path. This is because I have no experience of Kṛṣṇa consciousness. You may prefer to say that I have forgotten my relationship with Kṛṣṇa.

Six-Month Experiment

Our process of Kṛṣṇa consciousness does not allow blind following. So I request that you make an experiment to try our system seriously for six months without making any permanent commitment. At the end of the six months you can judge whether you want to continue or quit.

Do you live near any of our worldwide ISKCON centers? Attending one of them will give the best chance to jump-start your experiment.

How to Realize the Truth?

Does there really exist a road, a path to reality? Can a disciplined, goal-oriented mind ever be free to come face-to-face with reality? Shouldn't freedom of the mind be at the beginning and not at the end of the journey? If so, then why do we search? What are we looking for?

If we have an idea of it, then there will be no research. If we can recognize it, that means we have seen it before. So what we find will be a projection - the will, the desire of the mind, and not the truth.

Can there be a middleman between you and the truth? Can God be found through someone else? Is not the understanding of oneself the "road" to God?

The ego cannot be suppressed and substituted with spirituality. It is only through the understanding of the Self that we will let go, without any preconceived ideas. I feel that the *Gītā* can only be understood by a mind that has rid itself of all that it has accumulated. We have to go beyond the mind, and this can only come about through understanding and passive observation. The *Gītā* cannot be interpreted by a thinking mind, as all knowledge, no matter how vast, will always be limited. Thoughts come from memory, from all that we have accumulated. So will chanting Kṛṣṇa's name, suppressing all other thoughts, liberate me?

Dovetail Through Chanting

Here are your questions with answers:

Question: But does there really exist a road, a path to reality?

Answer: Yes, why not?

Question: Can a disciplined, goal-oriented mind ever be free to come face-to-face with reality?

Answer: Yes, why not?

Question: Shouldn't freedom of the mind be at the beginning and not at the end of the journey?

Answer: Yes, but you have to understand what is actual freedom of the mind, not the so-called freedom of a wild, uncontrolled mind.

Question: Then why do we search?

Answer: If you have lost something, you need to search for it. You have lost your original enlightened state of consciousness; therefore you must search for it. But if you meet someone who can tell you precisely how to revive it, there is no need for further searching. You simply have to follow his instructions. That's all. You will quickly attain enlightenment.

Question: What are we looking for?

Answer: Perfect realization of the Absolute Truth. This is the original, natural energy of the living being. It is called Kṛṣṇa consciousness, and is also known as Christ consciousness, Allah consciousness, etc. It is attained by dovetailing your individual consciousness with the universal consciousness. Just as a bicycle rider traveling at ten miles per hour can become one in speed with a car by grabbing onto it and not letting go, we can attain our original, enlightened consciousness simply by dovetailing our individual consciousness with the universal consciousness.

Your comment: If we have an idea of it, then there will be no research. If we can recognize it, it means that we have seen it before. So what we will find will be a projection, the will, the desire of the mind, and not the truth.

Our response: No research is necessary. The Absolute Truth is already there within you. You have seen it before and you will be able to recognize it. It is not a projection. It is the original, underlying reality of all existence. Right now you are caught up in mental projections. You have to become free from mental projections by dovetailing your individual consciousness with the universal consciousness.

Question: Can there be a middleman between you and the truth?

Answer: If you are lost, can someone who knows the way give you directions? That person does not stand between you and your destination. His directions are the means of attaining your destination.

Question: Can God be found through someone else?

Answer: See the answer above. God is found through the mercy of God. If He chooses to send His mercy delivered to you by His representative, the bona fide spiritual master, that is His business. You cannot dictate to God what shall be His means of delivering you. He decides that, not us.

Question: Is not the understanding of oneself the "road" to God?

Answer: Yes, but you must understand what is the actual nature of the self, not a pseudo-self that has been imposed upon you by the material world.

Your comments: The ego cannot be suppressed and substituted with spirituality. It is only through the understanding of the Self that we will let go, without any preconceived ideas. I feel that the *Gītā* can only be understood by a mind that has rid itself of all that it has accumulated. We have to go beyond the mind, and this can only come about through understanding and passive observation. The *Gītā* cannot be interpreted by a thinking mind, as all knowledge, no matter how vast, will always be limited. Thoughts come from memory, from all that we have accumulated.

Our response: Genuine spirituality revives the original ego which has been suppressed by the material world. What is that original ego? "I am not this body. I am an eternal spirit-soul, the eternal servant of God." It is a fact that we have to give up all preconceived ideas and that the *Gītā* can only be understood by a mind that has become free from all accumulated dirt. But if you use your mind to try to go beyond your mind, you will find that you are still stuck on the platform of the mind. Even if you are thinking that you must turn off your mind, you are still on the mental platform because you are thinking that you have to turn off your mind. So such a system of passive observation, although helpful to a point, will in the ultimate issue be unable to deliver you to the transcendental platform.

Question: So will chanting Kṛṣṇa's name, suppressing all other thoughts, liberate me?

Answer: You do not need to make any separate endeavor to suppress all other thoughts. All you have to do is absorb yourself fully in chanting the Hare Kṛṣṇa *mahā-mantra* according the prescribed method. This will automatically dovetail your individual consciousness with the universal consciousness and thus liberate your mind from all the material thoughts that have polluted it in your millions of lifetimes in the cycle of birth and death. You will revive the original, dormant, enlightened consciousness that has been sleeping within you since time immemorial. You will enter into an eternal state of bliss of knowledge.

Initiation into the Sect?

Is it possible that one can be a devotee without being initiated into the Hare Kṛṣṇa sect?

Kṛṣṇa Consciousness Is Not a Sect

Kṛṣṇa consciousness is not a sect. It is the original, natural, pure consciousness of every living being. Kṛṣṇa consciousness is the essence of existence shared by all. Kṛṣṇa consciousness is the highest level of spiritual enlightenment experienced by fully awakened spiritual beings. When we clear out all the crud that has been accumulating and clogging up our consciousness for countless eons, we have attained that rarely attained state of spiritual perfection known as Kṛṣṇa consciousness.

The rarity of awakening one's Kṛṣṇa consciousness is described as follows by Lord Śrī Kṛṣṇa in the *Bhagavad-gītā*:

manuṣyāṇāṁ sahasreṣu
kaścid yatati siddhaye
yatatām api siddhānāṁ
kaścin māṁ vetti tattvataḥ

"Out of many thousands among men, one may endeavor for perfection, and of those who have achieved perfection, hardly one knows Me in truth."
Bhagavad-gītā 7.3

Please Share...

How long was the time period from your first "chemistry lesson" - experiment with *bhakti-yoga* - to your first self-realization blessing? Also, I would like to know ANYTHING else you wish to share so generously.

Search for Self-Realization

My self-realization search began when I was freshman in college. This was the same time my eventual guru, His Divine Grace Śrīla Prabhupāda, set foot on American soil for the first time. I attribute the intense yearning awakened in my soul to discover the meaning of life to my guru's arrival in the West. His physical presence in America had the potency to inspire me to reawaken my original, dormant consciousness. This is the power of a great spiritual master.

This was in the fall of 1965. By the fall of 1968 my yearning for spiritual enlightenment was so intense that I decided to completely abandon the material world and go to India to live there as a renunciate for the rest of my life. But then I realized that denying everything was not the answer. To deny everything means that you must also deny denial itself. There has to be a point where one finds something that is pure and wonderful that one can embrace and accept with all of one's heart and soul.

I felt a divine calling that I was to go to San Francisco instead. So I hitchhiked from Houston to San Francisco in December of 1968. It was there that I first met the disciples of my eventual guru. When you try seriously to adopt the self-realization path, Śrīmatī Māyādevī, the personification of the Lord's illusory energy, will do everything in her power to keep you in illusion. This is her duty. She is there to make sure that no superficial pseudo-spiritualists enter the kingdom of God. So Māyādevī tempted me by giving me some temporary local fame and prestige as a singer/songwriter. This was in 1969, in San Francisco and Berkeley. But by early 1971 I realized that this was not where it was at, that I had to again become absolutely serious about the self-realization path. By that time I had moved back to Austin, Texas.

I took to studying the Bible because I understood that Jesus Christ was fully self-realized. I also wanted to become like that. So I studied the Bible every day to try to understand what his secret was. Then one morning the answer dawned on me like a million tons of flowers. Christ says,"Father, not my will, but Thy will be done." I understood and realized that henceforward I must do what God wants me to do, not what I want to do.

So I began intensely praying on a daily basis, "Dear God, please guide me as to how I can be your perfect servant." And then one of the most highly advanced disciples of my eventual guru, His Holiness Viṣṇujana Swami, shows up in town and explains to me the philosophy of ultimate self-realization, Kṛṣṇa consciousness, in a manner that was so crystal clear that my intelligence could accept how profound and wonderful it was. His sweet, wonderful, loving dealings and the deep and obvious peace and happiness I could see in him were breathtakingly convincing.

I opted to follow all the guidelines of *bhakti-yoga* that he was teaching as an experiment for six months. After adopting all the practices, I found that I was experiencing a reality completely beyond this material world. It was so sweet and profound that there was no question of ever going back to material consciousness.

So at that point, in order to absolutely solidify my fixed position in the transcendental dimension, I decided to accept formal initiation from His Divine Grace A.C. Bhaktivedanta Swami Prabhupāda. On August 12, 1971 His Divine Grace sent me a letter from London accepting me as his disciple and giving me the name Sankarshan Das.

Since that time the profound spiritual consciousness that was awakened within me by my guru, with the help of his followers, has simply continued to expand and evolve beyond my wildest dreams. And it will continue to do so for all of eternity. I am inviting you, Jen, and all of my students, to be with me eternally in this most sublime state of existence beyond the cycle of birth and death, millions of light years beyond the suffering and illusion of this material world.

You are most dear to me since you are one of my very sincere students. I hope and pray that you can fully realize and adopt this supremely wonderful life of Kṛṣṇa consciousness and be unlimitedly blessed, just as I have been. If you can fully take shelter of these teachings, I can assure you that this will be your last birth in this material world. All of your suffering of material existence will very quickly be extinguished. There will be no happiness in this material world that will be able to even remotely compare to an insignificant, infinitesimal fragment of your divine, spiritual bliss.

Transmigration of the Soul
– Reincarnation – Law of Karma

Are Muslims Subject to the Law of Karma?

I was born as a Hindu, and I want to die as a Hindu. But suddenly I converted to Islam. I am wondering, since the Muslims do not believe in *karma*, if my *karma* will be the same. Will I have to be reborn? What is your advice to save me from taking birth again?

Karma Has Nothing to Do with Material Designations

Kṛṣṇa has nothing to do with Hindu or Muslim designations. In the *Bhagavad-gita* He does not say that you should designate yourself either as a Hindu or a Muslim. All He asks is that you should fully surrender yourself unto Him. This is all that is required to be saved from the repetition of birth and death.

Karma is a fact whether one believes in it or not. Hindus suffer *karma*. Muslims suffer *karma*. Everyone suffers from *karma*. But Kṛṣṇa states that if you surrender unto Him that He will free you from your *karma*.

Reincarnation

I am about to start studying the science of Kṛṣṇa consciousness. Is it possible that you can help by enlightening me regarding reincarnation? What really is reincarnation? How does reincarnation affect our soul?

You Are Changing Bodies

Reincarnation is a very simple principle to understand. Just as you have changed bodies in this lifetime many times - from a baby's body to a little girl's body, from a little girl's body to a young girl's body, from a young girl's body to a teenager's body, from a teenager's body to a young adult body, etc. - in a similar way you, the living being, have been changing bodies lifetime after lifetime.

Nature has facilitated you with many varieties of bodies to satisfy your desire to enjoy in many varieties of ways - sometimes as a human being, sometimes as an animal, and sometimes as a plant. But in each and every bodily situation you have not been fully satisfied because your actual identity is situated far, far beyond the body. None of the millions of different types of bodies that you have accepted over millions of lifetimes could satisfy your desire for an eternal existence full of bliss and knowledge.

To achieve that platform you must realize that you are not that body, that you are instead an eternal spiritual being, the eternal servant of Kṛṣṇa, or God. And then, under the expert guidance of the bona fide spiritual master, you should gradually master the art of rendering pure devotional service unto the Lord.

Comprehending that We Are Not This Body

How can we have the perfect comprehension than we are not this body?

The Self Beyond the Body

We can perfectly comprehend our existence beyond this body by seeing how this body is constantly changing while the self, within the body, remains the same. Your body is in a constant state of flux. At every second the old blood corpuscles are dying and new blood corpuscles are taking their place. But you remain as the constant observer of so many bodily changes.

This understanding regarding the self and the body is confirmed by Lord Śrī Kṛṣṇa in the *Bhagavad-gītā* as follows:

dehino 'smin yathā dehe
kaumāraṁ yauvanaṁ jarā
tathā dehāntara-prāptir
dhīras tatra na muhyati

> "As the embodied soul continuously passes, in this body, from boyhood to youth to old age, the soul similarly passes into another body at death. A sober person is not bewildered by such a change."
>
> *Bhagavad-gītā* 2.13

What Happens in the Next Life?

I know that once we die, we either go to Lord Kṛṣṇa (if we have done good deeds this life) or take another life. If a person takes another life, does he/she remain a Hindu or take birth into another religion (like Christianity, etc.)?

That Depends on Your Consciousness at the Time of Death

One who takes birth again will take birth according to their consciousness at the time of death. This is confirmed by Lord Kṛṣṇa in the *Bhagavad-gītā*:

yaṁ yaṁ vāpi smaran bhāvaṁ
tyajaty ante kalevaram
taṁ tam evaiti kaunteya
sadā tad-bhāva-bhāvitaḥ

> "Whatever state of being one remembers when he quits his body, O son of Kuntī, that state he will attain without fail."
>
> *Bhagavad-gītā* 8.6

The living being may take birth as a human, an animal, a plant, or, if he is extremely sinful, even as a bacterium. If he takes birth as a human being it can be in any country or in any religion according the mental state he had when he left his previous body.

But please try to understand in this connection that the concept of different religions is a manmade conception. On the spiritual platform, religion is one: to love God.

Simply doing good deeds is not sufficient for elevation to the kingdom of God at the time of death. Good deeds will give you a better position in your next life in this world. But if you want to attain the eternal kingdom of God, you must fully surrender yourself at the lotus feet of the Lord. You must fully dedicate every thought, word, and deed in the Lord's service under the guidance of the expert spiritual master in order to achieve the supreme perfection.

What Happens When a Soul Departs from a Body?

What happens when a soul departs from a body? Does it enter another body immediately? What happens if there is no body to enter? I need clarification on this.

He Immediately Enters Another Body

The next body is already determined by superior control. The living entity immediately gives up the present body and enters another. Material nature can produce unlimited bodies to facilitate the material desires of the living beings now living in this material world.

Demigod or Kṛṣṇa?

What should one do when instructions from a demigod conflict with what Kṛṣṇa tells one to do? Should one do what Kṛṣṇa says instead? Is it always so?

Also, I was wondering, what is Kṛṣṇa's stance on abortions? Are they sinful, and if so, how great is such a sin?

Kṛṣṇa and the Law of Karma

Since Kṛṣṇa is the supreme authority, we are meant to surrender only to Kṛṣṇa, not to the demigods.

Since the soul enters the womb at the time of conception, abortion is murder. The *karma* for murder is to be murdered. If someone aborts a baby, that person must be aborted in their next life as a karmic reaction.

When Does the Soul Get Realization?

At what moment after death does the soul realize that he has wasted his life? Is there any moment when he regrets not giving his life to Kṛṣṇa consciousness? Does this realization come after entering into the womb of another living entity?

In the Human Form

The soul might not come to any realization for millions of lifetimes, depending on how sinful he was. It is very sad situation. This is why we have to inundate this entire planet with Kṛṣṇa consciousness.

If the living being was pious enough to get another human birth, it is described in the *Śrīmad-Bhāgavatam* that after seven months he prays to the Lord to be released from the horrible situation that he is in. In this connection Śrīla Prabhupāda explains, "As long as the child is within the womb of his mother, he is in a very precarious and horrible condition of life, but the benefit is that he revives pure consciousness of his relationship with the Supreme Lord and prays for deliverance. But once he is outside the abdomen, when a child is born, *māyā*, or the illusory energy, is so strong that he is immediately overpowered into considering his body to be his self."

Therefore, you should consider yourself most fortunate to have a human birth and to be conscious of your relationship with Kṛṣṇa. Now fully take advantage of this very rare opportunity with which you have been blessed, and make your life perfect by complete surrender unto the lotus feet of Lord Śrī Kṛṣṇa.

Innocence in the Material World?

I have a question concerning *karma*. Since everyone on the material platform is suffering the results of his activities, *karma*, how is it that there can be innocence in the material world? What I am asking is, since the laws of *karma* are cruel yet exacting in carrying out justice to the sinful living entities, is there any innocence in the material world? Or is it as one of my teachers would say, "Everyone gets their just deserts"?

Ultimately, There Is None

Strictly speaking, there is no innocence in this material world. This explains why even a little baby can be born with birth defects. Of course, there is relative innocence here. Relatively speaking, compared to adults, little children are quite innocent. Gradually, as they grow up and engage in more and more sinful activities such as meat-eating, they lose that childhood innocence and become more and more jaded. Strictly speaking even children are not completely pure. They are also enjoying and suffering their *karma*, the results of their activities from previous lifetimes.

Is Mercy Killing Justified?

Could you please enlighten me on what the scriptures say about killing of animals generally and more specifically, killing to put an end to their suffering?

In the West, animal shelters humanely euthanize dogs and cats. Is this right from the spiritual point of view?

If it is wrong to practice mercy killing, then what is the justification to see the prolonged suffering of the animal? Do animals have *karma*?

Humane Killing?

It is a very noble ideal to want to relieve living beings from their suffering. If we have a desire to do this, it is very nice. But we must learn how to do it properly so that we do not prolong or increase their suffering. Every living being in each species has an allotted amount of suffering and enjoyment it is meant to experience in that species. Once that is finished, they then move on to the next higher species on the evolutionary ladder. In this way they gradually move up to the human form, in which they revive their original divine consciousness and once and for all escape the cycle of birth and death.

Euthanization simply postpones their misery and delays that time when they can become completely free from all suffering by becoming a self-realized soul. Therefore, if we really want to do good for others we should give them Kṛṣṇa consciousness, not euthanization. We should let them hear the holy names of the Lord and taste Kṛṣṇa prasādam. This is beneficial for the spiritual emancipation of all souls whether they are embodied in a human form, an animal form, or a plant form.

If someone came to kill you humanely, would you accept it?

Meaning of Birth and Death

Can you explain what is the real meaning of death and also what is the meaning of birth?

Like Trading In an Old Car for a New Car

Kṛṣṇa explains birth and death in the *Bhagavad-gītā*:

na jāyate mriyate vā kadācin
nāyaṁ bhūtvā bhavitā vā na bhūyaḥ
ajo nityaḥ śāśvato 'yaṁ purāṇo
na hanyate hanyamāne śarīre

> "For the soul there is neither birth nor death at any time. He has not come into being, does not come into being, and will not come into being. He is unborn, eternal, ever-existing and primeval. He is not slain when the body is slain."
>
> *Bhagavad-gītā* 2.20

From this we can understand that birth and death are something external to the living being. Just like one trades in an old car and buys a new car, he gives up one body (death) and takes on a new one (birth).

At the time of conception the soul enters into the mother's womb by means of the semen injected by the father. Then within the womb his body gradually develops, and after nine months he comes out at the time of birth.

After some time, when the body becomes old, worn out and useless, he leaves the body to take on another one according to his *karma*. If, however, one becomes enlightened in the science of Kṛṣṇa consciousness, he does not take birth again. He revives his original spiritual body, which is eternal, ever-youthful, full of bliss, and full of knowledge. He thus no longer suffers the miseries of material existence.

What Survives Death?

When we die, what part or parts of us will survive?

The Particle of Subatomic, Indestructible, Pure Anti-Material Energy

The answer is that we do not die. Simply the material body perishes, while the spirit-soul remains. You are the spirit-soul. The body is not you. It's just something that you are passing through. The spirit-soul is a particle of subatomic, indestructible, pure anti-material energy qualitatively one with God. This is the real you. It is not destroyed at the time of death. It simply travels to a new body according to its consciousness at the time of death. Or, if one is in a state of pure Kṛṣṇa *bhakti* at the time of death, that spiritual particle remanifests its original spiritual form in the spiritual world, giving up the transmigration from one body to another in this material world to become an eternal associate of the Supreme Personality of Godhead in His unlimited pastimes.

Why Do We Easily Forget?

Why is it that we don't ordinarily have past-life memories, except on rare occasions? Why are we thus limited to only one lifetime of memories? What causes us to forget so easily?

Because We Chose to Forget Kṛṣṇa

Ever since we chose to forget Kṛṣṇa, our memory has been very meager.

You mention our having one lifetime of memories. But the fact is that we do not even have that. Can you tell me what you were doing at this time exactly one year ago? Can you tell me what you were thinking, what you were saying, and what you were doing? No. You cannot.

Our nature is that we are forgetful. Remembering our past lives would not be any more helpful for getting us out of the cycle of birth and death than remembering what we were doing a year ago today. So why should we be interested to know our past lives? This is not very important.

When we walk down the street do we look forward or do we look backward? We look forward because that is how we will make progress. Looking behind at the places we have been will not allow us to move forward. So it is better that we look forward to see how we can advance in Kṛṣṇa consciousness. This is the proper utilization of the human form of life, not trying to figure out who we were in our last lives.

What Happens to the Soul at the Time of Death?

Can you explain what happens to the soul at the moment of death? Where does it go? Is it that the soul gets into another body immediately? I imagine the journey would be different for someone who has transcended this material world before death, but can you please explain the different pathways - the path for the devotee and the path for someone who has not realized Kṛṣṇa?

He Is Transferred to Another Body

At the time of death, the soul is either transferred to the spiritual world or it takes another body within this material world. This depends on the consciousness he is absorbed in at the time of death. This point is confirmed as follows in the *Śrīmad Bhagavad-gītā*:

yaṁ yaṁ vāpi smaran bhāvaṁ
tyajaty ante kalevaram
taṁ tam evaiti kaunteya
sadā tad-bhāva-bhāvitaḥ

"Whatever state of being one remembers when he quits his body, O son of Kuntī, that state he will attain without fail."

Bhagavad-gītā 8.6

How does one attain that state? This is described in the *Bhagavad-gītā* as being like the air carrying aromas.

śarīraṁ yad avāpnoti
yac cāpy utkrāmatīśvaraḥ

gṛhītvaitāni saṁyāti
vāyur gandhān ivāśayāt

> "The living entity in the material world carries his different conceptions of life from one body to another as the air carries aromas. Thus he takes one kind of body and again quits it to take another."
>
> *Bhagavad-gītā* 15.8

We have gross bodies composed of earth, water, fire, air, and ether. We also have subtle bodies composed of mind, intelligence, and false ego. The gross body dies, but the subtle body continues. Whatever nature you have cultivated during this lifetime is fully manifested in your subtle body. If you have cultivated material desires, at the time of death your subtle body will enter into a human or non-human form according to what sort of material desires you have cultivated. If you have fully absorbed yourself in spiritual desires, the subtle body will be discarded at the time of death, and you will regain your original, long-forgotten form and identity in the spiritual world.

Why Untimely Death?

When someone meets with an accident, why does the soul sometimes leave the body? As the soul is eternal, since it is an unnatural death, why does the soul leave the body in an untimely death?

According to Karma

The soul will remain in the body as long as it is destined to remain, according to the laws of material nature. When time comes for the soul to leave, it must leave.

Normally the soul does not leave the body until one becomes old. But sometimes, according to one's *karma*, one must leave the body even when one is young. All of these things are going on according to the laws of *karma*, action and reaction.

Near-Death Experiences

Scientists say that near-death experiences are the result of dying brain cells in a body. Christians believe that they are real experiences that occur because the soul leaves the body. What are your thoughts/beliefs on this subject? Does your literature make any mention of this subject?

Because of the Soul's Departure

The Vedas give us precise scientific information regarding death and near-death. It is a fact that death and near-death experiences occur because the soul leaves the body. In death, the soul leaves the body for good, never to return. In near-death, the soul leaves temporarily and then returns. Since the soul is the powerhouse which energizes the body, when it leaves the body, the body loses its energy source. This causes the brain cells and the other cells to start dying. So dying brain cells are not the cause of death. They are a symptom of death.

How Does a Soul Reincarnate?

How does a soul reincarnate? Why does a soul have to take up one body after another? Why does a soul go into ignorance? What happens exactly at the time of death? How can we get out of the chain of action-inaction-reaction?

Carried by the Subtle Body

The soul is carried by the subtle body to his next gross body. This is confirmed in the *Bhagavad-gītā* as follows:

śarīraṁ yad avāpnoti
yac cāpy utkrāmatīśvaraḥ
gṛhītvaitāni saṁyāti
vāyur gandhān ivāśayāt

"The living entity in the material world carries his different conceptions of life from one body to another as the air carries aromas. Thus he takes one kind of body and again quits it to take another."

Bhagavad-gītā 15.8

śrotraṁ cakṣuḥ sparśanaṁ ca
rasanaṁ ghrāṇam eva ca
adhiṣṭhāya manaś cāyaṁ
viṣayān upasevate

"The living entity, thus taking another gross body, obtains a certain type of ear, eye, tongue, nose and sense of touch, which are grouped about the mind. He thus enjoys a particular set of sense objects."

Bhagavad-gītā 15.9

The soul does not have to take body after body after body. He only does so if he still has material desires at the time of death. In such a state he is awarded a particular type of body by which he can fulfill his desires. If his only desire is to be a loving servant of God, he does not take birth again in this material world. He instead enters into the transcendental kingdom of God to enjoy an eternal life full of bliss and knowledge in the direct, personal association of Kṛṣṇa, or God.

The soul only goes into ignorance when he wants to be in ignorance. It is sometimes said, "Ignorance is bliss." There are certain persons who prefer the artificial comfort of ignorance over knowing and realizing the Truth as it is. For them ignorance is bliss, but not for the thoughtful person who is eager to know things as they actually are.

At the time of death the materially attached person is taken by the Yamadūtas to the abode of Yamarāja, where he accepts the karmic reactions for his past misdeeds before being carried by the subtle body to his next birth in accordance with what his mind was absorbed in at the time of death.

In the *Bhagavad-gītā* Kṛṣṇa gives us the formula of how to escape from the cycle of birth and death:

sarva-dharmān parityajya
mām ekaṁ śaraṇaṁ vraja
ahaṁ tvāṁ sarva-pāpebhyo
mokṣayiṣyāmi mā śucaḥ

"Abandon all varieties of religion and just surrender unto Me. I shall deliver you from all sinful reactions. Do not fear."

Bhagavad-gītā 18.66

Hellish Planets

If the spirit soul transmigrates from one body to another at the time of death, what part do the hellish planets play in this universe? How long does the spirit soul stay in that hellish place? And do the inhabitants get out, or are they destined to remain there, as in prison?

Stopping-Off Place for the Sinful

The hellish planets are a stopping-off point in the cycle of birth and death for those who have especially heavy sinful reactions to burn off. According to the volume of their *karma*, the sinful will have a longer or shorter sojourn there. But eventually they are released from the hellish planets, and through the process of transmigration in the 8,400,000 species, they will eventually end up with another human birth. Then if one's human birth is properly utilized by reviving one's dormant Kṛṣṇa consciousness, he will escape the dualities of material life and attain an eternal existence, full of bliss and full of knowledge in the unlimitedly wondrous spiritual sky.

What Happens to the Sinful at Death?

In the *Śrīmad-Bhāgavatam* it is described that people who are sinful are punished by Yamarāja, the God of Death, in his abode Yamaloka. But in the *Bhagavad-gītā*, Kṛṣṇa says that as soon as a soul leaves a body he enters into another body. So how is that he gets his punishment in Yamaloka? Who gets the punishment - the soul or the material body?

Yamaloka En Route to Next Body

Both things are true. The soul does enter into another body at the time of death. And he also is taken to the abode of Yamarāja to be punished for his misdeeds. He first enters the abode of Yamarāja in his subtle body - composed of mind, intelligence, and false ego - where he is punished, and then, after being sufficiently punished, he is assigned to his next gross body. The soul experiences the suffering due to his misidentification with the gross and subtle material bodies.

Living in the Material World

Is It Okay to Enjoy the Good Things in Life?

For the last couple of days, I have been completely absorbed in thinking about Kṛṣṇa, listening to Kṛṣṇa kirtans downloaded from your website, and reading His Divine Grace Śrīla Prabhupāda's *Bhagavad-gītā As It Is*, apart from my professional work time. I have not watched TV, nor have I listened to the radio. I perform *ārati* in my *pūjā* room and then again immerse myself in reading Śrīla Prabhupāda's "The Science of Self Realization."

Today a thought rose in me while I was reading the *Bhagavad-gītā As It Is*. There are so many good things in this world like good soul-stirring music, good and informative television programs and magazines, good scenic sights, good vegetarian food, etc. Is it true that I should not even enjoy these good things, that I should refrain from everything and direct all energy towards Kṛṣṇa, or is it enough to be away from evil deeds and be a good devotee of Kṛṣṇa? If I am not supposed to do anything other than thinking of Kṛṣṇa and praying to Kṛṣṇa, why has Kṛṣṇa created so many things for the living entity to experience and enjoy?

Why has Kṛṣṇa allowed me to go away from Him and not kept me on the right path, the path of Kṛṣṇa consciousness, always? Why has Kṛṣṇa placed me at a certain economic level so that I have to work and not focus 24 hours a day on Kṛṣṇa? I have read in the *Bhagavad-gītā* that Kṛṣṇa wants all living entities to be devoted to Him, and that He is very much pleased if a devotee pleases His senses rather than his or her own senses. If this is the case, why is Kṛṣṇa testing the living entities? Why can't He make us please Him directly? He is the most merciful, ever-attractive, all-opulent and controller of all senses.

Why am I being tested, for what reason?

Please guide me and bring me out of the darkness and into the light of Kṛṣṇa consciousness.

We Have to Know What Actually Are the Good Things in Life

Kṛṣṇa allows this material world to exist for those who want to try to enjoy separately from Him. Because you stubbornly wanted to go away from Kṛṣṇa, He allowed you to do so. Kṛṣṇa can make us do anything by force except for one thing: love Him. Love by its very nature must be voluntary. It cannot be forced. His mercy is that He gives you the free choice to love Him or leave Him. This is the only way that real love can exist. Now you must utilize your free will properly.

There are no good things in life outside of Kṛṣṇa consciousness. They may appear to be good, but in fact they are all bad. How can I make such a heavy, sweeping statement? The reason is that although many things give us a temporary sense of pleasure, they keep us entangled in the fourfold miseries of birth, death, old age, and disease.

The good things in life are those things which give us permanent deliverance from all material miseries by allowing us to enter and remain in the sweet atmosphere of pure love of Godhead, where all material miseries are conspicuous by their absence.

Whatever level we are at economically is what we have earned by our past *karma*. If we analyze our karmic situation philosophically, this will give us great impetus for being free from *karma* by taking complete shelter at the Lord's lotus feet. Therefore you should engage yourself 24 hours a day in pure Kṛṣṇa *bhakti* under the expert guidance of the spiritual master and the advanced Vaiṣṇavas.

If you want to graduate from the university, you must be tested. If you want to graduate from birth and death, you must be tested. If you take and follow our guidance very seriously, you will easily pass all tests.

I Need Power and Money

I have a serious problem and I don't know how I will solve it. My friend told me about your course, so that is why I visited your website. I need power and money.

Money and Power Are Nothing

Our system is not for getting power and money. It is for developing pure love for God. Once you realize God, you will no longer hanker for money and power. You will be fully satisfied by your surrender at the Lord's lotus feet. Power and money are nothing compared to realizing God.

Dealing with the Mentally Ill

In your Kṛṣṇa consciousness movement how do you deal with the mentally ill?

Everyone is Mentally Ill without Kṛṣṇa Consciousness

The first thing to understand is that everyone in this material world is mentally ill. That's why we are here. This material world is a place for those who are suffering from the mental disease of thinking that they are God, that they are the center of the universe.

Within this material world there are certain people who we say are mentally ill, and there are certain people who we describe as being sane. But this is a misunderstanding. This misconception is a sign of our mental illness.

The sane person is the one who realizes that he is the eternal servant of God and fully engages himself in the service of God. If we are blessed by the association of such a pure devotee of God, then we come out of our mental illness and achieve the actual platform of sanity, pure Kṛṣṇa *bhakti*.

Why Does One Lose His Faith in Kṛṣṇa?

I would like to know why one tends to lose his faith in Kṛṣṇa when he is in moments of great sorrow/distress. How does one develop full faith in Śrī Kṛṣṇa in spite of the sufferings one has to undergo because of his *karma*?

Lack of Philosophical Understanding

If we lose our faith in great moments of sorrow and distress, it is due to our lack of proper philosophical understanding. Those who are learned in transcendental knowledge take pleasure in times of distress because such times greatly facilitate remembering the Lord. In such times their faith becomes even stronger. It reminds them that this material world offers no hope of happiness, that only by taking complete shelter of the Lord can they become happy.

Why Did God Put Me into Depression?

I was under depression all of last year. Now I am all right. I want to know why God put me under depression. Now my career and studies have come to a standstill. My depression is not fully over. I am still taking medication. What should I do or think so that God will help me improve my condition?

You Put Yourself into Depression

God did not put you into depression. You put yourself in depression by turning away from God. All you have to do is fully absorb yourself in His loving service and you will never be depressed again.

Is There Any End to the Evil in the World?

I am surrounded by people who are greedy for material things. They are getting evil to get more and more of things. Sometimes they do evil things to hurt others. We see and realize the bad things they are doing to others, but we cannot do anything. Is there no end to these evil-minded people and their doings?

The Best Shot at Conquering Evil

The living entity has the free will to be either selfless or selfish. One who chooses the miserly path of selfishness will never find peace or satisfaction in this life or the next. The selfless lovers of God are pained greatly in their hearts to see the needless sufferings of those who choose the path of selfishness. They are also disturbed to see the sufferings that selfish persons inflict upon others.

Therefore, these loving souls selflessly dedicate themselves to inspiring the selfish souls to take up the liberating path of selfless service to God.

Whether the selfish souls will end their selfishness or not is up to them. All that can be done is that the pure devotees of God try to inspire them by perfect example and try compassionately to uplift them by sharing with them the enlightening words of wisdom from the revealed scriptures.

Stress and Strain

Please advise me how to prevent daily stress and strain that comes from doing routine work.

Love Defeats Stress and Strain

If we truly love someone and we are serving them, then even when there is stress and strain, we will not find it to be disturbing. We will see it as a wonderful opportunity to show our beloved our genuine love. In this way, if you truly love Kṛṣṇa and you are doing everything for Him, you will always be happy in all circumstances, whether stressful or peaceful.

Is Suicide the Ultimate Solution?

If someone commits suicide, what is his future? Will he suffer more than he is suffering now? Most people commit suicide to get out of their problems forever. What is the ultimate solution for our problems, if not suicide?

Surrender to Kṛṣṇa Is the Ultimate Solution to All Problems

Many people foolishly commit suicide thinking that it will be the ultimate solution to all of their problems. Nothing could be further from the truth. Suicide opens the door to ghostly life - the most unbelievably hellish, nightmarish existence, worse than anyone can even imagine.

The ghost has all the desires for bodily sense pleasure that he had when he was previously incarnated in a gross physical body. But he does not have the gross senses with which to fulfill those desires. Therefore, he must constantly search for weak-minded persons in gross bodies whom he can overpower by taking over their bodies so that he can enjoy gross sense pleasure vicariously through their senses.

But in spite of all his attempts, he is never satisfied. He simply becomes ever-increasingly more and more frustrated. Thus, someone who commits suicide simply increases his suffering even more. He is forced by the law of *karma* to take birth as a ghost for a very, very long time. He will be much, much more miserable as a ghost than he was in the body in which he committed suicide.

The ultimate solution for all varieties of suffering conditions is to fully surrender oneself unto Lord Kṛṣṇa under the expert guidance of scriptures, devotees, and the bona fide spiritual master. If you will surrender fully in this way, all of your desires for peace and happiness will be fully satisfied, and at the time of death you will not have to return to this world of birth and death. You will enter into the eternal spiritual sky, where life is full of bliss and full of knowledge.

Why Are We Imperfect and So Egotistical?

Since Kṛṣṇa is perfect, we, being part and parcel of Him, are also perfect by nature. So how did we become imperfect? Why are people so egotistical? I notice that wherever I go, people are so egotistical. Why is this?

This Is Part of Lord Kṛṣṇa's Perfect Arrangement

The perfection of Kṛṣṇa's creation is that He gives the living beings free will to love Him or leave Him. Love cannot be forced. It must be voluntary. Therefore, without this free will it would be impossible for love to exist.

A creation without love would certainly be missing something. It would not be satisfying. To the extent that love is manifested, to that extent there is happiness. Without love there can be no happiness.

Happiness depends on love, which depends on free will. Since Kṛṣṇa is an enjoyer by nature, He wants to taste the enjoyment of loving relationships with us, His part and parcel expansions. Therefore, He gives us free will to act as we please, either in His service or outside of His service.

Since free will exists, there must exist the possibility that it can be misused. Otherwise there is no free will. As long as there exists the possibility of misuse, there must also exist a certain degree of probability. If we apply even the most infinitesimal degree of probability against the infinite number of living beings who inhabit the spiritual world, we end up with an infinite number of living beings who fall from the spiritual world. Kṛṣṇa's perfect arrangement is to bring them all back to Him through the reformatory nature of this material existence. Sooner or later everyone here will get tired of the unrelenting repetition of birth, death, old age and disease. Sooner or later everyone will decide to go back to home, back to Godhead, never to return to this reformatory, covered existence.

In this material world everyone is egotistical because this is the place where all the egomaniacs are sent by God in order to learn how to become humble and return to His kingdom.

When Will I Become Free from Difficulties?

I would so much like to have a friend. This never-fulfilled desire always makes me lament. I am so lonely. If only I could have few friends, or even one, with whom I could reveal my heart, feel at home, and also advance in Kṛṣṇa consciousness - but every relationship I've had before just made me feel dirty.

I need to learn more about how I can apply Kṛṣṇa-conscious knowledge. I read so much, but I do not know what to do with my life to make it somehow useful and satisfying. What can I do? What will bring change?

I'm always waiting for that someone who will come and change my life, so that I will become happy and never face difficulty - but that person never comes. What is wrong with me? Why, in spite of so much struggle, do I not see any hope that my difficulties will ever end?

When You Flip On the Switch Within Your Heart

If you want to receive friendship, you must give friendship. You need to place yourself on the giving end. You must give of yourself before you are worthy to receive.

You will only suffer if you are not Kṛṣṇa conscious. If you are Kṛṣṇa conscious, you will not suffer in any condition. You should accept whatever situation Kṛṣṇa arranges for you and try to be fully surrendered in that situation.

Do not think of trying to change your situation. Simply you must change your consciousness. You keep wanting to change your external circumstances instead of your internal circumstances. Simply focus on the within, and the without will take care of itself automatically.

The wonder you are awaiting is at your fingertips right now. You simply have to flip on the switch of Kṛṣṇa consciousness within your heart. Simply you must affirm, "My Dear Lord Kṛṣṇa, from this moment on, I belong to You and nobody else. Please bless me that I can henceforward be fully absorbed in Your pure devotional service with my every thought, word and deed, for all of eternity."

Help Me Get Out of Māyā

I feel like I am getting into the clutches of *māyā* (illusion) again and again. I beg you, please help me out, please give me a good concrete solution.

If Kṛṣṇa says that where there is Godhead there is no *māyā*, then why am I getting into the clutches of *māyā*?

Increase the Quality and Quantity of Your Chanting

If you are being overwhelmed by the influence of the illusory energy, you simply have to increase the quality and quantity of your chanting of the Hare Kṛṣṇa mantra, and by the power of Kṛṣṇa's transcendental mercy you will be delivered.

Chant these names as much as you can with the full attention and devotion:

Hare Kṛṣṇa, Hare Kṛṣṇa, Kṛṣṇa Kṛṣṇa , Hare Hare
Hare Rāma, Hare Rāma, Rāma Rāma, Hare Hare

The result will be amazingly sublime.

Why "Lotus Feet"?

What is the meaning of "lotus feet"? When Kṛṣṇa created the material world for those who want to enjoy independently, why did He create suffering in it? He could have created a world with no suffering just like the spiritual world for those who wanted to enjoy independently.

They Enable Easy Crossing Over the Material Ocean

Kṛṣṇa's feet are called lotus feet because they enable one to easily cross over the vast ocean of material existence as confirmed in the following verse:

samāśritā ye pada-pallava-plavaṁ
mahat-padaṁ puṇya-yaśo murāreḥ
bhavāmbudhir vatsa-padaṁ paraṁ padaṁ
padaṁ padaṁ yad vipadāṁ na teṣām

> "For those who have accepted the boat of the lotus feet of the Lord, who is the shelter of the cosmic manifestation and is famous as Murāri, the enemy of the Mura demon, the ocean of the material world is like the water contained in a calf's hoof-print. Their goal is *paraṁ padam*, Vaikuṇṭha, the place where there are no material miseries, not the place where there is danger at every step."
>
> *Śrīmad-Bhāgavatam* 10.14.58

Just as a fish can never be satisfied out of his natural habitat, the water, the material world must necessarily be a place of suffering because it is not our nature to enjoy independently from God.

Kindly Guide Me

I am regularly chanting 16 rounds of the Hare Kṛṣṇa *mahā-mantra* daily and following other principles also. My wife is also doing some rounds daily. For the last two months I have been jobless, and I haven't got a suitable job in spite of my best efforts.

Now my problem is that my father isn't happy. He says that it's useless to chant 16 rounds since you are not doing your duty seriously, i.e. not working any job for last two months. He says that when you are not able to perform your duty sincerely there is no use of chanting, that you will not get benefit from chanting.

He also says that one should remember God from inside, from the heart, and that it is not necessary to chant names of God and show others that you chant this many rounds.

My father does not chant anything. Upon asking him the reason, he says that God is in his heart, that he remembers Him daily from inside, and that since he is performing his material duties it is not required for him to chant.

Hear from Your Original Father

Sometimes Kṛṣṇa puts His devotees into difficulty just to increase their feelings of dependence upon Him. But He will never let them starve. You don't have to worry. Something will open up for you.

According to the authoritative Vedic literatures, your father's understanding is very incorrect. According to the order of the Supreme Personality of Godhead, it is our duty to chant His holy names as much as possible every day. Sixteen rounds daily is the minimum standard.

Many people claim to be constantly remembering God on the inside while we see that externally they are fully absorbed in material attachments. If we could see what was actually going on their minds, we would see that they hardly think of God at all.

The fact is that anyone who is constantly thinking of God will also be constantly chanting His names, bowing down to Him, and rendering service unto Him. Those who refuse to chant His names may claim they are God conscious, but their "God consciousness" will tend to be to think that they are God and that by serving themselves they are serving God.

So, such so-called God consciousness may be very popular with those who want to continue their material attachments while at the same time proudly they think that they are already liberated, but it will not liberate us from this material world. It will keep us entangled in the cycle of birth and death.

We have been doing materialistic duties for millions of lifetimes. And where has it gotten us? We are still caught up in the repetition of birth, death, old age, and disease. If we want to escape the cycle of birth and death, we must maximize hearing and chanting and do our material duties only insofar as is required to cover our basic material necessities.

Why Does a Person Feel Helpless?

Why does a person feel helpless in front of God's decisions? Why is it very difficult for a person to forgive that human being who hurts his/her inner soul?

Such Feelings Are Born out of Ignorance Only

If one feels helpless, this is ignorance. The Lord's pure devotees never feel themselves helpless. They are always feeling how they are under the full protection of the Lord even in the most dangerous circumstances. If we feel helpless it means we do not trust the Lord to take care of us. God helps those who help themselves. The best help we can give ourselves is to develop full faith and trust in the Lord.

Persons who cannot forgive are infected by pride.

The Purpose of Our Existence

I was wondering about a question that someone asked me. It has been bothering my mind, too. The question regards our reason for existence. I am still blindfolded on this one!

If the only purpose of our coming to this material world is to get cured and become one with the Supreme, then my question is, why did we get separated from the Godhead and come here in the first place?

When we came here at first, I hope we were pure Self. Is it that then, over several lives, we become impure by performing karmic activities under the influence of *māyā*? Is my understanding correct?

When you say "spiritual plane/world that is full of bliss and happiness" - is this another plane of our existence where we are one with God yet not God Himself?

If we can become one with God, then is there any meaning to our existence? Don't we lose our identity to experience that Supreme Self? After we become one with the Supreme, then what were we before we merged?

Will it be like we never existed?

To Have a Loving Relationship with God

Just as a foolish child sometimes sticks his hand in a fire out of curiosity to see what it is like, sometimes the living entity foolishly decides to taste the forbidden fruit of trying to be God. Why does the child do this against the advice of his parents? This is the exercise of his free will, his independence.

We are impure from the very instant we enter this material existence. And by engaging in sinful activities, we become more and more impure. By taking to the devotional service of the Lord, we gradually become free of all of our impurities and can then return to our original position in the spiritual world as servants of the Lord.

The living being never becomes one with God. He always maintains his separate identity so that he can lovingly serve the Lord. Those who are perfect in spiritual consciousness deride the conception of becoming one with God.

The way to experience the Supreme Self is similar to the way you would experience the association of any great personality. You don't experience the association of Mahatma Gandhi by becoming Mahatma Gandhi. You experience Mahatma Gandhi by meeting him and talking with him. Similarly, you do not experience God by becoming Him. You experience God by associating with Him.

Does a woman want to serve her husband or become her husband? She wants to share the joys of family life with her husband. She does not want to annihilate the separate existence of herself and her husband by merging into him. Similarly, the devotee never wants to lose his individual existence by merging into God. Nor does God want this.

The purpose of your existence is to have a loving relationship with Kṛṣṇa, the Supreme Personality of Godhead. When we misuse our free will by trying to become God, we come to this material world to undergo sufficient sufferings to convince us to go back to our original position of being a servant of God.

Why Didn't God Do Better?

I get very upset when I look at the animal kingdom. It affects me so badly when I watch documentaries on television. If God is beauty and has made everything so beautiful on this earth, then why do animals need to kill one another for their survival?

Yes, I agree everything is balanced because of these food chains, but I am not happy with the food chains. God is the source of intelligence. Why couldn't He come up with a different plan where there would be no blood mess?

He Did, But We Didn't Accept It

God does have a different plan: the spiritual world. But we are such rascals that we have not agreed to accept His plan. We wanted to manufacture our own plan. Hence we have a world where one living entity is food for another type of living entity:

jīvo jīvasya jīvanam

"One living being is food for another."

Śrīmad-Bhāgavatam 1.13.47

Now if we will utilize our God-given free will, we can leave behind this world of violence and enter into the all-peaceful spiritual world forever.

How Do Animals Know God?

I am so thankful for the letter written to you expressing concern for the bloodbath that takes place in the animal kingdom. I have been wanting to write to you about this for some time but didn't know how to pose my concern.

I understand your reply but it hasn't really satisfied my sorrow. I guess I want to understand how to take the killings into perspective. It's true, you can't turn on a non-fiction television channel without seeing documentaries that show the cruelty and harshness of predator-over-prey situations. I hurt so badly inside, I can't switch the channel quickly enough. Even when I am not watching it I am aware of what is going on, and the immense sorrow I feel for what I see as pain and suffering and fear is overwhelming.

How do I use the *Bhagavad-gītā*'s words to help me not to feel sorrow for this?

I try to say to myself, "Well, in the next life, this innocent animal will come back stronger, or loved and happy." Is this correct? How do the animals know God?

By Evolution of Consciousness

Because of your nice, saintly qualities you are finding the inevitable suffering of this material world to be intolerable. There is no material solution for these miseries. The only solution is a spiritual solution. Everyone has to be killed today or tomorrow by the stringent laws of the material nature. The plants also have consciousness and are not happy about being killed.

Therefore, Kṛṣṇa tells us to get out of this miserable place and come back to His abode. This is the only real solution.

ā-brahma-bhuvanāl lokāḥ
punar āvartino 'rjuna
mām upetya tu kaunteya
punar janma na vidyate

> "From the highest planet in the material world down to the lowest, all are places of misery wherein repeated birth and death take place. But one who attains to My abode, O son of Kunti, never takes birth again."
>
> *Bhagavad-gītā* 8.16

There is a natural evolutionary system that gradually brings every living being to the human form of life in which he can realize God and return to the Lord's eternal abode. This is the good news. Everyone gets a chance to become liberated from this world of death.

The saddest thing is when after the living being evolves to the human form he does not utilize it for self-realization. In such a case he is forced by the laws of nature to head back down to the animal kingdom, where he awaits his chance to again become a human being.

Mind and Intellect

Could you please explain the difference between intellect and intelligence, and also the difference between mind and intellect?

Driving Instrument and the Driver

Intelligence and intellect are synonyms. The relationship between the mind and the intelligence is described in the following verses:

ātmānaṁ rathinaṁ viddhi
śarīraṁ ratham eva ca

buddhiṁ tu sārathiṁ viddhi
manaḥ pragraham eva ca

indriyāṇi hayān āhur
viṣayāṁs teṣu gocarān
ātmendriya-mano-yuktaṁ
bhoktety āhur manīṣiṇaḥ

"The individual is the passenger in the car of the material body, and intelligence is the driver. Mind is the driving instrument, and the senses are the horses. The self is thus the enjoyer or sufferer in the association of the mind and senses. So it is understood by great thinkers."

Kaṭha Upaniṣad 1.3.3-4

Regarding Skepticism

Since we are all skeptical on certain things, how can you say that we should not be skeptical?

Materially Handy, Spiritually Impeding

Skepticism is handy when dealing with the material energy, but it is an impediment when we are dealing with Kṛṣṇa.

Why Is There Suffering Even After Chanting?

I read with interest the answer given to Rajesh in the 6 August 2007 "Thought for the Day." You advised that although I have the body of a man or a woman, the body is not me. It is simply a covering, a garment which is being worn by the eternal spiritual being who lives within. If we can revive our original spiritual nature through reviving our lost loving relationship with God, we will enter into an eternal, all-blissful, all-knowing existence.

My question is: then why is there so much suffering when something happens to this unworthy body? We have diseases like cancer, heart attacks, blockages, kidney stones, liver problems, etc. When we are attacked by any one of these, we have mental setbacks in addition to financial ruin. All of one's family members have mental worries.

I know we can avoid these diseases by chanting the great Hare Kṛṣṇa Mantra and not taking birth again, but why is it that even after chanting God's names people still suffer?

Art of Chanting

As long as we have a material body we are going to face the dualities of material existence: heat and cold, happiness and distress, poverty and wealth, sickness and health, etc. However, one who becomes solidly fixed in Kṛṣṇa consciousness, although apparently still suffering these dualities, is no longer disturbed by them because his consciousness is situated on a platform completely transcendental to this material existence.

Such a transcendental attainment requires that one be carefully trained by the expert spiritual master in how to chant the names of God in a state of pure *bhakti* consciousness. Although casual chanting of God's name with some material motives is beneficial for the gradual spiritual elevation of the living being, it does not situate him on the transcendental platform beyond all material miseries.

How Can You Be So Optimistic?

I do not understand the optimism of devotees who say the world can be perfected through the chanting of Hare Kṛṣṇa. No doubt, as the Christians say, "All things are possible with God," yet the current state of the world would contradict that the world is a perfectible place. Right now, within most recent memory, there are reports in the media of mothers chopping off the limbs of their babies; of one mother who hanged her three children and then herself. I work with mentally ill people, and the state of their rooms is squalid, deplorable and abominable beyond belief. To my mind, Kali-yuga has never been so bad on this planet. Presently within the past year, 19 million people have been displaced by the monsoons in Bangladesh. Crime is rampant and the cities are infested with thieves, and there is a drug dealer on every street corner. Not to speak of the so-called "War on Terrorism" perpetrated by the Americans on the rest of the world. To my mind, things will get worse before they get better. Perhaps we have 10,000 years ahead of us in which Lord Caitanya's *saṇkīrtana* movement will better the world, but will there not always be war and gross evil in this Kali-yuga?

Why Not Be Optimistic?

You are most probably right that things will get worse before they get better. But things getting worse will actually be favorable for things eventually getting much better. Why? Because the more this material world becomes painfully obvious as a hellish existence, the more people are going to be serious about a spiritual alternative.

The predicted anomalies (irregularities) of this quarrelsome age will certainly come to pass as well as the 10,000-year golden era of Śrī Caitanya Mahāprabhu. The good news is that as the golden era becomes more and more prominent, the anomalies of this troublesome age will decrease to the point of nil. The bad news is that after 10,000 years, the golden era will disappear and the anomalies will come in full force much worse than anything we've experienced so far. In fact, it will be so bad in those times that the troubles we now face will seem like a Sunday school picnic in comparison. This is why we advise everyone to get out of the cycle of birth and death as soon as possible by fully surrendering to Kṛṣṇa, or God, and going back the Spiritual Sky. Who wants to be eaten by cannibals?

Those persons who are enlightened by Vedic wisdom must necessarily be optimistic regarding the potential for a massive global paradigm shift through the wide-scale dissemination of Kṛṣṇa consciousness. Why? Because the authoritative predictions are there in revealed scripture that the entire globe will indeed be transformed by a tidal wave of Kṛṣṇa *bhakti*. Of course, considering the present state of world affairs, it may take many thousands of years before this sublime transformation becomes universal in scope.

But this does not mean that we should not try for it now. The fact is that the more sincerely and intelligently we try to fully bring in Lord Caitanya's golden era, the faster it will happen. So why not try for it with full enthusiasm? We've got nothing to lose and everything to gain! And since, as Śrīla Prabhupāda stated "impossible is a word in fool's dictionary," if we are sincere enough, pure enough and intelligent enough, it could even happen in our lifetimes that we can see all the high court judges throughout the entire world wearing Vaiṣṇava *tilaka*. If our preaching were to become this successful, we could give Śrīla Prabhupāda a pretty nice preaching report when we go for his *darśana* after rejoining him in the spiritual world. Just imagine what kind of blissful, beaming, merciful smile he would bestow upon us then!

Material Relief from Anxiety?

Sometimes, so much anxiety can occur that a person involves himself in sense-pleasure activities (like reading newspapers, hearing movie songs, etc.) not for the sake of enjoying those sense pleasures, but just to feel relieved of anxiety – believing that if he didn't engage in those activities, his anxiety would get out of control, and he might need medications to have a normal day.

If Kṛṣṇa consciousness does not provide such quick relief from anxiety to that individual, then is it justified for him to involve himself for a few minutes (about 15 minutes) a day to get anxiety relief and then get back to Kṛṣṇa consciousness?

Why Worsen the Disease?

Would a doctor prescribe a temporary remedy that will only make the disease worse?

One simply has to learn how to enjoy Kṛṣṇa consciousness. Kṛṣṇa consciousness and only Kṛṣṇa consciousness brings immediate and lasting relief from all kinds of material distress.

If someone is turning to such remedies for anxiety, it means that he does not know how to enter into the blissful world of Kṛṣṇa consciousness. Such a person needs to take shelter of bona fide spiritual master who can then guide him in how to enter into that realm which is completely free from all forms of anxiety.

Why Did Kṛṣṇa Create Māyā?

Why did Lord Śrī Kṛṣṇa create *māyā*, the illusory energy? This *māyā* makes a lot of people deeply entangled in material desires and gets them totally engrossed in material happiness, which is perishable.

To Facilitate Those Who Choose to Be in Illusion

Why does a state build prisons? Because it wants that there should be criminals? No. It builds the prisons to facilitate those who choose that they would like to be criminals.

In a similar way, Kṛṣṇa provides the material energy for those who desire to be in the illusion that they are the center of existence. Kṛṣṇa does not put anyone into *māyā*. *Māyā* is there, provided by Him, for those who want it.

Urgent Request for Your Advice

For the last 15 days, I've been getting endless thoughts of ending my life. I am unable to think of anything else, 24 hours a day. I read an online article on the complications of diabetes and, as I am myself a diabetic, I was shocked by what I read. It has left a horrific impact on my mind. I am continuously thinking, if I get one of these symptoms, how could I cope with it? I am unable to concentrate on my *japa* and day-to-day activity. My wife is also desperately worrying about my mental condition even though I have not told her completely about what kind of thoughts are running in my mind.

Kṛṣṇa Consciousness Is the Best Medicine

There is no sense in thinking about ending your life, because you are eternal. The root cause of your suffering is not your diabetes. You are suffering because your mind is not properly situated in Kṛṣṇa consciousness. With diabetes or without diabetes, you will still be in the suffering condition of birth, death, old age, and disease if your mind is not properly situated.

Of course you should aggressively pursue all medical and alternative medical avenues for dealing with your diabetes disease. And at the same time, you should realize that Kṛṣṇa has blessed you with an opportunity to very intensely take shelter of Him.

So now your duty is to make a two-pronged attack against your distress by, on the one hand, taking all medical help, and on the other hand, completely taking shelter of Lord Śrī Kṛṣṇa and depending on Him for the result.

You can pray to the Lord, "My dear Lord, if you want my body to die right now, that's all right. I am simply your surrendered servant. Whatever you want to do with me is Your mercy. But my one prayer is that you kindly allow me to always be absorbed purely, 24 hours a day, in hearing, chanting, and remembering your glorious names, fame, teachings and pastimes."

If you sincerely pray like this from the innermost core of your heart again and again until this mood becomes firmly established in your heart, I can assure you that all of your anxiety will go away and that your peaceful mind will facilitate the healing of your body. A disturbed mind is one of the causes of disease. So there is nothing worse than mental anxiety for making the body more diseased. And there is no better medicine than Kṛṣṇa consciousness for helping your body to regain its health. Of course, at the same time, you must follow all medical advice for dealing with the diseases of the body.

Why Do People Hide from Truth?

I would like to know about truth. Why do people hide or run away from truth, and what are the negative consequences? This type of person, even after lying, is successful in life. Why do such things happen? These people also study *Bhagavad-gītā*, but they do the opposite of its instructions.

They Are Conditioned by Lies

People run away from the truth because they are conditioned by the lies of the materialists to believe that this material nature is the all in all. They do not realize the truth, that there is a transcendental existence full of bliss and knowledge beyond the cycle of birth, death, old age, and disease. The consequence of running away from the truth is that they remain entangled in the cycle of birth, suffering the miseries of material existence.

Materialistic people who are currently enjoying material success are only doing so as a reaction resulting from their past pious activities. As soon as they burn up the stock of their good *karma*, they will be forced by the laws of nature to suffer so many varieties of hellish conditions. If one wants to become permanently free from all forms of material reactions, he must take shelter of the Supreme Personality of Godhead in full surrender.

The *Bhagavad-gītā* orders that we must study the *Bhagavad-gītā* from the bona fide spiritual master who is coming in disciplic succession. If we disobey the *Bhagavad-gītā* and try to understand it according it to our speculation, we will not properly understand what the *Bhagavad-gītā* is and how to correctly follow its teachings.

Solution for Global Warming

The world is complaining increasingly about global warming. This morning I was stunned to read an article on the subject about the dangerous future our posterity will have. Do you see anything improving? Do you have any suggestions from the scriptures? It disturbs me. I think *go-sevā* (serving the cow) and agriculture offer a partial solution to this difficult situation.

Global Cooling

Because of the ever-increasing volume of sinful activities, the natural balance of the earth's atmosphere is being more and more disrupted. No matter how much they may reduce or offset the carbon dioxide emissions, as long as the sin emissions continue to spiral out of control, the world will be unavoidingly plunged into an ever-increasingly nightmarish situation. This is all going on under the stringent control of the law of *karma*.

If they want to restore balance to the earth's atmosphere, the first thing they must do is close the slaughterhouses and the abortion clinics. And then by the wide-scale introduction of *nāma-saṇkīrtana*, congregational chanting of the holy names of God, the fire of lust and greed burning in the hearts of the human society will gradually cool, and the entire planet will gradually transform into a paradise.

At that time, a new, sustainable economic system based on the cow, the bull, and family farms will naturally emerge.

Appreciation

Anyone who takes a few seconds to thoughtfully read and understand your direction can surely attain self-realization. It is wonderful that this message is presented to 7,000 individuals daily. . . just think of the magnitude if seven billion tasted this sweet nectar!

Message to Deliver the Entire World

What you have stated regarding the potency of the bona fide spiritual master's teachings is certainly correct. Because the pure message of Kṛṣṇa that has been received from Śrīla Prabhupāda is being presented, the potency is there in our message to deliver the entire world. In his purport to the *Śrī Caitanya-caritāmṛta, Ādi-līlā*, Chapter 7, Text 25, Śrīla Prabhupāda states, "The Kṛṣṇa consciousness movement of Śrī Caitanya Mahāprabhu is so powerful that it can inundate the entire world and interest all classes of men in the subject of love of Godhead."

Billions are out there dying for want of this nectar that we are making easily available to them. The difficulty is that they don't know where to look for the nectar, and thus they are trying to squeeze it out of the all the wrong places, like trying to get fruit juice out of a rock. This is why we must disseminate this knowledge as widely as possible so that everyone can be exposed to this most sublime knowledge. We have practically experienced that any thoughtful, sensitive person who open-mindedly considers these teachings will be convinced to surrender their life to Kṛṣṇa, the Supreme Personality of Godhead.

One Religion – World Religions – Universal Harmony

Can Gods of Past Beliefs Be a Hindrance?

Can gods of one's past beliefs/practices, such as Christianity, be a hindrance to pursuing Hinduism/one's self-realization? What would you recommend?

There Is Only One Supreme God

There is only one Supreme God. He is totally beyond any conceptions of Hindu, Christian, Jew, or Muslim. It is man's foolishness to try to drag God down to some sectarian, dogmatic level. The Lord always remains pure and transcendental, beyond any designations of this material world. The self-realization science is transcendental to all designations such as Hindu or Christian and can, therefore, be practiced by anyone, whether they be Hindu or Christian or whatever.

Genuine devotion to Lord Jesus and Lord Kṛṣṇa is the same because Jesus is the son of God and Kṛṣṇa is God, the Father. Whether I am devoted to the son or the father, I automatically become devoted to them both because their purpose is the same - to spread love of God all over the world and deliver everyone back to the kingdom of God.

The whole point is to become perfect in your relationship with the Supreme Person. Whether you address God as Kṛṣṇa or Christ does not matter. What does matter is that you become fully surrendered unto that Supreme Person in loving service.

What Are Your Teachings?

Thank you for the inspiration and comfort your lessons and daily thoughts bring me. I noticed in a recent "Thought for the Day" that you mention your Christian Brothers and Sisters. I am confused about what your teachings are. Christian, Muslim, Indian Spirituality - how would I explain what to call these beautiful teachings? I am, very slowly, reading the *Bhagavad-gītā* which you graciously mailed to me. I am sure my question is answered there, but I have not as yet come to a decision on a name.

Kṛṣṇa Consciousness Is the Universal Religion for Everyone

In the *Bhagavad-gītā* Kṛṣṇa says:

sarva-yoniṣu kaunteya
mūrtayaḥ sambhavanti yāḥ
tāsāṁ brahma mahad yonir
ahaṁ bīja-pradaḥ pitā

"It should be understood that all species of life, O son of Kuntī, are made possible by birth in this material nature, and that I am the seed-giving father."

Bhagavad-gītā 14.4

This means that Kṛṣṇa is the father of all of us and that we are all brothers and sisters. So we are brothers and sisters with all types of people. Do you understand?

The point I was making in the "Thought for the Day" is that Kṛṣṇa consciousness, what we are teaching, is the universal religion for everyone. All can come together on the common platform of Kṛṣṇa consciousness and create a new world order of peace and prosperity.

Will People of Other Religions Reach Heaven?

Hare Kṛṣṇa people always say that they respect all religions and that there is one God, but with different names in different religions. If people of another religion - for example, Muslims or Christians - if they truly follow their own religion, follow its instructions, will they get the main goal of reaching Heaven?

There Is Only One Religion: To Love God

Any bona fide name for God, such as Kṛṣṇa, Allah, or Christ, may be uttered to achieve spiritual perfection. So actually there is only one religion: to love God. Just like the sun is referred to by different names in different languages, but still there is only one sun. But no matter which names of God you prefer to chant, you must give up sinful activities and lead a saintly life. It's not that you can simply label yourself as a Christian, a Hindu, or a Muslim and expect to be saved. Saintly life includes honoring and respecting all of God's children, including the animals. It does not include eating them. The process of self-realization is not so cheap.

Seeking Clarification about the Truth

What's the truth and how to prove it? Are the various religions the truth?

The Original Source/The Absolute Truth

Nothing comes from nothing. Everything comes from something. The original thing from which everything is coming directly and indirectly is an object of great interest both to theologians and scientists.

That original source is known as the Absolute Truth. You cannot negate the existence of the Absolute Truth in any absolute terms because that would be logically contradictory. Therefore, since the nonexistence of Absolute Truth is logically absurd, the Absolute Truth must in fact exist.

Just as the Absolute Truth is one, similarly Religion is one. Religion means to reconnect yourself with the Absolute Truth.

As soon as we talk about different religions we have descended into the dark, murky waters of untruth. There is one Absolute Truth and one Religion, to reconnect with that Absolute Truth. This one Religion has been taught by all the great masters in history, but we unenlightened fools have totally misunderstood their teachings and fought countless wars because of our gross ignorance.

Should We Resist Religious Conversion?

Why do people want to convert to other religions? What are their advantages? Should we or should we not resist religious conversion?

Convert from Irreligion to Religion

The whole concept of converting from one religion to another is an illusion. Religion is one: to love God. The only conversion you can actually make is from being irreligious to being religious. Those people who "convert" from one "religion" to another "religion" are actually simply converting from one form of irreligion to another form of irreligion.

Should I Go with Internal Guidance?

Previously you wrote, "By submissively hearing from and serving the bona fide spiritual master, one can quickly achieve the supreme perfection of Kṛṣṇa consciousness. However, those who criticize the bona fide spiritual master, taking him to be an ordinary person, will make no progress in their spiritual life, no matter how much they make a show of being an advanced devotee of the Lord."

The Muslims believe that the word of Allah is only propagated by the Qur'an, which contains Muhammad's discourses from 610-632. The Christians believe that only Jesus is Lord and Savior, that he died for our sins, and that there is no salvation except via this belief. The Jews believe that they are God's chosen people. And now you tell me that "by submissively hearing from and serving the bona fide spiritual master, one can quickly achieve the supreme perfection of Kṛṣṇa consciousness." Can you tell me why I should adopt your belief and shun all others? Would it not be more advisable to check all of them out, and then go with internal guidance?

Yes, But Only After Becoming Self-Realized

I appreciate very much your genuineness, intelligence, and sincerity reflected in the way you are inquiring. You have asked me why you should accept our beliefs and shun the beliefs of all others. Please try to understand in this regard that the bona fide spiritual master never talks about beliefs. Beliefs are the residential quarters of sentimentalists. The genuine guru speaks on the level of science, not blind faith.

There is one universal science of God. It is equally applicable whether one addresses the Lord as Allah, Christ, Jehovah, or Kṛṣṇa. That all the names are valid does not mean that any one of them by itself is invalid. They can all stand on their own as valid nomenclatures for the Supreme Godhead. Whether you follow Christ, Buddha, or Kṛṣṇa does not matter. What does matter is that you pick one path and do it perfectly. Don't be a jack of all trades and a master of none.

If I'm driving from Austin to Houston I can take either Highway 290 or Highway 71. Either highway will take me there. But if I try to take a little of Highway 71 and a little of Highway 290 instead of proceeding directly on either highway my journey will become very difficult indeed.

Internal guidance is fine once you've become self-realized, but right now the voice of the guide within you is garbled by the static of millions of lifetimes of mental conditioning. You are not pure enough to accurately discern the voice of the Lord who is guiding you from within your heart. This is why a fully realized spiritual master is absolutely essential. The fully realized guru is the external manifestation of the guide within you. By hearing and learning from the fully realized guru you are easily and perfectly connected with the guide within.

It doesn't matter if that guru is in the line of Allah, Jesus, Buddha, or Kṛṣṇa. What does matter is that he is fully realized. If he is not fully realized he will not be able to connect you with the guide within. If he is fully realized he will be able to connect you very nicely with that inner voice. By learning from such a guru you will become totally reconnected with your eternal spiritual nature and thus you will become absolutely ecstatic. The proof of the pudding is in the eating!

That guide within is described in Christian scripture as the Holy Ghost. He is described in the most detailed and complete way in the ancient Vedic scriptures of India. There He is known as the Supersoul or Paramātmā, and His exact appearance is described in detail.

Philosophy alone can only give theoretical realization of the Absolute Truth. Full realization only comes when one puts that philosophy into practical action. Are you ready?

Enquiry about Buddhism

When you include Buddha in "sacred names," do you mean sacred names in correlation to God, or sacred names in general? If Buddhists are atheists, please explain to me how devotees of Kṛṣṇa include Buddha and by what degree. I understand the appreciation of the state of perfect enlightenment. Wasn't Buddhism started by Siddhartha Gautama between 500-400 B.C.? If Buddhism is voidism it seems to me to be a contradiction to include Buddhism in relation to God.

Please explain to me how the correlation was intended to be interpreted.

Buddha Is an Incarnation of God

Because Buddha is an incarnation of God, His name is indeed sacred in the same way as the names of Kṛṣṇa or Rāma. Lord Buddha appeared for the specific purpose of putting a stop to the abuse of the Vedic scriptures. At the time He appeared the Vedas were being interpreted in a twisted way to justify animal-killing. In order to save the poor animals, Buddha denied the Vedas and established the principle of *ahiṁsā*, nonviolence, on the basis of the law of *karma*. He convinced the people to become atheists but to follow Him. In this way He tricked them into following God, because He was Himself God. It's a fact that, technically speaking, Buddhism is not a religion because it denies the existence of God, presenting Void as the ultimate reality.

But the Buddhists unknowingly are getting the benefit of worshipping God when they revere and worship Lord Buddha. Buddhism is actually a sub-religious system of moral upliftment. Historically in India it helped to pave the way for the full-fledged introduction of Kṛṣṇa consciousness which took place from 1486 onward after Lord Caitanya appeared.

Biblical References to Meat-Eating

I have some more questions that have me confused with the intentions of the *Bhagavad-gītā* in comparison to the Bible. If one approaches both with open arms, as if there were a parallel between them, then one would be able to distinguish the contrasts as well. There are a few contrasting views in the Bible when compared to the *Bhagavad-gītā* in regard to which I would like your interpretation: Romans 14:2-3, 1 Tim 4:1-4 and Romans 14:17.

Thou Shalt Not Kill

You have inquired regarding the following passages from the Bible:

<u>Romans 14:2-3</u>

- One man's faith allows him to eat everything, but another man, whose faith is weak, eats only vegetables.
- The man who eats everything must not look down on him who does not, and the man who does not eat everything must not condemn the man who does, for God has accepted him.

<u>1 Tim 4:1-4</u>

1. Now the Spirit speaketh expressly, that in the latter times some shall depart from the faith, giving heed to seducing spirits, and doctrines of devils;
2. Speaking lies in hypocrisy; having their conscience seared with a hot iron;

3. Forbidding to marry, and commanding to abstain from meats, which God hath created to be received with thanksgiving of them which believe and know the truth.
4. For every creature of God is good, and nothing to be refused, if it be received with thanksgiving.

Romans 14:17

17. For the kingdom of God is not meat and drink; but righteousness, and peace and joy in the Holy Ghost.

If we accept the above verses as accurate translations, the first point is that these are not the teachings of Jesus. They are Paul's personal opinion. They are not the words of God, nor the words of Jesus Christ. They are the words of Paul, who joined the Christian movement some time after the departure of Jesus.

Even if we accept them as gospel, we still cannot reject the Ten Commandments on the strength of the above verses. In the Ten Commandments we are strictly prohibited from killing. Therefore, if a Christian chooses to exercise what he considers as his option to eat meat in light of the above verses, he will have to restrict his meat-eating to animals that have died naturally, not ones that were killed. If he violates the Ten Commandments we do not condemn him. He condemns himself by his own willful disobedience to the laws of God.

Some people who are attached to eating the flesh of killed animals have stated that the real meaning of "Thou shalt not kill" is "Thou shalt not murder." Therefore, they say, it is okay to kill and eat animals. But if we look at the original Hebrew for Exodus 20:13, i.e. "Thou Shalt Not Kill," we find the Hebrew is "lo tirtzack," which accurately translates as "any kind of killing whatsoever." Another point is that Christians are very critical of devotees of Kṛṣṇa who do not eat meat even though they are strictly forbidden to look down on us per Romans 14:3. If they do not even follow their own scriptures, why and how do they expect us to take them seriously? They talk very big and do not follow their scriptures. We strictly abide by ours. That should tell you something about the difference between so-called Christianity and Kṛṣṇa consciousness. My father was a Christian but he very much respected me that I strictly follow my scripture, the *Bhagavad-gītā*. And he rendered very much service also to help the Kṛṣṇa consciousness movement.

God said in Genesis: "Behold, I have given you every herb-bearing seed, which [is] upon the face of all the earth, and every tree, in which [is] the fruit of a tree-yielding seed; to you it shall be for meat."

If you look in the Merriam-Webster online dictionary you will find that the first definition for meat is "food," not animal flesh. If someone is addicted to eating meat, they will interpret the word meat as animal flesh, but we see that God defined meat as vegetarian food.

Someone who cannot see the spark of divinity within a living creature and wants to kill it and devour its flesh is a very low-class person at best. Such persons are addicted to the temporary titillation of their temporary taste buds. According to the law of *karma* described in the Vedic literatures and according to the Biblical principle, "as you sow, so shall you reap," someone who eats an animal that was killed in a slaughterhouse will in the future meet a similar fate. This is why Kṛṣṇa explains in the *Bhagavad-gītā*:

ye hi saṁsparśa-jā bhogā
duḥkha-yonaya eva te
ādy-antavantaḥ kaunteya
na teṣu ramate budhaḥ

> "An intelligent person does not take part in the sources of misery, which are due to contact with the material senses. O son of Kuntī, such pleasures have a beginning and an end, and so the wise man does not delight in them."
>
> *Bhagavad-gītā* 5.22

What I have thus far explained is only the tip of the iceberg. If you have any questions regarding the above points do not hesitate to write or call me, and I can explain these matters to you in much fuller detail.

Christianity and Kṛṣṇa Consciousness

I have been reading the knowledge of Kṛṣṇa consciousness now for over three years. I have read *Bhagavad-gītā As It Is* twice. I just completed *Kṛṣṇa Book*, which was one of the deepest and most revealing of books. I have chanted on my *japa* beads as much as 16 rounds per day for a six-month period. But I keep falling back to the two blocks that keep me from stepping from the bridge of reason into utter surrender to Kṛṣṇa.

First, I read in the first volume of *Memoirs: Anecdotes of a Modern-Day Saint* that the spiritual master is to be considered or looked at as God. This I find very difficult to swallow. I know intellectually that I want to be God, so that it is hard for me to look upon another as God. I understand the disciplic succession all the way back to Kṛṣṇa as well. But to look upon another human as God is impossible for me and keeps me blocked from complete surrender.

Second, I am a Christian living a set of spiritual principles that are also guided by the regulative principles of Kṛṣṇa consciousness. I do not gamble, drink alcohol, take drugs, or partake in illicit sex, and I sometimes don't eat meat. I never eat the cow. Śrīla Prabhupāda said once, "If you must eat meat, please do not eat the cow." I keep that promise to him for myself.

But what is really blocking me is the Deities. In the New Testament Acts 21:25 it states, in part, the following: "They should not eat food offered to idols, nor consume blood, nor eat meat from strangled animals, and they should stay away from all sexual immorality." The word "idols" keeps glaring back at me, and as I look at the Deities, They appear to be idols that food is offered to. Of course, I have read the analogy about the mailbox being a bona fide receptacle, but that doesn't shake my gut instincts. I keep reading the Bible and the *Bhagavad-gītā* and I see the similarities between the two.

I guess I am asking, how do I bring my consciousness around to fully surrender to Kṛṣṇa? How do I get to that place where in my heart and soul I can see and feel the truth?

There Is Only One Absolute Truth, Equally Applicable to All

I appreciate very much your genuine sincerity in regard to becoming a fully surrendered, pure devotee of the Lord. Your bringing forward your doubts to the spiritual master for clarification is the authorized process for clearing away the stumbling blocks on the path of devotion.

When we read in the authoritative scriptures that the spiritual master is to be accepted AS God it does not mean that we should think that he IS God. Note the distinction between the word "is" and the word "as." There is a gulf of difference. We accept the spiritual master AS we accept God. It means that just as we accept God as our spiritual authority, we also accept the spiritual master as our spiritual authority because he is the authorized representative of the Lord.

When a policeman turns on his siren and blinking red lights and starts following you down the highway, you have to accept him as being as good as the government. Actually he is a citizen just like you are. He has to obey the laws of the state just like you do. But when he is on duty and he commands you to pull over, he has to be accepted AS the government, even though he personally IS NOT the government. As long as he is properly executing his duties as a policeman, you are duty-bound to obey him. Is this clear?

Another example: in Christian theology Christ is considered the Son of God, but still he is accepted with the same veneration and devotion and surrender that is offered to God the Father because he purely represents God. The Son is considered as good as the Father, even though he is a different person. We don't take Christ to literally be the Father because that would make the Lord's Prayer absurd - Christ talking to himself. In the same way, we take the spiritual master to be the most confidential servant of God who connects us with God.

When I was with Śrīla Prabhupāda in New Vṛndāvana in 1972, he gave the example of the British viceroy during the British rule of India. He was not the king, but he was given the same honor and respect that was given to the king because he was the king's representative. Whatever gifts were offered to him were not accepted as his personal property. He would send those gifts to the royal treasury in London.

We also agree about not offering food to idols. "Idols" means "false gods." The authorized Deity manifestation of Lord Krsna is not an idol. It is the special mercy of Kṛṣṇa that He has agreed to accept our offerings in this way. Even according to Christian theology God is omnipresent. So if He is present everywhere, then certainly He is also present in His authorized Deity form. You cannot say that He is present everywhere except in the form of the Deity. That would be absurd. Just as in the Bible the Lord manifested His divine presence within the material manifestation of a burning bush, similarly the Lord fully manifests His divine presence within the form of His Deity so that His devotees can practice the art of rendering personal service to Him.

Are these points clear? If not, please inquire further. I am simply your humble servant to help you fully realize the Absolute Truth. There is only one Absolute Truth. It is neither Christian nor Hindu. It is equally applicable to all. When you realize that Absolute Truth you become the best Christian, the best Hindu, the best Muslim, the best humanitarian, the best everything.

To fully surrender to Kṛṣṇa you must fully surrender yourself to his representative, the bona fide spiritual master. By practical surrender in this way, you will see and feel how you are living in pure communion with God at every moment. The skeptical person can try this on an experimental basis for a period of time and then make a judgment based on the results. You have nothing to lose and everything to gain from surrendering to Kṛṣṇa. You should do it right now.

Why wait? Time and tide wait for no man. At any moment we could die by the stringent laws of this material nature. Therefore, surrender should not be postponed. It should be done immediately!

Who Do I Pray to Now?

I had always felt drawn to spirituality even though I felt like a caged bird. Then a Reiki teacher introduced me to healing treatments via meditation. I have been meditating regularly, reading scriptures, and learning about Reiki. I am now taking a course in Reiki healing.

Then a few days ago, I felt as if I didn't know who to worship any longer. I was brought up in the Christian faith, so I have always worshipped the God in the Bible. But then I started to feel that I had the power in me. It was like a living, breathing entity with a mind of its own. And, if I didn't meditate, it seemed to grow weak. I feel so awkward not knowing who to pray to. All of my life I have been degraded and humiliated by others who seemed to be intimidated by me. They acted as if I were convicting them of their sin, and because of this they were going to do everything they could to put me down. I'm still going through this, but it is not as bad as it was before. What is happening to me?

The Supreme Person

I have noted your awkwardness of not knowing who to pray to, and I am very pleased that you are inquiring from me in this way. To know who to pray to is the most important question we can ask in this human form of life. That person to whom you should pray is described as follows in the *Kaṭha Upaniṣad*:

nityo nityānāṁ cetanaś cetanānām
eko yo bahūnāṁ vidadhāti kāmān

> "There is one singular eternal amongst the plural eternals. And there is one singular conscious being, amongst the plural consciousness beings. The difference is the singular is maintaining the plurals, and the plurals are being maintained by that singular."
>
> *Kaṭha Upaniṣad* 2.2.13

By further research into Vedic teachings, we discover that the Supreme Person is Viṣṇu, and that in His original form He is known as Kṛṣṇa. Therefore you should accept Lord Kṛṣṇa as that person to whom you should pray. The best prayer is given in the *Kali-Santaraṇa Upaniṣad* as follows:

Hare Kṛṣṇa, Hare Kṛṣṇa, Kṛṣṇa Kṛṣṇa , Hare Hare
Hare Rāma, Hare Rāma, Rāma Rāma, Hare Hare

In this prayer we are begging the Lord (Krsna or Rāma) and His energy (Hare) that They kindly, both of Them, engage us in Their service. This chanting will bestow upon you all desirable things and make your life absolutely perfect and sublime.

Which Is the Best Religion?

There are different religions in the world, such as Hinduism, Christianity, Islam, Buddhism, Sikhism, Jainism and a few other religions. Kṛṣṇa says in the *Gītā* that He is supreme, and similarly Christ and Allah say in their religious books that they are supreme. How does an average, neutral human being judge the major religions and decide which is the best way forward? I feel confused. Each religion is telling that their God is superior and that one should accept their particular ideology. Kindly advise me on this. Does this mean that if a person accepts Kṛṣṇa consciousness he is liberated, and if he follows other religions he is not on the right track?

Pocket Dictionary and Unabridged Dictionary

In the Christian Bible and Islamic teachings there are statements indicating that there is more knowledge beyond what those teachings are revealing. For example, in the Bible, Christ states, "There is so much that I have yet to tell thee, but you cannot bear to hear it now."

Compare this with what Kṛṣṇa states in the *Bhagavad-gītā*:

jñānaṁ te 'haṁ sa-vijñānam
idaṁ vakṣyāmy aśeṣataḥ
yaj jñātvā neha bhūyo 'nyaj
jñātavyam avaśiṣyate

"I shall now declare unto you in full this knowledge, both phenomenal and numinous. This being known, nothing further shall remain for you to know."

Bhagavad-gītā 7.2

So according to what the Christian, Islamic, and Vedic teachings say about themselves, the Vedas are giving the complete, full knowledge and the Christian and Islamic teachings are giving a portion of it. This does not deny the validity of the Christian and Islamic teachings. This is simply to establish the more complete nature of the Vedic teachings. It is just like the difference between a pocket dictionary and an unabridged dictionary. Do you understand? Both dictionaries are valid, but one is more complete than the other one.

This is not our bias. This is according to the version of the teachings themselves. This is why I am following the Vedic teachings. If the Bible or Islamic teachings were more complete, I would follow them instead. I am not attached to any particular religion or any particular organization. I am simply attached to realizing and living the Truth in its most complete form.

My membership in ISKCON, the Hare Kṛṣṇa Movement, is utilitarian, not blind. I participate in ISKCON because they have the most perfect and complete conception of the Absolute Truth and the most perfect and complete methodology for realizing the Absolute Truth.

Can Man Make Up a Religion?

Can man make up a religion, if it has love of God in it? Or must he be a qualified and pure messenger of God like Śrīla Prabhupāda was?

Religion Can Only Be Given by God

Man cannot make up a religion. If a religious system is concocted, it will not be effective in liberating its followers from the cycle of birth and death. It is confirmed in the *Śrīmad-Bhāgavatam* that religion can be given only by God.

dharmaṁ tu sākṣād bhagavat-praṇītaṁ

"Real religious principles can only be given by God."

Śrīmad-Bhāgavatam 6.3.19

Even though Śrīla Prabhupāda is a most highly qualified and pure messenger of God, he did not make up a religion. He simply purely presents what Kṛṣṇa is giving in the *Bhagavad-gītā*.

If a postman delivers you a letter, you want to receive it in its original, pure form. You do not want the postman to change it or to concoct a letter that is supposedly from your friend when your friend factually wrote you something else. In the same way, we must learn religion directly from God Himself in the *Bhagavad-gītā* or from his pure messenger who does not adulterate it in any way. The highly qualified and pure messenger will deliver God's teachings to you in their original, pure form without even a slight tinge of adulteration - 100% pure. In spiritual life 99.99% pure is not good enough. We must be following a system that is 100% pure if we want to go back to Godhead.

Correlation Between Christianity and Vaiṣṇavism

Since we are in the season of Christmas, I thought I would get your perspective on Jesus' birth.

1. Is it true that Vaiṣṇavas celebrate Janmāṣṭamī in the same way that Christians celebrate Christmas Day?
2. Is it possible to be a Christian and a Vaiṣṇava at the same time?
3. Can one be a Vaiṣṇava and worship Christ as God, rather than Kṛṣṇa (at least as a chosen ideal)?
4. Isn't that the position of Śrīla Prabhupāda, who said the guru is the same as God? Hare Kṛṣṇa.

Jesus Christ Is a Pure Vaiṣṇava

There are similarities between Janmāṣṭamī and Christmas in that they are both days of great spiritual happiness for devout Kṛṣṇites and Christians respectively. On Janmāṣṭamī devotees of the Lord will hear and chant the glories of the Lord all day long and will fast all day up until midnight, at which time a feast and *ārati* are offered to the Lord. After the *ārati* the devotees will break their fast by honoring Janmāṣṭamī *prasādam*.

A true Christian must necessarily be a Vaiṣṇava also - automatically - because (as confirmed by Śrīla Prabhupāda) Christ is a pure Vaiṣṇava. The heavenly Father that Christ prayed to is revealed in the *Bhagavad-gītā* as Lord Śrī Kṛṣṇa. Śrīla Prabhupāda explains: A Vaiṣṇava is unhappy to see the suffering of others. Therefore, Lord Jesus Christ agreed to be crucified - to free others from their suffering. But his followers are so unfaithful that they have decided, "Let Christ suffer for us, and we'll go on committing sin." They love Christ so much that they think, "My dear Christ, we are very weak. We cannot give up our sinful activities. So you please suffer for us."

Jesus Christ presented himself as the Son of God, one in purpose with his father but a different person from his father. We follow his teaching. We do not concoct some idea that he is God, the Father. He would never have approved of being described as being God, the Father. We cannot separate the conception of Kṛṣṇa from the conception of God because Kṛṣṇa is God, the original father, the Supreme Person. We can in one sense say that the spiritual master and Jesus Christ are Kṛṣṇa or God because they are as good as God in the sense that they act with the full potency of God for delivering the fallen, conditioned souls of this material world.

Because Jesus and the bona fide spiritual master purely represent Kṛṣṇa, or God, they are considered to be non-different from Him. This does not mean they are one and the same as Him. It means that they are simultaneously one with and different from Him.

I Cannot Believe In Eternal Damnation

I was raised in a culture of Christianity, mostly Baptist and Methodist. I've never really claimed either. I was always put out by their seeming arrogance and hypocrisy. One thing is for certain: there is a substantial preoccupation with death and the afterlife in this culture. They warn everyone that you must love and follow Christ, or you will meet your fate in eternal damnation.

That's hard to get out of my psyche. Yet I've always questioned how a loving creator could allow such a thing.

Is it that we are expected to love and forgive, but our creator is not? All these rules and policies seem so made-up - as if God were some kind of Czar in the heavens raining his fury down on the human race.

I see a lot of truth in your lessons. I see the path to possible happiness. But those people's voices are in the back of my mind telling me that if I do this I'll burn for sure. Why would God want us to love him out of fear? Does that not make the love counterfeit?

Can you help me with this? What is your view of Christianity? Did Christ die for our sins, or was it mostly for his disciples? Is Kṛṣṇa the same thing as Christ? Doesn't God incarnate himself to come to the earth and help us?

Kṛṣṇa Attracts Us with the Enchanting Sound of His Flute

You are right. The idea of eternal damnation is a bogus idea. God is the most kind and forgiving person. In fact, love and forgiveness exist simply because Kṛṣṇa is so very, very kind.

The big-nasty-cop-in-the-sky concept is not at all correct. God is the most beautiful, sweet, kind-hearted Lord Kṛṣṇa who doesn't have to scare anyone into surrendering to Him. He attracts us all back to home, back to Godhead, with the enchanting sound of His beautiful flute and His inconceivably amazing pastimes with His devotees.

Christ was very unhappy to see the suffering of others. Therefore, he agreed to be crucified to free others from their suffering. But his followers are so unfaithful that they have decided, "Let Christ suffer for us, and we'll go on committing sin." They love Christ so much that they think, "My dear Christ, we are very weak. We cannot give up our sinful activities. So you please suffer for us." This is not love of Jesus. This is love of sin.

Kṛṣṇa is God, the Father. When Jesus prays, "Our Father, Who are in heaven," he's praying to Kṛṣṇa.

Lord Kṛṣṇa has now manifested on the earth in the form of the Hare Kṛṣṇa *mantra* to deliver everyone from their suffering. The entire world can now be delivered from the quagmire of delusion if they will simply chant:

Hare Kṛṣṇa, Hare Kṛṣṇa, Kṛṣṇa Kṛṣṇa , Hare Hare
Hare Rāma, Hare Rāma, Rāma Rāma, Hare Hare

How Does Kṛṣṇa View Other Religions?

I come from a Christian background and find the sectarianism present in Christianity to be very unattractive. Many different sects of Christians are always at odds as to who has the rightful claim to Jesus' teachings. From my brief foray into Christian history I have noted that many scriptures from the early Christians were removed from their belief system, and that what we have at present is not at all like the original teachings. Many of the Gnostic texts were considered heretical and a concerted effort was made by the established church to eliminate their teachings. Not only were their scriptures vilified, but anyone who believed in them was persecuted. So my question is: How does Kṛṣṇa view other religions? And how do the followers of Kṛṣṇa not fall into the same trap of creating a sectarian religion? By sectarian I mean thinking that anyone who does not follow the way of Kṛṣṇa as presented by the Hare Kṛṣṇas is wrong and will forever be condemned to live in hell.

"Many Religions" Is a Man-Made Conception

Kṛṣṇa-conscious philosophy rejects the concept of many religions as a man-made conception. Kṛṣṇa, or God, has given us only one religion: to develop our love for Him. This same religion has been taught by Lord Kṛṣṇa and all the great religious leaders of history. The *Bhagavad-gītā* enjoins us to give up the idea of different religions and fully surrender ourselves unto the Supreme Lord. That one Supreme Lord is known as Kṛṣṇa, Rāma, Govinda, Allah, Jehovah, etc.

What Is Hinduism?

I want to know about Hinduism. Why did they name it Hinduism? What does it mean?

The Religion of Those Living East of the River Sindhu

The Muslims mispronounced the river Sindhu as Hindu. They came to refer to those people who lived on the other side of the Sindhu river at Hindus. So Hindu technically means someone who lives east of the Sindhu River. It is not a term that appears anywhere in the Vedic scriptures. And Hinduism is said to be their religion. But there are so many different religion systems practiced by those who live east of the Sindhu River.

The actual word for the ancient culture of India is "*sanātana-dharma,*" which means the eternal nature of the soul. Someone who follows this path is known as "*sanātana-dharmī.*"

"Thought for the Day" Inspires a Christian

I read your daily messages eagerly every day. This course has made such a difference in my life as a Christian. I repeat what I said to you last year: I wish every Christian minister preached as you do.

This Proves that Our Message Is Transcendental

I am very, very happy to hear how enlivened you are to read my daily messages. That your life as a Christian has been transformed by these messages is proof of their transcendental nature.

I pray that your wish will come true. If every Christian minister and the ministers of all faiths can capture the true spirit of *sankīrtaṇa*, the congregational chanting of the holy names of God, it will create a spiritual revolution that will completely transform the human society. This entire earth planet will become a paradise.

Is Jesus the Only Way?

I noted in your response, "Many Religions to God Are Man-Made," there was no mention about Jesus being the door to a relationship to God, Jehovah etc. In 1 John 2:23 of The Holy Bible it states, "Whosoever denieth the Son the same hath not the Father; but he that acknowledgeth the son hath the Father also." Does this mean that Jesus is the only hope we have for a true, eternal relationship with God? What do you think about this verse?

The Way of Jesus, Pure Bhakti, Is the Only Way

This verse establishes the principle that our only hope for a true eternal relationship with God is to approach God through the transparent via medium of the bona fide spiritual master. It is fact, as confirmed in this Bible verse, that God cannot be approached directly. We can only approach him by the mercy of the bona fide spiritual master.

Since Jesus Christ is in fact one of the greatest spiritual masters in the history of the world, we Kṛṣṇites certainly accept his position of being our savior. In fact, it was Jesus Christ who inspired me to take to the pathway of *kṛṣṇa-bhakti*. God the Son, Lord Jesus Christ, blessed me by giving me the pathway to God the Father, Lord Sri Kṛṣṇa. By accepting the guidance of Jesus I was blessed with Kṛṣṇa consciousness.

Why Did You Choose Kṛṣṇa Consciousness?

What is it about Kṛṣṇa consciousness that made you choose to follow it above other paths? There are many great traditions, i.e. Islam, Christianity, Judaism etc. I would like to know what stands out about Hare Kṛṣṇa that made you follow it as opposed to others.

The Greatest Good Fortune

I am very happy to hear that my humble attempt to pass on the enlightened wisdom I have received from my beloved spiritual master is helping and inspiring you. Of course, this does not surprise me because I know how much it benefits me at every minute. Your appreciation simply tells me that you are a very sincere recipient of this most sublime wisdom.

An enlightened spiritual being does not perceive that there are different paths. He perceives one path with different levels of advancement along that one path. He also sees that some are going in the wrong direction on that path.

When we create sects such as Hinduism, Christianity, Judaism, Islam, etc, we are definitely heading in the wrong direction on the path. We are not seeing things on the enlightened spiritual platform. Rather we are seeing things on the miserable and illusory material platform.

In this connection it is stated in the *Śrī Īśopaniṣad*:

yasmin sarvāṇi bhūtāny
ātmaivābhūd vijānataḥ
tatra ko mohaḥ kaḥ śoka
ekatvam anupaśyataḥ

> "One who always sees all living entities as spiritual sparks, in quality one with the Lord, becomes a true knower of things. What, then, can be illusion or anxiety for him?"
>
> *Śrī Īśopaniṣad* Mantra 7

The great Vedic sages clearly perceived and followed that one path, and if we are fortunate we will carefully follow in their footsteps. If we are fortunate, we will not remain in the realm of relativity, where life is temporary and full of ignorance and misery. We will take the mercy of those sages and become elevated into that sweet realm of eternity, knowledge and bliss.

Whether we choose to label this as Allah consciousness, Christ consciousness, Jehovah consciousness, Universal consciousness, or Kṛṣṇa consciousness is not the point. The point is that we must revive our original, loving relationship with the Supreme Person, the source of all that exists.

Because His Divine Grace A.C. Bhaktivedanta Swami Prabhupāda had shown himself to be the most highly realized master in this universal science of the soul, I enrolled in his training program while I had the chance. I grabbed it in 1971 while the getting was good.

This is a decision which I have been celebrating for the last 35 years. By his grace I have achieved the greatest good fortune. Now if you like I can bestow that greatest good fortune on you. Would you like it?

Can't Somebody Explain the Koran As It Is?

My wife is a Muslim but she is chanting 16 rounds now and reading Śrīla Prabhupāda's books. I am reading a lot about Islam, and certainly there is a lot to be learned. Can't somebody truly explain the Koran as it is and make this world a better place?

Lord Caitanya Has Already Done That and Now So Should You

I am very happy to hear that your Muslim wife is so nicely adopting the universal, non-sectarian, nectarean process of Kṛṣṇa consciousness. The great *ācārya* (spiritual master who teaches by example) of chanting the Hare Kṛṣṇa *mantra*, Haridāsa Ṭhākura, also came from a Muslim family. That did not stop him from becoming *nāmācārya*, the greatest chanter of the Lord's holy names.

You are hoping that someone can explain the Koran as it is and make the world a better place. This was already done 500 years ago by Śrī Caitanya Mahāprabhu. This He did in a famous conversation with a Muslim scholar. The Lord explained as follows:

"The Koran accepts the fact that ultimately there is only one God. He is full of opulence, and His bodily complexion is blackish. According to the Koran, the Lord has a supreme, blissful, transcendental body. He is the Absolute Truth, the all-pervading, omniscient and eternal being. He is the origin of everything. Creation, maintenance and dissolution come from Him. He is the original shelter of all gross and subtle cosmic manifestations. The Lord is the Supreme Truth, worshipable by everyone. He is the cause of all causes. By engaging in His devotional service, the living entity is relieved from material existence. No conditioned soul can get out of material bondage without serving the Supreme Personality of Godhead. Love at His lotus feet is the ultimate goal of life. The happiness of liberation, whereby one merges into the Lord's existence, cannot even be compared to a fragment of the transcendental bliss obtained by service unto the Lord's lotus feet. In the Koran there are descriptions of fruitive activity, speculative knowledge, mystic power and union with the Supreme, but ultimately all this is refuted and the Lord's personal feature established, along with His devotional service. The scholars of the Koran are not very advanced in knowledge. Although there are many methods prescribed, they do not know that the ultimate conclusion should be considered the most powerful. Seeing your own Koran and deliberating over what is written there, what is your conclusion?"

The saintly Muslim replied:

"All that You have said is true. This has certainly been written in the Koran, but our scholars can neither understand nor accept it. Usually they describe the Lord's impersonal aspect, but they hardly know that the Lord's personal feature is worshipable. They are undoubtedly lacking this knowledge. Since You are that very same Supreme Personality of Godhead Himself, please be merciful upon me. I am fallen and unfit. I have studied the Muslim scripture very extensively, but from it I cannot conclusively decide what the ultimate goal of life is or how I can approach it. Now that I have seen You, my tongue is chanting the Hare Kṛṣṇa *mahā-mantra*. The false prestige I felt from being a learned scholar is now gone."

I am requesting that you kindly fully dedicate your life for spreading the Kṛṣṇa consciousness movement all over the world. You should be that person who explains the Koran as it is and makes the world a better place.

Isn't It Better to Sing the Name of Jesus with Love?

Isn't it better to sing the name of Jesus with love than to chant the Hare Kṛṣṇa *mantra* without love?

If You Truly Love One, You Will Automatically Love the Other

How can someone love the son without the loving the father? Or how can someone love the father without loving the son?

If someone thinks that they only love the son and not the father, their love for the son is imaginary. It is not real. Such pseudo-love is not accepted by the son, nor is it accepted by the father.

Similarly, if someone thinks that they only love the father and not the son, their love for the father is also imaginary, not real, and not acceptable by either the father or the son.

God, the Son, in the form of Jesus Christ, taught that we must love his father. Therefore if we actually love Jesus, we will obey his order to love his father, Lord Śrī Kṛṣṇa. God, the Father, Lord Śrī Kṛṣṇa, teaches us to love everyone, especially His pure devotees such as Lord Jesus Christ. Therefore if we actually love Kṛṣṇa, we must also love Lord Jesus Christ.

If you truly love one, you will automatically love the other. Is this clear to you?

Regarding Christ and Kṛṣṇa

I was raised as a Christian, in fact a Catholic, but now I am so in love with Kṛṣṇa that I think I may be doing Jesus a disfavor. Do you think that he minds that I am so into Lord Kṛṣṇa? Isn't his "job" to bring us to the Father, to Kṛṣṇa? I am a little confused as to whom I should owe my allegiance. They are both *avatāras*, forms of Godhead, equal in all respects. So, maybe I am worrying about nothing. I can still pray to either, or both; although my favorite Deity is still Lord Kṛṣṇa.

Develop Actual Pure Devotion

Lord Jesus Christ is most pleased with you that you have approached his father, Lord Kṛṣṇa, because, as you say, his job is to bring everyone to Kṛṣṇa. There is no question of whether you should have allegiance to one or the other. If you are devoted to Jesus, he will lead you to Kṛṣṇa. And if you are devoted to Kṛṣṇa, He will order you to worship His pure devotees such as Lord Jesus Christ.

That they are both *avatāras* is a fact. *Avatāra* means one who descends into the material world from the spiritual world. But because they are different types of *avatāra* they are not equal in all respects. Lord Jesus is known as a *śaktyāveśa-avatāra*, an associate of the Lord who was ordered by the Lord to come here to spread love of God, and Lord Kṛṣṇa is *Avatāri*, the source of all the *avatāras*.

It is a fact that by surrendering unto Lord Kṛṣṇa that you have nothing to worry about. By doing so you will become a perfect follower of Christ. Whether you approach the spiritual world through Kṛṣṇa or Christ, either way you are in good shape. But you must develop actual pure devotion, not the pseudo-devotion which is nothing more than covered materialism that is being deceptively peddled as pure devotion these days in the age of Kali.

Religion and Faith

I think you are doing very good work just like Śrīla Prabhupāda. Somebody asked me some questions, and I was unable to answer them. Could you please help me?

My questions are:

What is religion and what is faith?

Is Kṛṣṇa consciousness a faith or a religion?

How many forms of religion exist?

Real Religion Is Beyond This Faith or That Faith

It is nice that you are appreciating my humble attempt to push forward Kṛṣṇa consciousness all over the world. But please try to understand in this connection that I can take no credit for what I am doing. Whatever I am accomplishing is all by the mercy of Śrīla Prabhupāda. If I have any credit, it is simply that I am faithfully carrying out the instructions I received from Śrīla Prabhupāda.

Religion is generally taken to be a kind of faith that develops according to time and circumstances, just like someone may say that I am member of the Christian religion, the Islamic religion, etc. But that is not the real meaning of religion.

The English word "religion" comes from the Latin word "religio," which means "reverence." Religion is a combination of the Latin "re," which means "again," and "ligare," which means "to connect" (as in the English word "ligament"). So the actual meaning of "religion" is to reconnect with God, the source of our existence.

Just as we reconnect with another human being through love, the reconnecting process with God is through loving service to Him. This reconnecting process is completely transcendental to any conception of this religion or that religion. Thus, real religion is to completely surrender ourselves unto the Supreme Person. It is completely transcendental to this faith or that faith. Therefore, Kṛṣṇa states in the *Bhagavad-gītā*:

sarva-dharmān parityajya
mām ekaṁ śaraṇaṁ vraja
ahaṁ tvāṁ sarva-pāpebhyo
mokṣayiṣyāmi mā śucaḥ

> "Abandon all varieties of religion and just surrender unto Me. I shall deliver you from all sinful reactions. Do not fear."
>
> *Bhagavad-gītā* 18.66

Kṛṣṇa is not telling us to abandon religion. He is telling us how we can fully embrace real religion by rejecting all pseudo-religion that is masquerading as religion and fully surrendering ourselves to Him.

Kṛṣṇa consciousness is actual religion because it is teaching us simply to surrender to the Supreme Person. It is not a kind of faith. A Kṛṣṇa-conscious person recognizes the validity of all the different names for God. He does not say that the Supreme Being can only be known as Kṛṣṇa.

Just as there is only one sun in the sky although it has hundreds of different names according to different languages, actual religion is one, to become a lover of God, whether this universal science is taught in Vedic terms, Christian terms, or Islamic terms.

The final test of whether or not someone is actually religious is that he is no longer attracted by any type of material sense gratification and has become completely endowed with all saintly qualities. One does not become religious by adopting this label or that label and condemning all those who have not accepted the same label. One becomes actually religious by abandoning the labels and fully giving oneself to the Supreme Person, Kṛṣṇa, under whatever authorized scriptural name one chooses to address Him.

How Can One Enlighten Others?

I have a question regarding so-called 'religious conversion.' People of every religion (going by the legal definition rather than a philosophical definition of religion) accuse other religions of conversion. In fact, this has become the cause of hatred and bloodshed in many parts of the world.

How will you reach such people to explain this wonderful truth and convince them?

Four Ways to Help Spread Truth

If you want others to realize these sublime truths of the science of Kṛṣṇa, you must fully dedicate your life, according to your own capacity, for helping us to spread Kṛṣṇa consciousness all over the world. For the greatest effect, you should give the maximum amount of energy possible for this purpose.

There are four ways you can dedicate your energy:

1. Give your life: You can dedicate your entire life to serving this mission by becoming an initiated disciple.

2. Give your money: You can help us by donating financially to help us cover the expenses of spreading Kṛṣṇa consciousness all over the world.

3. Give your intelligence: Engage your intelligence in helping us to awaken others to the science of *bhakti*.

4. Give your words: Tell everyone you meet about Kṛṣṇa.

If possible, do all four of the above. If that is not possible, do three of them. If that is not possible, do two of them. And if that is not possible, do at least one of them. In this way engage yourself in the topmost activity of assisting this mission of delivering the world population from ignorance.

Who Can Practice Kṛṣṇa Consciousness?

Can one practice Kṛṣṇa consciousness and be a Christian, Buddhist, Hindu or even a Muslim?

Everyone Is Welcome!

Anyone and everyone can remain in their present designation and practice Kṛṣṇa consciousness. For example, one of the members of our course is a Baptist minister. The science of self-realization does not belong to any one designation. We are all children of the same God, regardless of what we may call Him. To develop pure love for Him is the purpose of our existence. This is the universal science, the universal religion for all of mankind. Anyone who seriously takes up chanting the Hare Kṛṣṇa *mahā-mantra* under the expert guidance of the bona fide spiritual master will achieve the perfection of human existence, pure love for God.

How to Tackle Evil-Doers?

Please clarify how, in this dense Kali-yuga, noble people should deal with evil-doers. Śrī Kṛṣṇa would just finish the wicked people, but we cannot do so. So what should we do?

First Conquer the Evil in Your Heart

First conquer the evil in your own heart.

Once you've done that, Kṛṣṇa will empower to teach others how to conquer the evil in their hearts. Then the whole world will be saved.

How Can You Say the World Is a Mess?

Regarding something you wrote previously in "Thought for the Day," how do you think contemporary society has gone way off track? How do you suppose that we have made a "royal mess" out of the world? If you are referring to pollution, that is something we have already discussed. Then again, if you are discussing how people practice their religion, I think each one is acting according to his or her own faith.

What has caused the mess? How do you see that there is a mess in the first place?

Read a Newspaper

"Society off track" means that human life is meant for self-realization, not sense gratification. Yet we see and entire civilization dedicated to sense gratification. "Royal mess" means that instead of serving God, as we are meant to be doing, we are serving our senses.

It is a fact that different people are acting according to their different religious faiths. One man's religious faith is that you should be tortured and killed because you are not a Muslim. In the name of religious faith so many atrocities are being committed against living beings on a daily basis.

This is why we have to rise beyond the false platform of different religious faiths and understand that religion is one, to reconnect with that Supreme Person Who is the source of all existence. To be truly religious means to be 100% reconnected with that Supreme Person. Such a reconnected person will never give any unnecessary harm to other living creatures. Yet we see that the so-called religious people of varying faiths are, in the name of the religion, causing so much suffering to other living beings.

Such persons are not actually religious in the true sense of the term because they are obviously not reconnected with the Supreme Person, the source of all existence. If they were reconnected, they would never commit the atrocities they do against other human beings, against unborn children in the womb, and against the innocent animals.

The mess has gradually compounded itself more and more throughout the various *yugas* (ages) as mankind has strayed further and further away from the teachings given in the *Bhagavad-gītā*. Any intelligent, sensitive person can see the world is a mess just by reading a newspaper.

Your previously expressed idea that pollution can be solved by stronger legislation would be true if there were governments strong enough and intelligent enough to enact and enforce the proper legislation. For example, one of the biggest polluters on this planet is the slaughterhouse industry. If the governments were actually strong and proper, they would immediately shut down the slaughterhouses. But there are no such enlightened and strong governments on this planet. So your idea of solving pollution by stronger legislation is not at all practical. We must first have strong, enlightened governments. Then and only then can your principle of stronger legislation be effectively applied. Until then, we are stuck with an ever-increasingly polluted planet.

Christ and Kṛṣṇa

Could you tell me what the difference is between Christ and Kṛṣṇa?

Son and Father

Christ is God, the Son. And Kṛṣṇa is God, the Father. The word "Christ" is an etymological derivation of the word "Kṛṣṇa." They share the same name just as a father and a son share the same last name.

Nature of the Soul – Our Eternal Constitutional Position - Kṛṣṇa, the Ultimate Lover – Free Will

Does the Soul Merge with the Universal Conciousness?

Does the soul (*ātmā*):

(1) merge with universal consciousness absolutely (like, say, sugar mixes with water and becomes a clear solution)

(2) does it remain as a separate entity (like oil in water)?

If (1) is true, then upon reincarnation, how does it go to a specifically better or worse birth?

If (2) is true, does this mean that the souls can be counted?

Simultaneous Oneness and Two-ness

The soul remains separate after liberation. Unless there is two-ness, love cannot exist within the oneness of perfect harmony with Kṛṣṇa, or God. As Śrīla Prabhupāda said, "Love means two. Kṛṣṇa and you." The oneness of spiritual perfection is when the devotee attains a state of perfect harmony with God, total agreement with the Lord. It is not that at any stage of spiritual emancipation that one becomes God.

The individual souls are real and substantial. Therefore, we can definitely count them. But because they are infinite in number, we will never come to the end of our counting, even if we go on counting for all of eternity.

Regarding Unconditional Love

In your article on unconditional love, you said that we should do the things that God likes. How will we find out what God likes and what He does not like? What does God get from our doing what He likes? Instead, we should do the good things that humanity demands.

In my view God has given everything to us. We should properly use it. Certainly, doing good things like worshiping and chanting the Hare Kṛṣṇa *mantra* have a positive impact on our day-to-day lives, but God doesn't want anything from it.

God's Unlimited Kindness Upon Us

Your views are not completely correct. By serving the demands of humanity you will remain in the cycle of birth and death. From *sādhus* (saintly teachers), scriptures, and the spiritual master we can learn what God wants. By doing what God wants we will escape the cycle of birth and death.

God has given you everything; therefore, you must use everything in His service. This is your duty. God has directly instructed you to chant His names and bow down to Him. He states this directly in the *Bhagavad-gītā*.

It is a fact that God has nothing to gain by our service. He is blessing us with this opportunity to serve Him so that we can regain our original, pure consciousness that is eternal, full of knowledge, and full of bliss. This is His unlimited kindness upon us.

Searching for the Ultimate Lover

For 15 years I have been searching for someone who loves me. After my marriage I thought that this would be my husband for whom I was searching all these years. But I find myself still in search of somebody. I do not know who exactly he is.

Many times I tried to convince myself that it is the Lord for whom I am hankering. But still I am not convinced.

It has become a big problem for me. I cannot share this with anyone, because nobody can understand me. Please help me to convince myself that the person I am searching for is none other than Lord Kṛṣṇa Himself.

Kṛṣṇa Is the Ultimate Lover

It is a fact that the person you have been searching after for millions of lifetimes is none other than Lord Śrī Kṛṣṇa, the Supreme Personality of Godhead. There is no one else who can fully reciprocate your love and thus fully satisfy you. Now, armed with the understanding that all of your love should be exclusively reposed in Lord Śrī Kṛṣṇa, fully surrender yourself at His lotus feet. You will taste the inconceivable nectar of Kṛṣṇa *bhakti*.

What Is Desirable?

What is the composition of the *ātmā*, the soul?

What is the abode of the *ātmā* after liberation from the cycle of birth and death?

What is desirable - to take birth again and again and to remain in Kṛṣṇa consciousness (dualism), or to aim for liberation and remain like a dot in the universe? (Here "dot" denotes *ātmā*.)

Returning to the Kingdom of God

The *ātmā* is composed of eternity, knowledge and bliss.

The abode of the *ātmā* after liberation is residence in the Kingdom of God as the Lord's eternal servant.

You are wrong to categorize Kṛṣṇa consciousness as dualism. It is simultaneous oneness and difference. You are also wrong to think that liberation means to become like a dot in the universe. The "dot-in-the-universe" liberation conceived by the impersonalists is imaginary. Real liberation means to reawaken one's original, eternal identity as a servant of God. This is what is actually desirable, and nothing else.

I Am Unable to Understand

Śrīla Prabhupāda writes in his purport to *Bhagavad-gītā* Chapter 2, verse 12: "The Māyāvādī argues that the plurality mentioned in this verse is conventional and that it refers to the body. But previous to this verse such a bodily conception is already condemned. After condemning the bodily conception of the living entities, how was it possible for Kṛṣṇa to place a conventional proposition on the body again?"

I'm not sure what Śrīla Prabhupāda is saying in these lines. What is the convention that he is talking about? I've looked up the word "convention" in the dictionary; however, I am still unable to understand.

The Meaning Is Clear

Thank you very much for your sincere endeavor to carefully read and fully understand each and every word of our beloved Śrīla Prabhupāda's purports to the *Bhagavad-gītā*. There is nothing more essential for our spiritual lives than to understand and fully implement the instructions given by Śrīla Prabhupāda in his books.

Conventional means "ordinary" or "in the ordinary material sense." In our ordinary, everyday, worldly existence we experience a sense of individuality in relation to our individual material bodies. The Māyāvādī philosopher foolishly concludes that because we have a sense of individuality in our conditional existence, we must therefore have no sense of individuality in the liberated state.

There is no Vedic evidence for this false theory. This is like saying that the way to cure a headache is to cut off your head. The Māyāvādī philosophy is that if your individual existence is painful, you should end it. The Vaiṣṇava philosophy is, "Don't end it, mend it." Purify your sense of individuality by reawakening your eternal, original, spiritual individuality as a servant of God. This is the supreme perfection of existence, not an artificial denial of your individuality.

The Origin of the Jīva

There are some questions that have always been haunting me since I started understanding myself through Śrīla Prabhupāda's ultimate guidance. The questions are, "From which abode does the *jīva* (the individual spiritual being) come into existence?" and "Immediately after the jīva comes into existence, out of four types of *rasas* (relationships of servitude, friendship, parenthood, or conjugal love), in what kind of *rasa* is he situated?"

He Is an Eternal Emanation of the Lord

There is no time that the *jīva*, the individual spiritual being, comes into existence, because he always exists as an eternal emanation of the Lord. This is confirmed in the second chapter of the *Bhagavad-gītā*, that there was never a time that the *jīva* did not exist.

Each individual being has his own unique *rasa*, or relationship with the Lord. Just as there are no two snowflakes that are exactly alike, there no two *jīva* souls who have exactly the same *rasa* or relationship with the Lord. According to their particular relationship, they have their particular eternal place of residence, either in Goloka Vṛndāvana (the topmost planet of the spiritual world where the Lord is served with great intimacy) or on one of the unlimited number of Vaikuṇṭha planets where the Lord is served with great awe and reverence.

Forgetting their eternal relationship as a servant of the Lord, the *jīva* souls foolishly struggle to be happy in a dungeon of demons; but no matter how much they may appear to be happy and successful here, they are ultimately frustrated. Therefore, the sane person takes shelter of the lotus feet of Lord Śrī Kṛṣṇa and returns to his eternal position in the spiritual world.

Aren't There Many Enlightened People?

How do we know that 99.99% of people are lost and in a state of illusion? There are surely many good people from many different backgrounds, whether they be Hindu, Muslim, Christian, etc.

Are there not many enlightened people in the world?

No. Their Number Is Very Rare

The fallen nature of the souls in the present age of Kali is described as follows in the *Śrīmad-Bhāgavatam*.

prāyeṇālpāyuṣaḥ sabhya
kalāv asmin yuge janāḥ
mandāḥ sumanda-matayo
manda-bhāgyā hy upadrutāḥ

"O learned one, in this iron age of Kali men have but short lives. They are quarrelsome, lazy, misguided, unlucky and, above all, always disturbed."
Śrīmad-Bhāgavatam 1.1.10

By noting the difference between goodness and spiritual enlightenment, it is easy to discern that practically the entire world is in a state of illusion. How many enlightened newspapers are distributed and read? How many enlightened movies are a box-office success? How many enlightened books are on the best seller list? How many enlightened government leaders are leading their nations in such a way that all of their citizens are becoming enlightened? If spiritual enlightenment were common, there would be a dramatic difference in the world atmosphere. The world would be practically free from terrorism and crime.

There is a distinct difference between being good and being enlightened. The quality of goodness is known as *sattva-guna* and is the highest position within the material modes of nature. Those who are in the mode of goodness take birth again in this material world. Although they are in a very advantageous position to cultivate spiritual enlightenment, if they do not seriously do so, they must remain in the cycle of birth and death.

That very rare number of souls who come to the spiritually enlightened platform are situated in what is known as *śuddha-sattva,* or pure goodness. Such souls are 100% free from the all the qualities of material existence and do not take birth again. The rarity of spiritually enlightened persons is described by Kṛṣṇa in the *Bhagavad-gītā* as follows:

manuṣyāṇāṁ sahasreṣu
kaścid yatati siddhaye
yatatām api siddhānāṁ
kaścin māṁ vetti tattvataḥ

"Out of many thousands among men, one may endeavor for perfection, and of those who have achieved perfection, hardly one knows Me in truth."

Bhagavad-gītā 7.3

Spiritual enlightenment has nothing to do with one's designation as a Hindu, Christian or Muslim. It is simply a matter of whether or not one has become completely sold out to the Lord as evidenced by his complete detachment from all forms of material sense gratification.

Ātmā, Jīva, Prāṇa

Can you please explain the difference between *ātmā*, *jīva* and *prāṇa*? When we say that a person is suffering or enjoying, 'who' is actually suffering or enjoying?

Jīva Floats within Prāṇa

Ātmā is the spirit-soul. This term is more or less synonymous with *jīva*, the living entity. The *ātmā* and the *jīva* are the same. *Prāṇa* is the life air that is flowing within the material body. In our conditioned state of consciousness, the *ātmā* or the *jīva* is situated in the body floating within the *prāṇa*, the life air.

The *jīva*, the *ātmā*, is the one who is suffering or enjoying. If he misidentifies with matter, he suffers. If he remembers his spiritual nature and acts accordingly, he factually enjoys unlimited bliss.

Not Hate Anybody?

Is it true that we must not hate anybody?

Devotee Naturally Loves

It's not a question of being required to not hate anyone. A person who is fixed in Kṛṣṇa consciousness will naturally not hate anyone because he feels unlimited love for all living beings.

yas tu sarvāṇi bhūtāny
ātmany evānupaśyati
sarva-bhūteṣu cātmānaṁ
tato na vijugupsate

"He who sees systematically everything in relation to the Supreme Lord, who sees all living entities as His parts and parcels, and who sees the Supreme Lord within everything never hates anything or any being."

Śrī Īśopaniṣad Mantra 6

Is There Proof of Spiritual Reality?

What is the proof that a spiritual reality exists?

Can you surrender to illusion and to God as well, meaning some percent to illusion and some percent to God? In other words, what happens before one is completely enlightened as yourself? Can he be in Kṛṣṇa consciousness and still be to some extent in illusion while he is practicing Kṛṣṇa consciousness, through chanting Hare Kṛṣṇa, remembering the Lord, etc?

Desire for Immortality Is the Proof

If the only reality were this temporary material body, there would be no desire in the living being for immortality. His desire for immortality is the proof of the spiritual reality.

Yes, there can be a mixture. You can be 1% in illusion and 99% Kṛṣṇa conscious. But if you have even 1% material desires at the time of death, you will take birth again in this material world to fulfill that desire. Therefore, you must become 100% absorbed in Kṛṣṇa consciousness without even a slight tinge of material desire, not even 0.00001%.

If one is sincerely executing the principles of Kṛṣṇa consciousness as an initiated disciple of a bona fide spiritual master, that means that he is step by step diminishing his illusion and advancing his Kṛṣṇa consciousness all the way to the point of unalloyed devotional service, 100% Kṛṣṇa consciousness.

So now you must sincerely and carefully absorb yourself 24 hours daily in Kṛṣṇa consciousness so that you can as soon as possible achieve the goal of pure Kṛṣṇa *bhakti*.

Does the Soul Feel Pain?

The soul cannot be killed by any means. But will the soul feel difficulty or pain when the body is harmed?

If He Identifies With the Material Body

The soul feels difficulty or pain if he identifies with the material body. To the extent that he is realized in his eternal spiritual identity, he becomes aloof from the pains and pleasures of the material body. The sensations are still there for a realized soul, but he is not disturbed by them. Because the self-realized soul is fully situated in the Lord's internal energy, for him the pains and pleasures of this world are just something happening 'out there' in the external energy.

Origin of the Living Being

I heard that we are part and parcel of Kṛṣṇa, but that still we and Kṛṣṇa are different, that we (the *ātmās*) and Kṛṣṇa (the *Paramātmā*) cannot be of the same identity. Kṛṣṇa says in the *Bhagavad-gītā* that there is no time when we do not exist, nor is there a time when He does not exist. But the *ātmā* should also have a source from which he comes. So why are we different from our source? Actually I want to know about the origin of the *jīva*, the individual living being.

Simultaneously One and Different

Even though the complete whole and its part are one, there is a difference. Just like you are part of India, therefore, you are one with India. However, there is vast difference in the population of you, namely one, and the population of India, many, many millions.

The *jīva* is eternally being emanated from Lord Śrī Kṛṣṇa. Therefore, Kṛṣṇa is his source. But there is no time when he did not exist because Kṛṣṇa has always been emanating the *jīva* and He will eternally continue to do so.

Consciousness After Death

I am in confusion about the nature of consciousness after death. People from the Māyāvādi/Advaita camp have told me that after death a person's ego/mind dies and merges with God. I do not want to believe this, but I feel that I do not grasp the differences between the ego, mind and soul. It's not that I doubt the survival of the soul, but I have a hard time refuting those who say that consciousness ends at death.

You Exist for a Good Reason

Why should we take someone's opinion when God Himself, the ultimate authority, under whose direction everything is happening, has clearly stated the eternal existence of the living being?

Here are Lord Kṛṣṇa's words:

na tv evahaṁ jātu nāsaṁ
na tvaṁ neme janādhipāḥ
na caiva na bhaviñyāmaḥ
sarve vayam ataḥ param

"Never was there a time when I did not exist, nor you, nor all these kings; nor in the future shall any of us cease to be."

Bhagavad-gītā 2.12

If your ultimate perfection were to merge into God, why would you ever exist as a separate being to begin with? What purpose would your temporary illusory sense of separate existence serve? It would serve no purpose.

The eternally separate identity of the living being does make sense. The two-ness allows for an exchange of love between the Lord and the living beings. Do you think God wants to live in a world without love and without any association?

The Māyāvādis say that everyone is one, but then they immediately contradict themselves by making a distinction between being Māyā and being Brahman.

The soul is the actual person, the actual self. The mind and the false ego are two of the subtle coverings of the self. The mind is the channel for our sensual desires. In this regard Śrīla Prabhupāda describes it as "the pivot of the active sense organs." The false ego is that which foolishly misidentifies with a rotting material body. The real ego is the soul.

Isn't That a Contradiction?

The soul is eternal, full of knowledge and full of bliss, but the independence of the soul is minute. Isn't that a contradiction?

The Absolute Truth Must Be Devoid of Contradiction

You have asked, "The soul is eternal, full of knowledge and full of bliss, but the independence of the soul is minute. Isn't that a contradiction?"

The Absolute Truth must be devoid of contradiction. Therefore, the answer is that it is not a contradiction.

How so?

Here's how:

The amount of water in the ocean is so vast that it is immeasurable. And the amount of water in a tiny drop of ocean water is minute, easily measurable. In spite of the minuteness of the drop of ocean water and the vastness of the entire ocean, both of them share the same chemical composition. This is easily understood.

So in the same way, the Lord, like the ocean, is inconceivably vast, unlimitedly independent while the living entity, like the drop of ocean water, is tiny, minutely independent. Yet both of them share the same chemical composition of being eternal, full of knowledge, and full of bliss.

Is there any difficulty for you to understand this simple explanation?

What Is True Love?

Love is precious. What is love? Could you explain in your own words in detail what true love is?

When You Love God

True love is when you love God, because when you love God your love goes automatically to everyone, just as when you water the root of a tree all the leaves and branches are nourished.

What Happens to Atheists?

What happens to those who do not accept Lord Kṛṣṇa as the Supreme Personality? I am referring to the people who are atheists.

Everyone Gets Exactly What They Want

Kṛṣṇa is the supreme benevolent person. He gives everyone exactly what they want. Those who want to serve Him with love are given the facility to do just that in His eternal planet, Goloka Vṛndāvana. The atheists, who desire to completely forget that He is the Supreme Personality of Godhead, are given to facility to do just that in a world in which is His supremacy is ignored and denied - this material world of birth and death.

Can We Live Without the Word "I"?

When we say we are part of the great God, we always say, I am a part of God (*aham brahmāsmi*). But in reality who am I? If we say always 'I, me, and mine,' then it it is a word, "self." Some gurus say we should leave aside the word "I." When we say, "I am a part of God," "I" always comes. Can we live without the word "I?"

Awaken the Real "I"

The gurus who say to eliminate the word "I" are incomplete in their knowledge. They do not know that along with the false "I" there is also a real "I." The false "I" is, "I am this body." The real "I" is, "I am the eternal spirit-soul, servant of Kṛṣṇa."

To try to completely eliminate "I" is not practical. It is artificial. It will not solidly situate one on the spiritual platform. The best it can do is to give one a sense of temporary relief. But then after some time one will come back to the false "I."

It is only when one becomes situated solidly on the platform of the real "I" that one will never again go back into the trap of the false "I." Under the cloud of the false "I" one thinks, "I am male. I am female. I am American. I am Indian. I am white. I am black. I am old. I am young." And so many other false things. It is only when one fully reawakens his eternal servitor relationship with Lord Śrī Kṛṣṇa, the Supreme Personality of Godhead, that he can become completely free from the false sense of "I." As soon as the false sense of "I" is there, there will also be a false sense of "mine." And one becomes completely entangled in the cycle of birth and death.

If one will regularly chant the Hare Kṛṣṇa *mantra* with love, he will fully re-awaken the dormant, real "I" which has been sleeping within the heart since time immemorial. He will enter into an eternal existence which is full of knowledge and full of bliss.

Hare Kṛṣṇa, Hare Kṛṣṇa, Kṛṣṇa Kṛṣṇa , Hare Hare
Hare Rāma, Hare Rāma, Rāma Rāma, Hare Hare

Free Will or Kṛṣṇa's Plan?

We have free will. We choose to go closer to Kṛṣṇa or away from Him, to do things for Him or for ourselves. Yet all that happens is Kṛṣṇa's plan, and nothing is by chance. How can one reconcile this?

If I have free will, then Kṛṣṇa doesn't have a plan because if my will is really free, how would He know what I'm going to do? If he has a plan, and my so-called free will is only a facet of His plan, then my will is under His control, not really free.

Both

Both points are true. Everything is happening by Kṛṣṇa's arrangement, and at the same time we have the free will to be part of Kṛṣṇa's plan or to rebel against Kṛṣṇa's plan. Of course, even if we try to rebel we are still under His plan. We are just under a different aspect of it. We can voluntarily agree to be the under the wonderful spiritual nature, which is eternal, full of bliss, and full of knowledge. Or, by stubbornly trying to be independent, we can be under the control of the material nature and experience instead temporality, ignorance and misery.

Just like a nation has a system of government under which all of its citizens live. Everyone is under the national government. At the same time everyone is free to obey the laws or disobey the laws. Those who choose to disobey the laws are still under the law. They must go to the prison and be subjected to a most unpleasant set of laws. Those who voluntarily agree to abide by the laws of the state live a happy life full of so many freedoms, even though it is all done within the context of the state laws.

So we have a choice: whether we would like to be law-abiding citizens of God's eternal kingdom, or whether we would try to prove that we are so-called independent and end up in the prison of material existence until we come to our senses and realize that we should get out of this nasty place and go back to our original home.

Responsible Non-Doer?

In *Bhagavad-gītā*, Chapter 2, verse 47, Kṛṣṇa tells Arjuna, "You have a right to perform your prescribed duty, but you are not entitled to the fruits of action. Never consider yourself the cause of the results of your activities, and never be attached to not doing your duty."

Since I am not the cause of the results of my activities, how is it I am considered to be responsible for those actions?

Responsible for Choosing Māyā

We have a choice whether to act under the influence of the material energy or the spiritual energy. If we place ourselves under the material energy, we are carried along helplessly on the roller-coaster of material existence. However, because we voluntarily chose the material energy over the spiritual energy, we have to take responsibility for everything that we do while under its influence. Just like if someone becomes very intoxicated, they may become completely unaware of what they are doing. But still they are responsible for everything they do in that intoxicated state.

So the best thing is to embrace a life of full freedom in the Lord's service by taking complete shelter of the Lord through the agency of His spiritual energy.

Why Doesn't Kṛṣṇa Force Everyone to Be a Devotee?

As Kṛṣṇa is the supreme power completely beyond *māyā* (the material energy), and everyone chants His holy names and glories, why can't He make all the *jīvas*, the living beings, to be His devotees?

Why did He make the *jīvas*? How did He create the *jīvas*? Before the *jīvas* were created, where were they and what was their consciousness?

Love Is Voluntary

You are wondering why, if Kṛṣṇa is all-powerful, can He not force all living beings to be His devotees. The answer is that devotion is not something that can be forced. Love is something that one voluntarily offers to someone else.

The *jīvas*, the living beings, exist for the sole purpose of expanding the Lord's happiness by their having loving relationships with the Lord. The Lord wants to enjoy the happiness of having a sweet, loving relationship with each and every living being throughout the entirety of existence. Therefore, He comes to this material world again and again and sends His representatives here again and again just to try to attract us to serving and loving Him. This is His great kindness upon us.

The *jīvas* are eternal emanations of the Supreme Person. There was never a time when He did not emanate them, nor will there ever be a time when He will not emanate them. Simply by His sweet will they are eternally emanated from His transcendental body, just as the rays of the sun emanate from the sun.

Pictures of Kṛṣṇa

Regarding pictures of Kṛṣṇa, is it really so important to have a photograph or picture of something? Of course, like everyone else I am also dependent on visualizations. But sometimes I feel, enough is enough. Memories, for example, are much more intensive than photographs.

"Re-ligion" comes from "re-ligare," to reconnect. Did God give us this option of having many ways to reconnect? Or is this manmade? And, can you tell me why we have to pray since God might know what we need basically? Do you think an agnostic person or even an atheist is a worse person than others? Why is an atheist an atheist? Doesn't he need to reconnect to God?

Nurturing Love

If someone has a girlfriend and he wants to keep his fire of love burning, he will definitely keep her photograph handy. Even though he already has memories of her, the photograph will help him to keep those memories strong. So the Lord's devotee applies the same principle to nurturing his love for God.

Reconnecting with God is reconnecting with God. It does not matter what label you give to it, it is still the same thing. Man has invented so many different labels, and then he fights over the labels. In this way, he misses the point of religion and is not able to connect with God.

We do not need to pray to God to tell Him what we need. That is a fact. We only need to pray to Him for the sake of reconnecting with Him.

The closer we are to the fire, the warmer we get. The further away from the fire we are, the colder we get. The closer we get to God, the more we become saintly. And the further away we get from God, the more we are unsaintly.

Everyone, even the atheist, is connected with God at every minute, but the atheist does not realize it; therefore, he is in a suffering condition. So when we say "reconnect with God," what we are actually saying is to once again be aware of our eternal connection with God.

Imperfect Love

I read one of Śrīla Prabhupāda's articles in which he said that there is no love in this material world even though many people glorify it. There are so many people who glorify the love between young couples, between parents and children, between friends, and love for the country, etc. Śrīla Prabhupāda says that this is not love, it's *kāma* - material desires. In Sanskrit there is no such word as "love;" the only similar word is "*prema*"- love for Godhead. Is it a fact that the so-called "love" in the material world is only a distorted reflection of *prema* - the spiritual love?

I have personal experience of this. My parents "love" me, so they bind me and do not allow me to do anything that is against their will; they do not allow me to serve Kṛṣṇa. This is *kāma*, not love.

What about the love between devotees? Is this *kāma*, is it spiritual love, or is it a mixture of both?

The Perfection of Love

The so-called love in this material world is *kāma,* or lust. But when one loves Kṛṣṇa, he can then genuinely love Kṛṣṇa's devotees and all living beings. When we water the root of the tree, all the leaves and branches are nourished. That love of a devotee for other devotees and all living beings is completely devoid of *kāma*. It is a manifestation of *prema*, because he loves everyone, seeing them in relationship with Kṛṣṇa.

Why Do I Feel Such Bliss?

Why is it that I feel such ecstasy, including weak knees and vibrations through my spirit-soul and body, when I hear Lord Śrī Kṛṣṇa's words from *Bhagavad-gītā*?

I feel wonderful joining in with *kīrtana,* and it's great doing *japa*... But it's not anything like hearing our Lord's words. Is it okay that I desire to hear Kṛṣṇa speak more than anything else?

Consciousness Revival

You are feeling such ecstasy because you are reviving your original consciousness, which is eternal, full of bliss, and full of knowledge.

Every devotee has his particular way in which he is especially inclined towards Kṛṣṇa consciousness. If you feel especially inclined to hear the *Bhagavad-gītā*, that is very nice.

Immovable Soul?

In *Bhagavad-gītā* 2.24 Lord Śrī Kṛṣṇa states:

"This individual soul is unbreakable and insoluble, and can be neither burned nor dried. He is everlasting, all-pervading, unchangeable, immovable and eternally the same."

Please explain what Kṛṣṇa means by "the soul is immovable." If the soul is situated in the region of heart and we move every day, how is the soul immovable?

Immovable Within That Body

In the original Sanskrit the word given is *acalah*, which means "fixed," "immovable;" it also means "mountain" because a mountain is fixed in one place, immovable.

Immovable means "immovable within that body," just as driver is immovable within the car, always remaining in the driver's seat. The car may be moving a hundred miles per hour, but within the car the driver is in a fixed, stationary position.

Similarly, throughout the entire life the soul is always situated within that particular body. Therefore, it is known as immovable.

What Is Consciousness?

Will you please enlighten me on the concept of consciousness?

The Sense of "I Am"

Consciousness is the sense of "I am" that you possess. Just like you asked me to enlighten you regarding what is consciousness. This means you have a sense of being a person who wants to be enlightened. It is this sense of individuality that is your consciousness.

Am I a Body Without a Spirit?

How can I find out for myself that people are not the material bodies but are spiritual beings? From my personal experiences of the connection between material body states and mental states, I can't help but conclude that the two are one and the same and inseparable. Likewise, scientific research corroborates this view: There is not a need for a spirit to explain the functions and behavior of a human being. Brain imaging technologies have shown the higher states of consciousness to be the result of physical changes and functions within the brain, caused by dedication to the meditation practice. The grand illusion appears to be not the material world but the spiritual world. Could it be that I'm a body without a spirit?

I want to believe otherwise, yet the material is all I see. The fear of death is persuasive, but it doesn't convince me.

Try to Understand the Animating Principle

If you were simply a bag of chemicals, there would be no reason for you to be afraid of death. What is the difference between an inanimate bag of chemicals and an animate bag of chemicals? Chemicals are chemicals, nothing more. There is no reason to give more value to the animate bag over the inanimate bag. So just try to understand why every living being, even the plants and animals, give more value to the animate bag than to the inanimate bag. In this way you can begin to understand what the actual self, the animating principle within the body, is.

Why Did God Create the Universe and the Human Beings?

If in the beginning there was only Lord Kṛṣṇa, why did He create the universe and the human beings? He advises everyone to follow the *Gītā* by surrendering to Him, but at the same time He creates His inferior, illusory energy known as *māyā* that deludes everyone. Is this considered to be a testing phase for human beings? If yes, then what is the need of doing all these things if finally everything is going back to Him?

For His Enjoyment

The first thing you should try to understand is there was never a time when there was only Kṛṣṇa and no one else. Kṛṣṇa is eternally emanating the living beings from Himself in order to enjoy loving relationships with each and every one of them. But since love by its very nature must be voluntary, Kṛṣṇa gives each living being the freedom to choose whether to love and serve Him as the Supreme Person or whether to try to imitate Him by foolishly considering himself to be the Supreme Person.

If the living being chooses to try to imitate the Lord, he cannot try to do so unless he is the under the illusion that he is the supreme. Therefore, for such a fool, the Lord provides His *māyā*, His illusory energy, which enables the living being to actually think that he is the center of the universe.

It is wrong to think that everyone is deluded by *māyā*. The vast majority of the living beings remain eternally absorbed in the Lord's service in His eternal kingdom. It is only an infinitesimal fraction of the innumerable living beings in the spiritual world who opt out of an eternal life full of knowledge and bliss because of a foolish desire to be the center of existence.

Everyone has a choice of one of two destinies. One can choose to think that he is the center of enjoyment and thus try to be an enjoyer of this material world. Such an unfortunate soul will be caught up in the cycle of birth and death, living one temporary existence full of ignorance and misery birth after birth, until he finally wises up and comes back to the Lord's service.

Or one can choose to be an eternal servant of God in His transcendental kingdom and live an eternal life full of knowledge and bliss. Everybody gets to make this choice. This material world is the place for those who make the wrong choice. The living beings who choose not to serve the Lord will remain eternally in this material existence, but they can rectify themselves whenever they want to.

Is Everyone Kṛṣṇa's Servant?

You said, "*jīvera svarūpa haya kṛṣṇa nitya-dāsa*" which means that in his own original form the *jīva* soul is situated as the eternal servant of Kṛṣṇa. Considering that when he is conditioned the *jīva*, due to his false ego, will not accept that he is the eternal servant of Kṛṣṇa, or God - does this principle also apply for those living beings who are in a conditioned state of consciousness?

Yes

Even the conditioned souls are the eternal servants of Kṛṣṇa. It is simply that they have forgotten it. That's all.

Who Is the Doer?

If we ourselves are not the doer, then we are so many puppets on strings being pulled by God. We have no free will. Who, in fact, is the doer in my local field of activity? Is it me, or is it the Cosmic Puppeteer? I don't mean to sound offensive.

I am simply confused. Please help me to understand the true nature of this reality, that of the doer in the field.

Supreme Doer and Subordinate Doer

Both you and God are the doers. He is the supreme doer because He is the master programmer who has programmed both the spiritual world and the material world. And you are also the doer, the subordinate doer, because you have full freedom to flip between the two different channels at will. You are the subordinate doer because although you have complete, total freedom to choose which program you want to be tuned into, it is God who makes the programs, not you.

Everyone is acting under the direction of God. That's a fact. But we have a choice in how we want to be directed. In a state, the citizens have a choice of being law-abiding citizens or criminals. If they choose to be law-abiding citizens, they voluntarily co-operate with the laws of the state and enjoy the full benefits of citizenship. But if they choose to be criminals, they are brought under the stringent control of the state by being placed in the prison.

So we have a choice. Do we want to voluntarily place ourselves under the Lord's direction, or do we want to try to defy His authority and be placed under the stringent control of His material energy? In either case we are under the Lord's control. But the devotee chooses voluntarily to serve the Lord and thus relishes an eternal life full of knowledge of bliss, while the non-devotee chooses to defy the Lord and thus suffers birth after birth in the cycle of birth, death, old age, and disease.

Brahman, Paramātmā, Bhagavān – Different Features - Different Levels of Realization

Does God Really Witness Everything?

It is said that the Supersoul (God) is present in all living entities along with the souls. How can I understand that the Supersoul is able to witness and remember everything that every soul does? To make it more complex, there are infinite living entities. I can't find any logical explanation anywhere! At the same time, Kṛṣṇa enjoys in Goloka.

Is there any scriptural reference that explains how the Supersoul works?

He Easily Does

Krsna in His expanded form, the Supersoul, easily observes what is going on everywhere. His omniscience is confirmed as follows in the *Śrīmad-Bhāgavatam*:

vāsudeve bhagavati
sarva-jñe pratyag-ātmani
pareṇa bhakti-bhāvena
labdhātmā mukta-bandhanaḥ

SYNONYMS

vāsudeve—to Vāsudeva; *bhagavati*—the Personality of Godhead; *sarva-jñe*—omniscient; *pratyak-ātmani*—the Supersoul within everyone; *pareṇa*—transcendental; *bhakti-bhāvena*—by devotional service; *labdha-ātmā*—being situated in himself; *mukta-bandhanaḥ*—liberated from material bondage.

TRANSLATION

He thus became liberated from conditioned life and became self-situated in transcendental devotional service to the Personality of Godhead, Vāsudeva, the omniscient Supersoul within everyone.

Śrīmad-Bhāgavatam 3.24.45

Krsna can easily know everything because everything is His energy and He is all-powerful.

Is God is unlimited or is He limited? If He is unlimited, He can do anything and everything and know anything and everything. If He cannot do and know anything and everything, He is not unlimited and He is not God. But God has to be God. He cannot not be God.

It is also confirmed in the *Bhagavad-gītā*:

vedāhaṁ samatītāni
vartamānāni cārjuna
bhaviṣyāṇi ca bhūtāni
māṁ tu veda na kaścana

SYNONYMS

veda—know; *aham*—I; *samatītāni*—completely past; *vartamānāni*—present; *ca*—and; *arjuna*—O Arjuna; *bhaviṣyāṇi*—future; *ca*—also; *bhūtāni*—all living entities; *mām*—Me; *tu*—but; *veda*—knows; *na*—not; *kaścana* —anyone.

TRANSLATION

O Arjuna, as the Supreme Personality of Godhead, I know everything that has happened in the past, all that is happening in the present, and all things that are yet to come. I also know all living entities; but Me no one knows.

Bhagavad-gītā 7.26

Attaining Paramātmā Realization

Is it necessary that Paramātmā realization be accompanied by visualizing the Viṣṇu *mūrti* (form) within? And does that realization stay, or is it momentary, as Śrīla Prabhupāda has described it as momentary in his *Gītā* commentary?

Krsna Consciousness Is Higher

Those who are on the path of *Paramātmā* realization are described as follows in the *Śrīmad-Bhāgavatam*:

kecit sva-dehāntar-hṛdayāvakāśe
prādeśa-mātraṁ puruṣaṁ vasantam
catur-bhujaṁ kañja-rathāṅga-śaṅkha-
gadā-dharaṁ dhāraṇayā smaranti

"Others conceive of the Personality of Godhead residing within the body in the region of the heart and measuring only eight inches, with four hands carrying a lotus, a wheel of a chariot, a conchshell and a club respectively."

Śrīmad-Bhāgavatam 2.2.8

Paramātmā realization is not permanent. Even though it is only attained after great difficulty and many, many lifetimes, it is still imperfect. Therefore, it is better that you focus your attention on becoming Kṛṣṇa conscious. Through Kṛṣṇa consciousness you can easily attain perfect self-realization in this very lifetime.

Are There Different-Sized Manifestations of the Paramātmā?

It is mentioned that the *Paramātmā* (Supersoul) resides within the body in the region of heart and measures only eight inches. Does that make the size of *Paramātmā* bigger in small forms of animals, like an ant or a single-celled animal?

Yes

The Supersoul (*Paramātmā*) takes a larger or smaller size proportionate to the size of the particular material body that He inhabits.

Brahman and Paramātmā

How is *Brahman* different from *Paramātmā*?

Perfect and More Perfect

Brahman is the impersonal aspect of the Supreme. It is the shining effulgence which emanates from the Lord's transcendental body. The *Paramātmā* is the four-armed form of the Supreme Lord Who is dwelling within your heart, within the heart of all living beings, within every atom, and also between the atoms.

Brahman realization is considered perfect and *Paramātmā* realization is considered more perfect. The *Brahman*-realized soul realizes the eternity aspect of the Supreme. The *Paramātmā*-realized soul realizes the eternity and knowledge aspects of the Supreme. Beyond *Brahman* realization and *Paramātmā* realization is *Bhagavān* realization, which is said to be most perfect. One who achieves *Bhagavān* realization realizes all three aspects of the Supreme: eternity, knowledge, and bliss.

There is a very nice story in this connection. Formerly in India there were no trains. The trains were introduced by the British. So one village was included on the new train route. The tracks were laid, the station was built, and the villagers were curiously waiting for the first train to arrive so they could see what is this thing that is called a train.

Finally, late one evening, the first train arrived. One villager who was waiting on the edge of town saw the train from a distance coming down the tracks approaching the village. He came running into the village declaring that he had seen a train. He said that a train is a bright moving light. Another villager who lived near the station saw the train. He declared that the train has many, many cars connected together that are all identical. Another villager was there at the station when the train stopped. He examined the train carefully and said that there was one car with an engineer that pulled the entire train and he described in detail what each of the cars were like.

Each of the villagers had seen exactly the same train and had honestly described what they saw. Yet each of them had a different experience according to how closely they were able to examine the train. In the same way, there is one Absolute Truth, but it is understood differently as *Brahman*, *Paramātmā*, or *Bhagavān* according the degree of closeness of the realized *yogī*. The nondual yet variegated nature of the Supreme is confirmed in the *Śrīmad-Bhāgavatam* as follows:

vadanti tat tattva-vidas
tattvaṁ yaj jñānam advayam
brahmeti paramātmeti
bhagavān iti śabdyate

"Learned transcendentalists who know the Absolute Truth call this nondual substance *Brahman*, *Paramātmā* or *Bhagavān*."
Śrīmad-Bhāgavatam 1.2.11

We train our students how to achieve *Bhagavān* realization. When one realizes *Bhagavān*, his realizations of *Brahman* and *Paramātmā* are automatically included without any extra endeavor.

Why Roam the World Seeking God?

If God is within us, why roam around the world in search?

Realize God at Home

It's a fact that God is within us. He dwells within us in the form of the four-armed *Paramātmā*, the Supersoul. But we are not able to perceive and hear Him because at the present moment our consciousness is completely covered by the three modes of material nature. This point is confirmed as follows by Lord Sri Kṛṣṇa in the *Bhagavad-gītā*:

tribhir guṇa-mayair bhāvair
ebhiḥ sarvam idaṁ jagat
mohitaṁ nābhijānāti
mām ebhyaḥ param avyayam

"Deluded by the three modes [goodness, passion and ignorance], the whole world does not know Me, who am above the modes and inexhaustible."
Bhagavad-gītā 7.13

Since we have been covered by these modes since time immemorial, it is no easy task to become free from their influence. However, if we will surrender ourselves to God according to the instructions He gives us in the *Bhagavad-gītā*, the Lord will deliver us from covering influence of the modes of material nature and reveal Himself to us according to the degree of our surrender.

daivī hy eṣā guṇa-mayī
mama māyā duratyayā
mām eva ye prapadyante
māyām etāṁ taranti te

"This divine energy of Mine, consisting of the three modes of material nature, is difficult to overcome. But those who have surrendered unto Me can easily cross beyond it."

Bhagavad-gītā 7.14

Therefore, you are right in stating that there is no need to roam all over the world seeking God. All we have to do is surrender unto Him at home as He instructs us to in the *Bhagavad-gītā*. In this way our lives will be successful. The method He gives for realizing Him is to approach the bona fide spiritual master, inquire submissively from him, and render service unto him. The self-realized soul can empower us to realize God because he has seen the truth.

Since the entire world is suffering greatly due to a lack of God consciousness, that person who has realized God voluntarily leaves aside the comforts of home life and accepts the austerity of traveling extensively all over the world for enlightening people in this most sublime transcendental science of how to realize God. There is no greater kindness, no greater compassion than this.

Kṛṣṇa Is In and Not In Everything?

In your "Thought for the Day" you quoted this verse:

yo māṁ paśyati sarvatra
sarvaṁ ca mayi paśyati
tasyāhaṁ na praṇaśyāmi
sa ca me na praṇaśyati

"For one who sees Me everywhere and sees everything in Me, I am never lost, nor is he ever lost to Me."

Bhagavad-gītā 6.30

But in *Bhagavad-gītā* 9.4, Lord Kṛṣṇa says:

mayā tatam idaṁ sarvaṁ
jagad avyakta-mūrtinā
mat-sthāni sarva-bhūtāni

na cāhaṁ teṣv avasthitaḥ

> "By Me, in My unmanifested form, this entire universe is pervaded. All beings are in Me, but I am not in them."

So should we also consider that Kṛṣṇa is not in everything simultaneously? Please help me understand the differences between these two verses.

Here's How

Yes, it is a fact that Kṛṣṇa is within everything and not within everything, both at the same time.

It may appear contradictory that Kṛṣṇa in one verse says that He is everywhere and in another describes that He is not present within the living beings. We also know from other verses that Kṛṣṇa is present within all beings as the Supersoul.

So what could Kṛṣṇa possibly mean when He says that He is not within the living beings?

He is saying that although He is everywhere, He is simultaneously aloof from this material creation. This is something like a wealthy factory owner who has set up the managerial systems in his factory so expertly that every employee feels the owner's presence and does his job expertly even though the factory owner is aloof from the day-to-day activities on the assembly line while he is somewhere else engaged in other activities such as meeting with dignitaries, etc. Of course, any employee who is very keen to have a personal relationship with the owner can, by sincere service, become his intimate associate and even be allowed to participate in the owner's private family affairs.

Is Everyone Cheated by Their Mind?

I have read your articles every day for two months. I really admire what you do for what you believe. I have to confess that I'm not good at English writing so you must forgive me if I cannot express my opinion correctly.

Your thoughts have very much inspired me. However, when I try to do as you said to approach the Kṛṣṇa consciousness, I just see my own mind in an unspeakably blank emptiness.

I think that people with different religions can only find different shapes of God according to what they believe, and that this is why the world needs many different religions - because our pure or true mind (or soul) will automatically show the picture a person is eager to see. I'm not disagreeing with what you believe. I just wonder: Is everyone being cheated by their own mind, by what one's own mind shows to him or her?

Under this theory, there is only one truth, which is our pure mind (sometimes called the Buddha nature).

Perfection of the Pure Mind

I am very happy to hear from you of your admiration for my beliefs. But in this connection I humbly beg to point out to you that what I am writing is not my beliefs. What I am presenting is the timeless knowledge of existence, which has been carefully transmitted by great, fully realized spiritual masters since time immemorial. Anyone who would like to become fully realized in this ultimate knowledge can do so simply by taking advantage of the guidance of the bona fide spiritual master.

As long as we take the Supreme according to our imagination or mental speculation, we remain within the realm of impure mind. Therefore, we should not allow ourselves to be cheated by the impure mind. We should instead take advantage of the mercy of the bona fide spiritual master who ushers us into the realm of the pure mind, which is described in the following verse of the *Bhagavad-gītā*:

> In the stage of perfection called trance, or *samādhi*, one's mind is completely restrained from material mental activities by practice of yoga. This perfection is characterized by one's ability to see the self by the pure mind and to relish and rejoice in the self. In that joyous state, one is situated in boundless transcendental happiness, realized through transcendental senses. Established thus, one never departs from the truth, and upon gaining this he thinks there is no greater gain. Being situated in such a position, one is never shaken, even in the midst of greatest difficulty. This indeed is actual freedom from all miseries arising from material contact.
>
> *Bhagavad-gītā* 6.20-23

Regarding the state of pure mind/Buddha nature, please note that there are three stages:

- Pure mind (*Brahman* realization)
- Purer mind (*Paramātmā* realization)
- Purest mind (*Bhagavān* realization)

These are described as follows in the *Śrīmad-Bhāgavatam*:

vadanti tat tattva-vidas
tattvaṁ yaj jñānam advayam
brahmeti paramātmeti
bhagavān iti śabdyate

"Learned transcendentalists who know the Absolute Truth call this nondual substance *Brahman, Paramātmā* or *Bhagavān*."

Śrīmad-Bhāgavatam 1.2.11

If one becomes *Bhagavān* realized, then he is situated in the highest, most complete realization of the Buddha nature. Such a most-perfectly realized soul fully surrenders himself at the lotus feet of the Supreme Personality of Godhead.

Demigods, Incarnations and *Avatāras*

Are Śrīla Prabhupāda's Teachings a Myth?

Not to be offensive, but how can I know for certain that Prabhupāda's writings/ teachings are not "just another myth?" Why should I cling to Kṛṣṇa when there are so many other gods and goddesses crying out for my attention?

Worship the God of Your Choice

It is not a question of Śrīla Prabhupāda's writings/teachings. It is rather a question of Kṛṣṇa's teachings in the *Bhagavad-gītā*. This is because Śrīla Prabhupāda is not presenting his own teachings. He is simply presenting the teachings of Kṛṣṇa without any adulteration, without any addition or subtraction. Kṛṣṇa clearly states in the *Bhagavad-gītā*:

yānti deva-vratā devān
pitṝn yānti pitṛ-vratāḥ
bhūtāni yānti bhūtejyā
yānti mad-yājino 'pi mām

> "Those who worship the demigods will take birth among the demigods; those who worship the ancestors go to the ancestors; those who worship ghosts and spirits will take birth among such beings; and those who worship Me will live with Me."
>
> *Bhagavad-gītā* 9.25

You are welcome to cling to any god or goddess of your free choice. But you should know you will attain the abode of whichever god or goddess you cling to. Kṛṣṇa also explains:

antavat tu phalaṁ teṣāṁ
tad bhavaty alpa-medhasām
devān deva-yajo yānti
mad-bhaktā yānti mām api

> "Men of small intelligence worship the demigods, and their fruits are limited and temporary. Those who worship the demigods go to the planets of the demigods, but My devotees ultimately reach My supreme planet."
>
> *Bhagavad-gītā* 7.23

The pantheon of gods and goddesses is situated within this material existence. If you cling to one of them you will attain a residence on a planet that will be destroyed at the time of the universal destruction. If, on the other hand, you cling to the Supreme Personality of Godhead, you will attain residence on the Kṛṣṇaloka planet, which will never be destroyed.

So you can decide whether you would like temporary shelter or permanent shelter, and then worship the god of your choice.

What Is the Relationship Between Śiva and Viṣṇu?

Can you explain to me the relationship between Śiva and Viṣṇu? Some sources say, "Śivaya Viṣṇurūpāya Śivarūpāya Viṣṇave—Śiva is the same as Viṣṇu, and Viṣṇu is the same as Śiva." And some other sources say that Śiva is a servant of Viṣṇu, that he carries out the will of Viṣṇu. Can you explain this?

Like Milk and Yogurt

I am very happy to note that at such a young age as 14 you are very keen to become learned in Vedic wisdom. You should perfect your understanding of the Vedic wisdom and become a pure devotee of Lord Kṛṣṇa.

It is not true that Śiva is the same as Viṣṇu, and that Viṣṇu is the same as Śiva. The real fact, according to the revealed Vedic wisdom and the great enlightened teachers, is that Śiva and Viṣṇu are simultaneously one and different, just like milk and dahi (yogurt).

How is that so? Milk can be transformed into yogurt; indeed yogurt is nothing but a transformation of milk. But while it is true that milk can be transformed into yogurt, it is not true that yogurt can be transformed into milk.

So Viṣṇu is like milk and Śiva is like yogurt. Śiva is nothing but a transformation of Viṣṇu, but he cannot be transformed into Viṣṇu.

Lord Śiva possesses 84% of the qualities of *Bhagavān*, Lord Viṣṇu 97%, and Lord Kṛṣṇa is 100% *Bhagavān*.

Isn't Lord Viṣṇu the Ultimate Godhead?

I read all your daily thoughts for the day. I am a bit confused about Viṣṇu and Kṛṣṇa. If Kṛṣṇa is an incarnation of Lord Viṣṇu, isn't Lord Viṣṇu then the ultimate Godhead?

Yes, But...

Yes, Lord Viṣṇu is certainly the ultimate Godhead, but we have to understand exactly Who Lord Viṣṇu is and how He is the ultimate Godhead. He is the ultimate Godhead because He is the source of all that exists. Everything emanates from Him. All material universes, all living beings, and all forms of Viṣṇu emanate from

Him. There are millions and millions of Viṣṇu forms emanating from the original Viṣṇu form. That original Viṣṇu form is known as Kṛṣṇa.

Just as one candle can be used to light another candle, which can then light another candle, which can then light yet another candle millions and millions of times—Kṛṣṇa is the original form of Godhead, and multi-millions of Viṣṇus are His expansions. Everything that exists is an emanation from Kṛṣṇa. He is the original source of everything, as confirmed by Lord Sri Kṛṣṇa Himself in the *Bhagavad-gītā*:

ahaṁ sarvasya prabhavo
mattaḥ sarvaṁ pravartate

"I am the source of all spiritual and material worlds. Everything emanates from Me."

Bhagavad-gītā 10.8

When Did Lord Rāma Appear?

Śrī Caitanya Mahāprabhu appeared five centuries ago, and Lord Kṛṣṇa appeared fifty centuries ago. Are there time records of the appearances of Lord Rāma, Lord Nṛsiṁhadeva and so forth?

Mahābhārata Gives Us a Hint

We can understand something about when Lord Rāmacandra appeared by consulting the *Mahābhārata* (*Śāntiparva* 348.51-52) as follows:

tretā-yugādau ca tato
vivasvān manave dadau
manuś ca loka-bhṛty-arthaṁ
sutāyekṣvākave dadau
ikṣvākuṇā ca kathito
vyāpya lokān avasthitaḥ

"In the beginning of the millennium known as Treta-yuga this science of the relationship with the Supreme was delivered by Vivasvān to Manu. Manu, being the father of mankind, gave it to his son Mahārāja Ikṣvāku, the king of this earth planet and forefather of the Raghu dynasty, in which Lord Rāmacandra appeared."

From these verses we can understand that Lord Rāmacandra appeared in the dynasty of Mahārāja Ikṣvāku, the son of Manu. Manu heard the *Bhagavad-gītā* from Vivasvān at the beginning of Treta Yuga, some 2,005,000 years ago.

In this way through scriptural research we can learn more about the different incarnations of Lord Śrī Kṛṣṇa.

Why Doesn't Kṛṣṇa Appear?

There is a lot of discussion about when Kṛṣṇa's incarnation as the Kalki *avatāra* will make His appearance on earth. We see now that after Lord Kṛṣṇa made his appearance and then departed 5,000 years ago that mankind has gone from bad to worse with no apparent limit to how much injustice and immorality can become manifested around us. Why doesn't Kṛṣṇa make an appearance now to put an end to all this? I know that it has already been stated in the Vedas that the age of Kali yuga is going to last for another 427,000 years, and this is bound to happen. But isn't all this going beyond tolerance? Isn't there a need for God to intervene to make man realize his purpose for being here, and how misguided he is?

He Has Appeared

You are absolutely correct in understanding the dire need for the Lord to appear. He has mercifully done so at the present time by manifesting Himself in the form of the Hare Kṛṣṇa Movement. Kindly take advantage of this by fully dedicating your life to this movement.

What Did God Look Like?

What did God look like the very first time he incarnated himself on earth? Was it his two-armed version with skin the color of clouds?

Why is it still so difficult to break free from *māyā* even when a strong attempt is being made?

What do you think Kṛṣṇa would say if you asked Him what you should do if you are struggling with depression and anger?

He Was a Gigantic Fish

The first incarnation of Kṛṣṇa within this universe is described as follows in the *Śrīmad-Bhāgavatam*:

oṁ namo bhagavate mukhyatamāya namaḥ sattvāya
prāṇāyaujase sahase balāya mahā-matsyāya nama iti.

"I offer my respectful obeisances unto the Supreme Personality of Godhead, who is pure transcendence. He is the origin of all life, bodily strength, mental power and sensory ability. Known as Matsyāvatāra, the gigantic fish

> incarnation, He appears first among all the incarnations. Again I offer my obeisances unto Him."
>
> *Śrīmad-Bhāgavatam* 5.18.25

It is difficult to break free from *māyā* because we have been conditioned to be her slave for millions and millions of lifetimes. Becoming Kṛṣṇa conscious is to declare war against *māyā*, the illusory energy. If your endeavor to break free from *māyā* is not successful even when a strong attempt is made, you must make an even stronger attempt. And if that is not successful, you must make an even stronger attempt. In this way you must make your attempt stronger, stronger, stronger, stronger, until finally you break free from the clutches of the material energy.

Depression and anger are the symptoms of a person who is under the influence of the material modes of passion and ignorance. In the *Bhagavad-gītā*, Kṛṣṇa orders us to be transcendental to the influence of the three modes of material nature.

Why Did Kṛṣṇa Come as a Fish?

What has me curious is why Kṛṣṇa came to earth as a fish? Was there a specific reason?

To Protect the Vedas

Your question is answered in the first verse of the *Daśāvatāra-stotra* as follows:

pralayo payodhi-jale dhṛtavān asi vedaṁ
vihita-vahitra-caritram akhedam
keśava dhṛta-mīna-śarīra jaya jagad-īśa hare

> "O Kesava! O Lord of the universe! O Lord Hari, who have assumed the form of a fish! All glories to You! You easily acted as a boat in the form of a giant fish just to give protection to the Vedas, which had become immersed in the turbulent sea of devastation."

Differences Between Kṛṣṇa, Nārāyaṇa, and Viṣṇu

Would you please kindly explain the differences, if any, among Śrī Kṛṣṇa, Śrī Viṣṇu and Śrī Nārāyaṇa? Since Śrī Kṛṣṇa is the source of all, Śrī Kṛṣṇa would be the source of Śrī Viṣṇu and Śrī Nārāyaṇa if they are not the same as Śrī Kṛṣṇa.

God at the Office, God at Home

Kṛṣṇa is the source. They are His expansions.

God at the office is Nārāyaṇa or Viṣṇu. He is engaged in official duties of universal management. But God at home is Kṛṣṇa. He is simply enjoying intimate pastimes with His most confidential devotees.

Are Kṛṣṇa and His Expansions the Same Person?

Could you please tell me whether the various expansions of Lord Kṛṣṇa are each a separate personality, or are they all the same One, the same person?

Simultaneously One and Different

The answer is that they are *advaita*, they are non-different. They are one and the same person, yet at the same time that one Supreme Person manifests Himself as different personalities for the sake of unlimitedly expanding His enjoyment.

For example, Lord Balarāma is Kṛṣṇa Himself, yet He is manifested as a different person so that Kṛṣṇa can enjoy having a brother. In this material world many people enjoy having a brother. So would we think that God is lacking something, that He cannot enjoy having a brother? No. God cannot be lacking in any way. Therefore, even though everything that exists is nothing but His own personal expanded energy, He manifests it full of unlimited varieties of personal relationships for the unlimited expansion of His personal pleasure.

The Lord manifests two types of expansions. The integrated expansions, such as Lord Balarāma and Lord Rāmacandra, are the same person as Kṛṣṇa. The separated expansions are the living entities such as us. We are distinct, individual persons. We are not Kṛṣṇa.

Does Nārada Still Come to Earth?

Does the great sage and liberated spaceman Nārada Muni not come to this planet any more, or does he only come here for devotees?

That's Up to Him

Nārada Muni can appear anywhere according to his sweet will and to anyone whom he chooses. We should not assume that he is no longer coming here. He can appear for devotees whenever he wants and he can also appear for non-devotees any time he chooses, just as he appeared to Mṛgāri, the hunter.

Worship Only Kṛṣṇa?

I have been praying to Lord Gaṇeśa, Lord Hanumān, Lord Śiva, Lord Viṣṇu, Lord Rāma and the Supreme Personality of Godhead Kṛṣṇa since childhood. Should I forget the rest and worship only Kṛṣṇa?

Watering the Root Waters the Entire Tree

When you water the root of a tree, all the leaves and branches are automatically nourished. Watering the leaves and branches will not be effective in giving the tree the water it needs. If you want the tree to get sufficient water, you must water the root. Only by watering the root will the tree be healthy. If you neglect to water the root, the tree will die.

According to the Vedic scriptures, there is a clear distinction between the Supreme Lord and the demigods. Lord Kṛṣṇa is the original form of the Supreme Lord. Lord Viṣṇu and Lord Rāma are His expansions. The demigods are highly elevated devotees of the Lord who serve the Lord within this material world. There is no need to worship the demigods separately. When we serve the Supreme Lord, the demigods are automatically satisfied.

So the answer to your question is, yes. You may give up all other forms of worship and simply fully surrender yourself to Kṛṣṇa. This is why Kṛṣṇa states in the *Bhagavad-gītā* that we should give up all other duties and simply fully surrender ourselves to Him. However, if you are not able to do this, you may continue to worship the demigods for the purpose of begging them to bless you that you can fully surrender yourself to Lord Kṛṣṇa.

You may worship any and all forms of the Supreme Lord, as any worship of the Supreme Lord is effective for delivering us from this material existence. Just like when we chant the Hare Kṛṣṇa *mahā-mantra* we are worshipping both Lord Kṛṣṇa and Lord Rāma. But demigod worship is described by Lord Kṛṣṇa as the activity of those who have lost their intelligence.

Are All Great Teachers Avatāras?

Are all the great spiritual teachers of the world (Christ, Buddha, Mohammed, etc.) *avatāras* of Kṛṣṇa? And if so, what kind of attention should we pay to their teachings? Should we honor them and learn from them as well?

Avatāras or Śaktyāveśa Avatāras

All the great teachers of the world are either incarnations of God or pure devotees of God. In either case they are equally venerable or worshipable because the pure devotee of God is meant to be worshipped on the same level as God. Because the pure devotee is fully invested with the *śakti* or energy of Kṛṣṇa for uplifting the global consciousness, he is known as a *śaktyāveśa avatāra*.

The various incarnations and pure devotees appear again and again throughout history for the purpose of reestablishing religious principles. They sometimes speak the full truth, sometimes partial truth, and sometimes focus on sub-religious principles, as in the case of Lord Buddha.

If you will carefully study the *Bhagavad-gītā* as it is, you will understand the full truth and then see how all the incarnations and pure devotees taught their students in such a way as to bring them closer to the highest truth.

Sometimes the great teachers present principles which are against the higher principles of Vedas for the purpose of regulating sinful men so that they gradually come to the ultimate standard of pure devotion. So in terms of what principles and teachings to embrace and which ones to leave aside, by studying and following the teachings of the *Bhagavad-gītā* you will realize everything.

Neglecting Sītā and Rāma?

In the Hare Kṛṣṇa *mantra*, there is a mention of Rāma, which I believe is Lord Rāma. If I understand clearly, Rāma and Kṛṣṇa are both *avatāras* of Viṣṇu. So Rāma, Kṛṣṇa and Viṣṇu are actually one and the same.

In none of your lectures or emails have you ever mentioned about Lord Rāma or Mātā Sītā. You have always described the pastimes of Lord Kṛṣṇa and Rādhā. Why do you mention about Rādhā and Krsna and not mention about the life and teachings of Sītā and Rāma?

Watering the Root Nourishes the Branches

You are right that Rāma, Kṛṣṇa, and Viṣṇu are one and the same. But you are incorrect to think that Kṛṣṇa and Rāma are *avatāras* of Viṣṇu. The actual situation is that Viṣṇu and Rāma are *avatāras* of Kṛṣṇa. This is confirmed in the *Bhagavad-gītā* in which Lord Śrī Kṛṣṇa states that He is the source of everything, that everything emanates from Him.

While it is not true that we never mention Sītā and Rāma, the fact is that we mention Rādhā and Kṛṣṇa a lot more than we mention Sītā and Rāma. However, this does not mean that we are neglecting Sītā and Rāma. Just as when we water the root of a tree all the leaves and branches are nourished, when Rādhā and Kṛṣṇa are glorified Sītā and Rāma are automatically glorified.

If you will hear more of my lectures, you will find that I sometimes do mention Sītā and Rāma.

Technical Terms

I have a question regarding the actual meaning behind primary manifestation, secondary manifestation, expansion, incarnation, plenary portion etc. For example, in the following śloka or verse:

pañca-tattvātmakaṁ kṛṣṇaṁ
bhakta-rūpa-svarūpakam
bhaktāvatāraṁ bhaktākhyaṁ
namāmi bhakta-śaktikam

> "I offer my obeisances unto the Supreme Lord, Kṛṣṇa, who is nondifferent from His features as a devotee, devotional incarnation, devotional manifestation, pure devotee and devotional energy."
>
> *Śrī Caitanya-caritāmṛta, Adi-lila* 1.14

Similarly, in many other places I encounter these technical terms but am not able to comprehend what are the similarities or differences between them.

Features of the Lord

The different features of the Lord are as follows:

1. Devotee— *bhakta-rūpa*: Kṛṣṇa Himself in the form of a devotee, i.e. Lord Caitanya, the original Personality of Godhead
2. Devotional incarnation— *svarūpakam*: Lord Caitanya's first expansion, Lord Nityānanda
3. Devotional manifestation— *bhakta-avatāram*: Lord Caitanya's incarnation, Śrī Advaita Ācārya
4. Pure Devotee— *bhakta-ākhyam*: the Lord's pure devotee, Śrīvāsa
5. Devotional Energy— *bhakta-śaktikam*: Śrī Gadādhara, who represents the internal energy of the Lord for the advancement of pure devotion.

The Cause of All Causes – The Origin of All:
Kṛṣṇa – The Absolute Truth

The Study of Me

My goal is to evolve spiritually and come closer to God. My plan is working on myself: the study of me; being conscious/aware of my actions and the suffering I may be creating for myself and others through my material nature.

To live in harmony and peace, I meditate, practice yoga and read spiritual literature. I have been searching all my life.

The More We Surrender, the Better We Feel

I am very happy to hear of your desire for self-knowledge. In the Sanskrit language this is called *ātma-tattva*, the science of the self.

Any study of the self will always remain incomplete unless the origin of the self is thoroughly investigated also. That origin of all selves has thoroughly revealed Himself in the Vedic literatures as Lord Śrī Kṛṣṇa, the Supreme Personality of Godhead.

If you study thoroughly who Kṛṣṇa is, your self-knowledge will be perfect, and you will achieve unlimited freedom and happiness.

When Did Kṛṣṇa Create This World?

Can you please advise me about when Kṛṣṇa created this world, and when this world will end?

Do you have any evidence in the form of *ślokas* (verses) to quote?

155 Trillion Years Ago

This particular universe and all the multitude of universes were created by the exhalation of an expansion of Kṛṣṇa known as Mahā-Viṣṇu 155 trillion years ago. After another 155 trillion years Mahā-Viṣṇu will inhale and the material nature will go into a state of suspended animation until His next exhalation.

This is confirmed in the *Brahmā-saṁhitā* as follows:

yasyaika-niśvasita-kālam athāvalambya
jīvanti loma-vilajā jagad-aṇḍa-nāthāḥ
viṣṇur mahān sa iha yasya kalā-viśeṣo
govindam ādi-puruṣaṁ tam ahaṁ bhajāmi

"Brahmā and other lords of the mundane worlds, appearing from the pores of hair of Mahā-Viṣṇu, remain alive as long as the duration of one exhalation of the latter [Mahā-Viṣṇu]. I adore the primeval Lord Govinda of whose subjective personality Mahā-Viṣṇu is the portion of portion."

Brahma-saṁhitā 5.48

How Do You Explain Creation?

How do you explain to someone how they were created if they don't accept the Big Bang theory or the Adam-and-Eve thing? How do you explain the planets and how we were created by Kṛṣṇa or Lord Viṣṇu?

The Original Something

You simply ask them if they have any experience of something coming out of nothing. The fact is that everything comes from something, and each something that a thing comes from also has a something that it has come from. If we trace back, back, back until we come to that something that does not come from another something, that is the Supreme Being. It is not difficult to understand. Any person with a cool brain can understand this.

What Is the First Language of the Universe?

1. Can I know what the first language of the universe was?
2. How was the universe created, and secondly, in the Bible and Koran they say that Adam was the first man in the world. Is it true? Who was the first man in the world, and in which country was he created?
3. Kindly tell me how many years have passed since the creation of the universe.
4. Let us know about the principle God in the world.
5. What is the difference between the *Bhagavad-gītā*, the Bible and the Koran, and how many years' difference is there between these books?

Sanskrit Is the Original Language of the Universe

Sanskrit is the original language of this universe. Just after the creation of this universe 155 trillion years ago, Lord Brahmā was thinking in the water and heard the two syllables "*ta*" and "*pa*" from the Sanskrit alphabet.

sa cintayan dvy-akṣaram ekadāmbhasy
upāśṛṇod dvir-gaditaṁ vaco vibhuḥ
sparśeṣu yat ṣoḍaśam ekaviṁśaṁ
niṣkiñcanānāṁ nṛpa yad dhanaṁ viduḥ

> "While thus engaged in thinking, in the water, Brahmājī heard twice from nearby two syllables joined together. One of the syllables was taken from the sixteenth and the other from the twenty-first of the *sparśa* alphabets, and both joined to become the wealth of the renounced order of life."
>
> *Śrīmad-Bhāgavatam* 2.9.6

The universe in which we reside has come out from the breathing of Mahā-Viṣṇu. The original person in this universe was Lord Brahmā. He does not live in any country of this planet Earth. He has his own planet, Brahmāloka.

As confirmed by Lord Brahmā, Kṛṣṇa is the Supreme Godhead:

īśvaraḥ paramaḥ kṛṣṇaḥ
sac-cid-ānanda-vigrahaḥ
anādir ādir govindaḥ
sarva-kāraṇa-kāraṇam

> "The Supreme Personality of Godhead is Kṛṣṇa, who has a body of eternity, knowledge and bliss. He has no beginning, for He is the beginning of everything. He is the cause of all causes."
>
> *Brahma-saṁhitā* 5.1

The Bible goes back 2,000 years, and the Koran is more recent than that. The *Bhagavad-gītā* was spoken to the Sun God millions of years ago. The difference in the books is that the Bible and the Islamic teachings state that there is something more than what they have so far revealed. The *Bhagavad-gītā*, however, states that there is nothing more to be known than what is revealed in the *Bhagavad-gītā*:

jñānaṁ te 'haṁ sa-vijñānam
idaṁ vakṣyāmy aśeṣataḥ
yaj jñātvā neha bhūyo 'nyaj
jñātavyam avaśiṣyate

> "I shall now declare unto you in full this knowledge, both phenomenal and numinous. This being known, nothing further shall remain for you to know."
>
> *Bhagavad-gītā* 7.2

Is Experiential Truth Relative?

If Truth exists within the realm of experience, wouldn't that make Truth relative and not absolute?

Truth Is Not Relativized by Experiencing It

Experience can be both relative and absolute. Just like we can experience something in a dream state or in an awakened state. If we experience Truth within the realm of relativity, this does not make Truth relative. Rather, the experience of Truth within the relative world elevates us to the absolute plane. The relative plane is a manifestation of the absolute plane, just as the clouds which cover the sun are a product of the sun. They come into being by the influence of the sun to evaporate the ocean water. Just as the sun can penetrate through the clouds, Truth can penetrate through relativity and fully manifest itself anywhere it chooses. The Absolute Truth is Kṛṣṇa, the Supreme Personality of Godhead.

Who Created God?

What existed when God was not there? Who created God?

God Created God

Nothing could have existed if God had not been there because He is the manifester of everything. Nothing exists without His manifesting it. Since He has always existed and because of His desire to enjoy a manifestation, His manifestation has also been existing along with Him as His subordinate energy for all of eternity.

If anyone created God, it would have to be God Himself, because He is the origin of everything. He is not created by anything or by anyone else because He is self-manifested. There is no meaning to the idea of being God unless He is self-manifested. If He were created by anyone or anything else, He would not be God. God means that He is the Supreme. He is not dependent on anyone else or anything else for His existence.

Does God Exist?

Does God exist? If so, where does He exist?

Of Course

Yes, of course God exists. How could He not exist? If He did not exist, nothing could exist, and you wouldn't exist to be able to ask me if He exists. The fact that you exist to ask me if He exists proves that He exists.

He exists in His own abode, in the hearts of all living beings, within every atom, and between the atoms. Because everything is His expanded energy, there is nowhere that He does not exist, and at the same time He is beyond everything.

Śrīla Prabhupāda describes Kṛṣṇa in this way:

"There is nothing but Śrī Kṛṣṇa, and yet nothing is Śrī Kṛṣṇa save and except His primeval personality."

So now you should qualify yourself to meet God face-to-face, eye-to-eye. In this way you will never again be confused, wondering if God exists and where He exists.

Challenge: You Have Not Proved that God Exists

You said (by way of proof) that the fact that we exist is proof that God exists. A little more thought would tell you that the fact that we exist only proves that WE exist, not that God exists.

Your Existence Proves God's Existence

The Vedic conception of God is that God is the source of all that exists. This is why I claim that our existence proves God's existence. In other words, I am making the point that we cannot exist without having a source for our existence. I make this claim because we are not self-manifested. If you can manufacture yourself out of nothing, then you have some rational grounds for defeating my argument.

Who Is Kṛṣṇa?

Please tell me, who is Kṛṣṇa? I am new with understanding self-realization. When I pray (chant, meditate) I am speaking directly to God and also to His son Jesus and the Holy Spirit. But in your chants you are calling on other names. Please tell me who they represent and why you call upon them.

The Origin of All That Exists

Kṛṣṇa is the most perfect and complete name for the Supreme Personality of Godhead, that Supreme Person Who is the origin of all that exists. He is known by different names according to different languages. In English He is called "God." In Sanskrit He is called "Kṛṣṇa."

In English we call water "water." In Spanish it is known as "agua." Whether we refer to it as water or as agua, the substance is the same. Similarly, whether we address the Supreme Person as God, Kṛṣṇa, Allah, or Jehovah, the person is the same. What matters is not the particular name we use. What matters is that we approach Him selflessly with pure love.

Each and every one of the unlimited names for God describe different aspects of His various attractive qualities. The name "Kṛṣṇa" is most perfect and most complete because it refers simultaneously to all of His attractive qualities and therefore contains all of the other names for God within the two syllables "kṛṣ" and "ṇa."

We chant His name with love, calling for Him to deliver us from the repetition of birth and death by accepting us as His eternal servants.

Does God Exist?

How can one believe in the existence of God?

A Scientific Proof

We have no interest in believing in God. Belief can be changed just as easily as the wind changes directions. We want to KNOW whether God exists or not. Once we know this, our position will be very solid. While beliefs can be whimsically changed at any moment, knowledge is unshakable. Because modern-day science is constantly being changed, we can understand that the scientists have not yet arrived at the point of knowledge.

"God" simply means "the source of all that exists." From practical experience we can see that everything comes from something, that nothing comes from nothing. Therefore, the universe must come from a source. Just as we have a name for this thing and that thing, we also have a name for the original source of existence. We call that source by the word "God." Therefore, just as certainly as the universe exists, as confirmed by our perception of it, we can know positively that God exists.

To say that the universe simply exists on its own without having a source is not scientific because that is not the pattern we observe within nature. Everywhere we can observe that one thing comes from another thing, which comes from another thing, which comes from another thing. If we trace all back to the original source of all that exists, we find God.

Proof of God's Existence?

Can you prove to me that God exists? I know I can't prove that He does not exist. But I would like to know whether you can prove the existence of God.

In your writings, you have argued that everything comes from something and that the original source is God. This is not logical since it also means that God too must have an origin. Then He/She is not an all-powerful God, but rather just somebody who has more power than we have. This doesn't make that person God.

Absolutely!

If someone has already decided there is no God, we cannot prove anything to them. If, however, someone is truly open-minded we can easily prove to them that God exists.

We can observe by practical experience that every machine requires an operator. No machine can start itself. There must be an operator. We also observe that this universe functions as a gigantic machine. Therefore, we can guess that the universal machine must also have an operator.

God has an origin. That origin is Himself. He is self-manifested, and everything else that exists is God-manifested.

Proof of God's Existence

If we are searching for God, then it seems logical to say that God would be the origin. However, if we were not specifically searching for God, then we could also say that everything originated from some base chemicals and that too would be logical. This type of reasoning does not indicate any presence or lack of God.

You have now hinted at a possible answer to my question, i.e. reciprocation from God. Now that would seem tangible proof of His existence. But, so far I don't seem to have had any kind of communication from God. Can you please explain what form this reciprocation would take?

According to One's Surrender

But where did the base chemicals come from? That you have not explained. All we are saying is that there is some original source from which everything is coming. The name by which we refer to that original source is not as important as understanding that there is an original source and understanding what our relationship is with that original source.

How God reciprocates with a person depends on that person's degree of surrender. This is explained as follows by Lord Śrī Kṛṣṇa in the *Bhagavad-gītā*:

ye yathā māṁ prapadyante
tāṁs tathaiva bhajāmy aham
mama vartmānuvartante
manuṣyāḥ pārtha sarvaśaḥ

"As all surrender unto Me, I reward them accordingly. Everyone follows My path in all respects, O son of Pṛthā."

Bhagavad-gītā 4.11

Acintya Bhedābheda Tattva

What is the meaning of "*acintya bhedābheda tattva*?"

Simultaneously One and Different

Acintya bhedābheda tattva means that the Absolute Truth is simultaneously, inconceivably one and different. Just as a drop of the Atlantic Ocean is qualitatively one with the Atlantic Ocean and quantitatively different from it, the living being is qualitatively one with God and quantitatively different from God.

Viṣṇu, the Source of Kṛṣṇa?

Why is Lord Kṛṣṇa's name greater, more powerful than Lord Viṣṇu's names, even though Lord Viṣṇu is source of Lord Kṛṣṇa?

No. Kṛṣṇa, the Source of Viṣṇu

It is a very common misconception in India that Viṣṇu is the origin of Kṛṣṇa. This indicates how much out of touch modern-day Hindus are with their own scriptures.

The actual fact is that Kṛṣṇa is the original Supreme Personality of Godhead. All other incarnations emanate from Him.

It is very clearly stated by Lord Kṛṣṇa in the *Bhagavad-gītā*:

ahaṁ sarvasya prabhavo
mattaḥ sarvaṁ pravartate

"I am the source of all spiritual and material worlds. Everything emanates from Me."

Bhagavad-gītā 10.8

Lord Brahmā states in the *Brahma-saṁhitā*:

īśvaraḥ paramaḥ kṛṣṇaḥ
sac-cid-ānanda-vigrahaḥ
anādir ādir govindaḥ
sarva-kāraṇa-kāraṇam.

"Kṛṣṇa who is known as Govinda is the Supreme Godhead. He has an eternal blissful spiritual body. He is the origin of all. He has no other origin and He is the prime cause of all causes."

Brahma-saṁhitā 5.1

It is furthermore stated in the *Śrīmad Bhāgavatam*:

ete cāṁśa-kalāḥ puṁsaḥ
kṛṣṇas tu bhagavān svayam

"All of the above-mentioned incarnations are either plenary portions or portions of the plenary portions of the Lord, but Lord Śrī Kṛṣṇa is the original Personality of Godhead."

Śrīmad-Bhāgavatam 1.3.28

Some people think that because the Lord first appeared as Viṣṇu within the prison of Kaṁsa and then took the form of baby Kṛṣṇa, Viṣṇu is His original form. This is not a fact, as confirmed by the authoritative Vedic literatures. Kṛṣṇa spoke to His mother Devakī shortly after His birth revealing to her why He had manifested the Viṣṇu form:

etad vāṁ darśitaṁ rūpaṁ
prāg-janma-smaraṇāya me
nānyathā mad-bhavaṁ jñānaṁ
martya-liṅgena jāyate

"I have appeared in this Viṣṇu form just to convince you that I am the same Supreme Personality of Godhead again taken birth. I could have appeared just like an ordinary child, but in that way you would not have believed that the Supreme Personality of Godhead had taken birth in your womb."
Śrīmad-Bhāgavatam 10.3.44

Why Did All This Come to Be?

Should all living beings seek devotional love for the Supreme?

Understanding from the Buddhist point of view, if everything is included in one and one is included in everything, then why did all this come to be?

Who created love, and why? Since it takes two for a loving relationship, isn't this a form of dualism?

All Exists Eternally for the Pleasure of the Supreme Person

Yes, devotional love for the Supreme is that for which all living beings should seek. This is not a matter of blind faith or blind following. It is a matter of proper understanding of how we can restore our original, natural consciousness - the one that we had before we became conditioned by illusion and entered into a life of suffering in the cycle of birth and death.

You have mentioned that from the Buddhist point of view, everything is included in one; but the philosophy of oneness is another philosophy separate from Buddhism. In Buddhism the highest philosophical principle is zero, or void. Buddhism accepts "zeroness" as the Supreme Truth, not oneness.

You are wondering why everything exists. If everything were one, there would be no need for anything at all to exist except for homogenous oneness. The fact that we see so many varieties before us negates the very conception that everything is one, because such a conception gives us no logical way to explain what we are experiencing.

The conception of the Supreme Person - Who wants to expand His enjoyment by expanding innumerable living beings from Himself for the purpose of enjoying loving relationships with them - provides a solid, logical basis for understanding reality.

This paradigm, which is elaborately described in the Vedic wisdom, can neatly, in one package, account for all aspects of reality as we know it and give us access to being elevated to a higher level of reality far beyond our current range of perception.

Some people consider dualism to be a bad word because they have suffered so many anxieties here in this dualistic material world. But just consider the word harmony, which implies peacefulness and unity. Harmony means that there are two or more things that resonate well together. They are separate, but there is no clash between them. If all is one, harmony cannot exist, because there must be different things or persons to harmonize with one another. The perfection of existence is not to merge into oneness with the Supreme. The perfection of our existence is to enter into a state of perfect harmony with the Supreme. In that perfectional stage, one reciprocates transcendental love with the Supreme Personality of Godhead for all of eternity.

How Do We Know God Exists?

I have a question for you. How do we know God exists? How can you prove it?

How Could God Not Exist?

I am very happy that you are inquiring how we can know that God exists. My question for you is, "How could God not exist?"

Are you the Complete Whole, the Total Existence? Or are you a part of it? Because you are not the Complete Whole and are only a part of it, you are only conscious of the pains and pleasures in your body. On the other hand, the Complete Whole, the Total Existence, is conscious of the pains and pleasures within all living beings.

How can we deny the reality of the Complete Whole, the Total Existence, when we are living within it at every moment? That would be a most preposterous proposition. Only a mindless fool would deny the existence of the Complete Whole. So we must first, on the basis of common sense observation, accept the reality of the Complete Whole, the Total Existence.

The next step is then to understand the nature of that Complete Whole. It is described as follows in the *Śrī Īśopaniṣad*:

oṁ pūrṇam adaḥ pūrṇam idaṁ
pūrṇāt pūrṇam udacyate
pūrṇasya pūrṇam ādāya
pūrṇam evāvaśiṣyate

"The Personality of Godhead is perfect and complete, and because He is completely perfect, all emanations from Him, such as this phenomenal world, are perfectly equipped as complete wholes. Whatever is produced of the Complete Whole is also complete in itself. Because He is the Complete

Whole, even though so many complete units emanate from Him, He remains the complete balance."

Śrī Īśopaniṣad Invocation

In Defense of Skepticism

Without a bit of skepticism how would you find the truth in things? After all, one should not be too gullible, as there are a lot of bogus things.

Science is not like the dogma of most religions, which is defined as (1) a doctrine or system of doctrines proclaimed true by a religious sect or (2) a principle, belief, or statement of an idea or opinion, especially one that is authoritatively, sometimes arrogantly, asserted as Absolute Truth. So I like to try and keep a balance, if you know what I mean, and not be too gullible.

Skepticism is very helpful in understanding things better, as you get both sides of the story. What do you think of the saying, "A lot of good can come out of bad"? For instance, some bad things that have happened in my life have pointed me in the right direction. Skepticism is like that, in a way. Without bad, how would you understand the purity of good or the spirit? So without skepticism it would be a lot more difficult to find the truth.

Skeptical of Skepticism

Skepticism is the philosophical position of doubting everything. In terms of being duped by false teachings, it is certainly helpful to a certain point. But just as the existence of counterfeit money indicates the existence of real money, falsity indicates that somewhere there is actual truth.

If one is overly skeptical regarding money, he will never be able to accept money from anyone due to his paranoia that all money is counterfeit. This is a highly unrealistic and impractical position. Similarly, if is one is overly skeptical regarding knowledge, he will never be able to accept anything as truth. But since truth exists, to take the philosophical position of the skeptics, to never accept anything as truth, would be ridiculous.

Science proposes to give us truth. Yet we do not see a consensus of opinion among scientists. What one scientist says is true is said by another scientist to not be true. So how we will arrive at the truth? This is the most important question we can ask in this human form of life. Therefore, the *Vedānta-sūtra* enjoins:

athāto brahma jijñāsā

"The purpose of the human form of life is to understand what is the Absolute Truth."

So how will we arrive at the Absolute Truth? We are living within it at every minute. Therefore, the Absolute Truth of existence can never be extinguished, although it may be temporarily covered by ignorance. If we are very sincere to reconnect ourselves with that Absolute Truth, then the Supreme Absolute Truth dwelling within us will bring us in contact with a bona fide spiritual master who will then fully reveal that Absolute Truth to us. When it comes to a direct experience of the Absolute Truth, skepticism would be a great hindrance for the progressive development of our intelligence. Therefore, under such a circumstance, we would be extremely foolish to hold onto our skepticism. Under such a circumstance skepticism must be abandoned.

The philosophy of skepticism dictates in the ultimate end that one must also doubt the validity of skepticism.

When one reaches the precincts of the Absolute Truth, to hold onto the crutch of skepticism is a gross violation of the principle of skepticism.

Devotion to Kṛṣṇa or Viṣṇu

Is Kṛṣṇa the *avatāra* of Viṣṇu, or is Viṣṇu the *avatāra* of Kṛṣṇa? I have been a devotee of Viṣṇu since my childhood. Do I now have to change my devotion? Usually now, when I chant Hare Kṛṣṇa, when I close my eyes I see the form of Viṣṇu. I face many problems on the Kṛṣṇa path.

There Is No Difference

There is actually no difference between Viṣṇu and Kṛṣṇa. He is exactly the same Supreme Person. When that Supreme Person is in the office taking charge of the universal affairs, He is called Viṣṇu. And when that same Supreme Person is at home having intimate dealings with His friends and family members, He is called Kṛṣṇa. Kṛṣṇa is a more intimate, personal name, and Viṣṇu is a more formal, official name for the same Supreme Person.

So whether Kṛṣṇa's or Viṣṇu's form comes to your mind when you chant does not matter. Simply fully absorb your mind in the transcendental sound vibration of *Hare Kṛṣṇa, Hare Kṛṣṇa, Kṛṣṇa Kṛṣṇa , Hare Hare Hare Rāma, Hare Rāma, Rāma Rāma, Hare Hare* - and regaining the association of the Supreme Person Kṛṣṇa or Viṣṇu in His eternal transcendental kingdom is assured.

The Bona Fide Spiritual Master – Instruction of Guru Guru Parampara/Disciplic Succession – Initiation – Transparent Via Medium

Is Sincere Effort Predestined?

Is whether or not I put sincere effort in following the instructions of the spiritual master predestined by my past *karma*, or is it according to my free choice? I mean, sometimes I am able to put in sincere effort and sometimes I am not.

Taking Advantage of Guru's Mercy Transforms Destiny

To what extent one is obedient to one's spiritual master is not predetermined by one's *karma*. It is totally up to you right now how much you will be surrendered to following the instructions of your spiritual master.

You can be neglectful and suffer the consequences, or you can be fully obedient and reap the supreme reward of going back to home, back to Godhead at the end of this lifetime. The choice is fully yours, no matter what your past *karma* may be. The spiritual master is giving you the opportunity to become liberated from the predestining influence of the laws of *karma*. This is his special mercy upon the disciple. It is fully up to the disciple whether or not he will take complete advantage of the guru's mercy. The choice is fully yours. Now what will you do?

If One Has No Information about Kṛṣṇa Consciousness

In "Thought for the Day" you wrote that God gives us everything we need, but because we do not follow him we are suffering. But what if one's *karma* is such that one is not able to get any information about Kṛṣṇa consciousness or anything spiritual? Is such forced suffering - under which we cannot even free ourselves, no matter how much we would want to - just another kind of *karma*?

Kṛṣṇa Will Send Him a Guru

Anyone who is sincerely seeking the highest truth beyond all suffering will be blessed by coming in contact with a devotee of the Lord, who will then reveal the Truth to him. In other words, the Lord within knows the person's desire to realize the highest truth and thus sends the spiritual master to plant the seed of *bhakti* within his heart. Anytime someone wants to become free from his *karma*, all he has to do is desire that freedom and then obey the instructions of the spiritual master who is sent by the Lord to deliver him.

How Can I Advance?

You have said that you must inquire submissively from a self-realized soul. But because of confusion I don't know what to ask. I feel that I've met a self-realized soul, but I still don't believe that this person can help me because of my own limitations. I feel that there are things inside myself that block me from having a true relationship with anyone. What can I do to make advancement at this stage?

Approach Guru in the Mood of Arjuna

Arjuna was confused when he approached Lord Śrī Kṛṣṇa, the supreme self-realized being. But after approaching the Lord he became free from all confusion. Therefore, if you want to be free from all confusion, all you have to do is approach the guru, self-realized soul, in the same way that Arjuna did. Here's how he inquired from the Lord:

kārpaṇya-doṣopahata-svabhāvaḥ
pṛcchāmi tvāṁ dharma-sammūḍha-cetāḥ
yac chreyaḥ syān niścitaṁ brūhi tan me
śiṣyas te 'haṁ śādhi māṁ tvāṁ prapannam

"Now I am confused about my duty and have lost all composure because of miserly weakness. In this condition I am asking You to tell me for certain what is best for me. Now I am Your disciple, and a soul surrendered unto You. Please instruct me."

Bhagavad-gītā 2.7

The self-realized soul can definitely liberate you from your entangled position within this material existence. He is specifically empowered by Lord Kṛṣṇa to do this. All you have to do is to fully surrender unto him, just as Arjuna fully surrendered unto Lord Śrī Kṛṣṇa. This will solve all of your problems very easily.

Why Do We Need Initiation?

Why do we need an initiation process by a guru for advancement in spiritual life?

Only a Liberated Soul Can Liberate Us

The absolute necessity of initiation by a spiritual master is confirmed in the Vedic injunctions as follows:

tad vijñānārthaṁ sa gurum evābhigacchet

"In order to understand the transcendental science, one must approach a bona fide spiritual master."

Muṇḍaka Upaniṣad 1.2.12

tasmād guruṁ prapadyeta
jijñāsuḥ śreya uttamam
śābde pare ca niṣṇātaṁ
brahmaṇy upaśamāśrayam

"Therefore any person who seriously desires real happiness must seek a bona fide spiritual master and take shelter of him by initiation. The qualification of the bona fide guru is that he has realized the conclusions of the scriptures by deliberation and is able to convince others of these conclusions. Such great personalities, who have taken shelter of the Supreme Godhead, leaving aside all material considerations, should be understood to be bona fide spiritual masters."

Śrīmad-Bhāgavatam 11.3.21

Without a guru we are nowhere. It takes a liberated soul to get us out of the cycle of birth and death. A conditioned soul cannot become liberated unless he takes shelter of a bona fide spiritual master.

How Should We Take Guru's Mercy?

How should we take the spiritual master's mercy? It is already there, but how does one take it? How is it possible to associate with a pure devotee of Kṛṣṇa?

Follow His Instructions

The most powerful mercy of the spiritual master is manifested in the form of the instructions which he gives to his beloved disciples. (They are all beloved.) The proper way to take this mercy is to accept each and every instruction you receive from your spiritual master as your very life and soul by faithfully and carefully executing it to the best of your ability. When you are associating with Kṛṣṇa's pure devotees you must always remember to respect them equally as you respect God. This is confirmed by Kṛṣṇa's instruction to Uddhava:

ācāryaṁ māṁ vijānīyān
navamanyeta karhicit
na martya-buddhyāsūyeta
sarva-deva-mayo guruḥ

"One should know the acarya as Myself and never disrespect him in any way. One should not envy him, thinking him an ordinary man, for he is the representative of all the demigods."

Śrīmad-Bhāgavatam 11.17.27

Finding a Spiritual Master

Much of your teaching requires that we approach a bona fide spiritual master and take instructions from him.

Is it acceptable to read *Bhagavad-gītā* and follow the teachings through purports from His Divine Grace Śrīla Prabhupāda? I guess my main question is: Can I regard His Divine Grace Śrīla Prabhupāda as my spiritual master, or must I approach someone directly?

Follow Prabhupāda's Instructions

What I present are not my teachings. I am simply a humble messenger presenting the teachings of Lord Śrī Kṛṣṇa as He presents them in the *Bhagavad-gītā*.

His Divine Grace A.C. Bhaktivedanta Swami Prabhupāda is most certainly your spiritual master because through his books he is guiding you in how to attain spiritual perfection. He is your *śikṣā guru*, instructing spiritual master, because his instructions are taking you from the darkness into the light.

Through carefully reading Śrīla Prabhupāda's books you will see that he teaches you that you also need a spiritual master whom you can approach with your personal questions and from whom you can receive personal guidance. This type of guru is known as the "initiating guru."

Śrīla Prabhupāda points out the absolute necessity of this type of guru in his *Śrīmad-Bhāgavatam* purport quoted below:

> The real fact is that a bona fide spiritual master knows the nature of a particular man and what sort of duties he can perform in Kṛṣṇa consciousness, and he instructs him in that way. He instructs him through the ear, not privately, but publicly. 'You are fit for such and such work in Kṛṣṇa consciousness. You can act in this way.' One person is advised to act in Kṛṣṇa consciousness by working in the Deities' room, another is advised to act in Kṛṣṇa consciousness by performing editorial work, another is advised to do preaching work, and another is advised to carry out Kṛṣṇa consciousness in the cooking department. There are different departments of activity in Kṛṣṇa consciousness, and a spiritual master, knowing the particular ability of a particular man, trains him in such a way that by his tendency to act he becomes perfect. *Bhagavad-gītā* makes it clear that one can attain the highest perfection of spiritual life simply by offering service according to his ability, just as Arjuna served Kṛṣṇa by his ability in the military art. Arjuna offered his service fully as a military

> man, and he became perfect. Similarly, an artist can attain perfection simply by performing artistic work under the direction of the spiritual master. If one is a literary man, he can write articles and poetry for the service of the Lord under the direction of the spiritual master. One has to receive the message of the spiritual master regarding how to act in one's capacity, for the spiritual master is expert in giving such instructions. This combination, the instruction of the spiritual master and the faithful execution of the instruction by the disciple, makes the entire process perfect. Śrīla Viśvanātha Cakravartī Ṭhākura describes in his explanation of the verse in *Bhagavad-gītā, vyavasāyātmikā buddhiḥ*, that one who wants to be certain to achieve spiritual success must take the instruction from the spiritual master as to what his particular function is. He should faithfully try to execute that particular instruction and should consider that his life and soul. The faithful execution of the instruction which he receives from the spiritual master is the only duty of a disciple, and that will bring him perfection. One should be very careful to receive the message from the spiritual master through the ears and execute it faithfully. That will make one's life successful.
>
> from the purport to *Śrīmad-Bhāgavatam* 3.22.7

Śrīla Prabhupāda will always remain your instructing guru, but now, as per his instructions quoted above, you must also accept a guru from whom you will receive personal guidance. This type of guru is called the "*dīkṣā guru*" or the "initiating spiritual master." When you become serious to follow the instructions given by Śrīla Prabhupāda to fully surrender yourself to the guidance of the spiritual master who practically engages you in devotional service to Kṛṣṇa, you must seek out such a spiritual master who perfectly represents Śrī Kṛṣṇa and Śrīla Prabhupāda and take complete shelter at his lotus feet as his initiated disciple.

Can Conscience Be Our Guide?

What, if anything, does the Vedic literature have to say about the human conscience, which gives us the ability to do "the next right thing?"

If We Can Properly Hear It

The Supreme Lord does not want any living being to act sinfully, and He begs him through his good conscience to refrain from sin. But the difficulty is that people act sinfully in spite of their good conscience, being impelled by the dictates of their senses, which burn with desire like a fire which is never satisfied no matter how much fuel is fed to it.

We have to learn how to clearly discern between our mind and our conscience. The mind is the pivot point for the senses. If we are not sufficiently careful and intelligent, our mind, being impelled by the senses, will drag us again and again into the dark realm of sense gratification. But if we listen very carefully to our conscience, it will take us into the brilliant, enlightened realm of complete shelter at the lotus feet of Lord Śrī Kṛṣṇa.

In this connection Śrīla Prabhupāda states, "Being present in everyone's heart, the Lord gives the living entities the conscience whereby they can accept the Vedas and the spiritual master. In this way the living entity can understand his constitutional position and his relationship with the Supreme Lord."

Qualification to Be Accepted as a Disciple

In your last letter you requested me to develop pure, unadulterated love for Lord Kṛṣṇa. I am sincerely attempting to do this. I am chanting 16 rounds daily of the Hare Kṛṣṇa *mantra* on *japa* beads. I am trying to serve devotees regularly. I am regularly donating a portion of my income to Kṛṣṇa-conscious services. I am reading Śrīla Prabhupāda's books and offering my food to Kṛṣṇa before I eat. I am also attending a number of temple programs, including lectures from visiting *sannyāsīs*, and associating with devotees as much as I can. I realize that in order to obtain unadulterated love of Kṛṣṇa I also need to surrender fully to a bona fide spiritual master. Is there anything else I need to be doing to become qualified to be accepted as a disciple of a bona fide spiritual master?

Now Notify the Spiritual Master

It sounds like you are doing very nicely. The next step is to notify the spiritual master that you would like to take shelter of him for becoming his disciple. He will then guide you further.

Why Do We Need an Outer Guru?

Several years ago I went off in search of my guru. A friend of mine told me, "Jesus is your guru." If we have the Holy Spirit as a guide, why do we also need an "outer" guru?

Telecommunication Link Required

Because you are not pure enough to receive direct transmissions from Lord Jesus or the Holy Spirit within, you therefore require the telecommunication link of the external bona fide spiritual master.

Just like if someone were standing in front of you, you could speak directly to him. But if he were at a great distance, you would require the telecommunication link of a telephone.

Effectiveness of Guru's Instructions

I'm not your initiated disciple, but I aspire to be. Are the replies I receive from Your Grace fully effective even though I am not yet initiated?

According to the Degree of Surrender

The instructions of the bona fide spiritual master are always fully potent. But their impact upon the heart of the disciple varies according to the degree of his surrender. For example, they become even more effective for the disciple after initiation because at that time the disciple is fully surrendered to executing whatever order he receives from the spiritual master. Of course, if the student is fully surrendered even before initiation, the spiritual master's instructions will be fully effective even before initiation.

Can the Guru Be Wrong?

I understand that the guru is not omniscient, that he is not the same as Kṛṣṇa, and that he is a representative of Kṛṣṇa. Sometimes my limited understanding disturbs me. For example: My guru might not know what is beyond the wall of his room but Kṛṣṇa knows and sees everything. As such, Kṛṣṇa is full in knowledge and guru is limited.

My question is: is there a possibility that a guru or his teachings may be wrong or that his instructions may be wrong?

The Bona Fide Guru Is Never Wrong

Although the guru is not omniscient, because he has a direct connection the Supreme Omniscient, he is as good as the Supreme Omniscient. Therefore, I always can understand and feel how my spiritual master is watching over me, blessing me and guiding me at every minute.

The bona fide guru does not invent his own teachings. He simply repeats the instructions of Kṛṣṇa without any adulteration. Therefore, there is never any flaw in his teachings. If he concocts his own message or presents a message which is not in accordance with the Vedic literatures, he is not bona fide and should be rejected. Such a bogus guru will do us more harm than good. We must be careful to only take shelter of the lotus feet of the bona fide spiritual master; otherwise our spiritual life will be a total disaster.

If Guru Is Not Bona Fide?

How can we know if our guru is bona fide one? Can we accept another guru if our guru is not bona fide one?

Reject Him and Accept a Bona Fide Guru

If the spiritual master purely repeats the words of Kṛṣṇa as given in the *Bhagavad-gītā,* without any addition or subtraction, then he is bona fide. Sadly, nowadays it is very rare to find such a bona fide guru. Most of the so-called gurus present some concocted ideas which differ from the teachings of Lord Śrī Kṛṣṇa, the original spiritual master.

If your guru is not bona fide, you must reject him and take shelter of the bona fide spiritual master.

What if Sankarshan Prabhu Gives Us Misinformation?

I feel that Sankarshan Prabhu should spend more time in India and understand the basic Hindu teachings by listening to the various spiritual masters before he spreads the same all over the world. Although he is doing a great job, what if, after doing all that, he preaches wrong and sends the incorrect message of *Bhagavad-gītā*?

I Only Speak the Pure Message of Kṛṣṇa

I appreciate very much that you feel I am doing a great job. I have also noted your concern that you fear that I might sometime speak something which is against the teachings of the *Bhagavad-gītā*. In this connection you may rest assured that I have fully surrendered myself at the lotus feet of the world's leading *Bhagavad-gītā* authority, His Divine Grace A.C. Bhaktivedanta Swami Prabhupāda. He has carefully imparted unto me the innermost understanding of the *Bhagavad-gītā* as confirmed by the great *ācāryas* who have guided India's Vedic civilization throughout the ages.

Thus I never give my own opinion regarding the message of the *Bhagavad-gītā*. I have no other activity than to repeat the teachings of the *Bhagavad-gītā* without adulteration - exactly as spoken by Lord Śrī Kṛṣṇa to Śrī Arjuna on the battlefield of Kurukṣetra 5,000 years ago - because I have been carefully trained by my Guru Mahārāja to never add anything or subtract anything from this topmost knowledge spoken by Lord Śrī Kṛṣṇa.

In this way, what I teach to my students is perfectly in line with the *Bhagavad-gītā*. Of course, in this connection I can take no credit whatsoever. I am simply the humble servant who is delivering the message of Lord Kṛṣṇa as confirmed by the greatest spiritual masters of Indian history. I cannot take any credit for the purity of the message I am delivering because all credit goes to my spiritual master, Śrīla Prabhupāda, who has enlightened me with the perfect knowledge of the *Bhagavad-gītā* and ordered me to spread it all over the world. If I have any credit at all in this regard it is simply that I am always strictly following the instructions given to me by my spiritual master and repeating whatever he has told me, without any deviation.

How to Please Guru?

If a disciple does not know what his spiritual master wants, what should he do in order to please his spiritual master?

Inquire and Render Service

Your question is very nice, because the secret of success in spiritual life is to successfully carry out the orders received from one's spiritual master. In order to do this, it is compulsory that the disciple know what his spiritual master wants him to do. The method is very simple. All you have to do is ask him.

Do not speculate what you think the spiritual master wants. You must directly ask him so that you can know for certain what he wants. Then you should faithfully do your best to serve his orders. In this way you will achieve the supreme perfection.

Who Succeeds Śrīla Prabhupāda?

Guru Nanak, after testing many of his disciples, selected Guru Angad as his successor and announced it before everyone by placing his hands on him and declaring Guru Angad as his representative and successor.

Did Śrīla Prabhupāda also select a person to represent him and be his successor, or is it that any of his disciples who are following the regulative principles could be a guru and initiate disciples? Even in the disciplic succession from Lord Kṛṣṇa to Śrīla Prabhupāda (mentioned in *Bhagavad-gītā*), only one guru is mentioned at each step. Or is there a chain of gurus at any of the steps?

Those Who Strictly Follow Him

Śrīla Prabhupāda instructed that all of his disciples who are strictly following him become gurus. He gave this instruction to us many, many times. For example, here is one such instance from a lecture he gave in Hyderabad:

> So we got this information from His Divine Grace Bhaktisiddhānta Sarasvatī Ṭhākura, and that knowledge is still going on. You are receiving through his servant. And in future the same knowledge will go to your students. This is called *paramparā* system. *Evaṁ paramparā prāptam*. It is not that you have become a student and you'll remain student. No. One day you shall become also guru and make more students, more students, more.

That is Caitanya Mahāprabhu's mission, not that perpetually... Yes, one should remain perpetually a student, but he has to act as guru. That is the mission of Caitanya Mahāprabhu.

Lecture —Hyderabad, December 10, 1976

Apparently you have not read the Guru *Paramparā* list very carefully. There are many instances in our Guru *Paramparā* when there was more than one present *ācārya* listed. The Guru *Paramparā* is like a tree. From the trunk come many branches, and from each branch comes many sub-branches, each with many sub-branches.

How Can I Know What Kṛṣṇa Wants?

I am 100% convinced that only vegetarian foods can be offered to Lord Śrī Kṛṣṇa. Nonetheless, while reading your reply, a number of questions kept arising in my mind. In my current state, my consciousness is not yet 100% devotional. It is surviving due to the fact you have emphasized that with spiritual gain follows material gain. While chanting, my mind is running through the house, to the chores and other things. Is this any good?

Secondly, how can I know what Lord Kṛṣṇa wants from me?

From the Spiritual Master, Scriptures, and Saintly Devotees

I always recommend that my students complete at least 16 rounds of *japa mālā* before sunrise because during this *sattvic* period of day the mind is far less likely to become distracted by thoughts of the day's activities.

We know what Kṛṣṇa wants us to do by consulting with the spiritual master. Just like if you go to work for a company, how do you know what the owner of the company expects of you in your job? You are trained by your immediate supervisor in how to do everything in such a way that the owner is pleased. In the same way, we have to learn how to please Kṛṣṇa with all of our thoughts, words and deeds through the training that we receive from the spiritual master, the *śāstras* (scriptures) and the Lord's devotees.

Have You Seen Kṛṣṇa?

I asked my father, "Have you seen Kṛṣṇa?" He answered, "No, but Kṛṣṇa helps me in many ways."

I want to know if you have seen Kṛṣṇa directly or not. If you have seen Him, have you talked to Him? I have been studying your emails for the past two years. I am satisfied with your answers. I asked so many people who are in Kṛṣṇa *bhakti*, "Have you seen Kṛṣṇa?" All of their answers are the same. They all say, "No." I want now to meet a person who is alive who has seen God. I know that your spiritual master, Śrīla Prabhupāda, could see God at every minute.

So I want for my guru a person who has seen Kṛṣṇa. I want to become his follower. But I do not want to leave home. I want to remain at home and serve Kṛṣṇa at my best. I also want to see Kṛṣṇa as early as possible.

You Are Asking the Wrong Question

You are mistakenly thinking that seeing Kṛṣṇa is the qualification for being a bona fide spiritual master. The demon Kaṁsa saw Kṛṣṇa, but he was not a guru, nor was he even a devotee. The actual qualification for being a spiritual master is to only repeat the words of Kṛṣṇa without any addition or subtraction. Nowhere in the scripture does it say that one is required to see Kṛṣṇa in order to be a spiritual master. You should not invent your own requirements regarding who is a bona fide spiritual master. You should leave this up to authoritative directions given in the Vedic scriptures. In this regard kindly note what the *Śrīmad-Bhāgavatam* states about the bona fide spiritual master:

tasmād guruṁ prapadyeta
jijñāsuḥ śreya uttamam
śābde pare ca niṣṇātaṁ
brahmaṇy upaśamāśrayam

> "Any person who seriously desires real happiness must seek a bona fide spiritual master and take shelter of him by initiation. The qualification of the bona fide guru is that he has realized the conclusions of the scriptures by deliberation and is able to convince others of these conclusions. Such great personalities, who have taken shelter of the Supreme Godhead, leaving aside all material considerations, should be understood to be bona fide spiritual masters."
>
> *Śrīmad-Bhāgavatam* 11.3.21

You may remain at home and become a first-class devotee, but only if you are willing to conduct your home life strictly under the guru's guidance.

Of course, by dint of his devotional service, the spiritual master perceives everything within Kṛṣṇa and Kṛṣṇa within everything. This is a natural by-product of his full absorption 24 hours daily in the Lord's service. But this is not the yardstick by which you determine who is a spiritual master. Anyone can falsely claim that he is seeing Kṛṣṇa. Therefore, you must judge the guru's qualifications by the above verse from the *Śrīmad-Bhāgavatam*. And when you find him you must take complete shelter of him by initiation. Is this clear?

How Can One Recognize a Guru?

You have thoroughly explained the qualities of bona fide gurus. But how can one recognize them and surrender himself to that person who will ultimately lead us to Lotus Feet of Kṛṣṇa?

He Only Repeats Kṛṣṇa 's Words

The spiritual master can be easily be recognized by seeing that person whose only business is to repeat the words of Kṛṣṇa, without any addition or subtraction, to everyone that he meets.

Surrendering to him can also be easily accomplished. All you have to do is inform the spiritual master that you want to be his disciple and then ask him what he wants you to do. "Disciple" means one who disciplines himself by always meditating upon and following the instructions that he receives from his spiritual master.

Strict Initiation Requirements

I would like to know from you why any person wishing to get initiated from you or any other guru in ISKCON is subject to pre-conditions for getting initiated. A person who is showing interest in *kṛṣṇa-bhakti* should be trusted by the guru outright and be immediately accepted as a disciple. By such a policy, many newcomers will come to Kṛṣṇa consciousness. With tough pre-conditions in place, a real devotee is discouraged from *kṛṣṇa-bhakti*.

An Inspiration for the Serious

Just as every university has entrance requirements, similarly there are also certain requirements for becoming initiated by the bona fide spiritual master. The candidate must be solidly fixed in chanting at least 16 rounds of Hare Kṛṣṇa *japa mālā* daily and following these four regulative principles:

1. No illicit sex life
2. No intoxication
3. No meat-eating
4. No gambling

These items must be followed strictly throughout the entire life of those who have taken initiation. Therefore, those who want to be initiated must clearly demonstrate their determination to remain fixed in these practices for life.

Most so-called gurus nowadays give initiation very cheaply without requiring their disciples to observe a daily vow of chanting God's names or following the above-mentioned regulative principles. Such so-called initiation is cheap and meaningless and does not enable the students to attain spiritual perfection. Sometimes ISKCON is criticized for its strict requirements, but actually ISKCON is to be glorified for having such strict requirements because this is a symptom of ISKCON's legitimacy.

Those who are sincere enough to want initiation will also be sincere enough to demonstrate that they can follow their initiation vows for life. We could give initiation very cheaply to anybody and everybody, even to strangers who walk in from the street. But such cheap initiation would not help the people to advance in Kṛṣṇa consciousness. Therefore, instead of giving cheap initiations, we test those who request initiation in order to make sure that they are fit candidates for a lifetime of strictly following their initiation vows.

In this connection my spiritual master, His Divine Grace A.C. Bhaktivedanta Swami Prabhupāda, has explained: "One must be able to pass the test of the spiritual master, and when he sees the genuine desire of the disciple, he automatically blesses the disciple with genuine spiritual understanding."

So the only real requirement is a genuine desire for spiritual life. If one has that sincerity, he will be happy to demonstrate his ability to follow the regulative principles.

Similar to the way that high-level universities with tough entrance requirements (like Harvard and Oxford) attract a large number of highly qualified applicants from all over the world, those spiritual masters who do not water down or cheapen the process of Kṛṣṇa *bhakti* attract many sincere and dedicated disciples from all over the world.

If one is serious about a life of complete surrender to Lord Śrī Kṛṣṇa, he will humbly submit himself to what the Lord's representative, the spiritual master, instructs him to do. He will not find fault with the spiritual master if the spiritual master asks him to wait for some time before the initiation ceremony.

If one is serious to take shelter of the bona fide spiritual master, the eternal bond between the disciple and the spiritual master begins from the first moment the disciple accepts the instructions of his spiritual master as his very life and soul.

Is Guru Really Required?

In the scriptures it is mentioned that a guru can help an aspiring devotee to get the right information to reach Kṛṣṇa by providing answers to questions that the aspiring devotee might have. But what is the need of a guru to a person who already knows answers to all his/her questions?

For example, a person who has *properly* read the books and articles written by Śrīla Prabhupāda and people like you would have all their questions answered already. For such people, there is no need of a guru as they have already got all the questions answered. In other words, they don't need to know anything more from the would-be guru.

Another point I would like to make is that, for a person who is 100% committed to Kṛṣṇa, the onus of getting the right guru lies more with Kṛṣṇa than the person himself/herself. When he/she is ready for it, the guru will come to his/her doorstep on his/her own. If the guru never comes, then Kṛṣṇa never intended for it.

Don't Take Without Giving

We must always remember that Kṛṣṇa says not only to inquire from the spiritual master. In the same verse in which he instructs us to inquire from the spiritual master, he also tells us that we must also serve the spiritual master.

tad viddhi praṇipātena
paripraśnena sevayā
upadekṣyanti te jñānaṁ
jñāninas tattva-darśinaḥ

"Just try to learn the truth by approaching a spiritual master. Inquire from him submissively and render service unto him. The self-realized souls can impart knowledge unto you because they have seen the truth."

Bhagavad-gītā 4.34

It is not a loving thing to do, to take knowledge from the spiritual master without giving him service in return. Without the exchange of love between the master and the student, transcendental realization will not take place. The knowledge gleaned will only remain book knowledge and the student will gradually lose interest in the knowledge because for him it will become dry and tasteless.

Kṛṣṇa is sending the guru for everyone. But the poor souls of Kali Yuga are so blind that they are not able to take advantage of Kṛṣṇa's mercy in the form of the spiritual master that He has sent them.

Is It Really Possible to Get Rid of Māyā 100%?

I have a problem. I am so much attracted to Kṛṣṇa consciousness, but I easily get carried away by material desires. This shows that I am still not very firmly fixed in Kṛṣṇa consciousness. After having fulfilled my material desire, I wonder why I got deviated so easily. I don't want to get carried away by *māyā*. Is it really possible to get rid of *māyā* 100%? How much time did it take you to come out of the clutches of *māyā*?

I have another question regarding an answer you previously gave. You wrote, "By perfecting the science of *bhakti* within any tradition, one will achieve the perfection of that tradition by becoming a perfect Muslim, a perfect Krishnite, a perfect Christian, etc."

How can a Muslim be a perfect Muslim? Where are the details of who, where and how? God is given only in the Vedas. The majority of the Muslims/Christians eat meat, so how can they be perfect in their devotional service when the scriptures they follow instruct them to eat meat (even cow)? I do not have anything against any religion, and most of my good friends since my childhood have been Muslims (I am materially a Hindu). But I have pondered this question in my mind for some time.

Dedication to the Spiritual Master

The turning point for becoming a steady devotee is when the disciple realizes how much the spiritual master loves him or her and thus becomes inspired to dedicate his is or her entire life in loving service to the spiritual master. This was the turning point in my spiritual life, and it will be the turning point in your spiritual life also, when that day comes.

A Muslim or Christian will not become perfect in his religion until he realizes that the animals are also, along with the human beings, the beloved children of God and should therefore not be murdered and eaten. Although the Bible, the Koran, and the Vedas all give prescriptions for animal-killing under restriction, these instructions are for those who are materially engrossed to minimize their sinful activities so that they can gradually give them up. Those who have understood the essence of all scriptural wisdom give up material sense enjoyment and focus 100% on developing pure love of God. Such persons do not partake of the flesh of animals.

On Gurus

It is my understanding that a guru is one who guides the initiate into a meaningful relationship with God. Do you acknowledge that there are gurus in the world who are not ISKCON devotees?

Whoever Has Fully Realized God

Anyone who teaches his students how to attain pure love of God can be accepted as a bona fide spiritual master. Being a bona fide spiritual master has nothing to do with being a member of a particular organization. It depends on being a fully God-realized being. The Founder-Ācārya of ISKCON, His Divine Grace A.C. Bhaktivedanta Swami Prabhupāda, was situated on the highest platform of God realization. Anyone who is fully surrendered to his instructions and has properly assimilated his teachings is qualified to guide us in how to become spiritually perfect. This does not mean that others who are not his students are not qualified. We simply have to see if the person has fully realized God. This is the criterion.

Is the Master Self-Realized?

How does one know if the spiritual master he is choosing is self-realized or not? Are you self-realized?

He Must Be

The spiritual master must be self-realized because if the spiritual master is not self-realized, he is not a bona fide spiritual master. The guru's duty is to teach his disciple how to become self-realized. If he is not self-realized, how can he teach his disciple to become self-realized? Such a so-called guru is a cheater, not a teacher. We must carefully avoid such cheaters and find the bona fide spiritual master.

So how do we know that the spiritual master is bona fide? The bona fide spiritual master never advertises himself as such. Therefore, we have to understand the bona fide spiritual by his symptoms as described in the revealed scriptures.

tasmād guruṁ prapadyeta
jijñāsuḥ śreya uttamam
śābde pare ca niṣṇātaṁ
brahmaṇy upaśamāśrayam

> "Any person who is seriously desirous of achieving real happiness must seek out a bona fide spiritual master and take shelter of him by initiation. The qualification of a spiritual master is that he must have realized the conclusion of the scriptures by deliberation and arguments and thus be able to convince others of these conclusions. Such great personalities, who have taken complete shelter of the Supreme Godhead, leaving aside all material considerations, are to be understood as bona fide spiritual masters."
>
> *Śrīmad-Bhāgavatam* 11.3.21

Guru's Willingness to Initiate Disciples in Spite of Taking Their Karma

When a guru initiates, does he take the *karma* of his would-be disciple? Is that the reason many gurus are not very willing to initiate? Sometimes the aspiring disciple has to wait for five years and more to get initiated.

Some gurus are willing to initiate easily, some are not. Why is it so? What happens if a disciple chants his prescribed 16 rounds and follows all the regulative principles, say, for six months, gets initiated, and after some time breaks the regulative principles and stops chanting the prescribed number of rounds?

It is said that if one does a wrong, one has to bear the results of it. But if one lets down a guru, it is a bigger offense. What happens in that case?

His Special Mercy

Yes, the spiritual master does take the *karma* of those that he initiates. Therefore, the spiritual master has to be cautious and make sure that the candidate can be strong and steady in his practice, that he will not fall down.

Sometimes the spiritual master will be very lenient and give someone initiation even if they are not very fixed up, just for the purpose of helping them to get fixed up. This is his special mercy that is sometimes given in specific circumstances. It is totally up to the spiritual master if and when he wants to give such special leniency.

If one takes initiation and then deviates from his initiation vows, the spiritual master will have to suffer by undergoing such things as bad dreams and diseases. The disciple who deviates from his spiritual master will find it impossible to advance on the pathway of spiritual perfection until he can realign himself with the orders received from his spiritual master.

The Happiness of the Lord

How can we definitely know when the Supreme Personality of Godhead is pleased with our service? We become happy by serving the Lord, but it does not necessarily mean that the Lord is also happy with our service. Please help me to realize the happiness of the Lord.

Please His Pure Representative

Just as the proper way to water the branches and leaves of a tree is to water the tree's root, in the same way the only way that we can be happy is to make the Lord happy. In other words, we are like the leaf and Kṛṣṇa is like the root.

Because Kṛṣṇa is still very remote and distant for the neophyte devotee, the scriptures state that to please Lord Kṛṣṇa one simply has to please his pure representative, the bona fide spiritual master. When one pleases his spiritual master, Kṛṣṇa is pleased. This is the amazing potency of the system of disciplic succession.

Ecstasy at Every Moment?

Unfortunately, I do not always feel very happy when chanting my rounds and doing my day-to-day activities. Is it possible to relish at every moment this great ecstasy and happiness that I feel when receiving your email or attending a *kīrtana*? How do I do that?

Associate with Guru Through His Instructions

You have asked, "Is it possible to relish at every moment this great ecstasy and happiness that I feel when receiving your email or attending a *kīrtana*?"

The answer is, "Yes, of course."

You have also asked, "How do I do that?" The answer is very simple. Always remain in the constant association of your spiritual master by meditating upon, worshipping, and sincerely trying to execute the instructions he has given you.

How Can the Common Man Surrender to Kṛṣṇa?

Bhagavad-gītā, Chapter 18, Verse 66 seems to be the essence of the *Bhagavad-gītā*. When we consider the position of the common man, what exactly does Lord Kṛṣṇa mean in this verse when He says that we should abandon all other duties and simply surrender unto Him?

The poor and the poorest of the poor are unable to reach the teachings of the *Bhagavad-gītā*. A lot has to be done to improve our guru system. Probably the process has begun, but it has to go a long way.

Through the Medium of Guru

It is not difficult for anyone, even a common man, to surrender to Kṛṣṇa. They must simply follow the instructions given by Kṛṣṇa in the *Bhagavad-gītā*. For example, in the *Bhagavad-gītā* Kṛṣṇa says that we should take shelter of Kṛṣṇa's pure representative, the bona fide spiritual master. If we place ourselves under the instructions of the spiritual master, he will instruct us exactly what to do to become fully surrendered to Lord Kṛṣṇa.

You mention unfortunate souls who are not able to reach the wondrous teachings of the *Bhagavad-gītā*. But the bona fide spiritual master makes these teachings easily accessible to the entire world population. All they have to do is be willing to hear from the bona fide spiritual master.

The guru system is already perfect. It is always perfect because it comes to us as the most wonderful gift from Lord Śrī Kṛṣṇa, the Supreme Personality of Godhead, for reconnecting us with Him through the healing mercy of the spiritual master. So instead of thinking of reforming the guru system, we should be thinking of reforming our corrupted hearts.

We were originally situated in the spiritual world in the transcendental pastimes of the Supreme Personality of Godhead. But due to envy of His position as the Supreme Lord we were forced to come to this material world and suffer endlessly in the cycle of repeated birth and death. The guru system is there to give us the means to escape this vicious cycle and return to our original position. But instead of thinking about rectifying our hearts, we foolishly think about rectifying the guru system. First things first. First we must become completely pure. Then we can rectify all the problems of the entire universe. The guru system is not one of the problems. It is the solution.

Modern and Vedic Culture

What are the differences and similarities between Vedic culture and contemporary culture?

Different Approach to Science

The modern-day culture and the Vedic culture are similar because both of them are scientifically oriented. Both of these cultures are trying to solve all the problems of life through the advancement of knowledge. The difference is in how each of them goes about trying to realize the knowledge. In the Sanskrit language there are described two approaches to knowledge:

1. *āroha-panthā*, the path of ascending knowledge, and
2. *avaroha-panthā*, the path of descending knowledge.

The contemporary society is following the way of ascending knowledge, *āroha-panthā*, and the Vedic culture follows the way of descending knowledge, *avaroha-panthā*. So what is the difference between theses two paths?

Through *āroha-panthā* we rely exclusively on what we perceive with our senses and the mental speculations based upon such perceptions. The difficulty is that our senses, including the mind, are imperfect. Even if we extend their reach with microscopes, telescopes, and other such instruments, we are still perceiving through our imperfect senses, and we can thus never gain conclusive knowledge. This is why the scientific textbooks are constantly being updated, and why the contemporary society still remains chaotic in spite of so much so-called scientific advancement.

The *avaroha-panthā* is quite different. On this pathway one purifies one's consciousness and senses through the *yoga* system, especially the *bhakti-yoga* system. Since each of us originates from the source of all existence, each one of us has our own innate, personal connection with God, the source of all existence. By purifying the senses through the *bhakti-yoga* system, and thus developing pure love for God, one gradually attains direct perception of the source of all existence, the Supreme Person. By thus knowing Him, one then gains perfect scientific knowledge of everything. This is confirmed by Lord Śrī Kṛṣṇa in the *Bhagavad-gītā*:

jñānena tu tad ajñānaṁ
yeṣāṁ nāśitam ātmanaḥ
teṣām āditya-vaj jñānaṁ
prakāśayati tat param

"When, however, one is enlightened with the knowledge by which nescience is destroyed, then his knowledge reveals everything, as the sun lights up everything in the daytime."

Bhagavad-gītā 5.16

Pure vs. Pseudo Surrender

When can someone know his/her worth and readiness for an eternal commitment and pure surrender to a guru, where there will not be any inner conflict after the surrender (or pseudo-surrender)? How pure should the devotee be? And how complete - without any chance of reservations about the self and also the guru - should a devotee be prior to initiation?

Accept Kṛṣṇa's Order

Your inquiry is very nice. You want to know the difference between pure and pseudo surrender. To know this difference is very important. Otherwise how can one make genuine surrender to the Lord, the prime duty of the human form of life?

The first thing is that one should thoroughly study the spiritual master to make sure that he is indeed bona fide. He must be a humble servant of the Lord, coming in an unbroken disciplic succession of spiritual masters originating with Lord Kṛṣṇa, whose only desire is to engage his disciples in the Lord's service. He must speak only the teachings of Kṛṣṇa as given in the *Bhagavad-gītā,* without addition or subtraction. If he does not present *Bhagavad-gītā* in this way - as it is - one should immediately reject him because he is not a bona fide spiritual master.

You also want to know how a person can understand if he or she is ready for taking complete shelter of the bona fide spiritual master by initiation. If one is willing to dedicate one's entire life to following the spiritual master's instructions, he or she is ready for initiation. The vow the spiritual master will ask the disciple to make at the time of initiation is that for the entire life, the disciple will strictly avoid illicit sex, intoxication, meat-eating, and gambling, and chant at least 16 rounds daily of the Hare Kṛṣṇa *mantra* on *japa mālā* beads. To make sure that the prospective disciple is ready for initiation, the spiritual master requests that he or she be recommended for initiation by the local ISKCON leader.

The purity required is that one has to have been able to strictly follow the above principles for at least one year. In the *Bhagavad-gītā* Kṛṣṇa says that we should cast aside all of our reservations and surrender to Him through the process of taking shelter of the bona fide spiritual master. So, if we are truly dedicated to Kṛṣṇa, we will follow His order and accept initiation from the bona fide spiritual master. In this way we will avoid pseudo-surrender and become purely surrendered to Śrī Guru and Śrī Kṛṣṇa.

Is Scripture Our Guru?

Can someone consider *śāstra* (the scriptures) as their guru?

Scripture Is Not a Guru Substitute

Our first birth is from our mother and father. Our second birth is from the guru, who is our second father, and from the Vedic scriptures, which are our second mother.

In conceiving a child both the father and mother play distinct, non-interchangeable roles. Similarly, on the pathway of self-realization the spiritual master and the scriptures both play distinct, non-interchangeable roles.

The scriptures are like a mega-pharmacy that contains hundreds and thousands of different kinds of medicines. The spiritual master is like the skilled physician who has realized the essence of the Vedic scriptures and who can specifically prescribe for each individual disciple a customized program that is the most suitable for that individual disciple.

When we go to the pharmacy we come with the prescription we have received from our doctor. Similarly, when we approach the Vedic wisdom we do so under the guidance of our spiritual master. This is how we are able to come to a proper understanding of the scriptural knowledge.

How Can You Find a Guru?

Can you have more than one guru? How can you find a guru?

How you can get and increase faith in guru and God?

You Already Have

While we have only one initiating guru, we may have an unlimited number of instructing gurus.

You do not need to go looking for a guru. You have already found one.

The way to increase your faith in guru and God is to chant the Hare Kṛṣṇa *mantra* on a regular, daily basis.

Why Do People Treat You Like God?

I have looked at your web site and seen your pictures, and I have to say:

Wow! People treat you like God, don't they? You sit in the midst of flower petals and on a raised platform. Why is that? Are you above the people you teach?

Guru Is Given Same Respect as God

Just as a policeman, even though just an ordinary citizen like you or me, is respected as being the government when he is on duty, similarly the spiritual master, even though he is also a living being like you or me, is given the same respect that we give to God because his duty is to act as God's representative.

The spiritual master never feels that he is above the people that he is teaching. Rather he considers himself below them. He sees them as his masters because he has to serve them by delivering them back to the spiritual world. He feels completely unqualified and unfit to sit on an exalted seat. But as a matter of duty he is required to accept the respectful obeisances and loving service being offered to him by his disciples. He has this duty because Kṛṣṇa orders His devotees to learn the science of *bhakti* by taking shelter of a bona fide spiritual master to whom they are to give the same honor and respect that they would give to Kṛṣṇa if He were personally present.

I Know Your Guidance Will Help

You must have many devotees by now, and I know your guidance will help them.

If I Can Help Just One Person

Although the number of enrollees in the course has now topped 5,000, my interest is still very much on the individual level. If I can help just one person to become a pure devotee of Lord Krsna I will consider my life to be a complete success. If there is any way that I can serve you by helping you to achieve the supreme perfection, that will be a great honor and privilege for me.

It's a fact, as you say, that my guidance can help people to achieve the perfection of Kṛṣṇa consciousness. But I can make no claim whatsoever to any kind of personal qualification in this regard. If there is any success in my feeble endeavor, it is only because I am trying my best to honestly serve the order of my spiritual master, His Divine Grace Śrīla Prabhupāda, to spread this Kṛṣṇa consciousness all over the world. Whatever result may come from my efforts is simply his kindest mercy upon me.

Thank You for Your Spiritual Guidance

Thank you for your concern and continuing spiritual guidance. I've been trapped in a box of darkness, and your daily emails are a ray of hope piercing the shadows, leading me toward the light of knowledge.

Your Understanding Is Very Nice

Your understanding of the spiritual master is very nice. The nice sentiment you have expressed is very similar to this beautiful prayer that Śrīla Prabhupāda taught us:

oṁ ajñāna-timirāndhasya
jñānāñjana-śalākayā
cakṣur unmīlitaṁ yena
tasmai śrī-gurave namaḥ

> "I was born in the darkest ignorance, and my spiritual master opened my eyes with the torch of knowledge. I offer my respectful obeisances unto him."

Missing You

I, for one, find myself missing you. Isn't that strange? I mean, I haven't ever met you personally but ever since you left on your journey away from Austin, I find myself missing your presence. How is this possible?

On a more positive note, in addition to following the four regulative principles, I have now increased my daily rounds from 8 to 10. Sixteen rounds seems so far off, but so did the amount that I am chanting now. One thing that I try to keep in mind is that "every expert was a beginner once."

On Separation from Śrī Guru

I am very happy to hear that you are feeling separation from the Spiritual Master. This is a sign of your making very nice spiritual advancement. The more we hanker for Śrī Guru's association, the more all of our material desires are burned away and the more we become completely happy and satisfied in Krsna consciousness. This happens by the grace of Śrī Krsna.

I am delighted by your spiritual progress. Continue enthusiastically as you are doing, and surely Kṛṣṇa will bless you.

We Don't Want to Overburden You

I was wondering how many emails you receive on an average day that require an answer, and if it would be better not to comment or ask too many questions. Is this too great an effort to answer all the emails? We do not want to overburden you with too many emails.

The Burden of the Beast vs. the Burden of Love

My daily emails can range from a few to many. Sometimes, owing to varying circumstances, I get several days behind on my correspondence, and it becomes quite an endeavor to catch up. However, I would much prefer to have this burden than to be relieved from this burden.

In this connection His Divine Grace Śrīla Prabhupāda explains as follows:

> "There are two kinds of burdens. There is the burden of the beast and the burden of love. The burden of the beast is unbearable, but the burden of love is a source of pleasure. Śrīla Viśvanātha Cakravartī describes the burden of love very practically. He says that the burden of the husband on the young wife, the burden of the child on the lap of the mother, and

the burden of wealth on the businessman, although actually burdens from the viewpoint of heaviness, are sources of pleasure, and in the absence of such burdensome objects, one may feel the burden of separation, which is heavier to bear than the actual burden of love."

So the point is that I want all of my beloved disciples and readers to know that they always have a fully open channel of communication with me. I am always ready to hear from and respond to my dear disciples and readers.

What Does "Sankarshan" Mean?

I was just wondering what the meaning of your name "Sankarshan" is. I hope you don't mind my asking personal questions instead of spiritual ones.

One Who Attracts All Living Entities

It is a fact that when we approach the spiritual master we are especially meant to inquire about how to advance ourselves in Kṛṣṇa consciousness, rather than ask personal questions. But since you have inquired I will try to answer to your full satisfaction.

Sankarshan means one who attracts all living entities. This, of course, refers to the Supreme Lord. My spiritual master, Śrīla Prabhupāda, has given me the name Sankarshan Das, which means the servant of Sankarshan. Even though I am the mere servant of Sankarshan, I am praying for His blessings that I can attract all living entities to Him.

Of course, they are already attracted to Him. But in this material world they are attracted to His illusory energy rather than to Him directly. Just as a hungry man cannot be satisfied by trying to eat the reflection of food, no one in this material world can be satisfied, no matter how hard they try to enjoy the Lord's illusory energy. Therefore, my prayer is that I can attract them directly to the Lord, away from His illusory energy. The illusory energy is especially manifested in the forms of illicit sex, meat-eating, intoxication, and gambling. The Lord Himself is manifested in the form of His holy names:

Hare Kṛṣṇa, Hare Kṛṣṇa, Kṛṣṇa Kṛṣṇa, Hare Hare
Hare Rāma, Hare Rāma, Rāma Rāma, Hare Hare

Chanting the Hare Kṛṣṇa Mantra

How Is One to Chant with a Focused Mind?

I am trying to practice Kṛṣṇa consciousness. I am chanting 16 rounds daily and following other regulative principles. From a lot of devotees I have learned that chanting is the most important activity we do in Kṛṣṇa consciousness. So I want to know how to chant properly or how to practice chanting so that I can slowly improve in my chanting. Right now it is really difficult for me to chant with a focused mind. I am reading *Bhagavad-gītā As It Is* regularly, trying to understand it slowly, as you always suggest in your course. But I have lot of trouble developing myself and applying the concepts in practical life.

My other question is: on my level, what thing should I stick with so that my development in Kṛṣṇa consciousness becomes sure?

Stay Rigidly Absorbed in the Names

In chanting, the two most important things are to keep your mind fixed on the names and to call out to the Lord like a child crying for mother. If your mind goes off, feelingly beg your spiritual master and Lord Kṛṣṇa that you want to chant purely but your mind is being dragged away by *māyā*. Strongly, intensely beg your spiritual master and Lord Kṛṣṇa to help your mind stay rigidly absorbed in chanting the holy names.

In practical life you must always remain introspective, that every thought in your mind, every word spoken from your lips, and every action performed with your body is pleasing to your spiritual master and to Lord Kṛṣṇa. Use everything for Kṛṣṇa, not in the service of *māyā*.

Why Do We Chant Hare Kṛṣṇa?

When we chant the Hare Kṛṣṇa *mantra*, what is it exactly that we are trying to do?

To Awaken the Dormant Love of God

We are trying to awaken the dormant love of God which is there within our hearts. This is explained very nicely by *Śrī Caitanya Mahāprabhu as* follows:

ceto-darpaṇa-mārjanaṁ bhava-mahā-dāvāgni-nirvāpaṇaṁ
śreyaḥ-kairava-candrikā-vitaraṇaṁ vidyā-vadhū-jīvanam
ānandāmbudhi-vardhanaṁ prati-padaṁ pūrṇāmṛtāsvādanaṁ
sarvātma-snapanaṁ paraṁ vijayate śrī-kṛṣṇa-saṅkīrtanam

"Glory to the congregational chanting of Lord Śrī Kṛṣṇa's Holy Names, which cleanses the heart of all the dust accumulated for years and extinguishes the fire of conditional life, of repeated birth and death. This saṇkīrtana movement is the prime benediction for humanity at large because it spreads the rays of the benediction moon. It is the life of all transcendental knowledge. It increases the ocean of transcendental bliss, and it enables us to fully taste the nectar for which we are always anxious."

Śikṣāṣṭaka 1

A Request for Tips to Improve Chanting

Please give us some tips on how to improve our chanting.

Ten Transcendental Tips

Here are tens tips for improved chanting:

1. Serve those who serve the Lord; don't criticize them out of envy or false ego.
2. Worship Kṛṣṇa as the "source of all spiritual and material worlds," "the ultimate beneficiary of all sacrifices and austerities, the Supreme Lord of all planets and demigods and the benefactor and well-wisher of all living entities." Show respect to demigods like Lord Śiva or Gaṇeśa and personalities like Hanumān as exalted devotees of Lord Kṛṣṇa.
3. Show full respect to the spiritual master in thoughts, words and actions, considering him to be a representative of the Lord. Carry out the orders of the spiritual master with enthusiasm and attention to detail.
4. Honor (and study) the scriptures as the instructions of the Supreme Lord (*dharmaṁ tu sākṣād bhagavat-praṇītam*) with the desire to understand how they are correct (not *if* they are correct).
5. Have faith that the Holy Name is not a mundane sound vibration, but is in fact transcendental sound, descending from the (pure) spiritual platform.
6. Have faith in the explanations and glorification of the Holy Name given by guru, sadhu and *śāstra*. This knowledge is given by those who have experienced the glories of the Holy Name and who have "seen the truth."
7. Root out the desire to commit sins. A sin is an action that is not connected to the Supreme Lord, something done for the gratification of the senses. Acting only for the pleasure of the material body takes you further from practical realization of your factual identity as an eternal spirit soul (separate from the temporary material body).
8. Give up ritualistic pious activities. Transcend feelings of duty and obligation, and perform all activities for the pleasure of Kṛṣṇa.
9. Discuss the glories of the Holy Name with servants of the Lord who will relish hearing about them.

10. Chant attentively, absorbing your full consciousness in the transcendental vibration of the Holy Name.

If you can seriously follow the above ten guidelines, your chanting will improve by leaps and bounds.

1,728 Mahā-mantras?

I was wondering: Is one round of chanting on the *japa* beads done 108 times so that 16 rounds would actually mean chanting the Hare Kṛṣṇa *mantra* 1,728 times?

Deeply Dive Daily

On each bead we chant the entire *Mahāmantra*:

Hare Kṛṣṇa, Hare Kṛṣṇa, Kṛṣṇa Kṛṣṇa, Hare Hare
Hare Rāma, Hare Rāma, Rāma Rāma, Hare Hare

Therefore, each time we chant around the 108 beads we chant the Hare Kṛṣṇa *mahā-mantra* 108 times. Every initiated devotee chants around the beads at least 16 times daily. Your math is correct: 16 x 108 = 1,728. So every day, the initiated devotees chant the Hare Kṛṣṇa *mahā-mantra* at least 1,728 times. In this way they deeply dive daily into that sweet, nectarean ocean of *nāma-rasa*, the taste of the name.

So now you must make your life perfect by giving up bad habits and chanting at least 16 rounds every day according to the expert guidance of guru, *sādhus* (saintly advanced devotees), and *śāstra* (scripture). Your life will be inconceivably sublime.

Chanting in One Sitting?

Is it okay if I chant the 16 rounds of the *mahā-mantra* on the beads throughout the day, or should it be done all at once, on one sitting? I find it hard to do it all at once, but am trying my best.

Easier and More Potent in the Early Morning

The rounds can be chanted any time of the day, but it is much more potent to chant in the early morning hours, before sunrise. It is also easier to focus the mind on the Lord's names during this time. If sitting for a long time is a problem, you may stand or walk while chanting your *japa*.

Chant Hare Kṛṣṇa, Not Hare Rāma

Lord Kṛṣṇa is the Godhead. He is Supreme. Then why in the *mahā-mantra* does the name of Lord Rāma appear? Repeated chanting of the first line only, I feel, should be more effective to put an end to this cycle of birth and death.

Do Not Invent Something New

Don't try to invent something new. What has been given to us by the *ācāryas* is perfect. Rāma is also a name for Kṛṣṇa. It means "the Supreme Enjoyer." It also refers to Lord Balarāma, Lord Rāmachandra, and Lord Paraśurāma, who are all different forms of Kṛṣṇa.

The *mantra* as it is was personally chanted by Lord Kṛṣṇa when He appeared in the form of Śrī Caitanya Mahāprabhu. Plus, it has been chanted since time immemorial by countless numbers of fully realized souls. Chanting only the first half of the *mantra* and leaving out the rest of it will greatly diminish its transcendental potency.

The *Kali-santaraṇa Upaniṣad* says there is no better means of self realization in this age of Kali than the chanting of:

Hare Kṛṣṇa, Hare Kṛṣṇa, Kṛṣṇa Kṛṣṇa, Hare Hare
Hare Rāma, Hare Rāma, Rāma Rāma, Hare Hare

Therefore, I am humbly requesting you to chant:

Hare Kṛṣṇa, Hare Kṛṣṇa, Kṛṣṇa Kṛṣṇa, Hare Hare
Hare Rāma, Hare Rāma, Rāma Rāma, Hare Hare

Please Help Me

I am facing a great hardship in chanting. I can listen or sing in a *kīrtana* (group singing of the holy names) for 24 hours, but whenever I try to chant with beads, my mind wanders, and I am unable to concentrate on the *mantra*.

Disciplined, Early-Morning Chanting

The key to focused *japa* chanting is to rise early in the morning and finish one's daily quota of *japa* chanting before sunrise. This time of the day is known as *brāhma-muhūrta*. It is a very spiritual time of the day when it is very easy to keep one's mind fixed on the holy names. At this time of day the mode of goodness predominates. This is why it is so easy to chant during this time period. Once the sun comes up, the atmosphere shifts into the mode of passion, a time for activity and productivity; then it becomes very difficult to sit and peacefully meditate on the holy names. If for some reason you cannot complete your *japa* before sunrise, then you must finish it before you take your morning meal. If you make this serious commitment and stick to it every day, you will be able to train your mind to stay absorbed nicely during your *japa* chanting. It is simply a matter of training and practice.

Why the Hare Kṛṣṇa Mantra?

Since all of Lord Kṛṣṇa's many names, forms and other attributes are considered nondifferent, why is the Hare Kṛṣṇa *mahā-mantra* recommended for chanting/singing, as if it were more important than any other *mantra*?

Hare Kṛṣṇa Is the Most Fully Potent

Even though it is a fact that each and every name of God has the full potency to deliver us from this material existence, still there is a difference between fully potent, more fully potent, and most fully potent. This is why it is clearly enjoined by Lord Brahmā as he is quoted in the *Kali-santaraṇa Upaniṣad*:

hare kṛṣṇa hare kṛṣṇa
kṛṣṇa kṛṣṇa hare hare
hare rāma hare rāma
rāma rāma hare hare

iti ṣoḍaśakaṁ nāmnāṁ
kali-kalmaṣa-nāśanaṁ
nātaḥ parataropāyaḥ
sarva-vedeṣu dṛśyate

> "In all of the Vedic literatures there is found no better method for freeing ourselves from the sinful contamination of the age of Kali than chanting these sixteen names: *Hare Kṛṣṇa, Hare Kṛṣṇa, Kṛṣṇa Kṛṣṇa, Hare Hare, Hare Rāma, Hare Rāma, Rāma Rāma, Hare Hare.*"

The Sanskrit language is crystal clear. It leaves no doubts as to the intended meaning. It is pointedly stated, *nātaḥ parataropāyaḥ* — "there is no better method."

Because we are in a very diseased state of consciousness at the present time (Kali Yuga), the spiritual master prescribes for us only the most potent medicine. When one is extremely sick, only the most potent medicine will do. The drug store is full of many varieties of bona fide medicines. But when we are very sick we take only that medicine prescribed for us by our physician, knowing fully well that we need to follow his prescription in order to recover quickly from our disease.

What Should Be Done First?

Kindly guide me. What should be done first in order to make progress on the path of devotion? Should one stop doing all things such as gambling? Or should one stop eating non-vegetarian food as well as onion, garlic etc.? Or should one strengthen one's chanting?

Chanting Gives the Higher Taste

The first thing is to chant, because by chanting you will experience a higher taste and easily be able to give up the lower tastes such as gambling, onions, garlic, and non-vegetarian food.

Chanting is stronger if you rise early and complete 16 rounds before sunrise.

Chanting and Exams

What is the best time for chanting the Hare Kṛṣṇa *mahā-mantra*? In time of a student's examination, how many rounds is compulsory? My exam is very near. How should I adjust time for chanting and also for my study?

First Chant, Then Study

The best time is in the early morning hours before sunrise. First chant 16 rounds, then study for school. You will have much better comprehension and retention of your studies.

Are Mundane Thoughts an Impediment?

Often when I chant, various mundane thoughts come up and distract me. Are these thoughts an offense or an impediment to pure chanting? Should they somehow be suppressed?

Spiritualize All of Your Thoughts

It is natural that at the beginning of our spiritual path the untrained mind will still be distracted by so many mundane thoughts. These thoughts are like weeds in the garden of our heart, and are certainly impediments for our spiritual progress. Therefore, we should determinedly and patiently engage ourselves in training the mind not to pay attention to such thoughts. Just as so many rivers are entering into the sea at every second while the sea level always remains at a constant level, we can remain unaffected by such thoughts. We should ignore such thoughts by bringing our mind to the higher level absorption in the beautiful sound of Kṛṣṇa's holy names:

Hare Kṛṣṇa, Hare Kṛṣṇa, Kṛṣṇa Kṛṣṇa, Hare Hare
Hare Rāma, Hare Rāma, Rāma Rāma, Hare Hare

In this regard Lord Śrī Kṛṣṇa states in the *Bhagavad-gītā*:

yato yato niścalati
manaś cañcalam asthiram
tatas tato niyamyaitad
ātmany eva vaśaṁ nayet

> "From wherever the mind wanders due to its flickering and unsteady nature, one must certainly withdraw it and bring it back under the control of the self."
>
> *Bhagavad-gita* 6.26

Don't be discouraged if such thoughts come. This is par for the course for a beginning practitioner of Kṛṣṇa consciousness. Now you must simply train your mind to remain 100% absorbed in the wonderful names of Kṛṣṇa.

Why Chant on Beads?

What is the significance of chanting "Hare Kṛṣṇa" on beads? Sometimes I chant without beads.

To Ensure the Greatest Absorption

Chanting on beads is very important. Lord Caitanya, who is Kṛṣṇa Himself appearing in the form of a devotee, also chanted on beads. This the practice of the all the great *ācāryas*, the spiritual masters who teach by practical example. The beads add extra depth to the process of chanting and enable the devotee to fix his mind fully in loving meditation on the holy names.

The beads are also a means of counting how many *mantras* are uttered on a daily basis. Every devotee is to make a fixed vow of how many *mantras* he will utter on a daily basis and remain fixed in that vow without fail. We ask each and every one of our initiated students to chant at least 16 rounds daily of Hare Kṛṣṇa *japa*. This equates to a minimum of 1,728 repetitions of the Hare Kṛṣṇa *mahā-mantra* every day.

Of course, we are meant to chant Hare Kṛṣṇa as much as possible, 24 hours daily, either on the beads or off the beads. But our daily vow of at least 16 rounds must be chanted on the beads to ensure the greatest absorption.

Śrī Viṣṇu Sahasrāṇām

Am I correct in my assumption that it is permissible for me to chant the Śrī Viṣṇu *Sahasrāṇām*, the thousand names of Lord Viṣṇu?

Incredible Leveraging Power of the Hare Kṛṣṇa Mahā-mantra

Although it is okay for you to chant Śrī Viṣṇu *Sahasrāṇām*, it is better that you chant the Hare Kṛṣṇa *Mantra*.

Why?

Because according to revealed scriptures, one utterance of Rāma is equal to 1,000 repetitions of the names of Viṣṇu, and 1 utterance of Kṛṣṇa is equal to 3 utterances of Rama. This means that if you say Kṛṣṇa one time you get the benefit of chanting 3,000 names of Viṣṇu. Considering how long it takes to get all the way through the Viṣṇu *Sahasrāṇām* one time, you can see that it is much more beneficial spiritually to simply focus on chanting Hare Kṛṣṇa.

If you simply utter the *mahā-mantra* one time –

Hare Kṛṣṇa, Hare Kṛṣṇa, Kṛṣṇa Kṛṣṇa, Hare Hare
Hare Rāma, Hare Rāma, Rāma Rāma, Hare Hare

– you will get what benefit?

4 Rāmas = 4,000 names of Viṣṇu, plus 4 Kṛṣṇas = 12,000 names of Viṣṇu

Therefore, one *mahā-mantra* equals 16,000 names of Viṣṇu.

If you chant one round of *japa*, you will get the benefit of chanting 108 x 16,000 names of Viṣṇu. And if you chant 16 rounds of *japa*, you will the benefit of chanting 27,648,000 names of Viṣṇu.

Thus we can understand the great leveraging power of the Hare Kṛṣṇa *mahā-mantra*.

Switching to the Mahā-mantra

I have been chanting the *mantra* given by my spiritual guru. But lately I have found that I feel more comfortable in chanting the *mahā-mantra*. Can I change my chanting totally to *mahā-mantra*?

Yes; It Is the Supreme Mantra

In the Vedic wisdom the chanting of the Hare Kṛṣṇa *mahā-mantra* is described as the topmost means of attaining spiritual perfection. Therefore, your teacher should have advised you in this regard. Yes, you may switch over to chanting the Hare Kṛṣṇa *mantra* instead of what you are currently chanting. Whatever benefit you may receive in chanting other *mantras* is automatically included when you chant Hare Kṛṣṇa.

The difference is that the Hare Kṛṣṇa *mantra* not only gives you the benefit of the other *mantras* - it gives millions and billions of times more benefit beyond that.

Why Do Deity Worship?

Why do Deity worship? When one chants Hare Kṛṣṇa or any holy names of the Supreme Lord, this is equivalent of Deity worship, as the holy name is non-different from the Deity.

It Empowers Your Chanting

In the Kali-yuga the *yuga-dhārma* is chanting the holy names. That alone is sufficient for self-realization. Even though the Deity and the holy names are non-different, Deity worship is also accepted because it helps one to become purified for properly chanting the Lord's holy names. It empowers your chanting.

Necessary to Chant in Lotus Posture?

I am 17 years old, and I want to start chanting the Hare Kṛṣṇa *mahā-mantra* on *japa* beads. But I cannot put myself into the yogic lotus posture, and I cannot even do the Japanese posture. When I try to do these postures I cannot concentrate because I feel so much pain. So what I should do? Is it necessary to chant in the lotus posture?

Sit Straight But Comfortably

Although it is recommended to sit straight while chanting *japa* (because it helps you to fix your mind on the Hare Kṛṣṇa *mantra*), it is not necessary to go into a formal posture such as the lotus posture. Sit comfortably and focus your energy on fully absorbing your consciousness in the all-attractive sound of Lord Śrī Kṛṣṇa's names.

Absent-Minded or Focused Japa?

Can *japa* be chanted absent-mindedly (such as when doing other work) or must it be with one-pointed mindfulness in order "to count"? Which is authentic *japa:* silent or aloud?

Focused Is More Beneficial

Although highly focused *japa* is more beneficial than absent-minded *japa*, whether *japa* is absent-minded or a highly focused meditation, in either form it is beneficial. It is simply a matter of degrees of benefit.

Those who take initiation vows commit themselves to 16 rounds of highly focused *japa* every day on their *japa* beads. (Each round is 108 repetitions of the Hare Kṛṣṇa *mantra.*) This minimal amount of focused *japa* is necessary for one who wants to completely purify his consciousness from all the dirt accumulated over millions of lifetimes.

Japa means to chant aloud but softly.

What Is the Significance of 108 Beads?

What is the significance of 108 beads in a single round of *japa*? For so long I have not come across the answer to this question. I am eager to know.

108 Gopīs

The 108 beads represent Kṛṣṇa's 108 chief gopīs.

What Is Considered Chanting?

Is saying the Hare Kṛṣṇa *mahā-mantra* while working or performing chores also considered chanting, or is it only when using the beads?

Vibrating the Holy Names on Your Lips

In the *Bhagavad-gītā* Kṛṣṇa says that we are to chant His names 24 hours a day. Whether we chant with beads or without beads it is still considered chanting. However, if we want to realize the full benefit of the holy names for completely freeing our hearts from all material desires, we must devote at least two hours daily to intensely chanting the holy names on *japa* beads without diverting our consciousness to anything else. In this connection Śrīla Prabhupāda states in his *Caitanya-caritāmṛta* purport:

> Although Mādhavendra Purī was not interested in eating and sleeping, his interest in chanting the *mahā-mantra* was as acute as if he were an aspiring transcendentalist rather than a *paramahaṁsa*. This means that even in the *paramahaṁsa* stage, one cannot give up chanting. Haridāsa Ṭhākura and the Gosvāmīs were all engaged in chanting a fixed number of rounds; therefore, chanting on beads is very important for everyone, even though one may become a *paramahaṁsa*. This chanting can be executed anywhere, either inside or outside the temple.
>
> from the purport to *Caitanya-caritāmṛta, Madhya* 4.125

So whether one is a *paramahaṁsa*, a highly elevated transcendentalist, or a beginner, everyone is meant to take advantage of chanting the Hare Kṛṣṇa *mantra* or any other bona fide names of God on chanting beads, *japa* beads.

Chanting for Material Success

I've heard that the spiritual energy from chanting the Hare Kṛṣṇa *mahā-mantra* can be utilized in a materialistic way. Does it mean that someone can repeat "Hare Kṛṣṇa" in order to reach his own material goals and be successful?

Not Good, Not Necessary

The Hare Kṛṣṇa *mahā-mantra* is undoubtedly the most powerful method of approaching and connecting with God. Any method of approaching God can be properly utilized for reviving our dormant enlightened consciousness, our Kṛṣṇa consciousness. Or it can be improperly utilized by petitioning the Lord to give us better facility for sense gratification. Unfortunately nowadays mostly we see that people are approaching God to improve their material facilities.

This is less intelligent because God is going to give us our material facilities anyway. Because He is our loving father, He will make sure that our material needs are met. Therefore, the intelligent person petitions the Lord for the revival of his Kṛṣṇa consciousness.

This is the best benediction to seek. Instead of begging for better facilities in a disaster zone, why not beg for that pure consciousness that qualifies one to be liberated from the disaster zone by being transferred to that place which is eternal, full of knowledge and bliss, where there is never any shortage of facilities? This is real intelligence. This is Kṛṣṇa consciousness.

To use the holy names for material advancement is a *nāma-aparādha*, an offense against the holy name. Our success or failure is going to come to us anyway as a result of our past pious and impious activities. So there is no sense in trying to manipulate our *karma* by chanting the names of God. The smart thing to do is to elevate your consciousness beyond the success/failure, karmic dimension by pure chanting of the Hare Kṛṣṇa *mahā-mantra*. This is the ultimate and eternal success.

How Does One Chant Without Offense?

Would you explain what the stages are in chanting and how it all works? I note that there are ten offenses that one should not commit while chanting the Holy Name. Should we achieve this at the first stroke, or does it happen gradually?

Is it that chanting with offense has no benefits, and therefore we should chant only if we are able to do so in the pure mode of goodness? How does one get to the stage of chanting the Holy Name without any offense - *tṛṇād api sunīcena, taror api sahiṣhṇunā*? It is hard to be 100% attentive. The mind wanders sometimes, although as much as possible we try to chant in the early morning. Please show your mercy upon us so that we might chant in the pure mode of goodness.

Chant in a Humble State of Mind

I will be most happy to answer your sincere inquiry. There are three stages of chanting:

1. Offensive chanting
2. Clearing stage
3. Offenseless chanting

We all start at the offensive stage, but as we sincerely chant, trying to avoid the offenses, we enter into the clearing stage. And then gradually, gradually, as we become solid in avoiding all of the offenses, we enter into the perfectional stage, the offenseless stage.

The ten offenses are as follows:

1. To blaspheme the devotees who have dedicated their lives for propagating the holy name of the Lord.
2. To consider the names of demigods like Lord Śiva or Lord Brahmā to be equal to, or independent of, the name of Lord Viṣṇu. (Sometimes the atheistic class of men take it that any demigod is as good as the Supreme Personality of Godhead, Viṣṇu. But one who is a devotee knows that no demigod, however great he may be, is independently as good as the Supreme Personality of Godhead. Therefore, if someone thinks that he can chant "Kāli, Kāli!" or " Durgā, Durgā!" and that it is the same as Hare Kṛṣṇa, that is the greatest offense.)
3. To disobey the orders of the spiritual master.
4. To blaspheme the Vedic literature or literature in pursuance of the Vedic version.
5. To consider the glories of chanting Hare Kṛṣṇa to be imagination.
6. To give some interpretation on the holy name of the Lord.
7. To commit sinful activities on the strength of the holy name of the Lord. (It should not be taken that because by chanting the holy name of the Lord one can be freed from all kinds of sinful reaction, one may continue to act sinfully and after that chant Hare Kṛṣṇa to neutralize his sins. Such a dangerous mentality is very offensive and should be avoided.)
8. To consider the chanting of Hare Kṛṣṇa one of the auspicious ritualistic activities offered in the Vedas as fruitive activities (*karma-kāṇḍa*).
9. To instruct a faithless person about the glories of the holy name. (Anyone can take part in chanting the holy name of the Lord, but in the beginning one should not be instructed about the transcendental potency of the Lord. Those who are too sinful cannot appreciate the transcendental glories of the Lord, and therefore it is better not to instruct them in this matter.)
10. To not have complete faith in the chanting of the holy names and to maintain material attachments, even after understanding so many instructions on this matter.

It's also offensive to be inattentive while chanting. Anyone who claims to be a devotee of the Lord must carefully guard against the above offenses in order to quickly achieve the supreme success - pure love of Kṛṣṇa, Kṛṣṇa *prema*.

In the beginning it is impossible to chant in a completely pure state of mind. Therefore we must chant, even though we do so offensively. Then gradually, gradually, by the unlimited power of the Lord's sweet holy names, all of offenses will melt away into oblivion.

The simple formula for achieving the pure stage of offenseless chanting is practice, practice, practice. The tongue must work. Try to clearly pronounce and hear each and every syllable of the *mahā-mantra*:

Hare Kṛṣṇa, Hare Kṛṣṇa, Kṛṣṇa Kṛṣṇa, Hare Hare
Hare Rāma, Hare Rāma, Rāma Rāma, Hare Hare

Chant in the mood of a small child calling out to his parents for help. This mood will attract the mercy of the Lord and his energy to quickly deliver us from the ocean of birth and death.

The key for perfect chanting is to always chant in a humble state of mind, thinking yourself lower than the straw in the street, being more tolerant than a tree, and offering all respects to others without desiring any respect for yourself. Chanting in this mood will quickly bring you to pure goodness, the offenseless stage in which you will relish the holy names of the Lord unlimitedly. In this connection Śrīla Rūpa Goswāmī has written as follows:

"I do not know how much nectar the two syllables 'Kṛṣ-ṇa' have produced. When the holy name of Kṛṣṇa is chanted, it appears to dance within the mouth. We then desire many, many mouths. When that name enters the holes of the ears, we desire many millions of ears. And when the holy name dances in the courtyard of the heart, it conquers the activities of the mind, and therefore, all the senses become inert."

A Request for Advice on How to Chant

Please give me advice on how to chant. I am of the Christian faith, but I realize that I need to initiate meditation in my own life in order to find peace in this "screaming, loud, aggressive" world.

Hare Kṛṣṇa in the Early Morning

Thank you very much for your sincere and wonderful inquiry. It is a fact that we must become expert at fully absorbing our minds in God 24 hours a day. Otherwise our minds will become dragged away by the mundane influence of this present, highly materialistic age.

In this age the recommended form of meditation is to chant as much as possible the holy names of God. The recitation of God's holy name is recommended in all the scriptures of the world. And in the *Kali-santaraṇa Upaniṣad* it is specifically mentioned that out of all the unlimited names of the unlimited Supreme Being, the most potent names to chant are these:

Hare Kṛṣṇa, Hare Kṛṣṇa, Kṛṣṇa Kṛṣṇa, Hare Hare
Hare Rāma, Hare Rāma, Rāma Rāma, Hare Hare

If you will rise early in the morning every day before sunrise, take your bath, and sit to peacefully chant these names for as much time as you can spare before you begin your day's activities, you will realize a new peace, happiness, and satisfaction in your life which you have never felt before.

How Do We Conquer Evil?

How do we conquer the evil in our heart?

Regular Chanting

Your question is very nice. There is no such thing as an evil heart. Every single living being throughout all of existence is basically good-hearted. Evil manifests when the pure heart becomes polluted by the six enemies: lust, anger, greed, illusion, madness, and envy. Through the process of giving up sinful activities and regularly chanting the holy names of God, any person, no matter how polluted his heart might be with these enemies, can gradually free the heart completely from these six types of contamination and become perfectly and unlimitedly blissfully situated in pure love of God.

How Do I Feel the Spiritual World?

By the grace of Kṛṣṇa consciousness, I now have tangible feeling that this material world is not my home. It's just a miserable camp for losers. But I haven't got a tangible feeling that the spiritual world is my hometown. When can I get a real, tangible feeling for this?

I want to take on a part-time job to make some money to buy Kṛṣṇa consciousness books or to donate money to pure devotees. I have tried to find a part-time job during college, but it seems that Kṛṣṇa has put up so many obstacles to prevent me from finding a job. I am still not financially independent. Why? What is Kṛṣṇa's arrangement?

Dive into the Names

Kṛṣṇa has greatly blessed you with the knowledge and the feeling that this material world is not your home. And although He has also blessed you with the knowledge that the spiritual world is your actual home, you are not yet feeling that it is your home. My best advice to you regarding how you can get this strong feeling in your heart is that you should dive deeper and deeper into the sweet nectar of Lord Kṛṣṇa's holy names by chanting the Hare Kṛṣṇa *mahā-mantra* with love as much as possible every day. The Lord's holy names and His transcendental abode are one and the same, so if you will focus your mind on diving deeper and deeper into the holy names of God, you will feel how you are living in the spiritual world at every minute, and you will see that the material world is just something happening out there in the Lord's external energy.

We cannot always understand how the arrangement of the Lord is being made for our ultimate benefit, yet it always is, 100% of the time. Keep trying for the part-time job and see what Kṛṣṇa arranges.

Does 108 Chants Equal 16 Rounds?

I have a rudraksha bead at home, and I am using it to chant Hare Kṛṣṇa *mantra* 108 times, as it takes that many times to complete one round. Is this equivalent to chanting 16 rounds daily?

Sixteen Times 108 is 16 Rounds

I am very happy that you are rising early and chanting the Hare Kṛṣṇa *mantra* 108 times before sunrise. This is very good news!

Regarding your chanting on the rudraksha beads, it is most pleasing to Lord Kṛṣṇa if we chant His holy names on sacred *tulasī* beads. If you go to your nearest ISKCON center you will find *tulasī* beads available for purchase at a nominal price. You may continue chanting on the rudraksha beads in the meantime, but you should replace them as soon as possible with *tulasī* beads.

Chanting around the string of beads one time completes 108 repetitions of the Hare Kṛṣṇa *mahā-mantra*. This is equivalent to chanting one round of *japa*. Those who are initiated by a bona fide spiritual master into the *bhakti* path make a lifetime commitment to chant at least 16 rounds a day. One-hundred eight repetitions of the *mahā-mantra* is one round; 1,728 repetitions is 16 rounds.

Now you are chanting one round on most days. This is a great beginning. Now try to make a firm commitment that EVERY day you must complete one round. Once this is solid, you can increase to two rounds every day. In this way gradually you can bring yourself to the point of chanting at least 16 rounds daily, and, if you can agree to follow some basic moral principles along with your chanting, you can become an initiated disciple of the bona fide spiritual master and become empowered for achieving spiritual perfection in this very lifetime.

Please keep me posted on your progress. I want to see that you become fully happy in this lifetime by complete surrender at Lord Śrī Kṛṣṇa's lotus feet, and that you can regain your original eternal identity in the spiritual world and thus escape the cycle of birth and death.

Is Chanting Hare Kṛṣṇa Recommended by Kṛṣṇa?

If chanting the Hare Kṛṣṇa *mantra* is the best way to achieve liberation, why didn't Lord Kṛṣṇa tell us that in the *Gītā*?

Yes, by Words and Actions

This is why Kṛṣṇa specifically orders in the *Bhagavad-gītā* that we should be chanting His names 24 hours daily, and why He personally appears in the Kali Yuga to demonstrate for us the best means of chanting His names:

Hare Kṛṣṇa, Hare Kṛṣṇa, Kṛṣṇa Kṛṣṇa, Hare Hare
Hare Rāma, Hare Rāma, Rāma Rāma, Hare Hare

God Himself has personally taught us both by words and example that we should always be chanting the Hare Kṛṣṇa *mantra* as much as possible, but the human society is so unfortunate that they ignore His wonderful instructions.

Offering Food to Kṛṣṇa - Prasādam

Question about Prasādam

I just had a quick question about *prasādam*. A devotee once told me that if you take *prasādam* once, you will be guaranteed a human form in your next life. But I read in Prabhupāda's transcendental diary that there is no guarantee. So if you take *prasādam* once, are you guaranteed a human form in your next life?

(Editor's note: *Prasādam* is a Sanskrit word which means "mercy." Vegetarian food that is offered to Lord Kṛṣṇa with love and devotion becomes transformed from matter into spirit. After being offered it is no longer ordinary food. It is transformed into pure spiritual energy and is called *prasādam*.)

Make This Your Last Lifetime in the Material World

Prasādam has such potency; there is no doubt. One time a young child named Dwarkadish Das, a disciple of Śrīla Prabhupāda, fed some ducks some *prasādam*. When he wrote Śrīla Prabhupāda about this, Śrīla Prabhupāda wrote him back that those ducks would become humans in their next birth.

For lower animals and animalistic humans to take birth again as human beings is certainly progressive. But those who have taken seriously to the path of Kṛṣṇa *bhakti* are fixed in their determination to make this their last birth in the material world. They have no interest in coming back again as human beings.

Therefore, my request to you is that you must make this your last lifetime in this material world. You must become very solidly determined to go back home, back to Godhead by fully surrendering to the lotus feet of guru and Kṛṣṇa.

Are Saying Grace and Offering Our Food the Same?

I was raised Catholic, and I say grace prior to eating. Is this the same or similar to the way one offers food to Kṛṣṇa for Kṛṣṇa *prasādam*?

Thanking God Is Not Enough

Saying grace or thanking God for the food is very nice, but it is not enough. One should offer the food to God before eating. Let Him enjoy it first. If you are a guest in my house, and you fill up my refrigerator with so many nice foods, and then I sit down to enjoy all these wonderful foods, thanking you while proceeding to eat without inviting you to eat, what kind of gratitude is that? Do you understand? God is omnipresent. He is here with us at every moment. He has given us all of our eatables. Therefore, it is quite rude if we do not offer Him the food before we eat. This is simply a matter of human decency. We offer everything to the Lord before we eat; otherwise we are no better than animals.

Is Eating Vegetables Also Sinful?

I understand that the Supreme is existing in every part and particle of all that exists, and that should live a gentler, compassionate life, respectful of all. But for life to continue, we eat food and use things which are made up of life taken from plants, grains, fruits, vegetable, herbs, animals, etc. I am a vegetarian, yet I do not feel right about plucking the life out of vegetation. I do not see the difference between animals and vegetation, as the life-force is incomparable! Whatever I eat and use in my daily life - even taken as God's *prasāda* - my conscience feels guilty! Can you please offer any insight?

Yes, If the Food Is Not Offered to Kṛṣṇa First

I am most pleased with you for realizing that it is also wrong to pluck the life out of vegetation, just as it is wrong to pluck the life out of animals, to satisfy our tongues. The Vedic scriptures enlighten us regarding the spark of divinity, the living soul, that is there with all variety of living things. The fact is that we are held accountable for murder whether we kill a well-to-do person or a pauper. We are held accountable for murder whether we eat a plant or an animal. So what to do?

Kṛṣṇa, our loving Father, has provided for us a system of sustaining our bodily existence without being tainted by sin. If we will eat foods from the categories of fruits, vegetables, dairy products, and grains and offer them to Him (Lord Kṛṣṇa) before we eat, this will free us from the karmic reaction of killing the vegetable. Not only that, when the vegetable gives up its life to be offered to Kṛṣṇa, it becomes blessed with a quicker ascension up the evolutionary ladder to the human species.

We cannot apply the same logic to eating meat, fish, or eggs because Kṛṣṇa forbids us to eat these foods. But as long as we restrict ourselves to the categories of fruits, vegetables, dairy products, and grains and always offer them to Kṛṣṇa first before eating, not only are we sinless in such eating, but such eating also frees us from the karmic reactions of millions of previous lifetimes. When food is offered to Kṛṣṇa, it is transformed from matter into spirit. It becomes a holy sacrament, and such eating cleanses our hearts of ignorance and suffering. Such sacrificial food is called "*prasādam*," which means mercy.

If we don't offer our food to Kṛṣṇa, we should feel guilty. Why? Because He has supplied us with all of our eatables, and because He is our roommate. He is living with us at every minute. Since He is our supplier and He is living with us, how can we be so ungrateful as not to ask Him to eat first when we partake of a meal? The best thing is to keep an altar at home with a picture of Kṛṣṇa. Whenever you eat, always prepare a special plate for Kṛṣṇa with all the items of the meal on it. Lay it before Him. Bow down. Chant Hare Kṛṣṇa. Invite Him to accept your offering.

Give Him a few minutes to peacefully enjoy the meal. Then you may transfer what was on the plate back into the cooking pots or onto your plate directly. Everything is now considered offered to Kṛṣṇa, even what was in the cooking pots. You can never offer something twice to Kṛṣṇa. You may save offered food in your refrigerator to heat up again and take at a later time.

Is There a Blessing We Can Use When Eating Out?

I know that we should offer our meals on our home altar using the formula given in the article "How to Offer Food to Kṛṣṇa" from the Ultimate Self-Realization website. My question is: Is there a blessing before meals that can be done if one is not eating at home (e.g. in a restaurant, packed lunches, etc)?

A Nice Prayer to Use Before Taking Prasādam

If you are in an awkward situation where you cannot bow down and offer prayers, you can offer your food within your mind by softly chanting Hare Kṛṣṇa.

Packed lunches should be offered to Kṛṣṇa at home. The foods are only offered to Kṛṣṇa one time and then they can be taken immediately or packed for taking to school, work or travels. They are not offered again before eating.

There is, however, a nice prayer from BhaktivinodaṬhākura that can be recited before taking *prasādam*:

śarīra avidyā-jāl
jaḍendriya tāhe kāl
jīve phele viṣaya-sāgare
tā'ra madhye jihvā ati
lobhamay sudurmati
tā'ke jetā kaṭhina saṁsāre
kṛṣṇa baḍa dayāmay
karibāre jihvā jaya
sva-prasādānna dila bhāi
sei annāmṛta pāo
rādhā-kṛṣṇa-guṇa gāo
preme ḍāko caitanya-nitāi

"O Lord! This material body is a lump of ignorance, and the senses are a network of paths leading to death. Somehow or other we have fallen into the ocean of material sense enjoyment, and of all the senses the tongue is the most voracious and uncontrollable. It is very difficult to conquer the tongue in this world, but You, dear Kṛṣṇa, are very kind to us. You have sent this nice *prasādam* to help us conquer the tongue; therefore, let us take this *prasādam* to our full satisfaction and glorify Your Lordships Śrī Śrī

Rādhā and Kṛṣṇa and in love call for the help of Lord Caitanya and Prabhu Nityānanda."

How Is Killing a Plant Different From Killing an Animal?

I have a question about killing and survival. It seems that there is no way to avoid killing; whether it is by breathing in microorganisms and killing them with our immune system or harvesting carrot plants and eating them. Obviously we have to continue breathing and eating to maintain our bodies. How is killing of a microbe or carrot spiritually different from killing an animal to eat?

They Are the Same

Killing a microbe or a carrot is the same as killing an animal. This is why we must engage ourselves completely in devotional service and why we must offer our vegetarian foods to Kṛṣṇa before eating. If we are acting under the higher authority of Guru and Kṛṣṇa then we are freed from all karmic reactions. This is just like an ambulance driver who can run a red light without getting a traffic ticket.

It's true that we must suffer karmic reactions for all forms of killing, even the microbial germs we kill by breathing. But if we are engaged in devotional service to Kṛṣṇa then we are freed from all karmic reactions. If we are practicing Kṛṣṇa consciousness and offering our vegetarian foodstuffs to Lord Kṛṣṇa before eating, we are freed from the karmic reactions of killing a carrot or a potato, etc. Otherwise even if we eat vegetarian foods that have not been offered to Kṛṣṇa before eating, we get the karmic reaction for having murdered a living being.

How Should I Offer My Food to Kṛṣṇa?

I have become a vegetarian after reading "Thought for the Day." I try now to offer all of my food to Kṛṣṇa, but I am not exactly sure how I should do this. How should I make the offering? Please guide me.

Follow This Simple Formula

The main thing when you offer food to Kṛṣṇa is that you must do it with love. First of all you should be bathed and wearing clean clothing. The kitchen and the cooking pots must also be very clean. In your home, make a nice altar with a picture of Kṛṣṇa on it. You should also keep a special plate that is only for Kṛṣṇa, nobody else. Whenever you cook (fruits, vegetables, milk products, and grains—no meat, fish, eggs, onions or garlic), you place a portion of that food on Kṛṣṇa 's plate and then place the plate on the altar for Kṛṣṇa 's enjoyment. Humbly bow down and ask the Lord to accept your offering and then chant the Hare Kṛṣṇa *mantra* three times. Give the Lord a few minutes to enjoy His meal. The remnants of the offering can then be transferred off the Lord's plate, which is reserved exclusively for Him, and can then be eaten. The remants of the offering are called *prasādam* (the Lord's mercy). We call this "honoring *prasādam*," to distinguish it from the ordinary, animalistic eating of materialistic persons. The foodstuffs that are on the Lord's plate have now been offered, as have also all portions of each dish still remaining in the cooking pots.

If you are away from home, you can carry a photograph of Kṛṣṇa for making your offerings or you can mentally offer your foods to Kṛṣṇa if you are in a place where you cannot set up a portable altar.

Offering Food at Work

Being a working person, I have to eat food in the office canteen. Such foods prepared give karmic reactions. Also they must have some things like onion, garlic etc. Though we take vegetarian food, still, sometimes we are not sure that the foods do not contain some non-vegetarian contaminations like egg by-products, etc. In this way we accept so many karmic reactions.

Before I take the food, I chant the Hare Kṛṣṇa *mantra* three times as an offering to Kṛṣṇa, and then I take it. Are we really taking away the karmic reaction by offering this way, even though the food contains some stuff which can't be offered? So what can we do in this situation where we can't offer our food in the purest way before we take as Kṛṣṇa *prasādam*? Is there is any way to get rid of the reactions?

Bring Prasādam from Home

You need to prepare your own foodstuffs at home and take them to work with you. You should cook them in a mood of devotion to Lord Kṛṣṇa and offer them to Him. If we eat food cooked by non-devotees, even if all the ingredients are pure, we are still adversely affected by the materialistic mentality of the persons who cooked the food. On the other hand, if we take food which was cooked with love and devotion for the pleasure of Kṛṣṇa, that eating will elevate our consciousness. If we take food cooked by non-devotees, that eating will cloud our consciousness.

Why Take Prasāda?

What are the benefits one gets when one takes *prasāda* and why should one take only *prasāda*?

For Release from All Kinds of Sins

The remnants of foodstuffs that have been offered to Lord Śrī Kṛṣṇa are known as *prasādam* or *prasāda*. The Sanskrit word "*prasādam*" literally means "mercy." When we offer the proper foods to Lord Śrī Kṛṣṇa with love and devotion, He accepts them and by His mercy transforms them from matter into spirit. Such foods are indeed the Lord's mercy and are, therefore, called *prasāda* or *prasādam*.

In the *Bhagavad-gītā* Kṛṣṇa explains the benefits of taking *prasādam*:

yajña-śiṣṭāśinaḥ santo
mucyante sarva-kilbiṣaiḥ
bhuñjate te tv aghaṁ pāpā
ye pacanty ātma-kāraṇāt

"The devotees of the Lord are released from all kinds of sins because they eat food which is offered first for sacrifice. Others, who prepare food for personal sense enjoyment, verily eat only sin."

Bhagavad-gītā 3.13

If we eat foods other than *prasādam*, even purely vegetarian foods, we are eating only sin. Such eating will oblige us to take birth after birth in this material world and should, therefore, be strictly avoided. Anyone who is serious about escaping the cycle of birth and death should become a strict Krishnatarian by only eating *kṛṣṇa-prasādam*. Such a diet is very tasty, very nutritious, and quite affordable also.

Are Vegetable-Eaters Killers?

Since plants also have life, doesn't eating vegetables also entail killing living beings?

Obeying the Lord Is Sinlessness

In this material world even by breathing we are killing so many microbial germs. And eating vegetables is also killing. In this world there is the law that one living being is food for another living being.

jivo jīvasya jīvanam

"One living being is food for another."

We simply have to take what is allotted to us by the Lord as our quota and offer it to Him first before eating. This will free us from the sin of killing. The Lord has allotted human beings to take fruits, milk products, vegetables and grains, provided we offer them first to Him before eating. We cannot take meat, fish and eggs because these have not been allotted to us as our quota.

Support for Vegetarian Diet

Can you give me the purport from the *Bhagavad-gītā* where Lord Śrī Kṛṣṇa's menu is given clearly eliminating non-vegetarian foods?

Bhagavad-gītā Verse and Purport

Here is the verse and purport:

patraṁ puṣpaṁ phalaṁ toyaṁ
yo me bhaktyā prayacchati
tad ahaṁ bhakty-upahṛtam
aśnāmi prayatātmanaḥ

"If one offers Me with love and devotion a leaf, a flower, fruit or water, I will accept it."

Bhagavad-gītā 9.26

Purport by Śrīla Prabhupāda

For the intelligent person, it is essential to be in Kṛṣṇa consciousness, engaged in the transcendental loving service of the Lord, in order to achieve a permanent, blissful abode for eternal happiness. The process of achieving such a marvelous result is very easy and can be attempted even by the poorest of the poor, without any kind of qualification. The only qualification required in this connection is to be a pure devotee of the Lord. It does not matter what one is or where one is situated. The process is so easy that even a leaf or a little water or fruit can be offered to the Supreme Lord in genuine love and the Lord will be pleased to accept it. No one, therefore, can be barred from Kṛṣṇa consciousness, because it is so easy and universal. Who is such a fool that he does not want to be Kṛṣṇa conscious by this simple method and thus attain the highest perfectional life of eternity, bliss and knowledge? Kṛṣṇa wants only loving service and nothing more. Kṛṣṇa accepts even a little flower from His pure devotee. He does not want any kind of offering from a non-devotee. He is not in need of anything from anyone, because He is self-sufficient, and yet He accepts the offering of His devotee in an exchange of love and affection. To develop Kṛṣṇa consciousness is the highest perfection of life. *Bhakti* is mentioned twice in this verse in order to declare more emphatically that *bhakti*, or devotional service, is the only means to approach Kṛṣṇa. No other condition, such as becoming a brāhmaṇa, a learned scholar, a very rich man or a great philosopher, can induce Kṛṣṇa to accept some offering. Without the basic principle of *bhakti*, nothing can induce the Lord to agree to accept anything from anyone. *Bhakti* is never causal. The process is eternal. It is direct action in service to the absolute whole.

Here Lord Kṛṣṇa, having established that He is the only enjoyer, the primeval Lord and the real object of all sacrificial offerings, reveals what types of sacrifices He desires to be offered. If one wishes to engage in devotional service to the Supreme in order to be purified and to reach the goal of life — the transcendental loving service of God — then one should find out what the Lord desires of him. One who loves Kṛṣṇa will give Him whatever He wants, and he avoids offering anything which is undesirable or unasked. Thus meat, fish and eggs should not be offered to Kṛṣṇa. If He desired such things as offerings, He would have said so. Instead He clearly requests that a leaf, fruit, flowers and water be given to Him, and He says of this offering, "I will accept it." Therefore, we should understand that He will not accept meat, fish and eggs.

Vegetables, grains, fruits, milk and water are the proper foods for human beings and are prescribed by Lord Kṛṣṇa Himself. Whatever else we eat cannot be offered to Him, since He will not accept it. Thus we cannot be acting on the level of loving devotion if we offer such foods.

In the Third Chapter, verse thirteen, Śrī Kṛṣṇa explains that only the remains of sacrifice are purified and fit for consumption by those who are seeking advancement in life and release from the clutches of the material entanglement. Those who do not make an offering of their food, He says in the same verse, are eating only sin. In other words, their every mouthful is simply deepening their involvement in the complexities of material nature. But preparing nice, simple vegetable dishes, offering them before the picture or Deity of Lord Kṛṣṇa and bowing down and praying for Him to accept such a humble offering enables one to advance steadily in life, to purify the body, and to create fine brain tissues which will lead to clear thinking. Above all, the offering should be made with an attitude of love. Kṛṣṇa has no need of food, since He already possesses everything that be, yet He will accept the offering of one who desires to please Him in that way. The important element, in preparation, in serving and in offering, is to act with love for Kṛṣṇa.

The impersonalist philosophers, who wish to maintain that the Absolute Truth is without senses, cannot comprehend this verse of *Bhagavad-gītā*. To them, it is either a metaphor or proof of the mundane character of Kṛṣṇa, the speaker of the *Bhagavad-gītā*. But, in actuality, Kṛṣṇa, the Supreme Godhead, has senses, and it is stated that His senses are interchangeable; in other words, one sense can perform the function of any other. This is what it means to say that Kṛṣṇa is absolute. Lacking senses, He could hardly be considered full in all opulences. In the Seventh Chapter, Kṛṣṇa has explained that He impregnates the living entities into material nature. This is done by His looking upon material nature. And so in this instance, Kṛṣṇa's hearing the devotee's words of love in offering foodstuffs is wholly identical with His eating and actually tasting. This point should be emphasized: because of His absolute position, His hearing is wholly identical with His eating and tasting. Only the devotee, who accepts Kṛṣṇa as He describes Himself, without interpretation, can understand that the Supreme Absolute Truth can eat food and enjoy it.

—end of quote—

Offering Restaurant Food to Kṛṣṇa

My question is: when a person takes vegetarian food from a vegetarian restaurant (sometimes prepared by non-devotees), can he offer the food to Kṛṣṇa with love? If he can, what would be his prayer for offering?

Better to Avoid Such Foods

As far as possible one should avoid taking even vegetarian food that has been prepared by non-devotees because the consciousness of the cook goes into the foodstuffs. If we eat food cooked by devotees, that food helps us to become Kṛṣṇa conscious. But if we eat foods cooked by non-devotees, this pollutes our consciousness.

Although I am flying regularly all over the world and the airlines nowadays have vegetarian dinners available, I never take the meal offered to me by the airlines. I am satisfied to eat whatever *prasādam* that I am able to bring on the airplane with me.

If under emergency condition you are sometimes forced to eat in a restaurant, it is better to simply take salad because that has not been cooked. If you have no other option for getting your meal, then you should beg Kṛṣṇa's forgiveness, chant the Hare Kṛṣṇa *mantra*, and beg the Lord to accept it. But this must be avoided as much as possible.

Prasādam Thrown Away?

My question is about *prasādam*. As I understand it, small portions of each food that is to be consumed should be correctly offered with prayer at the altar. Are these small portions also to be consumed? Or are they offerings that should be discarded?

Prasādam Should Always Be Honored

The special portions placed directly on the altar become the most potent manifestation of Lord Śrī Kṛṣṇa's mercy. They are so special that they have a special title also. All the food that it is offered to Kṛṣṇa is call *prasādam*, but the portion put on the Lord's plate is called *mahāprasādam* to signify its uniqueness. *Mahā* means great.

Mahāprasādam should be eaten with great devotion and relish. It must never be thrown away. Generally instead of using the word "eat," we use the word "honor" to describe the consumption of Kṛṣṇa *prasādam*. Partaking of Kṛṣṇa *prasādam* is a holy sacrament. It is not ordinary eating.

Proper to Eat a Lot of Prasādam?

When I go to eat *prasādam* here in the ISKCON Temple of Helsinki, why is it that I (and others) are allowed to eat as much as we want rather than eating only a little, the way *prasādam* is supposed to be eaten?

Eat Enough to Become Addicted

One who is fully absorbed in pure *bhakti* activities twenty-four hours a day relishes so much nectar from serving Kṛṣṇa that his bodily demands naturally become reduced. He becomes so completely addicted to Kṛṣṇa consciousness that he becomes naturally free from the bodily tendencies such as overeating or oversleeping.

However, most people who live outside the temple do not offer their food to Kṛṣṇa before eating it. Thus, according to the *Bhagavad-gītā,* they are eating only lumps of sin. When such persons come to the temple, we encourage them to eat as much as they can possibly hold so that when they leave the temple they will be so full they will not want to eat anything available outside the temple, which is generally not offered to Kṛṣṇa. And then we invite them to come back regularly for taking more Kṛṣṇa *prasādam*. In this way, we are trying to free people from the bad habit of eating unoffered foods by getting them fully dedicated to eating only Kṛṣṇa *prasādam*.

So kindly take Kṛṣṇa *prasādam* to your full satisfaction whenever you come to the temple. And do come often! In this way you will become completely, totally addicted to Kṛṣṇa *prasādam*. And we hope that you will also begin the process of offering your meals first to Lord Kṛṣṇa when eating at home (no meat, no fish, no eggs).

Bhakti Yoga – Devotional Service – Dovetailing - Real Renunciation

Selfish or Selfless Service?

Am I selfishly serving Kṛṣṇa because I want something in return (happiness) or am I experiencing happiness from trying to serve Him selflessly?

Advancing towards Selflessness

Your question - "Am I selfishly serving Kṛṣṇa because I want something in return (happiness) or am I experiencing happiness from trying to serve Him selflessly?" - is very nice.

In the beginning we come to Kṛṣṇa desiring happiness. This is unavoidable because we have no conception of pure devotional service. But then by the association of guru and Vaiṣṇavas we gradually come to understand that pleasing Kṛṣṇa is better than trying to please ourselves.

For someone who is on the path of progressive spiritual advancement, it is a combination of both - serving Kṛṣṇa for our pleasure and serving Him for His pleasure - that gradually transforms into deriving unlimited happiness by only thinking of Kṛṣṇa's pleasure. This is the supreme happiness.

How Do I Remain Always in Devotion?

Chanting the Hare Kṛṣṇa *mahā-mantra* and eating *prasādam*, the remnants of foodstuff offered to Kṛṣṇa, can be understood easily, but how do I remain always engaged in devotional service to the Lord?

Follow These Four Verses

Kṛṣṇa explains clearly in the *Bhagavad-gītā* how to always be engaged in devotional service. Kindly note the following verses:

tad viddhi praṇipātena
paripraśnena sevayā
upadekṣyanti te jñānaṁ
jñāninas tattva-darśinaḥ

His Divine Grace A. C. Bhaktivedanta Swami Prabhupāda
Founder-Ācārya of the International Society for Kṛṣṇa
Consciousness and the author's spiritual master.

The author pleads with the audience to consider spiritual life seriously.

Although sitting in an airplane in the stratosphere, the author flies beyond the entire universe riding high on the Hare Kṛṣṇa mahā-mantra.

The author composes a daily edition of the worldwide "Thought for the Day" email in serene British Columbia, Canada.

A student welcomes his teacher in Kaunas, Lithuania.

Kṛṣṇa shows His four-armed form.

Lord Kṛṣṇa becomes Arjuna's charioteer on the battlefield of Kurukṣetra.

Lord Caitanya with His primary associates Advaita Acārya, Nityānanda Prabhu, Gadādhara Pandita, and Śrīvāsa Ṭhākura.

Contemplating Kṛṣṇa at Mount Seymour, British Columbia, Canada.

Kṛṣṇa and His cowherd friends enjoy lunch together.

Devotees attend a lecture in London, England.

The author makes a point during a lecture in Estonia.

Kīrtana in Gurgaon, India.

The author leads an ecstatic Hare Kṛṣṇa *kīrtana* in Burgas, Bulgaria accompanied by devotees while passersby join in.

Class for practicing devotees in Pune, India.

Spiritual enthusiasts in Kaunas, Lithuania hear about Kṛṣṇa consciousness.

"Just try to learn the truth by approaching a spiritual master. Inquire from him submissively and render service unto him. The self-realized souls can impart knowledge unto you because they have seen the truth."

Bhagavad-gītā 4.34

Then under his expert guidance, one should carefully these following injunctions:

satataṁ kīrtayanto māṁ
yatantaś ca dṛḍha-vratāḥ
namasyantaś ca māṁ bhaktyā
nitya-yuktā upāsate

"Always chanting My glories, endeavoring with great determination, bowing down before Me, these great souls perpetually worship Me with devotion."

Bhagavad-gītā 9.14

yat karoṣi yad aśnāsi
yaj juhoṣi dadāsi yat
yat tapasyasi kaunteya
tat kuruṣva mad-arpaṇam

"Whatever you do, whatever you eat, whatever you offer or give away, and whatever austerities you perform — do that, O son of Kunti, as an offering to Me."

Bhagavad-gītā 9.27

man-manā bhava mad-bhakto
mad-yājī māṁ namaskuru
mām evaiṣyasi yuktvaivam
ātmānaṁ mat-parāyaṇaḥ

"Engage your mind always in thinking of Me, become My devotee, offer obeisances to Me and worship Me. Being completely absorbed in Me, surely you will come to Me."

Bhagavad-gītā 9.34

If you can sincerely follow the above four verses from the *Bhagavad-gītā*, you will become a perfect devotee, 100% absorbed in Kṛṣṇa consciousness 24 hours daily. And at the all-crucial time of passing away from your body, by such a dedicated life you will be guaranteed entrance into the spiritual world.

Solution to Stop Suffering

What is the solution to stop suffering?

I understand it is necessary to stop all my desires and focus only on God/Kṛṣṇa by chanting his holy names, associating with other devotees etc. Fair enough - it really makes me happy to tune into Kṛṣṇa consciousness.

But adapting my life so that Kṛṣṇa becomes my only desire is not very practical. I desire to move myself to a meeting in Brussels. I desire to buy clothes for my children. I desire so many things, because if I don't, they do not spontaneously materialize. Well... sometimes they do, but often they don't.

The thing is - now we are here in this material world anyway, why not make the best of it? Why not lead a Kṛṣṇa conscious life AND be a famous pop star like George Harrison? Why are devotees directed to a lifestyle that is so alienated from modern society? Especially since we are told so little about life in the spiritual world.

Doesn't *sanātana-dharma* need to be updated constantly into a vibrant lifestyle, celebrating the Supreme Personality of Godhead in all His manifestations?

Why don't we place more emphasis on the coming Golden Age and how it will be for the average soul?

Guru's Guidance

You have properly understood how to put a stop to suffering by becoming fully absorbed in Kṛṣṇa consciousness. But you are having difficulty realizing how to make this a practical reality when you deal with your day-to-day existence.

In this regard, kindly try to understand that you do not have to give up your material desires. All you have to do is spiritualize your material desires by connecting them with Kṛṣṇa. For example, if you can become a famous pop star, that is very nice. It is a mistake to give up one's material talents. They simply should be utilized in the service of Kṛṣṇa.

Devotees have an option of living a monastic life of full-time preaching and worship. Or if they prefer they can live a secular life working in the material society offering the fruits of their work to Kṛṣṇa. Either path is valid. But both paths should be carefully trodden under the guidance of the bona fide spiritual master. Then there will be spiritual success.

Sanātana-dharma, the eternal occupational duty of surrendering ourselves at the lotus feet of Lord Sri Kṛṣṇa, is always high-tech. Therefore, it does not require updating. This is a fact because *sanātana-dharma* exists in its pure form completely beyond the realm of time. Therefore, it is just as fresh and new now in 2007 as it was 5,000 years ago when Kṛṣṇa revealed it to Arjuna.

What we emphasize the most is how the individual can fully enter into the Golden Age right now by fully surrendering unto Lord Śrī Kṛṣṇa.

Where Am I Heading?

Whenever I am indulged in any activity that is in some way or other related to Kṛṣṇa, I experience immense happiness, pleasure and comfort which I could never experience otherwise. However, at the same time, there is some voice inside me that says, "You are doing these activities in order to seek happiness for your own self and not for Kṛṣṇa. Thus you are selfish and actually offending the Lord." Why am I facing such a dilemma?

Back to Your Original Existence

You should be prepared to execute whatever duties you are given for Kṛṣṇa's service by the spiritual master, never mind whether they are pleasing or displeasing to you. You should be neither attached to or averse to your own happiness and unhappiness. The devotee is not concerned for his own happiness. He simply wants to see that Kṛṣṇa is pleased. But because the devotee is part and parcel and Kṛṣṇa, he naturally becomes pleased when Kṛṣṇa is pleased.

There is nothing wrong in becoming happy by serving Kṛṣṇa because happiness is the natural result of devotional service to the Lord. But you should not become carried away by such happiness thinking that now you have become great. You should rather offer that joyful energy back into the Lord's service to improve the quality of your service to Him more and more and more. In this way you will be heading solidly back to your original existence, which is eternal, full of bliss, and full of knowledge.

When Can I Taste the Nectar of Pure Love?

I have more or less attained peace of mind through *bhakti-yoga*, even though I live in a terrible atmosphere. But I still don't love God. When can I rise to the stage of pure love for God as introduced in Śrī Caitanya's *Śikṣāṣṭakam*?

Why can't neophyte devotees love God immediately when they are engaged in devotional service?

You Can Begin Right Now

I am very, very pleased with you for your sincerity. I know that you are presently living in a situation in which it is very, very difficult to practice Kṛṣṇa consciousness. May Lord Kṛṣṇa bestow His special mercy upon you to help you through your present difficulties.

The perfectional stage of pure love of God is the ninth step and the culmination of the Kṛṣṇa consciousness pathway. It takes time to reach that stage. We have been in the cycle of birth and death for millions of lifetimes and are thus very,

very covered by the contaminating influence of the three modes of material nature. Therefore, we cannot expect to become 100% pure devotees immediately.

The nine steps of *bhakti* are described as follows in the *Bhakti-rasāmṛta-sindhu* (1.4.15-16):

ādau śraddhā tataḥ sādhu-
saṅgo 'tha bhajana-kriyā
tato 'nartha-nivṛttiḥ syāt
tato niṣṭhā rucis tataḥ
athāsaktis tato bhāvas
tataḥ premābhyudañcati
sādhakānām ayaṁ premṇaḥ
prādurbhāve bhavet kramaḥ

"In the beginning one must have a preliminary desire for self-realization. This will bring one to the stage of trying to associate with persons who are spiritually elevated. In the next stage one becomes initiated by an elevated spiritual master, and under his instruction the neophyte devotee begins the process of devotional service. By execution of devotional service under the guidance of the spiritual master, one becomes free from all material attachment, attains steadiness in self-realization, and acquires a taste for hearing about the Absolute Personality of Godhead, Sri Kṛṣṇa. This taste leads one further forward to attachment for Kṛṣṇa consciousness, which is matured in *bhāva*, or the preliminary stage of transcendental love of God. Real love for God is called *prema*, the highest perfectional stage of life."

Here are the above steps given in a list form:

1. *Śraddhā*—faith, the preliminary desire for self realization
2. *Sādhu-saṅga*—associating with devotees
3. *Bhajana-kriyā*—initiation by the bona fide spiritual master and adopting the practices of *bhakti yoga* under his direction
4. *Anartha-nivṛtti*—freedom from material attachment
5. *Niṣṭhā*—steadiness in self-realization
6. *Ruci*—taste for hearing about Kṛṣṇa
7. *Āśakti*—attachment for Kṛṣṇa consciousness
8. *Bhāva*—preliminary state of love of God
9. *Prema*—pure love of God.

In the *prema* stage there is constant engagement in the transcendental loving service of the Lord. So, by the slow process of devotional service, under the guidance of the bona fide spiritual master, one can attain the highest stage, being freed from all material attachment, from the fearfulness of one's individual spiritual personality, and from the frustrations that result in void philosophy. Then one can ultimately attain to the abode of the Supreme Lord.

You are wondering when you will attain *prema*. You should set your sight on attaining the third step as soon as possible, *bhajana-kriyā*. Once you do that, you will become very jolly and will make steady progress on the path to perfection.

You are also wondering why, as a beginner on the pathway, you cannot love God immediately. But you must be feeling some degree of love of God. Otherwise why are you spending so much time and energy practicing Kṛṣṇa consciousness? You are certainly not getting paid to do so. Therefore, you must be acting out of love. Higher stages of almost pure and completely pure love await you, but even at the present you must have some sense of loving Kṛṣṇa.

For example, when you see a painting of Kṛṣṇa, don't you find Him to be beautiful? This is love. Now you simply have to strengthen your feelings of love more and more toward the perfectional stage by going through the nine steps under the guidance of the spiritual master and the Vaiṣṇavas.

Nine Different Types of Bhakti

You spoke about nine different types of devotional service. Can you explain those, please?

Listed by Prahlāda Mahārāja

The nine different types of *bhakti* are listed as follows (by Prahlāda Mahārāja in the *Bhagavad-gītā*):

śravaṇaṁ kīrtanaṁ viṣṇoḥ
smaraṇaṁ pāda-sevanam
arcanaṁ vandanaṁ dāsyaṁ
sakhyam ātma-nivedanam

1. Hearing about the transcendental holy name, form, qualities, paraphernalia and pastimes of Lord Viṣṇu.
2. Chanting about the transcendental holy name, form, qualities, paraphernalia and pastimes of Lord Viṣṇu.
3. Remembering them.
4. Serving the lotus feet of the Lord.
5. Offering the Lord respectful worship.
6. Offering prayers to the Lord.
7. Becoming His servant.
8. Considering the Lord one's best friend.
9. Surrendering everything unto Him (in other words, serving Him with the body, mind and words).

Śrīmad-Bhāgavatam 7.5.23

Is Kṛṣṇa Consciousness Austerity or Joy?

Is Kṛṣṇa consciousness a practice in austerity or in joy and happiness?

It's Both

The answer is that it is both. Kṛṣṇa consciousness is simultaneously austere and supremely joyful. It is described in the *Śrīmad-Bhāgavatam* that austerity is the wealth of those who are renounced from this world.

Just as a businessman becomes more and more enlivened the more that he accumulates wealth, similarly the Kṛṣṇa conscious person relishes the austerities of practicing Kṛṣṇa consciousness as the sweetest, most sublime nectar.

Loving God

How is it possible to have a relationship with God? I do the chanting and read the books and associate with the devotees and follow the principles and offer my food, but I have no relationship with God, let alone a loving relationship. Surely, to develop a relationship with someone there needs to be personal interaction and two-way communication. So, how is it possible to have a relationship if I cannot see any reciprocation from God?

Why do you love God? What is it about Him that you love?

How do we know for sure that God loves us? And how do we see this in our lives, and not just in some scriptural quote?

What do the intimate loving affairs of Rādhā and Kṛṣṇa have to do with us?

How do I enjoy life?

By the Mercy of Guru and Kṛṣṇa

When you offer your food you are directly offering it to God. When you chant Hare Kṛṣṇa you are directly addressing the Lord and His energy to engage you in Their service. In this way, you should be developing a personal loving relationship with the Lord. You must always introspectively observe your thoughts, words and deeds to make sure that they are pleasing to the Lord. Don't do these things impersonally. Do them for the pleasure of Kṛṣṇa, the Supreme Personality of Godhead. Kṛṣṇa reciprocates by returning the offered foods back to us in the form of *prasādam*. He reciprocates with the chanting by showering us with transcendental bliss.

I love Kṛṣṇa because He is so beautiful and so wonderful and so absolutely amazing, and because He bestows upon me the highest happiness.

I know for sure that God loves us because I can feel the bliss He is showering upon me at every minute.

The intimate loving affairs of Rādhā and Kṛṣṇa are an invitation for us to become intimately involved in those loving affairs.

You enjoy life by adopting wholeheartedly the basic principles of *bhakti* given by Śrīla Rūpa Gosvāmī (as listed in *The Nectar of Devotion*) as follows:

How to Discharge Devotional Service:

1. Accept the shelter of the lotus feet of a bona fide spiritual master.
2. Become initiated by the spiritual master and learn how to discharge devotional service from him.
3. Obey the orders of the spiritual master with faith and devotion.
4. Follow in the footsteps of great *ācāryas* (teachers) under the direction of the spiritual master.
5. Inquire from the spiritual master about how to advance in Kṛṣṇa consciousness.
6. Be prepared to give up anything material for the satisfaction of the Supreme Personality of Godhead, Sri Kṛṣṇa. (This means that when we are engaged in the devotional service of Kṛṣṇa, we must be prepared to give up something which we may not like to give up, and also we have to accept something which we may not like to accept.)
7. Reside in a sacred place of pilgrimage like Dvārakā or Vṛndāvana
8. Accept only what is necessary, or dealing with the material world only as far as necessary.
9. Observe the fasting day on Ekādaśī.
10. Worship sacred trees like the banyan tree.

These ten items are preliminary necessities for beginning the discharge of devotional service in regulative principles. If in the beginning a neophyte devotee observes the above-mentioned ten principles, surely he will quickly make good advancement in Kṛṣṇa consciousness and enjoy life like anything.

Bhāva and Prema

In *Bhagavad-gītā* Chapter 4, Text 10 Srila Prabhupada says:

"The last stage of devotional life is called *bhāva*, or transcendental love of Godhead".

In the same purport, according with the *Bhakti-rasāmṛta-sindhu* (1.4.15-16), *bhāva* is defined as the preliminary stage of transcendental love of God. Real love for God is called *prema*, the highest perfectional stage of life.

Could you explain why we call *bhāva* both the preliminary stage and the last stage of devotion in the same purport?

What is the difference between *bhāva* and *prema*?

Is it enough to reach *bhāva* in order to love God?

Nectar and Highly Condensed Nectar

Bhāva and *prema* are both considered to be on the final stage. *Bhāva* is the beginning of that final stage, when ecstatic emotion fully awakens within the heart.

In this regard Śrīla Prabhupāda explains *bhāva* as follows:

> The *bhāva* stage is manifested by eight transcendental symptoms, namely inertness, perspiration, standing of hairs on end, failing in the voice, trembling, paleness of the body, tears in the eyes and finally trance.
>
> Purport to *Śrīmad-Bhāgavatam* 2.3.24

The difference between *bhāva* and *prema* is described as follows in the *Śrī Caitanya-caritāmṛta:*

samyaṅ-masṛṇita-svānto
mamatvātiśayāṅkitaḥ
bhāvaḥ sa eva sāndrātmā
budhaiḥ premā nigadyate

> "When that *bhāva* softens the heart completely, becomes endowed with a great feeling of possessiveness in relation to the Lord and becomes very much condensed and intensified, it is called *prema* [love of Godhead] by learned scholars."
>
> *Śrī Caitanya-caritāmṛta, Madhya* 23.7

Since *bhāva* is love of God in its preliminary stage, once one attains *bhāva* he should continue advancing to *prema*, the perfection of *bhāva*.

Rooting Out Sinful Desire

On one of your websites I read the following instruction: "Root out the desire to commit sins. A sin is an action which is not connected to the Supreme Lord; something done for the gratification of the senses. Acting only for the pleasure of the material body brings you further from practical realization of your factual identity as an eternal spirit soul (separate from the temporary material body)."

But how do I root out that desire?

Fully Occupied Heart

You have to completely fill your heart with spiritual desires in the service of the Lord. If the hotel of your heart is fully occupied with hearing, chanting, remembering and serving the Lord, when materially lusty and greedy desires come looking for a place to stay they will find that there is "no room at the inn." They will find instead a big sign that says "No Vacancy," and they will have to go somewhere else to find a place to reside.

How Can I Always Taste Happiness?

I understand that material happiness is temporary; but still, when it comes, I think it to be permanent and start trying to enjoy it. Even though I understand the illusory nature of material happiness, I find myself again and again falling into the trap of trying to enjoy it. How can I overcome this tendency and remain always fixed in transcendental bliss?

Always Make Kṛṣṇa Happy

If you want permanent happiness, stop trying to get it for yourself. Simply try to always give happiness to Lord Kṛṣṇa by your thoughts, words and deeds, in all times, places and circumstances. Then you will always be happy.

> "A person who neither rejoices upon achieving something pleasant nor laments upon obtaining something unpleasant, who is self-intelligent, who is unbewildered, and who knows the science of God, is already situated in transcendence. Such a liberated person is not attracted to material sense pleasure but is always in trance, enjoying the pleasure within. In this way the self-realized person enjoys unlimited happiness, for he concentrates on the Supreme."
>
> *Bhagavad-gītā* 5.20-21

Higher Pleasures

Pleasure is perceived by the mind mainly through the sense organs. Among the pleasures, the pleasure perceived as orgasm through genitalia is the most sought after.

The duration of these pleasures is very transient. Studying literature or listening to good music gives pleasure that lasts little longer than raw sense pleasure. So please enlighten me regarding long-lasting, higher pleasures.

Bhakti Is Pure Pleasure

Higher still is the pleasure of *bhakti*, which is ever-increasing and goes on eternally. The other pleasures are mixed with varying degrees of anxiety and are therefore not pure pleasures. Only *bhakti* is pure pleasure.

How Do We Love God?

My most humble question is: How do we love God?

It is easy to love a person or a thing that we see, but since we cannot see God, how can we love Him? Also, how do we know that he is reciprocating with our love? I do not doubt His existence, but I would like to know how to relate to Him.

By Engaging in His Service

You already have love of God lying dormant within your heart. All you have to do to revive it is engage yourself in His service. You can see God if you are willing to develop the eyes to see God. This is confirmed in the *Brahma-saṁhitā* as follows:

premāñjana-cchurita-bhakti-vilocanena
santaḥ sadaiva hṛdayeṣu vilokayanti
yaṁ śyāmasundaram acintya-guṇa-svarūpaṁ
govindam ādi-puruṣaṁ tam ahaṁ bhajāmi

"When one's eyes are anointed with the unguent, the salve of love of Godhead, he can see Kṛṣṇa everywhere, within and without."

Brahma saṁhitā 5.38

How is that salve applied? You must repeatedly hear the glories of the Lord through the mouths of His pure devotees.

If you sincerely give your love to Kṛṣṇa you will feel how He is reciprocating with you. In this regard the Lord speaks as follows in the *Bhagavad-gītā*:

patraṁ puṣpaṁ phalaṁ toyaṁ
yo me bhaktyā prayacchati
tad ahaṁ bhakty-upahṛtam
aśnāmi prayatātmanaḥ

"If one offers Me with love and devotion a leaf, a flower, fruit or water, I will accept it."

Bhagavad-gītā 9.26

So sincerely offer your vegetarian foods to Kṛṣṇa with love (no meat, fish, eggs, onions or garlic allowed), and when you partake of the remnants of the offering, you will feel how Kṛṣṇa is reciprocating with you in each and every bite.

Inaction in Action?

Please explain the meaning of *Bhagavad-gītā* 4.18: "One who sees inaction in action, and action in inaction, is intelligent among men, and he is in the transcendental position, although engaged in all sorts of activities."

Attaining True Inaction

"Action in inaction" refers to the impersonalists, whose goal is to become free from *karma* by completely stopping all activities. But the so-called inaction of the impersonalists is not doable. Even by their very breathing they are continuing to act in this material world. Even though they think that they are being inactive, still they are active. They are still accruing *karma*.

"Inaction in action" refers to the devotees of the Lord. Even though they are very active in this world, because they offer the fruits of all their activities to the Lord, they do not accrue any *karma* at all. So it is only the Lord's devotees who achieve the true position of inaction, i.e. freedom from all karmic reactions.

How Can I Conquer Anger?

How can I control the anger within me, and how can I be selfless when I deal with the outside world?

Also, how can I control temptations when it comes to material success or looking at nice *prasādam*?

My last question is: If any senior devotee chastises or scolds me, how can I take it as a blessing even if I have not made any mistake?

See What Kṛṣṇa Wants

Anger comes from unfulfilled desires. When things don't go the way we want them to go, we become angry. The easy way to conquer over anger is to stop seeing everything from the angle of what you want. If you will try to see everything from the angle of what Kṛṣṇa wants, you will easily conquer over anger.

The desire for material success becomes purified by offering the results of that success in the service of Kṛṣṇa. Arjuna was thinking that he did not want material success on the battlefield. But after Kṛṣṇa ordered him to fight the battle, he did so on the order of the Lord and achieved great success through his fighting, which was offered fully in Kṛṣṇa 's service.

There is nothing wrong if you are attracted to Kṛṣṇa *prasādam*. It is a very nice attraction. Simply take whatever *prasādam* you can easily digest and not beyond that. Overeating out of greediness leads to sickness and disease. Therefore, one should always control his tongue in the matter of eating by only taking Kṛṣṇa *prasādam* and by taking only as much as required.

Sometimes out of pride we think that we did not make a mistake, when factually we did make a mistake. But if we are being criticized for things that we have not done, we can tolerantly and respectfully ignore such criticism. However, be very careful in this regard. Remember to always curb down the strong tendency of false egotism. Most of the time we are wrong, but we stubbornly refuse to take the correction that we deserve.

Should I Relish the Nectar or Focus on Duties?

How does one handle keeping continual, daily physical balance when one's consciousness, because of its spiritual intoxication, will not come out of the Divine attention? For example, we may be preparing a meal or doing other duties, and although we may call our consciousness constantly into the physical "now" - especially knowing that what we are doing is for the Divine, and must therefore be done beautifully and with full, loving attention - consciousness suddenly skips away again to dance with the Divine and relish the nectar we receive therefrom. Which is the better way? Am I doing the right thing by calling my mind back from the Divine presence so often?

Focus on Pleasing Kṛṣṇa

Your question is nicely answered by the example of a great devotee of Kṛṣṇa named Dāruka. This devotee had the rare privilege of being one of the Lord's personal associates when He was on this planet 5,000 years ago. One day when Dāruka was fanning Lord Kṛṣṇa with a *cāmara* fan, he was filled with so much ectastic love that his consciousness was being carried away into an ocean of bliss. His mind became so surcharged with bliss that various ecstatic symptoms also became automatically manifested in his body. But Dāruka was so serious about doing a first-class job of fanning the Lord that he checked all of these ecstatic love manifestations so that he could continue doing his service for the Lord in the best possible way. In other words, he was more interested in giving the Lord happiness than he was in tasting it himself.

Of course, there is a vast difference between the unlimited ocean of ecstatic emotions experienced by Lord Kṛṣṇa's personal associates such as Dāruka and the emotions we experience ourselves. But still even for us neophytes, who may sometimes get a little "sneak preview" of spiritual emotion, the same principle applies. We do not want to selfishly enjoy whatever spiritual bliss may mercifully be bestowed up us. We prefer to offer the energy that bliss gives us back into the Lord's service. This is the secret of how to rapidly advance in Kṛṣṇa consciousness.

Kindly Help

Why do I always feel depressed? I do read your "Daily Thought" every day, and to some extent I get some strength, but only for a temporary phase. I have lost my appetite and feel my life is not worth anything. I feel weak and sleepy always. I try to wake up at 5:00 in the morning but always end up waking up late. I am 33 and not married, and this makes me feel more depressed. I do Kṛṣṇa *sevā* (devotional service to Lord Kṛṣṇa) every day, but still my mind is not at peace. How can I live a worthy life and get out of this material world?

Formula for Happiness

Although it is very nice that you are doing Kṛṣṇa *sevā*, that you are still not satisfied indicates that you not practicing Kṛṣṇa consciousness in a completely pure way. In other words, there must still be some tinges of self-centeredness in your service. What you have to do is completely put yourself in the shelter of Kṛṣṇa, accepting whatever situation he gives you as His mercy. Instead of thinking of your own happiness, always think of how you can make Lord Kṛṣṇa happy by your mood, your words, and your service. If you will fully adopt this attitude, you will become completely satisfied and happy. It is only when we put ourselves in the mood of unflinchingly loyal servants that we can truly be happy.

Is There Really Unlimited Bliss in Kṛṣṇa Consciousness?

In your daily "Thought for the Day" you often speak about "unlimited nectar of Kṛṣṇa consciousness" and "the reservoir of unlimited happiness." While I certainly have experienced to a certain extent the kind of happiness and bliss one experiences when performing activities in devotional service, I am moved to ask: How can you experience unlimited nectar, or delve into the reservoir of unlimited happiness? Do you really feel SO MUCH happiness all the time (unlimited reservoir) that at times it becomes difficult to contain it? I know that for one who remains 24 hours a day engaged in *bhakti*, life is always blissful; but is it not hyperbolic to go to such lengths as employing terms such as "unlimited" and "reservoir?"

I have another query as well. You mentioned in one "Thought for the Day": "If they want to restore balance to the earth's atmosphere, the first thing they must do is close the slaughterhouses and the abortion clinics. And then, by the wide-scale introduction of *nāma-saṅkīrtana*, congregational chanting of the holy names of God, the fire of lust and greed burning in the hearts of the human society will become gradually cooled, and the entire planet will gradually be transformed into a paradise. At that time a new sustainable economic system based on the cow, the bull, and family farms will naturally emerge."

Do you mean to say that if everyone starts chanting the holy names of God, the economic system will revert to the cow, bull and family farms, leaving aside the tractor, the automobile and all the sophisticated technological advancements of our time? I think this is pretty unrealistic, as there are other, non-regressive solutions to the global warming problem as I have pointed out earlier.

"Unlimited Bliss" Is an Understatement

We should not consider the glories of Kṛṣṇa consciousness to be a hyperbole, an extravagant exaggeration. The amazing descriptions of Kṛṣṇa consciousness given in the revealed scriptures are not imaginary, nor are they exaggerated. The scriptural descriptions regarding the unlimited bliss of Kṛṣṇa consciousness are perfect and complete. If a devotee is not experiencing Kṛṣṇa consciousness in this way, it simply means that he is not very advanced in Kṛṣṇa consciousness. He is only a beginner.

Even though the amazing descriptions of Kṛṣṇa consciousness seem unbelievable to one who is in conditioned consciousness, the fact is that even the most amazing descriptions are grossly understating the factual, inconceivable glories of Kṛṣṇa consciousness.

One who is licking the outside of a jar of honey may doubt the amazing descriptions he hears from others regarding the sweetness of the honey. But if he were to open the honey jar and put his tongue into the jar, he would gain factual confirmation of the truthfulness of all the amazing descriptions of the honey's sweetness.

Whatever percentage of bliss I am experiencing has nothing to do with how much bliss is there waiting to be experienced in the unlimited ocean of *bhakti*. As far as I am concerned, I am only tasting a few miniscule drops of that inconceivably and unlimitedly sweet ocean. But even a few drops of that ocean of *bhakti* are enough to bring peace and happiness to the entire world. Therefore, even though I consider myself to be completely unfit and unqualified, I have fully dedicated my life for trying to bring about the complete respiritualization of the human society by sharing whatever little bit I have realized about Kṛṣṇa consciousness with everyone.

If everyone becomes Kṛṣṇa conscious, we will see a natural gravitation towards a more sustainable economic system based on living in harmony with the earth instead of exploiting and raping the earth. This is not to say that we will throw away our technological advancement. What it means is that we will instead utilize our technological advancement for creating a socio-economic system which is in perfect harmony with the laws of God and nature instead of one so grossly opposed to these laws, as is the case with our present socio-economic system, which is creating a hell on earth.

Favorable Practice - Regulative Principles – Sadhana – Association of Devotees

Will Marijuana, Beer, and Liquor Help Meditation?

If one smokes marijuana in minute amounts for relaxation and meditative purposes, is this considered "intoxication" or is it acceptable? One may drink wine or beer and not drink until intoxicated; is this acceptable if it is done in moderation?

Don't Pour Water on the Fire

Marijuana and liquor do not take you to the real meditative state. Rather, they cloud the pure state of consciousness that is realized when one truly enters the meditative state. Why would you want to pour water on a fire while are while you are trying to light it?

Not Allotted as Our Quota

In an email you wrote, there is a phrase I did not understand. You stated, "We cannot take meat, fish, and eggs because these have not been allotted to us as our quota." Please explain to me how the maxim "not allotted to us as our quota" is related to our eating habits.

Kṛṣṇa's Prescription

"Not allotted to us as our quota" means that God has prescribed different kinds of foods for different kinds of species. For example, the tiger is allowed to eat flesh. If we study the body of a tiger we will see that his body is designed by God for flesh-eating. If we study in comparison the body of a human being, we will see that his body is not designed by God for flesh-eating. The human being is meant to subsist on a diet of fruits, grains, vegetables, and dairy products.

How Can I Check My Spiritual Progress?

How do I know whether I am fully Kṛṣṇa conscious? How can I check it?

See If You Have These Qualities

The more you become advanced in Kṛṣṇa consciousness, the more you will have nothing to speak about or hear about other than Kṛṣṇa. You will lose all attraction for the things of this world, and gradually you will more and more experience Kṛṣṇa within everything and everything within Kṛṣṇa.

Another sign is that the more you become full with Kṛṣṇa consciousness, the more you will see how fallen you are. In other words, you will become more and more humble.

Pulling of the Senses

I have been increasing the number of rounds that I chant, but along with each increase, I feel like my senses are trying even harder to keep me in this world of *māyā*. Are there any suggestions on how to get through those tough times?

Outpull Your Senses

Becoming Kṛṣṇa conscious means declaring war against the material energy. When we increase our onslaught against the material energy by increasing our chanting, it is natural that the material energy will counterattack to try to prevent us from making further progress. When we face these difficult moments in our progress, we have to push forward with renewed determination in spite of the obstacles.

The difficulties usually arise from having to sever our material attachments. But if anyone is able to tolerate such difficulties and continue pushing forward with great determination, surely his path to spiritual realization will become successful.

So no matter how hard your senses pull, you have to pull harder. He who pulls harder wins. If you let your senses pull harder, they will win. But if you will pull harder, it is you who will win. You have to be absolutely fixed in your determination to leave behind birth, death, old age, and disease for the attainment of an eternal life, full of bliss and full of knowledge.

Can I Associate with You Even Though I Am Still Doubtful?

Is it okay for me to associate with you and the other devotees, even like this?

You Are Always Most Welcome

You are most welcome to associate with us even if you are still "sitting on the bank." The more you experience how much nectar is being tasted by those who have "jumped into the water," the more your faith in the process of Kṛṣṇa consciousness will become strong. Simply by associating with those are fully submerged in the nectarean ocean of Kṛṣṇa *prema* (love of Kṛṣṇa) your dormant Kṛṣṇa consciousness will become revived. By repeatedly taking advantage of such association, you will one day will wake up and be amazed to discover that, much to your delight, you are now also fully immersed in the nectarean waters of Kṛṣṇa *prema*.

Is Solitude Better?

The explanation you gave in your last lesson about our relationship with God was clear and logical. In this regard, I want to know why it is very difficult to keep these feelings always intact. External factors like peer pressure in the workplace, passion, ailments etc. try to pull us away from the path of enlightenment.

Sometimes even in religious gatherings we are forced to discuss about material things rather than about God. In such a case, is solitude better for our Kṛṣṇa consciousness than to join the group for so-called *satsang*?

Better than Solitude Is...

Solitude is better than impure association, but better still is the association of pure-minded souls. The key to making solid spiritual progress is, as much as possible, to associate only with those persons who are practicing uninterrupted devotion, completely free from any material motivations. Unfortunately, practically all religious gatherings nowadays are 99% material with a little God consciousness added for the sake of a nice finishing touch. These sort of gatherings you must avoid. You need to find those rare religious gatherings that are 100% for the purpose of devotion.

If in a religious gathering you are forced to discuss material things, that means it is not a genuine religious gathering. That is a materialistic gathering disguising itself as a religious gathering. Beware of such wolves in sheep's clothing. Such association is our greatest enemy on the pathway to spiritual perfection.

You must find those persons who are purely pursuing devotion without any material motives and take complete shelter of their association. It is with this idea in mind that my spiritual master, His Divine Grace A.C. Bhaktivedanta Swami Prabhupāda, founded ISKCON, the International Society for Kṛṣṇa Consciousness, in a tiny storefront at 26 Second Ave in the Lower East Side of Manhattan, New York, in 1966. Now, by Kṛṣṇa's grace, this movement has expanded like wildfire all over the world to give every man, woman, and child on the face of this planet the opportunity to experience what is pure *bhakti*. By regularly associating with the ISKCON devotees, you can quickly and easily pick up the spirit of *bhakti* so strongly that it will carry you through those moments when you are forced to deal with so many external factors.

Regarding Ekādaśī

I have read a little recently about fasting and holy days, especially in regard to ekādaśī. How long should I fast - sundown to sundown? Is it better to fast completely, or just to omit grains and beans? Are there general guidelines to fasting that I can access? I do not mean to bombard you with questions, but you recommended that I fervently seek to be set free from the cycle of birth and death, and fasting is supposed to help with spiritual advancement.

As an Ingredient in the Back to Godhead Recipe

It's nice that you are desiring deliverance from the cycle of birth and death. To accomplish that, you need to do the following:

(These are the basic items of *sādhana-bhakti* to be executed by all those who are serious about being a devotee of Lord Kṛṣṇa.)

1. No illicit sex (sex other than for procreation)
2. No meat-eating (including fish and eggs)
3. No intoxication (including coffee, tea, and cigarettes)
4. No gambling
5. Chant at least 16 rounds of Hare Kṛṣṇa *mantra* every day on chanting beads
6. Only eat Kṛṣṇa *prasādam* (food which has been first offered to Lord Kṛṣṇa)
7. Regularly study the *Bhagavad-gītā As It Is* and the *Śrīmad-Bhāgavatam*
8. Develop an ongoing service relationship with your nearest ISKCON temple
9. Take shelter of and become initiated by a bona fide spiritual master

One of the items that enhances the above is the observance of Ekādaśī. Ekādaśī is observed from sunrise on the Ekādaśī up until the sunrise on the following morning. One must fast strictly from all forms of grains and beans, including anything cooked in a grain-based oil such as corn oil, or sweetened with a grain-based sweetener like corn syrup.

If one wants to do extra austerities for extra blessings, one can strictly fast by not taking anything except water. For even a stricter fast, one can avoid water also. And for even a stricter observance, one can stay home from work and spend the entire day and night, from sunrise to sunrise hearing and chanting the glories of the Lord.

Śrīla Prabhupāda engaged us in the simplest form of Ekādaśī, merely fasting from grains and beans. He also told us about the stricter forms. Many devotees have been inspired to observe Ekādaśī in the stricter forms, even though this is not mandatory.

Simply observing Ekādaśī, even in its strictest form, will not liberate you from birth and death unless you also observe the above-mentioned nine items. But the combination of above-mentioned nine items along with the faithful observance of Ekādaśī, either simply or strictly, will certainly deliver you from the cycle of birth and death.

Puzzled about Bhagavad-gītā

Kṛṣṇa says, "There is no possibility of one's becoming a yogī, O Arjuna, if one eats too much or eats too little, sleeps too much or does not sleep enough."

Bhagavad-gītā 6.16

Śrīla Rūpa Gosvāmī slept only two hours a day. Haridāsa Ṭhākura didn't even eat Kṛṣṇa *prasādam* until he finished his daily routing of chanting 300,000 holy names. I think they have set a good example for serving Kṛṣṇa 24 hours a day, and I want to learn from them. But this verse of *Bhagavad-gītā* doesn't approve of this sleepless life. Please clarify it.

Śravaṇam (hearing) is an important part of devotional service. Does it include reading? I am used to reading scriptures and your "Thought for the Day." Is this a kind of *śravaṇaṁ*? And does it include listening to a *kīrtana* video?

To Each His Own

To each his own. One man's food is another man's poison. What is too much or too little for one man may be different for another man. This is why every devotee needs to be guided by a bona fide spiritual master. In this way he can receive practical guidance to understand what is the proper amount of eating and sleeping to best facilitate his spiritual life. Even though great transcendentalists can get by with practically no eating no sleeping, if you try to artificially imitate them you will fall down.

Reading is a silent form of hearing. Listening to a *kīrtana* video is also hearing. Hearing your own *japa* chanting is also another form of hearing.

Who Makes More Progress?

There are devotees who stay in the temple and attend all *āratis* of the day. They also chant the prescribed number of rounds on their *japa mālā* beads every day and regularly study the *Śrīmad-Bhāgavatam*.

There are also devotees who do not stay in temples who do the prescribed chanting every day and study the *Śrīmad-Bhāgavatam*. These devotees also follow the regulative principles as do the devotees in the temple.

Is there any difference in the spiritual progress between these two types of devotees?

Whoever Is the Most Devoted

Although the temple atmosphere is the most favorable atmosphere for spiritual advancement, even more favorable is one's devotional attitude. Whoever has the most devotional attitude will make the most spiritual advancement, whether they live in the temple or outside the temple. Of course, there is no doubt that the temple atmosphere is the best place for cultivating a devotional attitude. But if one can have a powerful devotional attitude even while living outside of the temple, there will be no impediment for his rapid spiritual progress.

Is Kṛṣṇa Consciousness at a Distance Possible?

What is the end result for a student who completes these *Bhagavad-gītā* Lessons? Are we just dark shadows glimpsing the sun, with no hope of ever becoming devotees? Isn't it possible for students to worship Kṛṣṇa in their homes (since many of us live miles from temples) and to follow a home program that has been established by ISKCON? Do you not sanction initiation of students with this type of situation? Association with devotees is sometimes restricted by the physical distance and financial limitations of an individual. Please enlighten me with your views on these circumstances!

Yes

You can become initiated and become a pure devotee of Kṛṣṇa even if you live at a distance from any ISKCON center. You will simply need to follow these principles.

1. No illicit sex (sex other than for procreation)
2. No meat-eating (including fish and eggs)
3. No intoxication (including coffee, tea, and cigarettes)
4. No gambling
5. Chant at least 16 rounds of *Hare Kṛṣṇa mantra* every day on chanting beads
6. Only eat Kṛṣṇa *prasādam* (food which has been first offered to Lord Kṛṣṇa)
7. Regularly study authorized scriptures such as *Bhagavad-gītā As It Is* and *Śrīmad-Bhāgavatam*
8. Take regular guidance from senior devotees via correspondence, telephone, and personal meetings

Tools for Improved Chanting?

Sometimes while repeating the *mahā-mantra* I make a lot of *aparādhas* (offenses), and I do not feel good because of it. I cannot understand why one day my *japa* is okay but another day seems terrible. There is not any visible reason. Are there some additional tools which help to make my repeating of the *mahā-mantra* clearer?

Serve Pure Vaiṣṇavas

I am very happy to hear that you are endeavoring to improve the quality of your chanting. Because your taste for chanting has not yet become mature, you sometimes become very distracted from chanting. The *Śrīmad-Bhāgavatam* gives the perfect answer to your question as follows:

śuśrūṣoḥ śraddadhānasya
vāsudeva-kathā-ruciḥ
syān mahat-sevayā viprāḥ
puṇya-tīrtha-niṣevaṇāt

"O twice-born sages, by serving those devotees who are completely freed from all vice, great service is done. By such service, one gains affinity for hearing the messages of Vāsudeva."

Śrīmad-Bhāgavatam 1.2.16

In other words, if you will as much as possible serve pure Vaiṣṇavas you will naturally experience the Hare Kṛṣṇa *mantra* in an ever-increasingly wonderful way. The Hare Kṛṣṇa *mantra* will gradually become so amazingly sweet that your mind will naturally gravitate toward it 24 hours a day, just as the River Ganges naturally flows to the Bay of Bengal.

So whenever you have the opportunity to associate with and serve those who are purely practicing the science of *bhakti*, you must take advantage of it. This will greatly facilitate the awakening of the dormant *bhakti* which is currently sleeping within your heart.

Vegetarian Diet Clarification

I am a Muslim and would like you to clarify and enlighten us further on why an individual should consume vegetarian food. I feel that your reply - "if we want to be pure in our eating, we must first offer our food to the Lord before we consume it"- is specific to a sect or religion, and thus does not apply to everyone. I am not convinced by this answer, as I feel it is specific for members or followers of ISKCON; according to me, this is not a non-sectarian and scientific explanation to convince a person who is not associated with ISKCON.

My colleague could not give me a convincing reply, which he usually gives, and has thus asked me to contact you.

I find all of your other explanations and examples very scientific and universal, except the one mentioned above. I am sure you will help me to understand your explanation.

Compassion is Nonsectarian

I am very happy to hear that you are appreciating our presentation of the science of God. One of our leading saints is Namācārya Śrīla Haridāsa Ṭhākura, who comes from your Muslim community.

Compassion is a universal, nonsectarian principle. If you think eating an animal is an act of compassion, just imagine if you were the animal and someone came to kill you and eat you.

Meat-eating is allowed in the Bible, in the Koran, and in the Vedas, but under restriction. This is so that those low-class persons who lack compassion can gradually make some spiritual advancement. But the saintly class of men always show compassion to all living beings and give up the consumption of flesh and blood.

How to Be Centered?

Can you tell me how I can center myself when I travel a lot? Like you, I do a lot of traveling, and you are so centered. I have tried to attain serenity but cannot connect to my center when not in my chamber.

Know Who You Are and Be Who You Are

Centering is very simple. You have to tune in to your actual self. In other words, you simply have to know who you are and be who are. Always remember that you are not your body, that are the eternal servant of God. Carefully study the *Bhagavad-gītā* to hear directly from God Himself exactly how He wants you to live your life. Strictly abide by His instructions. If you do this, you always feel enlivened like anything because you will be perfectly centered at every minute with your every thought, word and deed in all times, places and circumstances.

This technique is equally effective whether you are traveling or remaining at home because it has nothing to do with your surroundings and everything to do with your relationship with God.

Apply this technique with determination, patience, and enthusiasm. Your life will be inconceivably sublime.

Continuing to Sin and Feeling Ashamed

I was following the regulations of the Vedic lifestyle, but recently I have started smoking again and having occasional drinks. I still don't eat meat. There have been occasions in the past few years when I've had illicit sex, but not nearly the way I used to. I was just wondering: If I continue to the best of my ability, will there come a time when I no longer will want these things? I feel very afraid that, because I make these mistakes, I'll never be able to have peace and to have a relationship with Kṛṣṇa. I'm sorry if I've offended you. Please give me any guidance you can.

Pick Yourself Up

When you fall down, pick yourself up and keep practicing Kṛṣṇa consciousness. Eventually you will become so strong that you will never fall down.

Humility and Self-Esteem

I am wondering if is it good to be as humble as grass, and if this humility has a negative effect on one's self-esteem. Is a devotee of the Lord allowed to love himself?

No One More Powerful

It is very good to consider ourselves to be lower than the grass because it is only in this humble state of mind that we can chant the holy names of the Lord constantly.

The more we become humble, the more we become powerful in self-esteem because as our humility increases so does our realization of our eternal spiritual identity. This is the perfection of self-esteem because there is no one more powerful than a self-realized soul.

No one loves himself better than the pure lover of God because he fully absorbs himself 24 hours a day in doing that which is most beneficial for himself, i.e. becoming a pure devotee of Kṛṣṇa, or God.

Confusion about Not Eating Animals

I am confused about not eating animals. They are children of God, too, but what about that the animals that the animals eat? Are animals less loved because many of them are carnivores? Is not God the Creator of everything? Where do we draw the line between deserving to live and deserving to be eaten? In order to live we have to eat what is in our nature to eat. The carnivores in the wild know what to eat. Why should we humans be any different? Life uses life. Life needs life. The Native Americans, who eat meat, thank the Sacred Power for the nourishment, clothes and supplies. I choose to eat prime rib, and you choose to condemn or criticize or judge me. If I judge someone, someone judges me. "Judge thee not, lest thee be judged." This moves us further and further away from Love. Thank you for listening to my concerns.

Live in Balance with Nature

Every species has its allotted quota of food by the laws of nature. You can understand this quota simply by studying the physiology of the human body. You will see a human body that is similar in all ways to the herbivores (herb-eating animals), not the carnivores (the meat-eating animals). If one goes outside of nature's balance, outside of his quota, he will lose his balance and thus be living in a disoriented state of consciousness. The wild animals have a natural sense of balance and therefore always eat within their quota. But modern man has drifted out of balance and thus does not know what to eat and what not to eat.

Today we live in a world that is very much out of balance because we human beings are consuming outside of our quota. Therefore, we see how polluted the rivers and the air are. We see how crime and brutal terrorism are running rampant. Now there is also a great fear of global warming. The environmental disruption, which is making big headlines every day, is the result of a human society run amok, not the animal society.

All these anomalies are due to our exceeding our allotted quota. If man can simply stick to his quota, the entire atmosphere of planet earth will be wonderfully transformed for the better.

Homosexual on Self-Discovery Quest

I am a homosexual man and I am battling with spirituality because I keep on thinking it is sinful to be who I am. The thing is that I did not choose to be attracted to the same sex. I am reading quite a number of books on a quest to discover who I am. Can you please advise?

Beyond Sexual Orientation

Actually whatever sexual orientation a person now has is in fact chosen by him according to his past *karma*. It is not by accident or chance that someone is heterosexually inclined or homosexually inclined. It is according to their previous life's activities.

But in this connection it is very important to understand that whether someone is homosexually inclined or heterosexually inclined, either type of sexual inclination is based on a false identification with the material body. It is this false sense of bodily identification which has been keeping us entangled in the cycle of birth and death for millions and billions of lifetimes suffering countless repetitions of birth, death, old age, and disease.

Therefore, the Vedic culture teaches us that whatever our sexual inclination is, we have to give it up. We must come the higher platform of realizing our identity beyond this material body as a pure spirit-soul and eternal servant of God. The self-realization process gradually brings one to becoming asexual, free of sexual inclination.

Our original state of consciousness is pure love for God. But when we come in contact with the material mode of passion, that pure love becomes transformed into lust. Whether we are homosexual, heterosexual, bisexual, or zoosexual, we are keeping ourselves entangled in countless sufferings due to our false sense of identifying with a rotting bag of stool, urine, pus, vomit, blood, guts, and bones.

My best advice to you is that you should now try to awaken your original divine enlightened consciousness, your Kṛṣṇa consciousness, by regularly chanting the holy names of God as much as possible:

Hare Kṛṣṇa, Hare Kṛṣṇa, Kṛṣṇa Kṛṣṇa, Hare Hare
Hare Rāma, Hare Rāma, Rāma Rāma, Hare Hare

If you do so, you will experience such unlimited bliss that you will realize that all sorts of sexual orientations are nothing but different sorts of nightmares only. You will gradually reach a state where you can personally associate with God face to face, eye to eye.

How Can One Advance with No Association?

You have kindly said that under proper guidance and spiritual association, one should reawaken one's original love for Godhead. But what if in certain circumstances one cannot associate with the devotees?

My second question is, how can one begin devotional service unto the Lord? It seems very difficult to regulate the mind, to keep it from hovering and getting attracted to material pleasure. Take the example of intoxication. It is not possible for me to avoid tea and coffee for more than two to four days. Consistency in keeping a spiritual attitude is practically a very, very difficult task. So please kindly suggest a permanent solution for this problem of mine.

Take Full Advantage of Whatever Association You Do Have

If you are away from devotee association, you should take more advantage of whatever association you do have. You have the association of Śrīla Prabhupāda through his books. You have the association of Kṛṣṇa through His holy names. You have Kṛṣṇa *prasādam*. My association is also there through my recorded videos and lectures and through my e-course. You may also personally inquire from me and be guided by me. If you take full advantage of whatever association you now have, Kṛṣṇa will see your sincerity and He will give you more and more association.

The beginning of devotional service is to chant the Hare Kṛṣṇa *mantra* and taste Kṛṣṇa *prasādam*. If you absorb your tongue in this way, you will get a higher taste and naturally lose your taste for the lower taste of tea, coffee, and other unnecessary things.

"4 Regs"

My question is one regarding the four regulative principles - specifically no intoxication. I have had much success with the other three, but I continuously struggle with intoxication. Please advise what the best way to defeat this problem is.

The Supreme Intoxication

If you can dive more deeply into the supreme intoxication - hearing and chanting the glories of Lord Śrī Kṛṣṇa - you will lose all interest in low-class types of intoxication.

Just imagine if I gave you $100,000. That would be very enlivening for you, would it not? But if I said that now you must return the $100,000 to me, this would no doubt be disappointing. But then if I said I will give you one billion dollars in exchange for the $100,000, you could very easily give up the $100,000.

So whatever intoxication you are attached to right now is a measly $100,000. It is mere pocket change compared to the one billion dollars' worth of pleasure that can easily be experienced through the supreme intoxication of chanting:

Hare Kṛṣṇa, Hare Kṛṣṇa, Kṛṣṇa Kṛṣṇa, Hare Hare
Hare Rāma, Hare Rāma, Rāma Rāma, Hare Hare

One realization I have also had is that if we casually described the four regulative principles as the "4 regs," as you did in the subject line of your email, it makes it harder to follow them. If we instead always respectfully refer them as Śrīla Prabhupāda always described them - as "the four regulative principles" - by this act of honoring them it becomes much easier to follow them.

When Problems Disturb Sādhana

It is said that one can be completely in Kṛṣṇa consciousness under all circumstances. But when material or monetary problems come, *sādhana* (devotional practice) is affected first - and when *sādhana* is affected, Kṛṣṇa consciousness is affected. So how can material problems be a blessing for an aspiring devotee?

Material problems are nice from one angle, as Kṛṣṇa gives realization that the material world is not a picnic. But how do we deal with them when they are having a negative effect on our practice of Kṛṣṇa consciousness?

Dive More Deeply into the Ocean of Bhakti

When material problems come, kindly remember that when the going gets tough, the tough get going. Great heroes thrive in times of difficulty. This is when they shine. Just as a powerful *kṣatriya* is enthused for battle when he is attacked by an enemy, a powerful Vaiṣṇava is enthused in his *sādhana* when he is attacked by *māyā*. Now he can show Kṛṣṇa how genuine he is in his desire to be a pure devotee.

Those who are enthused for *bhakti* only when things are going nicely are neophytes. In this connection there is a saying, "fair weather friend." In other words, only when things are going nicely is he your friend. Your devotion to Kṛṣṇa should not be conditional like that. And there is another saying, "Nobody knows you when you are down and out." So its not that we should only appreciate Kṛṣṇa when everything is going nicely and then abandon Him when things are turning sour.

If material problems are having a negative effect on your *sādhana*, you are not practicing your *sādhana* on a deep enough level. Dive more and more deeply into the ocean of *bhakti*, and you will reach a point where material problems enliven your *sādhana* just as they did for Queen Kunti.

Role of Willpower

What is your opinion on the role that willpower plays in spiritual life?

It's Absolutely Essential

It is not only my opinion. It is the opinion of Lord Śrī Kṛṣṇa, the Supreme Personality of Godhead, the source of all existence, that determination or willpower is required. In the recipe of Kṛṣṇa consciousness, willpower or determination is one of the most important ingredients. Without this determination or willpower, one cannot and will not be successful in going back home, back to Godhead.

Lord Śrī Kṛṣṇa states as follows in the *Bhagavad-gītā*:

sa niścayena yoktavyo
yogo 'nirviṇṇa-cetasā
saṅkalpa-prabhavān kāmāṁs
tyaktvā sarvān aśeṣataḥ
manasaivendriya-grāmaṁ
viniyamya samantataḥ

> "One should engage oneself in the practice of yoga with determination and faith and not be deviated from the path. One should abandon, without exception, all material desires born of mental speculation and thus control all the senses on all sides by the mind."
>
> *Bhagavad-gītā* 6.24

Śrīla Prabhupāda gives a nice example of the importance of willpower or determination as follows:

"As for determination, one should follow the example of the sparrow who lost her eggs in the waves of the ocean. A sparrow laid her eggs on the shore of the ocean, but the big ocean carried away the eggs on its waves. The sparrow became very upset and asked the ocean to return her eggs. The ocean did not even consider her appeal. So the sparrow decided to dry up the ocean. She began to pick out the water in her small beak, and everyone laughed at her for her impossible determination. The news of her activity spread, and at last Garuḍa, the gigantic bird carrier of Lord Viṣṇu, heard it. He became compassionate toward his small sister bird, and so he came to see the sparrow. Garuḍa was very pleased by the determination of the small sparrow, and he promised to help. Thus Garuḍa at once asked the ocean to return her eggs lest he himself take up the work of the sparrow. The ocean was frightened at this, and returned the eggs. Thus the sparrow became happy by the grace of Garuḍa. Similarly, the practice of yoga, especially *bhakti-yoga* in Kṛṣṇa consciousness, may appear to be a very difficult job. But if anyone follows the principles with great determination, the Lord will surely help, for God helps those who help themselves."

So become very strong in your determination that your life has one purpose and one purpose only, to become a pure devotee of Lord Śrī Kṛṣṇa. If you do so, your soon attaining the supreme perfection of going back home, back to Godhead is guaranteed.

How Can I Always Be Kṛṣṇa Conscious?

From one of your merciful lectures you instructed us that there should not be any gap for *māyā*, that we must fully engage our mind 24 hours in the thoughts and service of Lord Kṛṣṇa, the spiritual master, and the devotees. But these kind of thoughts do not come to my mind spontaneously. Even after the morning *sādhana* (meditation and worship), my mind is easily carried away by material thoughts, in spite of my sincerely trying to remember the Lotus Feet of Śrī Kṛṣṇa.

So how can I train my mind to be always focused in Kṛṣṇa Consciousness? And how can I instill the mind with thoughts pertaining to devotional service?

By Strong Faith

To keep your mind always focused on Kṛṣṇa you must have strong faith that by Kṛṣṇa consciousness you will be elevated to the highest perfection of life. Such focus of mind is called *vyavasāyātmikā*, being resolute in Kṛṣṇa consciousness. In this connection Lord Śrī Kṛṣṇa states in the *Bhagavad-gītā*:

vyavasāyātmikā buddhir
ekeha kuru-nandana
bahu-śākhā hy anantāś ca
buddhayo 'vyavasāyinām

> "Those who are on this path are resolute in purpose, and their aim is one. O beloved child of the Kurus, the intelligence of those who are irresolute is many-branched."
>
> *Bhagavad-gītā* 2.41

How Do I Control My Mind?

From your merciful lectures, I have learned that there are two bona fide ways to control our mind and keep it focused in Kṛṣṇa consciousness. One method is to lovingly persuade the mind to focus on Kṛṣṇa and the other way is to chastise the mind when it goes away from Kṛṣṇa.

I am sincerely trying hard to control my mind. Sometimes I can control it for up to two or three days keeping it engaged in thoughts of Kṛṣṇa. But then, out of impulse, it again starts engaging in lusty and greedy thoughts. This up-and-down process continues cyclically. I try to use my free time for studying Śrīla Prabhupāda's books and chanting the Hare Kṛṣṇa *mahā-mantra*. But if there are any gaps, these kinds of thoughts come to my mind and cause me severe distress. Kindly enlighten me: How can I always keep my mind focused on the lotus feet of Kṛṣṇa and His devotees?

Leave No Gaps for Māyā

The key is that you should not leave any gaps for *māyā*. One time His Holiness Viṣṇujana Mahārāja was with Śrīla Prabhupāda in Śrīla Prabhupāda's quarters in Los Angeles. Śrīla Prabhupāda explained to Viṣṇujana Mahārāja how he always remained in Kṛṣṇa consciousness. He pointed to his harmonium and said how, if there was any free time, he would play his harmonium and sing some Kṛṣṇa-conscious songs, and in this way leave no gaps for *māyā*. So you should very intelligently arrange your every moment so that there are no gaps for *māyā*.

Why No Intoxication?

I was speaking with one person over the weekend who claimed to be a Rastafarian. He asked me a question that I could not answer:

Where in our scriptures does it say intoxication is forbidden? What is the reasoning behind it?

The best answer I had was, "If you spend your time getting intoxicated, then you are not spending your time meditating on God." His reply was, "Why not use your intoxication to change your consciousness and meditate on God in this way?"

For the most part we were discussing marijuana, which he uses in his spiritual practice. It was a pleasant conversation, and nothing arose from it, but I could not call up any scripture that says "no intoxication." I just know it as one of the most dear regulated principles for achieving the Supreme.

Stay High Forever

The simple counter-argument is that as long as you rely on a chemical to alter your consciousness, you are still on the material plane. By buying into the idea of altering the consciousness by injecting a chemical, one is buying into a bodily conception of the self. Such a bodily conception of the self binds one to a state of illusion. The method for attaining and maintaining a genuine state of divine intoxication is to totally reject any sort of physical or material conception of the self by reviving one's original, pure state of divine intoxication. This method is known as Kṛṣṇa consciousness.

According to the *Śvetāśvatara Upaniṣad*, one is to have full faith in the words of the spiritual master. Hundreds and hundreds of times Śrīla Prabhupāda told us to strictly avoid any form of intoxication. These words coming from the mouth of the greatest spiritual master in the history of the universe are in themselves scripture.

Besides that, there are many scriptural statements indicating that intoxication should be given up. For example:

> Theft, violence, speaking lies, duplicity, lust, anger, perplexity, pride, quarreling, enmity, faithlessness, envy and the dangers caused by women, gambling and intoxication are the fifteen undesirable qualities that contaminate men because of greed for wealth. Although these qualities are undesirable, men falsely ascribe value to them. One desiring to achieve the real benefit of life should therefore remain aloof from undesirable material wealth.
>
> *Śrīmad-Bhāgavatam* 11.23.18-19

So you may inform such persons that if they think being intoxicated is a desirable state of consciousness, they should give the supreme intoxicant known as Kṛṣṇa consciousness a serious try. Stay high forever. No more coming down.

Arguments for Meat-Eating

I have a family friend studying in the UK. He is a Hindu working for McDonald's. He has been telling me that he gets free food, and that the cheese they use there is beef-based, and that also he started consuming beef. He has been arguing the following:

1. Why can Muslims, Christians, and Jews eat beef while Hindus cannot?
2. If everyone were to turn vegetarian, there would be an overpopulation of cattle, cows, hens, etc.
3. Herbivores have flat teeth and carnivores have pointed teeth. But humans have both. So it is a clear signal that we humans can eat both, as humans can easily digest non-vegetarian food.
4. Even plants and trees are living entities. But still we pluck and eat the fruits and vegetables.

I told him that cows are Kṛṣṇa's favorites, and that they provide milk, so they are our mothers. I also told him that Kṛṣṇa Himself says that consumers of beef will have to go through this repeated cycle of birth and death and be born 5000 times more in the worst lowly species. Then, he told me, "What is the proof that Kṛṣṇa said all this? *Bhagavad-gītā* was spoken so many years back, and at that time there was no copyright. Maybe the one who wrote it down is wrong, and has interpreted *Bhagavad-gītā* in his own way."

I did try my best, Mahārāja. Please excuse me if I made any offense. Please advise me as to I should answer him.

Arguments against Meat-Eating

Everyone can eat meat if they want to. But they will take the *karma* of becoming animals and being slaughtered and eaten by the very same animals that they ate. It does not matter how they designate themselves as Muslim, Christian, Jew, Hindu etc. Everyone is treated equally without any discrimination by the stringent laws of *karma*.

There would be no overpopulation of cows. The cattle are being artificially bred to support the beef industry. It is very simple to separate the cows and bulls into separate pasturing grounds.

Humans have two carnivorous teeth as a concession for the meat-eaters. That's a fact. But aside from that, their entire digestive system is herbivorous. When a human eats meat, it is very unhealthy because the rotting meat turns from fermentative to putrefactive while still present in the intestinal system. The carnivorous animals have a very short intestinal system designed to get the meat out before it turns putrefactive. It is because of meat-eating that we see so much colon cancer in the human society.

We are forbidden to consume even fruits and vegetables unless they are first offered to Kṛṣṇa to free us from the *karma* of killing them. We cannot offer meat to Kṛṣṇa because He specifically instructs us to offer Him vegetarian foods, not meat foods.

The words of Kṛṣṇa spoken 5,000 years ago have been passed down carefully, without any adulteration, through an unbroken chain of disciplic succession. Besides that, the proof of the pudding is in eating. When your family friend finds himself in the animal kingdom being readied for slaughter for as many times as there are hairs on the body of the cow that he eats, he will get his proof. But by then, it will be too late. It is more intelligent to learn by hearing than it is by being sent repeatedly to the slaughterhouse. But less intelligent fools are stubborn. They will only learn the hard way.

Do You Sightsee?

I was wondering: do you ever get to sightsee in places where you travel to preach?

We Are the Ultimate Sightseers

We certainly naturally see whatever sights are along the way wherever we go for preaching work. And we appreciate the amazing wonder of Krsna's material creation. When there are so many amazing sights in this material world, we can hardly begin to imagine how amazing the spiritual world must be.

But we do not go out of our way for any mundane sightseeing. For example, I have been regularly going to India for the last 25 years. Every time I go to India I go to Vṛndāvana, which is very close to the famous Taj Mahal. But in all these many visits, I have never gone to see the Taj Mahal because it has nothing to do with Kṛṣṇa consciousness. Even one time I went for preaching in Agra, the very city in which the Taj Mahal is located. But still I did not think it worth my time and energy to see the Taj Mahal.

The most beautiful sight wherever I go is the smiling faces of Kṛṣṇa's devotees and the beautiful form of the Lord's Deity in the temples. This is the ultimate sightseeing, to have the *darśana* of Kṛṣṇa and Vaiṣṇavas.

Self-Realization and a Job – Householder Life

How Are Children Viewed in Kṛṣṇa Consciousness?

How are children viewed in Kṛṣṇa consciousness? Are they seen as a distraction and detriment to spiritual progress, or as an opportunity to further one's relationship with Kṛṣṇa?

Children Can Be the Greatest Blessing

I am very happy that you are appreciating my humble attempt to present the teachings of Kṛṣṇa in the pure, unadulterated form given to us by Śrīla Prabhupāda.

Children in themselves are neither favorable nor detrimental for our Kṛṣṇa consciousness. It is how you relate with them that is either favorable or unfavorable for your Kṛṣṇa consciousness.

If you accept them as the Lord's greatest blessing upon you, that you have been awarded the opportunity of delivering these souls back to home, back to Godhead, then being a parent will be the most wonderful service that one can render to the Lord. This enlightened understanding of raising children is the real meaning of parenthood.

On the other hand, if you simply think of making all nice arrangements for their material bodies and neglect the eternal soul that resides within the body, your so-called parenthood will be a great hindrance not only for them, but for you also.

For the spiritual master it is a similar situation. He is the spiritual father. To have the responsibility of delivering his disciples back to the spiritual world is a great blessing because it fully absorbs him in Kṛṣṇa 's service.

Nowadays many charlatans pose as spiritual masters without even the slightest clue of how they or their disciples can achieve spiritual perfection. Such so-called spiritual masters are the greatest enemies of human society.

The parents who deliver their child from the cycle of birth and death are the greatest well-wishers. The parents who keep their children entangled in this cycle of birth and death are doing the greatest violence to those souls who have been placed under their care and protection by the Lord.

It is clearly affirmed in the *Śrīmad-Bhāgavatam*:

gurur na sa syāt sva-jano na sa syāt
pitā na sa syāj jananī na sā syāt
daivaṁ na tat syān na patiś ca sa syān
na mocayed yaḥ samupeta-mṛtyum

"One who cannot deliver his dependents from the path of repeated birth and death should never become a spiritual master, a father, a husband, a mother or a worshipable demigod."

Śrīmad-Bhāgavatam 5.5.18

Please Clarify My Confusion

I am confused. Since I have started going to the programs at my local ISKCON center, I am remembering Kṛṣṇa at every minute. I am even having dreams of Kṛṣṇa. I am thinking of Kṛṣṇa so much that I am even losing interest in my job. Is this normal, or am I missing something?

But I like to think about Kṛṣṇa. I used to have nightmares and I used to see things like shadows or what they call ghosts, but since I have read the *Bhagavad-gītā As It Is*, the nightmares have disappeared, and now I'm not afraid of ghosts (or whatever they are) anymore. I am beginning to like Kṛṣṇa.

Your Job Gives You an Opportunity to Do Practical Service for Kṛṣṇa

It is very nice that you are always remembering Kṛṣṇa. If we lose interest in everything else and are only interested in Kṛṣṇa, this is the perfection of our existence.

Kṛṣṇa consciousness frees us from all nightmares and ghostly influences. By Kṛṣṇa's unlimitedly sweet mercy we enter into an eternal existence full of bliss and knowledge.

You mention that you are becoming so much absorbed in Kṛṣṇa consciousness that you are losing interest in your job. But kindly try to understand that Kṛṣṇa consciousness means to engage everything in the service of Kṛṣṇa. So you should become now more eager to go to your job because it gives you a very nice opportunity to do practical service for Kṛṣṇa.

How can you serve Kṛṣṇa through your job? By engaging as much as possible of your monthly earnings in the service of Kṛṣṇa through regular donations to your local ISKCON center. This is the greatest blessing. You can now render devotional service by serving Kṛṣṇa through your job. This will help His movement become successful in blessing everyone with the same happiness and freedom of anxiety that you are now experiencing.

So now with a heightened sense of responsibility, go to your job and work in a first-class way for Kṛṣṇa. In this way you can show Kṛṣṇa how much you love and appreciate Him.

You are on the right track. There is no need for anxiety. The next step is to make yourself spiritually perfect by fully surrendering to Kṛṣṇa. This is accomplished by chanting at least 16 rounds of the Hare Kṛṣṇa *mantra* every day on *japa* beads, strictly avoiding illicit sex, intoxication, meat-eating and gambling, and fully taking shelter at the lotus feet of Kṛṣṇa 's representative, the bona fide spiritual master. This will completely free you from all confusion.

I Cannot Be Kṛṣṇa Conscious at Work

How can people concentrate on two things at a time - I mean, work as well as self-realization? If work needs complete devotion, then thinking about God is ruled out.

Yes You Can; Here's How

When we play the two-headed *mṛdaṅga* drum, the left hand and the right are playing separate beats, yet they are perfectly coordinated to make a nice, pleasing sound. In a similar way, by practice you can keep your Kṛṣṇa consciousness going on very nicely while at the same time you expertly perform the occupational duties at your job.

What to Do with a Spouse Who Is Not Kṛṣṇa Conscious?

I have been practicing Kṛṣṇa consciousness for some time. My spouse is not very keen on following this path. This acts as a hindrance to my progress and puts brakes on my active participation in the movement. What can I do?

Is it a must to have Deities (Gaura Nitāi / Laḍḍu Gopāla) at home if one takes initiation? We are told that the initiation commitment is for only for chanting 16 rounds daily and following the four regulative principles.

Inspire Her to Follow You by Serving Her with Love

Now that you are giving your love to Kṛṣṇa, your spouse may naturally feel neglected and discouraged. So you must now serve her with so much love that she will not feel in any way neglected and will become so much inspired and enlivened by your association that she resolves to follow you on the path of devotion to Lord Kṛṣṇa.

It is not required to have Deities at home, even if you are initiated. You may simply keep photographs of Śrī Kṛṣṇa, Śrī Pañca Tattva, Śrīla Prabhupāda, and your Guru Mahārāja on your home altar.

How Can I Do Full-Time Devotional Service?

I am an employee. I have a family and one child also. The child is one year old. My wife and I are both very keen on preaching. We want to put ourselves in loving devotional service all the time because the people in general are in such a dull and ignorant condition. I have lost interest in working a job. Can you suggest to me the way I should proceed?

By Following in the Footsteps of Śrīla Bhaktivinoda Ṭhākura

It is indeed wonderful that you and wife would like to be full-time preachers of Kṛṣṇa consciousness. There is truly no greater need than the spreading of Kṛṣṇa consciousness all over the world. Indeed, the entire world is suffering because of one problem and one problem only: lack of Kṛṣṇa consciousness.

However, since you are married with a one-year-old child, the best option will be for you to set the ideal example of earning your livelihood as a responsible *gṛhastha* (married man), supporting the Kṛṣṇa consciousness movement financially and donating your spare time to assist in the preaching work.

This ideal example will qualify you as a powerful preacher and a full-time devotee. In this way, you will be following in the footsteps of our great *ācārya*, Śrīla Bhaktivinoda Ṭhākura, who worked a job, raised a family, and powerfully preached the message of Kṛṣṇa.

Balancing Materialism and Spiritualism

I want to ask you about how to make a practical balance between materialism and spiritualism. I understand that the human birth is for developing love and devotion to Kṛṣṇa and for elevating oneself to Him (getting back to Godhead). But aren't our material requirements equally important?

If we get materially inclined, then we spend most of our time in earning for our material needs. So how do we make a balance? Should we suppress and curb down our material needs?

Also, why is chanting 16 rounds on *japa* beads prescribed? If I have faith in Kṛṣṇa and just take His name once a day, won't it give me *bhakti* and *mukti*?

Emphasize Spiritual Life

The principle of balance between spiritualism and materialism is presented in the ancient Vedic scripture, the *Śrī Īśopaniṣad:*

vidyāṁ cāvidyāṁ ca yas
tad vedobhayaṁ saha
avidyayā mṛtyuṁ tīrtvā
vidyayāmṛtam aśnute

> "Only one who can learn the process of material knowledge and that of transcendental knowledge side by side can transcend the influence of repeated birth and death and enjoy the full blessings of immortality."
>
> *Śrī Īśopaniṣad* Mantra 11

Since we are already solidly situated in material life from the day we were born, our balancing is to now give more emphasis to the development of our spiritual life. We must now focus our energies on awakening our dormant Kṛṣṇa consciousness.

Material requirements are important, but they are not as important as the spiritual requirements. Which is more important: to feed the bird within the cage or to polish the cage? Feeding the bird is more important. In the same way, this body is just a cage for the spirit-soul who is seated within. Along with keeping the body fit, we must more importantly focus on keeping our consciousness fixed on the Lord.

On the material side we should accept the basic comforts for keeping body and soul together. There is no need for extravagance. The balance of time and energy saved by plain living should be utilized for high thinking on the transcendental subject matter of the relationship between the individual being and the Supreme Being.

It's a fact that one pure utterance of the Hare Kṛṣṇa *mantra* is sufficient for our liberation. But at the present moment, we cannot chant with complete purity. Therefore, we must practice every day by chanting at least 16 rounds. By this daily practice, gradually our chanting will improve, and we will one day be able to utter the holy names with 100% purity. Even after reaching that stage, one will continue chanting on the *japa* beads to set a proper example for others who are trying to perfect their chanting.

Successful Career and Kṛṣṇa Consciousness?

Is it true that we must give up all material desires for attaining Kṛṣṇa's mercy before our death? This is important for me to know so that I may work toward it.

Is it permitted to be ambitious, to have a successful career while also cultivating my Kṛṣṇa consciousness?

Like Arjuna, Offer Your Career to Kṛṣṇa

Yes, we must be completely free from all material desires in order to qualify ourselves for the full mercy of Kṛṣṇa. But that does not mean that we cannot act successfully in this material world. Look at the classic example of Śrī Arjuna. He wanted to renounce his career. He wanted to call it quits. But after hearing Śrī Kṛṣṇa 's divine instructions, he realized that it was his duty to continue his career and offer its results to Kṛṣṇa.

So this is the perfection of renunciation. Not giving up your career.

If you are engaging your career in the service of Kṛṣṇa by donating as much as possible of your earnings for pushing forward the Kṛṣṇa consciousness movement, it is not considered material. It is considered spiritual. For example, a Kṛṣṇa conscious businessman can aspire to become the wealthiest businessman in the entire world.

Just imagine if Bill Gates were Kṛṣṇa conscious, how much good he could do for the suffering humanity. Therefore, whatever you are doing, offer it 100% in the service of Kṛṣṇa, under the guidance of the bona fide spiritual master. This will purify your heart completely and qualify you for going back to home, back to Godhead, at the time of death.

Realizing God in the City?

Is it possible to realize God while living in a city? The city life demands a lot of money (rent, fuel, bills). The material world is demanding almost my whole mind. If I were to focus my mind on God, my material world would become confused and would collapse. How can I escape from this money-demanding city life? It is tormenting me.

By Following Arjuna's Footsteps

The most conducive place for spiritual enlightenment is in a secluded place. But better still is in a temple of Kṛṣṇa in the association of devotees. So if you can regularly associate with the devotees at your nearest ISKCON temple and also transform your home into a temple of Kṛṣṇa, this will be the very best situation for your spiritual enlightenment, even if you are living in the most hellish of cities.

You are forgetting that Arjuna was fully focused on God in the midst of a hellish battlefield. Not only was he on a battlefield, he became supremely victorious on that battlefield also.

So if you will follow in the footsteps of Arjuna by fully surrendering at the lotus feet of Lord Śrī Kṛṣṇa - or in His absence, at the lotus feet of His pure representative, the bona fide spiritual master - you will be unlimitedly happy in perfect God realization, and you will also be highly successful in all of your material dealings as you battle it out every day with the material energy.

How Can I Fully Enjoy Kṛṣṇa's Blessings?

I have two jobs, and I am practically gone from home for 12 hours a day. I live with my wife and two beautiful children, ages two and seven.

A few years ago, Kṛṣṇa came into my life when a devotee sold me a copy of the *Bhagavad-gītā*. At that time a wonderful light dawned in my life, and I have been reading the *Bhagavad-gītā* and other writings of Śrīla Prabhupāda ever since.

But the daily routine and the burden, the economic problems and the stress that is produced from all this - even though it doesn't draw me away from Kṛṣṇa, it doesn't allow me to enjoy fully His blessings.

I would like you to guide me on my path, keeping in mind my life's activities which I cannot renounce (i.e. family, work).

Use Every Spare Minute in His Service

There is no question that your difficult material situation can prevent you from experiencing fully the Lord's blessings. A devotee experiences everything, both pleasant and unpleasant, as the Lord's blessings. You simply have to see how Kṛṣṇa has put you into a difficult situation in this material world to remind you that this is not your actual home, that your actual home is with Him in the spiritual sky. If you will fully utilize every spare second of the free time you have now to engage yourself in Kṛṣṇa-conscious activities - such as reading, chanting, and visiting your nearest ISKCON center - you will be amazed at how Kṛṣṇa will give you more and more free time to engage directly in Kṛṣṇa-conscious activities. In this way, you can gradually purify your consciousness completely and become a fully self-realized soul.

Are you chanting *japa* regularly and strictly following our regulative principles? They are: no illicit sex, no intoxication, no meat-eating, and no gambling. These activities must strictly be avoided by all those desiring to achieve spiritual perfection.

How Can One Think of Kṛṣṇa?

In most of your mails you have mentioned that we must always think of Kṛṣṇa. But I wonder how this is possible. As a student, one has to think of how to excel in studies. Once out of school, he has to think of getting into a good job. After getting into a good job, he thinks of getting a good position and so on. Once he is in a good post, he starts to think of getting married. Once married, he likes to have children and starts thinking of how to maintain them. In this way a person is always thinking of different things in his life. Now the question is, how can one think of Kṛṣṇa when he has so many other engagements and thoughts?

Offer Everything to Kṛṣṇa

The only way you can think of Kṛṣṇa while doing so many things is to do them for Kṛṣṇa. Doing them for Kṛṣṇa means that whatever fruits are gained as a result of those activities should all be offered to Kṛṣṇa. In this way, if you factually offer the results of all your activities to Kṛṣṇa, you can easily think of Kṛṣṇa no matter what you may be doing, whether as a student, a career man, or a family man.

Where Do I Begin?

Lately I have been straying away from becoming completely in bliss with God. I always tell myself I will have more time in the summer when school is out. I feel like I have no time. I feel a struggle between living in the material world and trying to surrender to God. I know it is my own material thoughts that tell me I have no time and that I will get to it in the summer. I want to start now. I want to be in complete bliss and complete happiness. Where do I begin? Why do I feel so restless? How do I know what will ease my restlessness?

Rise Early and Chant

The key is that you have to prioritize your spiritual life. Your material life comes and goes with the birth and demise of your material body. But your spiritual life is eternal. Therefore, your spiritual life is always more important than your material life.

Just like if you have a bird in a cage: which is more important, the bird or the cage? You are a spirit-soul. You are like the bird. Your material body is like the cage. Your first business is to see that the bird is well fed. Once you make sure the bird is healthy, then you can see about polishing the cage.

Begin by rising early every morning, taking your bath, and chanting the Hare Kṛṣṇa *mahā-mantra* on *japa* beads. This will fix your mind in Kṛṣṇa consciousness so that you can then engage in your ordinary daily duties while at the same time remaining fully absorbed in Kṛṣṇa consciousness.

Your feelings of restlessness are natural because you are neglecting your primary duty. Now if you seriously take up this chanting process, all of your restlessness will go away and you will become completely peaceful.

Should I Quit My Job?

I have been attending local ISKCON congregational programs regularly, which gives me immense peace of mind and pleasure. But when I get back to my job (company job), which is the source of my bread and butter, I really feel disillusioned and uncomfortable. So is it time that I should quit my job and give my full concentration to spiritual life? I have also family responsibilities, with my two daughters still to get married.

Become Internally Renounced

As long as you have family responsibilities, you must remain at your job. So there is no question of giving up your job. You cannot renounce your material duties. You can however, become internally renounced by offering yourself fully in Kṛṣṇa 's service.

As long as we have material bodies, we require some means of livelihood. If you will fully offer yourself to Lord Kṛṣṇa 24 hours daily, whatever means of livelihood you adopt will not be an impediment for your Kṛṣṇa consciousness. Job means earning money. And if that money is spent 100% in a Kṛṣṇa-conscious way, you will always feel blissfully connected with Kṛṣṇa, even when you are working your job.

So now you must master the art of how to spend your money perfectly in the Lord's service, without misspending even a small portion of it on material sense gratification. This will completely relieve you from your current sense of anxiety at your job.

Being Away from Devotees

In this material world, most people are non-devotees. We cannot avoid associating with them. For example, if you are a businessman, you have to do business with others. In short, we have to associate with non-devotees to make a living. We need social relationships to survive. How do we deal with such non-devotional association without being polluted?

There is nothing more bitter and painful than being separated from devotees. I wish that one day I can live with Kṛṣṇa-conscious devotees and serve Kṛṣṇa together. But at present, how do I deal with the bitter feeling that sometimes comes into my mind?

Connect Within the Heart

Devotees of the Lord do not artificially renounce this material world. Rather, they spiritualize this material world by engaging it in Kṛṣṇa's service. For this purpose you should always strictly follow the orders of your spiritual master and engage in your occupational duties in such a way that you become the leader of the people with whom you are associating. In this way you can lead them to Kṛṣṇa, just as your spiritual master is leading you to Kṛṣṇa

The taste of bitterness of being separated from devotees is actually a blessing in disguise because it is this intense hankering for devotee association that keeps the devotees always present with us within our hearts.

How Can I Advance?

I am a married man and belong to the Brahmin community, and I am from Andhra Pradesh, India. How can I advance in spiritual life, as I am a married man?

Chant under Guru's Guidance

If one chants the Hare Kṛṣṇa *mantra* under the guidance of a bona fide spiritual master, it does not matter whether he is married or single. In either case he can achieve the supreme destination.

Therefore, those who are serious about becoming liberated from the cycle of birth and death fully take shelter of the bona fide spiritual master through the process known as initiation.

Interacting with Non-Devotees

How Can I Become More Compassionate?

A difficulty I had with my family members raised a question for me. I have understood that the only actual compassion is to give someone Kṛṣṇa consciousness. But what is the meaning of compassion if one avoids accepting this Kṛṣṇa consciousness in all possible ways? If I am feeling compassion I should do something for it, not only say that I feel compassion. But what can I do for my family if they do not want to accept?

Another question is how to become more compassionate. For the time being I feel only a little compassionate to other people and their suffering, because not so long time ago I was terribly suffering myself and other people just made it more difficult for me to come out of it. For the time being, I think more of myself and developing my own happiness in Kṛṣṇa consciousness, not of others. So can you tell me, please, how can I develop more compassion? Or will it come later when I am more advanced?

First Become Expert in the Philosophy of Kṛṣṇa Consciousness

Even if people reject our attempts to be compassionate to them by giving them Kṛṣṇa consciousness, we can maintain our sincere love for them within our hearts and pray for that day when they will accept our compassion.

The way to develop compassion is to practice being compassionate. Try to develop your feelings of compassion by acting in a compassionate way to others. This will naturally stimulate the pure compassion that it is already there but currently lying dormant within your heart. And when you taste the supreme bliss of blessing others with Kṛṣṇa consciousness, you will naturally want to do it more and more and more. There is nothing more ecstatic than the original, pure compassion of giving Kṛṣṇa consciousness to others. It is the ultimate pleasure, divine intoxication.

The more you advance in Kṛṣṇa consciousness, the more your feeling of compassion for others will manifest. It is natural that now you should focus on developing your own Kṛṣṇa consciousness. This is not at all being selfish. This is required. Just like if someone wants to become a doctor to relieve people of their suffering, he must first go to medical school and become an expert doctor. So you must first become very expert in the practice and philosophy of Kṛṣṇa consciousness. In this way you will gradually, gradually become super-qualified to very expertly practice the ultimate compassion of injecting Kṛṣṇa consciousness into the hearts of the suffering people on this planet.

Lord Caitanya has ordered us, His followers, to perform the highest welfare work of saving the suffering humanity from the darkness of illusion. I want all of my disciples to be absolutely, totally committed to becoming 100% pure devotees themselves and performing the ultimate compassion of delivering the suffering humanity back to home, back to Godhead.

How Is It that We Are Limited and God Is Unlimited?

I shall be very grateful if you clarify one question which most people ask me:

As we all are parts and parcels of God, then how is it that we are limited and God is unlimited? Let's take the example of water. The properties of water remain the same whether we pour it in a glass or some another utensil. Please throw some light on this question.

These days I am finding it very difficult to complete my 16 rounds of *japa mālā*. Also, my parents are against it, and time and again they discourage me. Even though I have told them that it is my topmost priority, they don't agree. We are a combined family, but I am not giving in to this discouragement. I am completing my 16 rounds daily. Please guide me and bless me so that I may not fall. It has been almost one year since I started doing 16 rounds

Be Determined to Surrender to Kṛṣṇa

Water is of the same quality in small or large quantity. But a large quantity of water will support a ship, while the amount of water in your drinking cup will not. That is the difference. We are the small quantity of water, while God is the unlimited quantity of water. Although the quality is the same, the quantity is vastly different.

Parental problems while practicing Kṛṣṇa consciousness are nothing new. Look at the difficulty that Prahlāda Mahārāja went through with his father when he was practicing Kṛṣṇa consciousness. His father harassed him in so many different ways for practicing Kṛṣṇa consciousness. The persecution was so bad that Kṛṣṇa had to come and protect Prahlāda in the form of Lord Nṛsiṁhadeva.

We have to be very determined to surrender to Kṛṣṇa, even if our parents do not want us to. Although it would certainly be auspicious if you got your parents' blessing to practice Kṛṣṇa consciousness, you must not depend upon it. You must be determined to become Kṛṣṇa's pure devotee even if it is in defiance of their instructions.

People Sometimes Look Down on Devotees

I have subscribed to the Ultimate Self-Realization Course and feel truly privileged to receive Kṛṣṇa's divine mercy. (I am not, however so lucky to read it every day regularly.) I have a small query for which I would request your kind answer, please:

As we work toward Kṛṣṇa consciousness, the action of *māyā* is there in numerous ways. One of them is that the people around you start to look at you in a very lowly manner. They reduce their interactions with you such that one might take it for ignoring or disrespecting you. While one is moving toward Kṛṣṇa consciousness, one tends to get disturbed and feel frustrated at times when the world behaves in this manner. These and such feelings tend to put an impediment on achieving Kṛṣṇa consciousness. Please guide as to how to tackle this and continue our spiritual journey toward a more Kṛṣṇa-conscious life.

Ignore, Abhor, Adore

If others look down on you for your Kṛṣṇa consciousness, this is a great blessing from the Lord to help you break free from your material attachments and totally take shelter of Him. There is no reason to be disturbed. Even the greatest spiritual revolutionaries in history had to face similar impediments.

What happens is ignore, abhor, and adore:

In the beginning they ignore us.

Then when they notice that our example is a challenge to their life of unrestricted sense gratification, they abhor us.

But in the end, when they realize that Kṛṣṇa consciousness is the ultimate happiness, they will adore us.

How Does One Trust an Individual?

Again I have to approach you with my questions. I am wondering, how does one develop faith and trust in an individual? In the material world it sometimes just seems so difficult.

Only Trust Kṛṣṇa

One time Śrīla Prabhupāda said that the only person we can trust is Kṛṣṇa. So we really cannot trust anyone in this material world. What you should do, however, is trust people to the extent that they are surrendered to Kṛṣṇa and thus purely represent Him. This is why we put our complete trust in the spiritual master, because he purely represents Kṛṣṇa. So we can trust others, but only to the extent that they are fully surrendered to Kṛṣṇa.

Defeated in Debate

During conversation with my office friends at lunchtime yesterday, I presented the argument (which I had read a couple of times in your discourses) that since everything comes from something, there must be an origin for all that exists, and that that source is God. I presented the argument because I had thought it was good.

One of my friends said right away something to this effect: We can say that everything living and lifeless ultimately comes from molecules which come from atoms of elements, but nobody has disproved the possibility that atoms of hydrogen and carbon and other elements might have most amazingly existed forever - that is, that they never got created. He said that that possibility is equally awesome as the alternative possibility that atoms of some or all elements got created at either some single moment or over a time period in the distant past.

Then again, in the latter possibility, there might have been one creator of the atoms of elements or there might have been a committee of creators. All are conjectures. He said that he did not mind my presenting my whatever theology by identifying it as theology - that either a single God or a committee of Gods created atoms of elements and then molecules that form everything - but that he finds my presenting some flimsy argument as an irrefutable argument rather simple-minded.

I humbly admitted to him that what he said was right. I wanted to tell you what happened yesterday. So I am humbly writing you this note.

There Is Not One Shred of Evidence to Support His Theory

Don't ever admit that they are right just because you could not defeat them.

When we have practical experience that everything comes from something, it is more scientific to assume that this is a universal principle than it is to assume the opposite which has no basis in our practical experience.

His idea of matter having no origin is mere theory with not one shred of evidence. We have an entire universe full of evidence to establish the principle of cause and effect.

You cannot have a plurality of supreme beings because then they would no longer be supreme. Just like you cannot have many supreme courts; you can only have one supreme court. If there is more than one, none of them can be the supreme court.

Debating with materialists is a difficult but exciting art. Don't give up. Keep reading and chanting and pretty soon you will be able to defeat even the most erudite and stubborn of atheists!

Show Me that This Is Not a Cult

I've been hearing for many months from many people that this religion is a cult. I never entertained the thought, and I discarded it from my mind. But more and more I've been becoming concerned about this thought. More doubt and uncertainty has been wrapping itself around my mind. This religion has a few of the major qualities that it takes to be a cult. I'm a 12-year-old American looking for spiritual fulfillment and happiness (which this religion promises). There's nothing I want more than to be an eternal servant of the real God (which I'm unsure Who is) and to attain spiritual perfection. But I'm unsure if this is the right direction.

I want to believe this is the right way to go, but there is an enormous amount of confusion in my mind that can only be lifted by a true representative of the real

God. I don't want to waste my time, effort and money on what might be the wrong path to follow.

Please lift this doubt from my mind. I politely ask that you show me that this is not a cult. Convince me as if your life depended on it. If you can convince me, I'll endow as much energy as I possibly can into being 100% Kṛṣṇa conscious. But if you can't convince me, I'll consider cancelling my subscription.

Only Cheaters Label Genuine Religion as a Cult

When genuine religion is introduced in a world that is full of cheaters, the cheating so-called religionists will label it as a cult, a false religion. It is not proper to judge what is proper religion by popular votes. We take the words of God and the great spiritual masters of history to understand what is genuine religion.

I understand that you are not sure that Kṛṣṇa is God and are, therefore, hesitant to fully surrender unto Him. To alleviate your confusion you have to understand what is the proper definition for God. God is that person Who is the source of all that exists. In the *Bhagavad-gītā*, Kṛṣṇa clearly confirms that He is indeed the source of everything.

ahaṁ sarvasya prabhavo
mattaḥ sarvaṁ pravartate
iti matvā bhajante māṁ
budhā bhāva-samanvitāḥ

"I am the source of all spiritual and material worlds. Everything emanates from Me. The wise who perfectly know this engage in My devotional service and worship Me with all their hearts."

Bhagavad-gītā 10.8

It is not that only Kṛṣṇa declares that He is God. It is also declared by Lord Brahmā as follows:

īśvaraḥ paramaḥ kṛṣṇaḥ
sac-cid-ānanda-vigrahaḥ
anādir ādir govindaḥ
sarva-kāraṇa-kāraṇam

"Kṛṣṇa who is known as Govinda is the Supreme Godhead. He has an eternal blissful spiritual body. He is the origin of all. He has no other origin and He is the prime cause of all causes."

Brahma-saṁhitā 5.1

Arjuna reconfirms Kṛṣṇa's divinity as well:

arjuna uvāca
paraṁ brahma paraṁ dhāma
pavitraṁ paramaṁ bhavān
puruṣaṁ śāśvataṁ divyam
ādi-devam ajaṁ vibhum

āhus tvām ṛṣayaḥ sarve
devarṣir nāradas tathā
asito devalo vyāsaḥ
svayaṁ caiva bravīṣi me

"Arjuna said: You are the Supreme Personality of Godhead, the ultimate abode, the purest, the Absolute Truth. You are the eternal, transcendental, original person, the unborn, the greatest. All the great sages such as Nārada, Asita, Devala and Vyāsa confirm this truth about You, and now You Yourself are declaring it to me."

Bhagavad-gītā 10.12-13

Every other religious system in the world has some conception of God. The difference between this Kṛṣṇa consciousness system and the other systems is that in Kṛṣṇa consciousness we have clear, concise, precise, exact information about God. We know His most intimate names. We know the names of His close associates. We know exactly where He lives. We know exactly what His activities are, etc. Other religious systems are lacking in this detailed knowledge of God. They have only a vague understanding at best. Without clear knowledge of God, it is very difficult to achieve the perfection of existence, pure love of God. But if one has all detailed knowledge about God—about His unlimited power, beauty, renunciation, knowledge, wealth, and fame—it becomes very easy to develop pure love for Him and return to His eternal kingdom at the time of death.

If you are still having doubts regarding the authenticity of our process of self-realization, kindly let me know and I shall try my level best to destroy your doubts with the shining torchlight of transcendental knowledge.

Kṛṣṇa Equal to Everyone?

I have been so fascinated by Śrīla Prabhupāda's books, and now, due to your good job, I have taken to Kṛṣṇa consciousness. But my husband doesn't seem to like it. He is so engrossed in material things that he says he doesn't believe in Kṛṣṇa consciousness. I do my *japa* and go to the temple, but he doesn't like it. My question is: I am here today in this Kṛṣṇa consciousness because of Kṛṣṇa's mercy; so why is my husband an obstacle? If Kṛṣṇa made me Kṛṣṇa conscious, why not my husband? Please help me.

Some Take His Mercy, Some Don't

Kṛṣṇa is bestowing his mercy equally upon everyone so that they can all take to Kṛṣṇa consciousness and return home, back to Godhead. This is compared to the rainfall, which comes down everywhere without discrimination. But when the rain falls on a large, hard rock, it simply rolls off and does not penetrate that rock. And when the rain falls on the soft soil, it enters into that soil, thus enriching and nourishing it. In the same way, while those who are soft-hearted allow the mercy of Kṛṣṇa to enter into their hearts, those who are hard-hearted do not.

What makes one hard-hearted? Indulgence in sinful activities.

Then what can be done to soften the hearts of those who are hard-hearted, to give them a higher taste so they will give up sinful activities and chant the holy names? We must be soft-hearted towards them by giving them our loving kindness in the form of feeding them Kṛṣṇa *prasādam* (vegetarian food offered to Lord Kṛṣṇa with love and devotion) and telling them about their beautiful Lord Kṛṣṇa, Who will save them from all of their miseries. It is a special benediction of Lord Kṛṣṇa that the mercy of His devotee can act even more powerfully than His mercy alone. So you should always be very, very merciful to your husband and save him from his entanglement within the cycle of birth and death.

Difficulty with Spouse

I've been reading your emails since the beginning of this year, and I find them very inspiring. It is slowly changing my way of thinking for the better. I am now more conscious about my actions than before. I recently decided to abstain from eating meat, but the problem is that my spouse is having a problem with this. She does not want to accept this change of mine. How do I make her understand that all I am doing is following your teachings to improve my lifestyle? Please help, because this change of mine seems to be causing a strain in my relationship.

If She Truly Loves You

We take to Kṛṣṇa consciousness because it is the only way to become fully happy, free from all suffering. However, our family members may become unhappy with us when we adopt such an unfamiliar lifestyle. If that happens, we can ask them if they want us to be happy or not. Even if they do not want to follow this wonderful blissful pathway themselves, if they truly love us they will allow us to practice it so that we can become happy.

Surrendering to Kṛṣṇa– Transcending Karma - Cultivating Faith – Attaining A Higher Taste – Kṛṣṇa's Causeless Mercy

Wish Not Granted Is a Dilemma for Me

I have a very serious topic to discuss. We always hear success stories (followed by thanksgiving) about wishes granted to us by the Almighty. But suppose you have pledged something very dear to you, and the wish is not granted within a time frame in such a way that you 'missed the bus.' What do you do about your vow? This is a dilemma for me. Do advise me on this.

Make God's Wishes Your Wishes

The mistake we make when we approach God is that we approach Him with our wish list of what we want. This is the wrong approach. The proper way is that we should approach the Lord to see what He wants of us. We must give up our self-centeredness and become fully and purely God-centered. In such a state of mind, all our desires will be fulfilled, and we will feel complete peace and satisfaction at every minute for all of eternity.

How Can We Realize that Everything Belongs to Kṛṣṇa?

We know that everything belongs to Kṛṣṇa. But under illusion I think that I am independent. So how can we realize that everything belongs to Kṛṣṇa?

Only By Complete Surrender

The only way to realize practically that everything belongs to Kṛṣṇa is to offer everything you have to Kṛṣṇa. This is done by fully surrendering yourself unto Lord Kṛṣṇa's representative, the bona fide spiritual master.

What Would Kṛṣṇa Like Us To Do For Him?

I understand that we are the eternal emanations of Kṛṣṇa and that we are His eternal servants. We serve Kṛṣṇa in this life by serving His devotees, obeying the Spiritual Master, following the regulative principles, chanting, and becoming fixed in Kṛṣṇa consciousness. But how did Kṛṣṇa want us to serve Him before we rebelled and entered the material world, and how will we serve Him again when we attain the spiritual sky? In other words, what would Kṛṣṇa like us to do for Him?

Faithfully Follow His Instructions Given in the Bhagavad-gītā

You will find out how to serve Kṛṣṇa in your original spiritual identity only after you become a 100% pure devotee. In the meantime, to qualify yourself to reach that stage, you should fully surrender to following the instructions that Kṛṣṇa gives in the *Bhagavad-gītā*. You cannot artificially jump to the stage of knowing your original service and identity in the spiritual world.

What Does "Without Anxiety for Gain and Safety" Mean?

I am having difficulty understanding the verse in *Gītā* where Kṛṣṇa tells Arjuna that he should be beyond anxieties for "gain and safety." How does this relate to life in a world where one is always concerned with just that, "gain and safety?" One is always concerned with balancing one's checkbook, providing food for oneself and others, driving safely and protecting one's body, etc. So, in the regular state of human affairs, is one not to be concerned with "gain and safety?" I am particularly concerned with the safety issue, because I work in a capacity wherein I drive a vehicle transporting people to their jobs, and while in a way I understand that one should not be overly concerned with the possibility of an accident, for Kṛṣṇa has promised all protection, still, one must be alert not to cause or to be involved in an accident.

And, regarding the protection Kṛṣṇa promises Arjuna in verse 18.66 of the *Gītā*, I realize that the protection is concerning one's *sādhana* and the safety and security of the soul, and the protection He will give so we can render devotional loving service unto the pure devotee.

But in practical affairs in this world of *saṁsāra*, how does one strike a happy balance between being beyond anxiety for safety and being aware that, as Śrīla Prabhupāda says, "*padaṁ padaṁ yad vipadām*," there is danger at every step?

Do the Needful and Depend on Kṛṣṇa

Making proper arrangements for safety and being in anxiety about it are two different things. You do your best, and then depend on Kṛṣṇa. Just like now, I am flying to Europe. I have my seat belt on. This is a recommended safety procedure. However, this does not guarantee that I will arrive safely tomorrow morning in Amsterdam. I have taken all the safety precautions that are reasonable, but this material world remains a dangerous place in spite of my safety arrangements.

I know that I will not die unless and until Kṛṣṇa sanctions it. I put myself fully in His hands, that He is welcome to take my life whenever He wants to. Therefore, because I am fully dependent on Him, I am not in anxiety. But at the same time, as a matter of duty, I take whatever precautions are within my power. For the other things that are beyond my control, I depend fully on Kṛṣṇa.

My Love Is Not Accepted

I think that although I am trying to dedicate my life for Kṛṣṇa consciousness, I am not able to get Kṛṣṇa consciousness.

Sometimes - although I know that it is not real happiness - I am an addict for the materialistic world. Sometimes I am an addict for girls. I think that love is great, but the girl is not giving me her love. She is searching after someone else. I give my real love, but nobody is accepting my love. What can I do?

Give Your Love to Kṛṣṇa for Perfect Reciprocation

The only place you can give your love and be fully satisfied is to Kṛṣṇa. If we try to give and receive love only in this material world, it is sure and certain that we will be frustrated. Kṛṣṇa says in the *Bhagavad-gītā* that if you give all of your love to Him, He will personally protect whatever you have and personally deliver to you what you may be lacking.

So now just try to give your love fully and exclusively to Kṛṣṇa. When you water the root of the tree, all of the leaves and branches are nourished. In this way, when you give all of your love to Kṛṣṇa, your love becomes fully and perfectly distributed to all living beings, and you become unlimitedly happy.

How Can I See Kṛṣṇa?

I want to see Kṛṣṇa and talk to Him. How can I see Kṛṣṇa?

Anoint Your Eyes with the Salve of Love

If you want to see Kṛṣṇa you must fully surrender unto Him. Then that day will surely come when you will see Him face to face, eye to eye. This is described in the *Brahma-saṁhitā* as follows:

premāñjana-cchurita-bhakti-vilocanena
santaḥ sadaiva hṛdayeṣu vilokayanti
yaṁ śyāmasundaram acintya-guṇa-svarūpaṁ
govindam ādi-puruṣaṁ tam ahaṁ bhajāmi

"I worship Govinda, the primeval Lord, who is Śyāmasundara, Kṛṣṇa Himself with inconceivable innumerable attributes, whom the pure devotees see in their heart of hearts with the eye of devotion tinged with the salve of love."

Brahma-saṁhitā 5.38

You must anoint your eyes with salve of love. That salve is obtained by submissively hearing the topics of the Lord and rendering humble service to the Lord's servants.

How Will Following Kṛṣṇa Affect My Life?

I am a South Indian follower of Lord Śiva. How will following Lord Kṛṣṇa affect my life?

Marvelously

It will affect your life marvelously. By worshipping Lord Kṛṣṇa you will give the greatest pleasure to Lord Śiva. Lord Śiva is a devotee of Kṛṣṇa. Therefore, nothing gives him greater pleasure than to see that you are devotee of Kṛṣṇa.

In the *Śrīmad-Bhāgavatam* we find the following statement by Lord Śiva:

yaḥ paraṁ raṁhasaḥ sākṣāt
tri-guṇāj jīva-saṁjñitāt
bhagavantaṁ vāsudevaṁ
prapannaḥ sa priyo hi me

> "Any person who is surrendered to the Supreme Personality of Godhead, Kṛṣṇa, the controller of everything — material nature as well as the living entity — is actually very dear to me."
>
> *Śrīmad-Bhāgavatam* 4.24.28

Guarantee of Salvation?

You have stated in a recent lesson in the Ultimate Self-Realization Course that a person has to overcome *māyā* and leave aside the animal life, which relates to the material enjoyments.

Now my question to you is: For a person who becomes Kṛṣṇa conscious - or for that matter, follows the path of spiritualism - what is the guarantee that he will attain *mokṣa*, or salvation, from the cycle of life and death? As nobody knows what happens after death, there is no guarantee or assurance of the same.

Kṛṣṇa Guarantees

The guarantee is given by Lord Sri Kṛṣṇa. That all-attractive Lord states in the *Śrīmad Bhagavad-gītā*:

janma karma ca me divyam
evaṁ yo vetti tattvataḥ
tyaktvā dehaṁ punar janma
naiti mām eti so 'rjuna

"One who knows the transcendental nature of My appearance and activities does not, upon leaving the body, take his birth again in this material world, but attains My eternal abode, O Arjuna."

Bhagavad-gītā 4.9

So, on the absolute words of Lord Śrī Kṛṣṇa we can understand that if we fully absorb ourselves in Kṛṣṇa consciousness, we are 100% guaranteed to enter the spiritual world, the abode of Lord Śrī Kṛṣṇa, when we leave our present body.

What Is More Important?

What is more important: to love Kṛṣṇa or to take knowledge about Kṛṣṇa?

To Know Him Is to Love Him

Love of Kṛṣṇa is the ultimate perfection of existence, but knowledge of Kṛṣṇa is essential because it helps us to love Him. To know Him is to love Him. How can you love somebody you don't know?

Misfortune

When a material or spiritual misfortune happen to us, should we take it as a sign that we are committing offenses, be it material or spiritual?

No Such Thing for a Devotee

A devotee of the Lord humbly accepts all misfortune as the reactions due to him for his past misdeeds. And at the same time, he perceives all forms of fortune and misfortune as being the greatest good fortune because he sees how the Lord is bestowing unlimited mercy upon him at every step.

Whether he is suffering the reactions from his past misdeeds or being rewarded for his past pious activities, he takes either as the blessing of Kṛṣṇa to help him come closer and closer to Him. There is a beautiful verse from the *Śrīmad-Bhāgavatam* that helps us to understand this properly:

tat te 'nukampāṁ su-samīkṣamāṇo
bhuñjāna evātma-kṛtaṁ vipākam
hṛd-vāg-vapurbhir vidadhan namas te
jīveta yo mukti-pade sa dāya-bhāk

"My dear Lord, any person who is constantly awaiting Your causeless mercy to be bestowed upon him, and who goes on suffering the resultant actions of his past misdeeds, offering You respectful obeisances from the core of his heart, is surely eligible to become liberated, for it has become his rightful claim."

Śrīmad-Bhāgavatam 10.14.8

How Can I Get That Higher Taste?

Now I am trying to surrender to Kṛṣṇa. It is not easy, because I remember my old habits. How can I get that higher taste for Kṛṣṇa, and forget dark pleasures?

What can I do to better understand Śrīla Prabhupāda's books? How can I get more inspiration to read?

Serve Those Who Have It

I am very happy that you are trying to surrender to Kṛṣṇa because this is the purpose of our existence, to be fully surrendered unto Lord Śrī Kṛṣṇa.

The easy way to get a strong taste for Kṛṣṇa consciousness - strong enough to overpower all of our old material tastes - is to lovingly serve those devotees who have a very strong taste for Kṛṣṇa consciousness.

By getting this strong taste, you will naturally be inclined to read Śrīla Prabhupāda's books more, and with that increased reading will come increased understanding.

How Can I Give Up Lust?

How can I give up lust? Sometimes it is a very strong desire, and it is still there within my heart. I really want to give up this desire and to be Kṛṣṇa conscious. Please help me.

Experience Genuine Pleasure on the Spiritual Platform

Lust is a desire to enjoy the contact between your material senses and the object of the material senses in the form of a member of the opposite sex. In order for sex pleasure to be enjoyable, one has to come down to the platform of identifying the body with the self. This is a false concept which prolongs one's enslavement within the cycle of birth and death. By coming down to the bodily platform, on which there is only a perverted reflection of actual pleasure, one simply cheats himself out of factual happiness in the worst possible way. Why it is the worst way? Because there is no material pleasure greater than sex pleasure, there is nothing that reinforces the false bodily conception of the self more than sex. It causes one to have a very strong identity as a male or as a female, and thereby transcendental realization becomes impossible.

The first step in giving up lust is to remember that you are not your body and that sex pleasure does not actually touch the soul. You should realize that sex is superficial, not real pleasure, and that therefore it is tenth-class pleasure at best. Remember that the first-class pleasure, the real pleasure, comes from re-establishing one's lost relationship with the Supreme Personality of Godhead. There is no pleasure anywhere in the universe that comes even close to the pleasure derived at every minute by one who has awakened the dormant love of God within his heart. So if one is seeking real and lasting pleasure and satisfaction, he should know that the best pleasure and satisfaction comes from developing one's love for God.

The next step is to experience genuine pleasure on the transcendental platform. This pleasure, once tasted, will be experienced as a higher taste, a greater pleasure than what can be derived by any amount of material sense gratification. This pleasure can be easily experienced by one who engages himself in the *saṅkīrtana-yajña*, the congregational chanting of the Holy Names of God in the association of advanced transcendentalists.

Hare Kṛṣṇa, Hare Kṛṣṇa, Kṛṣṇa Kṛṣṇa, Hare Hare
Hare Rāma, Hare Rāma, Rāma Rāma, Hare Hare

How Can I Feel Kṛṣṇa?

How can I feel Kṛṣṇa? Can I see Him if possible? How can all my sins be washed away? Again and again I commit sins which Kṛṣṇa does not want me to do. How can I get out of this material world that I do not want to be part of?

Read Bhagavad-gītā Seriously

I am very happy that you are feeling that I am speaking to you according to the Lord's desire. Actually this is a fact. In our Kṛṣṇa consciousness movement we do not invent our own teachings. We simply deliver to our students the pure teachings of Kṛṣṇa exactly as they are spoken by the Lord in the *Bhagavad-gītā*. We do not add or subtract anything.

Therefore, because our words are the words of Lord Śrī Kṛṣṇa, they are fully potent to deliver our students from the clutches of birth and death.

You have asked how you can feel Kṛṣṇa. If you will read the *Bhagavad-gītā* very seriously, you will feel how Lord Kṛṣṇa is present before you and is instructing you.

In regard to seeing Kṛṣṇa, Lord Brahmā describes as follows in the *Brahma-saṁhitā*:

premāñjana-cchurita-bhakti-vilocanena
santaḥ sadaiva hṛdayeṣu vilokayanti
yaṁ śyāmasundaram acintya-guṇa-svarūpaṁ
govindam ādi-puruṣaṁ tam ahaṁ bhajāmi

"I worship Govinda, the primeval Lord, who is Śyāmasundara, Kṛṣṇa Himself with inconceivable innumerable attributes, whom the pure devotees see in their heart of hearts with the eye of devotion tinged with the salve of love."

Brahma-saṁhitā 5.38

The process for washing all your sins away is described by Lord Kṛṣṇa in the *Bhagavad-gītā*:

sarva-dharmān parityajya
mām ekaṁ śaraṇaṁ vraja
ahaṁ tvāṁ sarva-pāpebhyo
mokṣayiṣyāmi mā śucaḥ

"Abandon all varieties of religion and just surrender unto Me. I shall deliver you from all sinful reactions. Do not fear."

Bhagavad-gītā 18.66

If you want to stop sinning you must get a higher taste. We take to sinful activities as a less intelligent form of enjoyment. But those who are highly intelligent can easily stop sinful life because they derive unlimited pleasure from chanting the holy names of God:

Hare Kṛṣṇa, Hare Kṛṣṇa, Kṛṣṇa Kṛṣṇa, Hare Hare
Hare Rāma, Hare Rāma, Rāma Rāma, Hare Hare

Your final question is, how can you get out of this material world. If by Kṛṣṇa's grace one is fortunate enough to come under the shelter of the bona fide spiritual master, by the mercy of Kṛṣṇa he receives lessons on how to execute devotional service to the Supreme Lord. In this way, he receives a clue of how to get out of his continuous struggle, up and down, within the material world. Therefore, the Vedic injunction is that one should approach a spiritual master. The Vedas declare:

tad vijñānārthaṁ sa gurum evābhigacchet

"If you want to realize the transcendental science, you must approach the bona fide spiritual master."

Muṇḍaka Upaniṣad 1.2.12

Similarly, in *Bhagavad-gītā* (4.34) the Supreme Personality of Godhead advises:

tad viddhi praṇipātena
paripraśnena sevayā
upadekṣyanti te jñānaṁ
jñāninas tattva-darśinaḥ

"Just try to learn the truth by approaching a spiritual master. Inquire from him submissively and render service unto him. The self-realized soul can impart knowledge unto you because he has seen the truth."

Śrīmad-Bhāgavatam (11.3.21) gives similar advice:

tasmād guruṁ prapadyeta
jijñāsuḥ śreya uttamam
śābde pare ca niṣṇātaṁ
brahmaṇy upaśamāśrayam

"Any person who seriously desires to achieve real happiness must seek out a bona fide spiritual master and take shelter of him by initiation. The qualification of his spiritual master is that he must have realized the conclusion of the scriptures by deliberation and be able to convince others of these conclusions. Such great personalities, who have taken shelter of the Supreme Godhead, leaving aside all material considerations, are to be understood as bona fide spiritual masters."

Similarly, Viśvanātha Cakravartī, a great Vaiṣṇava, also advises:

yasya prasādād bhagavat-prasādaḥ

"By the mercy of the spiritual master one receives the mercy of Kṛṣṇa."

This is the same advice given by Śrī Caitanya Mahāprabhu:

guru-kṛṣṇa-prasāde pāya bhakti-latā-bīja

"By the mercy of Guru and Kṛṣṇa one receives the seed of *bhakti*."

Caitanya-caritāmṛita Madhya 19.151

So this is essential. To get out of this material world, one must come to Kṛṣṇa consciousness. This is achieved by taking shelter of a pure devotee. Thus one can become free from the clutches of matter go back home, back to Godhead.

Love of God

How can one know that he is in love of God?

No More Material Attractions

If one has actually developed love of God, he will no longer be attracted to anything in this world. He will fully surrender Himself for the rest of his life to only execute the will of the Lord.

Free Will or Karma?

Is whatever we do a result of our previous actions, is it due to our free will, or is it a mixture of both?

For example: One person, Kamal, goes to a temple to donate some money as charity, and other person, Madan, goes to some place and robs a bank. So was Kamal's decision to give charity due to his activities in his past life, or did he use his free will? And was Madan's decision to rob a bank due to his activities in his past life or to his free will?

Devotees Utilize Their Free Will

As long as we act for material sense gratification, we are under the stringent grip of *karma cakra*. But when we are engaged in any one of the nine types of devotional service, we are acting on the platform of free will.

How Can We Overcome Lust?

How can we overcome lust? Can you tell me the process for overcoming lust?

Beg Kṛṣṇa

The only way to overcome lust is to realize that the pleasure of *bhakti* is millions of times greater than the pleasure of lust, and then to beg Kṛṣṇa with great intensity to save you from lust every time lusty desires come.

Getting God's Love

Is it possible to have material desires and also get God's love?

In Different Forms

Everyone is getting God's unlimited love at every minute. Those who have material desires are getting His love in the form of the fulfillment of their material desires according to their *karma*. Those who have no material desires are getting His love in the form of the supreme reward of the Lord's direct association at every minute. So each of us decides which is more attractive to us: the Lord's material energy or the Lord Himself. In this connection Lord Śrī Kṛṣṇa explains in the *Bhagavad-gītā*:

ye yathā māṁ prapadyante
tāṁs tathaiva bhajāmy aham
mama vartmānuvartante
manuṣyāḥ pārtha sarvaśaḥ

"As all surrender unto Me, I reward them accordingly. Everyone follows My path in all respects, O son of Pṛtha."

Bhagavad-gītā 4.11

How Can I Be a Sincere Devotee?

I try every day to surrender my life to Kṛṣṇa, but I keep postponing it. So I need Kṛṣṇa to grant me favor in order to fully neglect this world of illusion.

By the Mercy of the Devotees

Kṛṣṇa has already given you the favor to become free from the world of illusion by bringing you into contact with His devotees. Now you must simply take full advantage of the association of the Lord's devotees by learning from them what is the science of *bhakti* and how to successfully execute it.

How Can We Control Desires?

How can we control our desires? Generally, people have desires to travel to new places, to wear new clothes, to eat delicious foods, to earn more money, to live a sophisticated life, to enjoy at every moment - the desires go on and on. It seems that we are more bodily conscious than spiritually conscious. But for everything there is an end. In order to lead a contented life, to be happy with what we have, we need the blessings of Kṛṣṇa and Guru.

If we get such desires, how can we control them? Many people around us say things like, "You will look good if you wear this. Why did you miss the chance to travel to new places? Why can't you eat all sweets?"

Desires multiply day by day. I want to know how to put a restriction on these desires. I seek your help to guide me better. I must realize that nothing is great other than being Kṛṣṇa conscious.

Go Deeper into Kṛṣṇa Consciousness

If you will simply go deeper into the nectarean ocean of Kṛṣṇa consciousness, you will taste so much nectar that nothing of this world will be able to compete with it.

This is confirmed in the following verse from the *Bhagavad-gītā*:

viṣayā vinivartante
nirāhārasya dehinaḥ
rasa-varjaṁ raso 'py asya
paraṁ dṛṣṭvā nivartate

> "The embodied soul may be restricted from sense enjoyment, though the taste for sense objects remains. But, ceasing such engagements by experiencing a higher taste, he is fixed in consciousness."
>
> *Bhagavad-gītā* 2.59

Will I Attain Higher Heights?

I have been following your guidance for over a year now and carefully reading "Thought for the Day." I am quite amazed at your ability to publish ever-fresh ideas and observations in your newsletter.

If I keep following, obeying, studying and chanting, will I be able to reach anywhere near those heights in thought? I reckon this sounds like a vain aspiration, but higher thoughts and higher levels of consciousness are something I desire. I feel I can come closer to understanding God in that way. How can I think like you?

If You Do What I Have Done

Yes, you will be able to advance in Kṛṣṇa consciousness to very high levels, where you will be having at every minute ever-fresh realizations about Lord Kṛṣṇa and your relationship with Him. This is not only possible - it is guaranteed that this will happen for you, if you will carefully chant your 16 rounds of the Hare Kṛṣṇa *mahā-mantra* every day and strictly follow the regulative principles of freedom.

If you want to be able to think like me, then you should do the same thing that I have done. You must fully surrender yourself to Guru and Kṛṣṇa.

How Can We Defy Our Destiny?

How can we defy our destiny? Am I really falling short of my expectations, or am I falling short of Kṛṣṇa's expectations?

Unlimited Room for Hope

There are two entirely different destinies awaiting you. And you have full freedom to make your choice. One is on the spiritual plane, and the other is on the material plane. Your destiny on the material plane is to experience birth, death, old age and disease repeatedly for an unlimited number of births through 8,400,000 different species. And your destiny on the spiritual plane is to live in full freedom an eternal, ever-youthful, all-blissful, all-existence, in the wondrous, divine atmosphere of the spiritual sky.

So which destiny do you prefer? You have to make your choice.

If you prefer to remain within the confining chains of *karma*, you do this by dedicating your life to the principle of material sense gratification both for yourself and for those with whom you associate.

If you prefer the unfettered freedom of eternal spiritual existence, you must take training in the self-realization science from a bona fide spiritual master. Kṛṣṇa would like you to return to His abode to eternally render Him loving service. But He does not force Himself upon you. Know for certain that whichever pathway you choose to follow will take you to your particular destination, either the repetition of birth and death or the supreme bliss of pure Kṛṣṇa consciousness. Now which one will it be for you?

How Do You Have So Much Enthusiasm?

You travel all over the world. You must see so many chaotic and miserable bodies, and souls who are completely drowned in material desires. I often wonder what a difficult task is being undertaken by you and others in ISKCON. I can only wish and pray to Śrī Hari that may He bless you all with His mercy and strength to save as many souls as possible by making them Kṛṣṇa conscious.

Don't you ever get tired or fatigued by such long journeys and constant traveling? How do you have so much enthusiasm, and where do you get this energy from? Do you never get troubled by any soul who might show disregard toward Śrī Hari? I am sure you must have come across lots of such fallen souls who openly criticize Śrī Kṛṣṇa. Don't you feel irritated when somebody says bad things about our beloved Śrī Hari? How do you keep yourself balanced in all situations? You travel so much, but you still get time to reply to your distant disciples' emails. This is just incomprehensible to me.

By the Mercy of Śrīla Prabhupāda

Yes, sometimes we become physically exhausted and must rest.

My enthusiasm is a blessing from Śrīla Prabhupāda. He ordered me to always be enthusiastic. We try to present Krsna so attractively, with the most intelligent and thoroughly honest marketing strategies, so that everyone will want to become His devotee.

Actually everyone does want to surrender to Kṛṣṇa. It's just that they have forgotten their eternal relationship with Him. If they are reminded in a compassionate way, they will gladly resume their original identity.

We may be irritated, but we respond with love and compassion, acting under the power and blessings of the previous *ācāryas*. This destroys any irritation that we may feel, and it destroys others' irritation, too.

Going Back to Godhead – Attaining Perfection – Pure Devotion

How Do We Know Kṛṣṇa Fully?

Lord Srī Kṛṣṇa states that even at the time of death, if one remembers Him one will attain salvation. But how will he get self-realization if he only remembers Kṛṣṇa at the time of death? And how will one know Him fully if he does not know him in this life?

A pure devotee, such as you, will know Him fully because you are fully engaged in Kṛṣṇa's service and are very dear to Kṛṣṇa. What will be one's position in the spiritual world compared to yours?

It has been stated that only through a spiritual master will one's prayers be effective. What about those people who pray every day but do not have a spiritual master? How will they attain salvation? There are millions of people who pray, yet they don't know that without a spiritual master their prayers will not be effective. What will happen to those people?

Remember Kṛṣṇa, Always

Your questions are very intelligent. The fact is that unless one practices remembering Kṛṣṇa throughout his life, he will not be able to remember Him at the time of death.

When a soul goes back to Godhead he regains whatever his eternal identity is in the spiritual world. It has nothing to do with what he was doing in the material world except that the bona fide spiritual master he surrenders to in this material world will remain as his eternal spiritual master in the spiritual world.

If one sincerely prays in a mood of total surrender to the Lord, he will be guided to take shelter of the Lord's representative, the bona fide spiritual master. The masses of people who are praying for material purposes do not receive this special mercy from the Lord. Because they are praying for material things, the Lord grants their prayers by keeping them in this material world birth after birth.

What Am I Working Toward?

I have a question about what happens after reaching the spiritual goal. I'm fairly certain that I understand what is required to be on the path to Godhead through your e-course and teachings. However, I'm not certain about what happens at the end of this material life if I become a perfect devotee. I understand the concept of not wanting to come back, but what am I working toward?

Also, there are some terms used frequently that do not make sense. What is "Godhead" and what is the relevance of "lotus feet?" Thank you for your assistance.

Being Fully Absorbed in Kṛṣṇa

If you are fully absorbed in Kṛṣṇa consciousness at the time of death, you will return to Kṛṣṇa. You will regain your original form in the spiritual world and eternally serve Lord Kṛṣṇa there in one of five different varieties of relationships.

"Godhead" literally means "divinity" as in "Godhood" or "God-ness." The term "Supreme Personality of Godhead" refers to any of the various *viṣṇu-tattva* forms. The original *viṣṇu-tattva* form is Kṛṣṇa, and the others are expansions from Him: Balarāma, Rāma, Nārāyaṇa, Mahā-Viṣṇu, etc.

"Lotus feet" means that those feet remove all fears of this material existence. In this connection Śrīla Prabhupāda has stated:

"The time of death is compared to crossing a vast ocean. It is very fearful. One doesn't know where he will go in the next life. And at every step there is danger in the material world. But for one who has taken shelter at the lotus feet of Lord Kṛṣṇa, that vast, dangerous ocean of birth and death becomes shrunk up to no more than the impression made in mud by a calf's hoof print. There is danger, but the devotee doesn't care for it. Just like if a gentleman is riding by in a carriage and he passes a small puddle, he considers it insignificant."

Am I Suffering from the "Grass is Greener" Syndrome?

I have been coming to the local ISKCON temple and reading the material written by Śrīla Prabhupāda (and few others). One recurring theme that I keep seeing is, "We are souls who have lost our identity, and our sole aim is to return Back to Godhead."

My question is: By having such desires, am I (are we) not suffering from the syndrome that is popularly known as "the grass is always greener on the other side"?

I've done that far too many times in life. For example, I used to feel that working life was better than student life. I used to feel that residing in US was better than residing in India, and so on.

I have to realize that each place in the material world has its own virtues and vices. None is absolutely better than any other in the material world. What is so different about Kṛṣṇa's abode? What have I forgotten?

Liberation from the "Grass is Greener" Syndrome

What you have forgotten is the difference between relative truth and Absolute Truth.

You have rightly observed how in this material world we have a tendency to think that the grass is greener on the other side of the fence, that some other situation is better than our present situation. I observed this tendency on my last world lecture tour. Many people think they would like to go to the Fiji Islands to enjoy the wonderful tropical atmosphere there. But I noticed in Fiji that the people want to get out of Fiji and go somewhere where they can earn more money. From this, someone might conclude that our desire to go back to the spiritual world is another manifestation of the "grass is greener" syndrome. But this is not the fact.

It is the "grass is greener" mentality that brought us to this material world in the first place. When we can finally fully give up this "grass is greener" tendency, we can then return to our original home in the spiritual world. The fish may think that the grass is greener on the land, but if he tries to live on the land, he will die a miserable death. In a similar way, we have abandoned our natural habitat in the spiritual world, thinking that the grass is greener somewhere else - and now we are suffering like anything.

The way out of this suffering condition is to free ourselves from this "grass is greener" mentality and return to our natural position in that wondrous Spiritual Sky. This makes perfect sense because no matter what our situation is in this material world, we are not fully satisfied with it. We can never be satisfied here because this is not our natural habitat.

If we say that every desire to change our position is a manifestation of the "grass is greener" tendency, this is tantamount to saying that there is no Absolute Truth, that everything is relative. But under careful analysis we can see that there must indeed be an Absolute Truth. Why? Because it is philosophically impossible to negate the existence of the Absolute Truth. If someone states, "There is no Absolute Truth," we will then ask him, "Are you absolutely sure?" He cannot say "yes," because to do so would be asserting an absolute, namely that there is no absolute. But according to his philosophy that there is no absolute, he cannot assert an absolute. Therefore, he cannot negate the existence of the Absolute, and there must indeed be an Absolute Truth.

So in conclusion, switching from one position to another in the relative world is a manifestation of the "grass is greener" syndrome. But the desire to return to our original, natural position in the realm of the Absolute Truth is the pathway of escaping the "grass is greener" syndrome, not another manifestation of it.

What Is the Final State of Realization?

What are the symptoms when one advances in Kṛṣṇa consciousness, and what is the final state of realization?

I am wondering what a devotee should aspire for when he remains steadfast in Kṛṣṇa consciousness. When a devotee chants *śuddha-nāma,* the pure name, what kind of mellow does he relish at the final state of realization?

What is the mood of the great Vaiṣṇava Ācāryas while chanting the Hare Kṛṣṇa *mahā-mantra*?

Is it possible for all devotees to be as perfect as Śrīla Prabhupāda? If one cannot attain that perfection, can he still attain the highest abode of Goloka-dhāma? Can you please give some insight as to what Śrīla Prabhupāda has instructed his disciples and what the ideal devotee should aspire for after he comes to Kṛṣṇa consciousness?

Pure Love of Godhead

You asked what are the symptoms when one advances in Kṛṣṇa Consciousness. The devotee will manifest the following symptoms:

1. He is very kind to everyone.
2. He does not make anyone his enemy.
3. He is truthful.
4. He is equal to everyone.
5. No one can find any fault in him.
6. He is magnanimous.
7. He is mild.
8. He is always clean.
9. He is without possessions.
10. He works for everyone's benefit.
11. He is very peaceful
12. He is always surrendered to Kṛṣṇa.
13. He has no material desires.
14. He is very meek.
15. He is steady.
16. He controls his senses.
17. He does not eat more than required.
18. He is not influenced by the Lord's illusory energy.
19. He offers respect to everyone.
20. He does not desire any respect for himself.
21. He is very grave.
22. He is merciful.
23. He is friendly.
24. He is poetic.
25. He is expert.
26. He is silent.

The final state of realization is Kṛṣṇa *prema*, pure love of Godhead.

When a devotee remains steadfast in Krsna consciousness, he should always aspire to faithfully carry out the instructions received from his spiritual master.

You asked what kind of mellow a devotee relishes at the final state of realization when he chants *śuddha-nāma,* the pure name. When we chant the Hare Kṛṣṇa *mahā-mantra*, then we are elevated to the platform of transcendental love.

The mood of the great Vaiṣṇava Ācāryas while chanting the Hare Kṛṣṇa *mahā-mantra* is that they are relishing the direct association of the Supreme Personality of Godhead.

All devotees can be as perfect as Śrīla Prabhupāda if they fully surrender to Lord Śrī Kṛṣṇa.

You ask that if one cannot attain that perfection, can he still attain the highest abode of Goloka-dhāma. One can attain that perfection. This is required for entering into Goloka-dhāma, the Lord's supreme abode.

Śrīla Prabhupāda instructed his disciples to become spotlessly pure devotees of Kṛṣṇa. This is what we all must aspire for: complete, total surrender at the lotus feet of Kṛṣṇa.

Is Hatred Wrong?

Is hatred against fellow human beings wrong?

The Enlightened Love All

Anybody who hates their fellow human beings is in a state of illusion because those who are enlightened with spiritual vision never hate anyone. This is confirmed as follows in the *Śrī Īśopaniṣad*:

yas tu sarvāṇi bhūtāny
ātmany evānupaśyati
sarva-bhūteṣu cātmānaṁ
tato na vijugupsate

> "He who sees systematically everything in relation to the Supreme Lord, who sees all living entities as His parts and parcels, and who sees the Supreme Lord within everything never hates anything or any being."
>
> *Śrī Īśopaniṣad* Mantra 6

Buy why do you mention only human beings? A Kṛṣṇa-conscious being loves everyone, including the animals, and therefore does not eat animals. One cannot eat the object of his affection.

Kṛṣṇa – The Form of Kṛṣṇa – Descriptions of the Spiritual World

Am I Living in the Spiritual World or in the Material World?

Sometimes it is becoming difficult to know whether I am living in spiritual world or material world. Sometimes I feel very spiritual and sometimes very material. Why is this world so contradictory?

How to Always Live in the Spiritual World

In this connection you should understand that in the ultimate issue there is only one world, the spiritual world. Within that spiritual world there is a covered portion known as the material world. Even while living in this material world, if a living entity's consciousness becomes uncovered by the mercy of Guru and Kṛṣṇa, that living entity is no longer living in the material world. He is living in the spiritual world.

That you are feeling sometimes spiritual and sometimes material means that your consciousness is not yet fully uncovered. You are still under the influence of the three modes of material nature. If you will stick very tightly to the process of Kṛṣṇa consciousness, especially the regular chanting of at least 16 rounds of *japa*, following our four regulative principles (no illicit sex, no intoxication, no meat-eating, no gambling), and using all of your free time for preaching Kṛṣṇa consciousness, I can assure you that very soon the covering cloud of *māyā* will be burned away by the brilliant Kṛṣṇa sun, and you will always feel that you are in the spiritual world.

There is nothing contradictory within the vast dominion of God. It is only when our consciousness becomes covered that we perceive things as contradictory.

What Is Kṛṣṇa Enjoying?

We all know that Lord Kṛṣṇa is Supreme Personality of Godhead. He is the origin of everything. He is the supreme enjoyer. But what is He enjoying? Would God feel lonely if He hadn't created us?

Kṛṣṇa Enjoys Everything

Kṛṣṇa enjoys everything. He enjoys being Himself. He enjoys wearing a peacock feather in His hair. He enjoys his relationship with Nanda Mahārāja and Mother Yaśodā. He relishes His pastimes with the cowherd boys and the cowherd girls. The list of the ways He enjoys and the relationships He enjoys is unlimited.

There is no question of Kṛṣṇa's being lonely because He has been eternally emanating us from Himself to enjoy loving relationships with us. When we say that God created us, it does not refer to a specific moment in time. It describes the relationship between us - souls who are being eternally manifested by God - and God Himself, the eternal manifester or creator of all that exists.

Why Did Kṛṣṇa Have No Children?

Though Lord Kṛṣṇa had eight wives, why did He not have any children? I am a beginner in the quest for spiritual freedom. I am still in my material consciousness. But this question has been bothering me for a while.

He Had Over 100,000

Kṛṣṇa had 16,108 wives of whom 8 were prominent, namely Rukmiṇī, Satyabhāmā, Jāmbavatī, Nāgnajitī, Kālindī, Lakṣmaṇa, Mitravindā and Bhadra. By each wife He had ten sons. Therefore, he had a total of 161,080 sons.

Did Kṛṣṇa Have Any Daughters?

In response to today's "Thought for the Day," you informed Ravi that Kṛṣṇa begot ten sons from each of his 16,108 wives. Why is it that Kṛṣṇa begot only sons? Why didn't he beget daughters?

Kṛṣṇa Had 16,108 Daughters

Kṛṣṇa did not only beget sons. He begot daughters also, more than anyone else. No one can compete with Him. He had 16,108 daughters, one by each of His queens. This is confirmed by the great Vaiṣṇava Bhāgavatam commentator, Śrīla Śrīdhara Swami.

Proof for Kṛṣṇa's Form

While I was talking with my friend, she asked me, "How can you prove that God has a specific Deity form? How can you be assured that He has that particular form of Kṛṣṇa - bluish-black in color, flute in hand, and wearing ornaments?"

Kṛṣṇa Proves It

Kṛṣṇa proves that He has a form by revealing Himself to those who worship Him with love. He reserves the right not to expose Himself to those who are envious.

If your friend is envious of God, there is nothing that you will be able to say that will turn her toward the Lord. Kṛṣṇa reveals Himself only to those who approach Him with love.

Can Our Relationship with Kṛṣṇa Be Changed?

Does the devotional relationship that each living entity has with Kṛṣṇa ever change - e.g. can the living entity change from loving and serving Him as a mother to loving and serving Him as a friend or conjugal lover?

Is there any degree of difference between the sound *oṁkāra* and the Hare Kṛṣṇa *mahā-mantra*?

Hare Kṛṣṇa, Hare Kṛṣṇa, Kṛṣṇa Kṛṣṇa, Hare Hare
Hare Rāma, Hare Rāma, Rāma Rāma, Hare Hare

If not, then why is it advised by Lord Caitanya to chant the *mahā-mantra* rather than the syllable *oṁ*?

Yes, There Is Full Freedom in the Spiritual World

Because there is full freedom in the spiritual world, if one chooses to change his relationship with Kṛṣṇa, he is free to do so. This is confirmed by my spiritual master, His Divine Grace Śrīla Prabhupāda.

One who is not able to chant the personal name of God may chant *oṁ* instead and still receive transcendental benefit. However, the personal name of God is more effective for attracting His mercy, just like the difference between someone addressing you, "Hey, you" or someone addressing you as "Rebecca." You will naturally be more favorably inclined towards someone who addresses you in a more personal way.

Can You Give a Glimpse of the Spiritual Realm?

Could you give us a quick glimpse into the scenery of the spiritual realm - our destination, Goloka Vṛndāvana, as described by our previous guru *paramparā*?

Meditation on Goloka Vṛndāvana

Your request is glorious. That supreme spiritual abode, known as Goloka Vṛndāvana, is wonderful - millions and billions of times greater than anything we can even begin to try to conceive of in our wildest imagination. Just as the lotus flower is the epitome of serenity and beauty here in this material world, that transcendental Goloka Vṛndāvana is the topmost lotus of all places of residence within the totality of existence. It is indeed the embodiment of the ultimate sweetness.

Lord Brahmā had a vision of Goloka Vṛndāvana and described it as follows:

"There exists a divine lotus of a thousand petals, augmented by millions of filaments, in the transcendental land of Goloka. On its whorl, there exists a great divine throne on which is seated Śrī Kṛṣṇa, the form of eternal effulgence of transcendental bliss, playing on His divine flute resonant with the divine sound, with His lotus mouth. He is worshiped by His amorous milkmaids with their respective subjective portions and extensions and also by His external energy [who stays outside] embodying all mundane qualities."

Every cubic inch of that all-wondrous transcendental abode is brilliant with the most dazzling splendor. It is magnificent, ever-fresh, and a place of unceasing enlivenment for all those who are so fortunate as to reside there. The source of its divine flavor is none other than the Supreme Personality of Godhead, Śrī Kṛṣṇa, who forever resides there engaged in unlimited varieties of all-attractive pastimes.

That all-merciful Original Person is described as follows by Lord Brahmā in the *Śrī Brahma-saṁhitā*:

veṇuṁ kvaṇantam aravinda-dalāyatākṣam-
barhāvataṁsam asitāmbuda-sundarāṅgam
kandarpa-koṭi-kamanīya-viśeṣa-śobhaṁ
govindam ādi-puruṣaṁ tam ahaṁ bhajāmi

> "I worship Govinda, the primeval Lord, who is adept in playing on His flute, with blooming eyes like lotus petals with head decked with peacock's feather, with the figure of beauty tinged with the hue of blue clouds, and His unique loveliness charming millions of Cupids."
>
> *Brahma-saṁhitā* 5.30

By hearing about, describing, and remembering that topmost planet in the Spiritual Sky we gradually develop more and more of an inclination for residing there, and thus qualify ourselves to eventually be transferred there.

Is Kṛṣṇa in the Fifth Dimension?

I once heard from a speaker at my local ISKCON center that, according to the *Śrī Brahma-saṁhitā*, God or Kṛṣṇa is situated in the fifth dimension, yet I find no such clear reference in that text - which I've read numerous times. Elsewhere I've read that the fifth dimension is where one comes face to face with Gopal Kṛṣṇa in Braj (Vraja Dhāma). Is this your understanding as well?

How to Enter the Fifth Dimension

Śrīla Prabhupāda very simply describes Kṛṣṇa consciousness as the fifth dimension after the previous four dimensions of *dharma* (religiosity), *artha* (economic development), *kāma* (sense gratification), and *mokṣa* (impersonal liberation).

As soon as one becomes initiated by the bona fide spiritual master, taking his instructions very seriously, he immediately enters the fifth dimension of eternity, knowledge and bliss - far, far beyond the three-dimensional, mirage-like reality of birth, death, old age, and disease.

Why Is Kṛṣṇa Blackish?

I have heard many reasons for Kṛṣṇa to be blackish, but what is the actual reason?

Because He Likes It

The color of the Lord has not been imagined by an artist. It is described in authoritative scripture. The color of the Lord is not poetical imagination. There are authoritative descriptions in the *Brahma-saṁhitā*, *Śrīmad-Bhāgavatam*, *Bhagavad-gītā* and many of the *Purāṇas* of the Lord's body, His weapons and all other paraphernalia.

Why does somebody prefer a certain color of shirt? It is a matter of taste. Kṛṣṇa is the supreme controller and supreme enjoyer. He is free to manifest any color according to his preference and taste. He is not obliged to follow anyone else's rules and regulations. He can be whatever color He wants to be, and He chooses the bluish-blackish complexion because that is what is most pleasing to Him.

Our Form in the Spiritual World?

When you say we enjoy or experience bliss in Kṛṣṇa's abode, I want to know: What will be our form or senses to experience that bliss (as we will not have any physical body or senses that we use in this material world)?

Eternity, Knowledge and Bliss

You have asked me, "What will be our form or senses to experience that bliss (as we will not have any physical body or senses that we use in this material world)?"

You will have a particular form composed of eternity, knowledge and bliss in the spiritual world - a form such as a cowherd boy or a cowherd girl. You will have fully spiritual senses in a fully spiritual body that never gets sick, never gets old, and never dies. You will enjoy life forever in the service of Kṛṣṇa, experiencing the most beautiful and wonderful things for all of eternity in unlimited varieties of loving pastimes with Lord Kṛṣṇa and His unlimited devotees. You will see, hear, feel, smell, and taste just like you do here, but in a way that is completely free of the difficulties experienced in the material world, such as birth, death, old age, and disease.

The Māyāvādī philosophers cannot imagine a happy state with functioning senses. Therefore, they say that after liberation one becomes senseless. This is a comparable to a sick man in the hospital who is nauseated by the thought of eating. Once he recovers his health, he regains his appetite and is very happy to enjoy eating many varieties of foods. While very ill he could not consider eating, but once recovered, he completely forgets the disgust he formerly felt for eating when he was very sick.

Is Kṛṣṇa Blue Because He Is Vast?

Maybe Śrī Kṛṣṇa is pictured as blue because He is as vast as the blue ocean and as vast as the blue skies. Could this be the reason?

No. He Desires to Be Blue

I am very happy to hear from you, as you are one of my very dear students who is rendering me tangible service to assist me in my mission.

Śrīla Prabhupāda amazed us, his disciples, when he told us about Kṛṣṇa's color. He told us that the sky is a reflection of Kṛṣṇa's bodily effulgence; therefore, it is blue. In other words, it's not that we imagine Kṛṣṇa as being blue because He is vast like the sky or the ocean. No, it's the other way around. Because the sky and ocean are reflections of Kṛṣṇa, therefore they are blue. Everything originates in God. All of the colors of the rainbow are present in Him. He can be any color that He desires to be. He manifests a bluish complexion because that is what He likes the best, and that is what His intimate devotees like the best.

Does Kṛṣṇa Have Form?

I have a perplexing problem. All my life, I was taught in the secular church that God/Kṛṣṇa has no form but is this brilliant white light - so beautiful that we could not look upon Him with our naked eye. This, of course, explains "pure awareness" to me. It makes much sense.

Now, within the *bhakti-yoga* teachings, I learn that Lord Kṛṣṇa took form in many ways and incarnations. We have pictures of Him. At the same time, we are not to attach ourselves to the physical, for we are not of this body. At this point, I cannot "attach" myself to any one picture of Lord Kṛṣṇa, no matter how beautiful, because of this earlier teaching. He is mightier than this "physical" form. In one sense I would say that this helps lead me away from physical attachment — period. Perhaps if I can keep my eye on this, then I can "detach" my mind from the shell and begin to realize that this is not the soul that resides within. Yet, I must keep the photos of Lord Kṛṣṇa upon my altar and accept them as "Him."

Forgive my ignorance, but I seem to be going through a state of confusion. Is there any way you could help clear this up for me?

Kṛṣṇa Has the Ultimate Form

You have stated that Kṛṣṇa is mightier than His physical form. In this connection please try to understand that Kṛṣṇa's form is not physical or material. Rather it is metaphysical, or transcendental. There is no question of Kṛṣṇa being mightier than His form because He and His form are one and the same. Kṛṣṇa's form does not in any way limit or restrict Him. That form is the source of all that exists.

Since Kṛṣṇa's form is not material, but rather fully spiritual, to meditate on His form does not cause bodily identification. It liberates the devotee from bodily identification. The brilliant white light is the beautiful aura emanating from Kṛṣṇa's transcendental form. In the *Śrī Īśopaniṣad* we find this prayer in which the devotee prays as follows:

pūṣann ekarṣe yama sūrya prājāpatya
vyūha raśmīn samūha
tejo yat te rūpaṁ kalyāṇa-tamaṁ
tat te paśyāmi yo 'sāv asau puruṣaḥ so 'ham asmi

> "O my Lord, O primeval philosopher, maintainer of the universe, O regulating principle, destination of the pure devotees, well-wisher of the progenitors of mankind, please remove the effulgence of Your transcendental rays so that I can see Your form of bliss. You are the eternal Supreme Personality of Godhead, like unto the sun, as am I."
>
> *Śrī Īśopaniṣad* Mantra 16

The devotee does not want to be blinded by the brilliant white light. He prays to see the form from which that light is coming. This is the perfection of the eyes. Kṛṣṇa's form is not physical. It is metaphysical. But this does not mean that He is formless. He has a form which is completely spiritual.

The Māyāvādīs teach that God is formless. But this is not a fact. The Lord has a form composed of eternity, knowledge and bliss.

Why Dhotīs and Sārīs?

Today I read "Thought for the Day" and the answer to the person who asked the reason for the Indian clothes and Indian names. Personally I love seeing people dressed like that and with names which all have a meaning connected with Kṛṣṇa.

Can you please explain how it helps facilitate their Kṛṣṇa consciousness? I did not understand that part.

I heard a follower say that a *sārī* is a spiritual dress and that according to Vaisnava etiquette it should never touch the ground. But why is a *sārī* a spiritual dress? And is a *dhotī* a spiritual dress, too? Is there a book that I can read on Vaiṣṇava etiquette? I would like very much to learn more.

Spiritual World Acculturation

Sometimes people mistakenly think that *sārīs, dhotīs* and devotional names are Indian. The real fact is that these are the culture of the spiritual world. Because Indian culture was formerly strongly connected with the culture of the spiritual world, *sārīs, dhotīs* and devotional names were also the fashion of the ancient Indian culture.

The ultimate self-realization science, Kṛṣṇa consciousness, is the process of reviving one's original, eternal identity as a resident of the spiritual world. Just as one who is going to relocate to a foreign country can prepare himself nicely for going there by practicing the language and culture of that country, one who would like to achieve the spiritual world can practice the culture of the spiritual world even while residing here in the material world by chanting Hare Kṛṣṇa and by adopting the style of the spiritual world.

It is not the system to choose a spiritual name for yourself. The spiritual name is given by the spiritual master at the time of initiation. Śrīla Prabhupāda revealed to us that a devotee's spiritual name is so potent that if he can simply remember his own spiritual name of the time of death, he will attain the supreme spiritual perfection of going back to home, back to Godhead.

The best guidebook on Vaiṣṇava etiquette is the *Śrī Caitanya-caritāmṛta.* In it you can read how the followers of Śrī Caitanya Mahāprabhu associated with each other in an amazingly transcendental way that was totally beyond this material world.

And - although you will feel that you are never touching the ground if you become solidly fixed in Krsna consciousness - there is no rule that a *sārī* or *dhotī* cannot touch the ground.

Proof of the Spiritual World?

I would like to know the proof of whether there really is any spiritual world and its topmost planet, Goloka Vṛndāvana. Sometimes I suspect its existence. I am sorry for my foolishness, but still want some proof so that my mind will be clear.

From the Reports of Others

How do you know for sure that there is a place called Russia? Have you ever been there? Perhaps not. But you know for sure that it exists from the reports of others who have been there.

In the same way, how do we know for sure that the spiritual world and Goloka Vṛndāvana exist? From the reports of others who have been there.

Does Lord Rāma Have a Separate Form?

I originally thought that Lord Rāma and Lord Kṛṣṇa are same. But in the purport of *Bhagavad-gītā* Chapter 15, verse 7, it is stated that Lord Rāma is a personal expansion of Lord Kṛṣṇa. So there must be separate *vigraha* (form) of Lord Rāma, as they are not same. Please explain.

Kṛṣṇa Manifests as Rāma

Kṛṣṇa manifests as Rāma. So Rāma is the same as Kṛṣṇa. This is just like a lit candle which can have its flame transferred to a second candle. It is the same flame although it appears to be a different flame. Kṛṣṇa is the "original flame," who also manifests Himself as Lord Rāma.

Three Spiritual Potencies

Would you elaborate on the three spiritual potencies – *sandhinī*, *saṁvit* and *hlādinī*?

Eternal Existence, Knowledge and Bliss

The material nature is displayed in three modes: goodness, passion and ignorance. Similarly the spiritual nature is displayed in three modes: *sandhini*, *saṁvit* and *hlādinī*.

Sandhinī is eternal existence

Saṁvit is knowledge.

Hlādinī is bliss.

Faceless God

You mentioned in yesterday's "Thought for the Day": "At my lecture last Saturday night in Reno, a member of the audience stated that God has no face. When I asked her how she can say that when Kṛṣṇa clearly reveals Himself as a person with a face, she said that Kṛṣṇa is just a vessel for the faceless God. Her philosophy does not make any sense."

Generally I can agree with both of you. But why do we need to have a picture of God? Nobody knows for sure what God looks like, nor what Kṛṣṇa looks like. Why do we need to have a picture at all? Islam refuses pictures of Allah. Also the Jews were punished by Moses when they started praying to the Golden Calf while Moses was on Mount Sinai receiving the Ten Commandments. Picturing gods was a very ancient method to make people believe or just to be afraid of some invisible power. It was a method of the upper class to keep the lower class under control. Even Jesus himself said: Those are blessed who believe (read the story of St. Thomas)!

There is a certain risk that a particular face or figure becomes more important than the message. And I think in our times, with out strong scientific background, praying to some fantasy pictures is far from reality. As a child I believed in God as an old man with a long big white beard and angry, powerful eyes (just like the picture in the Sistine Chapel in the Vatican, Rome). Is that wrong? A picture in the biggest and most absolutistic church? Or is your picture wrong? Finally, no one can tell the truth - all is a guess! It is fine if some people need an instrument for their faith; it is also okay if some people don't need anything but the feeling inside.

It will be always difficult for people of a different ethnological background to identify with the religion of a different culture and different time period. We would not pray to the sun anymore, but the Aztecs did. It was okay, but as we know today it was unnecessary because scientifically the sun is the sun. Not a god. We could think the same way about the picture of Kṛṣṇa. It's a picture, nothing more. We have to see everything in a historical context. Don't you believe that?

Facing the Reality of Kṛṣṇa's Face

You are incorrect in thinking that nobody knows what Kṛṣṇa looks like. Throughout the ages, pure devotees of the Lord have been able to see Him face to face. The paintings we have of the Lord have been confirmed as authentic by those who have actually seen the Lord.

As to why we are interested to see the Lord, the reason is that we are trying to develop our love for Him more and more. Everybody keeps photographs of their loved ones in order to remember and to stimulate their feelings of affection for them. This same thing can be done by keeping photographs of the Lord. By seeing such photos of the Lord we can nurture and increase our feelings of love for the Lord.

In an ordinary photograph of a person, that person is not present in their photograph. But because Kṛṣṇa, or God, is Absolute, He is personally present in His photograph. Therefore, those who keep and honor such photographs are greatly blessed by the personally present Lord on their pathway of spiritual perfection.

You have stated, "Finally, no one can tell the truth - all is a guess!" Thus according to your own philosophy, you are not in a position to judge the legitimacy or illegitimacy of the Lord's photographs. But in spite of your openly stating that no one can tell the truth, you are doing an about-face on your own statement by declaring such photographs to be fantasy pictures. If you feel that no one can tell the truth, then you must also feel that you are not qualified to tell the truth. Do you understand this simple logic?

Not everything is to be seen in an historical context, because Lord Kṛṣṇa exists eternally as an eternal youth in the spiritual world, completely outside of the limits of history. If we want to understand the Absolute Truth in full, we have to face the reality of Lord Kṛṣṇa's face.

Kṛṣṇa's Form According to Our Form?

On planet Earth, we have the image of Lord Kṛṣṇa similar to our own human form. On other planets, will the other inhabitants understand that Lord Kṛṣṇa has a form similar to theirs, as they see themselves?

Our Form According to Kṛṣṇa's Form

Some people argue that man imagines a form of God according to his own form. According to this philosophy, which is known as anthropomorphism, if dogs had a conception of God, they would imagine Him to be a super dog. And if cats had a conception of God, they would imagine Him to be a super cat.

But this is not at all the case. It is not true that we imagine the form of God according to our own form. The actual situation is that God has a form and we, being His children, have a form similar to His. Even in the Bible it is stated, "And God created man in His own image."

All living beings, no matter what species they are, have as their original spiritual form a human form.

So Kṛṣṇa has the same form for everyone. It does not matter which planet they live on or what kind of body they have. Anyone who develops pure love of God will be able to see and directly associate with that same person Kṛṣṇa, who has the most beautiful transcendental form.

Non-Physical Form?

I am having a hard time with "transcendental." Does this word mean basically "non-physical?" If so, then how is it that Kṛṣṇa has/is a transcendental body? I have always equated "body" with "form." I am schooled as an artist but also have mystical inclinations. How can something non-physical have a form?

Spiritual Form Is Permanent, Material Form Is Temporary

"Transcendental" means beyond this material existence. Kṛṣṇa's body is transcendental because it is not composed of material elements. It is instead composed of eternity, knowledge and bliss. This is confirmed as follows in the *Brahma-saṁhitā*:

īśvaraḥ paramaḥ kṛṣṇaḥ
sac-cid-ānanda-vigrahaḥ
anādir ādir govindaḥ
sarva-kāraṇa-kāraṇam

> "The Supreme Personality of Godhead is Kṛṣṇa. He has a body which is composed of eternity, knowledge and bliss. He has no beginning, for He is the beginning of everything. He is the cause of all causes."
>
> *Brahma-saṁhitā* 5.1

Even the Bible confirms that God has form because it says that man is created in the image of God.

Why do you think that something non-physical cannot have form? The spiritual elements also have tangibility. In fact, they are more tangible than the material elements because the material elements come into being at a certain time and then are destroyed at the time of the universal devastation. While countless phases of creation, maintenance and destruction are going on for the material elements, the spiritual elements of eternity, knowledge and bliss are always existing in an undisturbed way. Therefore, spiritual form is permanent, and material form is temporary.

Why Does Kṛṣṇa Wear a Peacock Feather?

Why does Śrī Kṛṣṇa wear a peacock feather in His hair instead of other kinds of feathers?

Because It's So Beautiful

Kṛṣṇa always wears a peacock feather in His hair because He is very fond of the peacock feather. Kṛṣṇa, or God, is a person. He has likes and dislikes. Because He has likes and dislikes, and because we are part of parcel of Him, we also have likes and dislikes. Because He has a taste for decorating Himself with a peacock feather, He does so. When we consider how beautiful the peacock feather is, we can immediately understand why Kṛṣṇa likes it so much.

Kṛṣṇa's Pastimes – The Spiritual Platform – Eternal Relationships

I Want To Know More About Sakhyam

I want to know more about *sakhyam*, spiritual friendship with Lord Kṛṣṇa. I have read an article about it in Back to Godhead Magazine and I'm really attracted to it.

Sakhyam, a Highly Advanced Stage of Devotion

Here's what Srila Prabhupada says about *sakhyam* (worshipping the Lord as a friend) in his purport to *Śrīmad-Bhāgavatam* 7.5.23-24:

> *Sakhyam*. In regard to worshiping the Lord as a friend, the *Agastya-saṁhitā* states that a devotee engaged in performing devotional service by *śravaṇam* and *kīrtanam* sometimes wants to see the Lord personally, and for this purpose he resides in the temple. Elsewhere there is this statement: "O my Lord, Supreme Personality and eternal friend, although You are full of bliss and knowledge, You have become the friend of the residents of Vṛndāvana. How fortunate are these devotees!" In this statement the word "friend" is specifically used to indicate intense love. Friendship, therefore, is better than servitude. In the stage above *dāsya-rasa*, the devotee accepts the Supreme Personality of Godhead as a friend. This is not at all astonishing, for when a devotee is pure in heart the opulence of his worship of the Deity diminishes as spontaneous love for the Personality of Godhead is manifested. In this regard, Śrīdhara Svāmī mentions Śrīdāma Vipra, who expressed to himself his feelings of obligation, thinking, "Life after life, may I be connected with Kṛṣṇa in this friendly attitude."
>
> —end of quote—

Sakhyam is a highly advanced stage of devotion realized by pure devotees who are eternally situated in a mood of friendship for the Lord. Such devotees are known as *siddhas*, or devotees who have already achieved perfection. In our present stage we are known as *sādhakas*, devotees who are striving to achieve perfection. The *sakhyam* described above cannot be artifically imitated or attained. It is awarded only to devotees who have been completely purified of all material contamination.

Inquiry About Life Under Kṛṣṇa

I can understand that this material life is very short and futile. Let me know how we can be happy in life under Kṛṣṇa, what will be in that world. Then I can be inspired. If we escape from the material life cycle, then where will we be?

Kṛṣṇaloka, The Spiritual Abode of Lord Sri Kṛṣṇa

When we surrender to Kṛṣṇa, He guarantees that we will have an eternal life, full of bliss and knowledge. The spiritual abode of Lord Śrī Kṛṣṇa is called Kṛṣṇaloka. It is the topmost planet in the spiritual world. Kṛṣṇa descended to this earth planet 5,000 years ago, bringing with Him many of His eternal associates from Kṛṣṇaloka. He came here for the purpose of manifesting a replica of His spiritual abode here on this planet in Vṛndāvana, India. His all-blissful Vṛndāvana pastimes on this planet give us a glimpse into the unlimitedly blissful pastimes going on at this very minute in Kṛṣṇaloka.

If you will fully surrender yourself now unto Kṛṣṇa, then at the time of death you will be transferred to Kṛṣṇaloka. If you will carefully read *Bhagavad-gītā As It Is* by His Divine Grace A.C. Bhaktivedanta Swami Prabhupada, you will gain perfect knowledge of how to surrender yourself to Kṛṣṇa.

Doubts About Goloka Vṛndāvana

I have a few doubts regarding Goloka Vṛndāvana (the topmost planet in the spiritual world).

What kinds of activities can we do when we reach Goloka Vṛndāvana (Kṛṣṇa's place), and what kind of service does God expect from us there?

How did we come into this material world for the first time?

Our Engagements in Goloka Vṛndāvana

When the spirit soul returns to his original home with Kṛṣṇa in the spiritual world, he will be engaged just like the devotees who served Kṛṣṇa in Vṛndāvana 5,000 years ago. These amazing relationships between Kṛṣṇa and His devotees are described in the *Śrīmad-Bhāgavatam* and the *Kṛṣṇa* book. The devotees participate with Kṛṣṇa in His various pleasure pastimes in a mood of unlimited enjoyment.

In the liberated stage we serve Kṛṣṇa according to our original natural tendency, in a mood of neutrality, servitorship, friendship, parenthood, or conjugal love.

We came to this material world because we revolted against the supremacy of Kṛṣṇa. This was our foolish mistake. We must, therefore, learn the art of how to fully surrender to Kṛṣṇa so we can go back to our original position in the spiritual world.

Why Does Kṛṣṇa Have Pastimes?

Kṛṣṇa is *ātmārāma*, in a self-satisfied state. But one of the primary reasons behind His having pastimes is to increase His own pleasure. If Kṛṣṇa is *ātmārāma*, then why does He want more pleasure?

To Please His Devotees

The fact is that Kṛṣṇa is *ātmārāma*; He is fully self-satisfied. He does not require anything else beyond Himself to be satisfied. He is fully self-sufficient because His very transcendental existence is total bliss. Therefore, He is not in need of anything. But out of His unlimited kindness upon His parts and parcels, the living entities, to enable them to be fully happy, He allows them to serve Him in multi-varieties of ways: in neutrality, as a servant, as a friend, as a parent, or as a conjugal lover.

Can We Be Purely Kṛṣṇa Conscious in Our Present Body?

Śrīla Prabhupāda says that should pray to Kṛṣṇa this way: "Dear Lord, please come quickly and bring me to your place."

How are we to understand "your place"? Can we be purely Kṛṣṇa conscious without leaving the body? Or must we be transferred to Goloka Vṛndāvana (the topmost planet in the spiritual world) to fully associate with Kṛṣṇa, the Supreme Personality of Godhead?

You Can See Kṛṣṇa Face to Face

When we pray to Lord Kṛṣṇa to take us back to His place, we are asking Him to take us back to the spiritual world. But it is also a fact that if we become purely Kṛṣṇa conscious even within this body, Lord Kṛṣṇa will personally reveal Himself to us. We will be able to see Him face to face.

This is described as follows by His Divine Grace Śrīla Prabhupāda in his purport to *Śrīmad-Bhāgavatam* 1.1.10:

> Similarly, the living entities, who are molecular parts of the whole spirit, are separated from the Lord by the artificial covering of *māyā*, illusory energy. This illusory energy, or the curtain of *māyā*, has to be removed, and when it is so done, the living entity can see the Lord face to face, and all his miseries are at once removed.

How Can New Govardhana be in Australia?

Kindly explain how New Govardhan can be created in Australia. Lord Kṛṣṇa lifted Govardhan in Vṛndāvana, and that is the original Govardhan. He did not lift it in Australia, so how can New Govardhan be recreated in Australia?

By Celebrating the Lord's Pastimes

To call this place New Govardhana is not at all inappropriate. This name was personally approved by one of the greatest spiritual masters in the history of the universe, His Divine Grace A.C. Bhaktivedanta Swami Prabhupāda. In a letter to Hari Śauri Das, dated 1 May 1977, His Divine Grace stated regarding this property where I am staying, "Yes, the name 'New Govardhana' will be very appropriate for your farm."

Because the devotee of the Lord always carries the remembrance of the Lord's pastimes within his heart, wherever he goes he is always living in the Lord's holy *dhāma*. By remembering Kṛṣṇa as the lifter of Govardhana Hill here, this place becomes transformed into Govardhana.

Anyone who understands the secret of transcendental meditation will appreciate how this place has become transformed into New Govardhana by being engaged in Kṛṣṇa's service. Although this may not make any sense from the mundane point of view, it is easily understood and realized by those who are on the transcendental plane.

How Shall We Know Our Rasa?

How shall we know our rasa, our eternal relationship with Kṛṣṇa in the spiritual world? Can we desire to know while we are still in this material body? Can we feel it?

Cultivate Pure Bhakti

Some are curious to know what is their *rasa*, their eternal relationship with the Lord in the spiritual world. In this connection there is a saying, "Curiosity killed the cat." Why is a strong statement made regarding what seems like a very spiritual desire, to know one's *rasa*?

The reason is this:

We must first focus our desire on becoming Kṛṣṇa's pure devotees. Then, after attaining pure devotional service, our *rasa*, our eternal relationship with the Lord, will be revealed. If we try to realize our *rasa* before we attain pure devotion, we will not be able to attain pure devotion, and thus we will never be able to realize what is our *rasa*.

In this connection Śrīla Narottama dāsa Ṭhākura has written:

rūpa-raghunātha-pade hoibe ākuti
kabe hāma bujhabo se jugala-pīriti

"When shall I be very much eager to study the books left by the six Goswāmīs? One has to learn of the conjugal loving affairs of Rādhā-Kṛṣṇa through the teachings of these six Goswāmīs."

If we want to know the intimate details of Śrī Śrī Rādhā-Kṛṣṇa's pastimes, including what is our eternal spiritual identity, we must cultivate pure *bhakti*, pure devotional service, by first humbly submitting ourselves as disciples at the lotus feet of the six Goswāmīs of Vṛndāvana and all the great Vaiṣṇava ācāryas.

It is only in this way that we will gradually, as we advance ourselves along the pathway of pure devotion, be able to understand the intimate details of the spiritual world and our relationship with the Lord there.

Are We Free to Choose Our Relationship with Krsna?

Is it true that we are completely free to choose what manner of relationship we want to have with Kṛṣṇa - devotee, friend, parent, etc.?

Only in the Perfectional Stage

When one attains the perfectional stage of pure Kṛṣṇa *bhakti* and thus becomes qualified to serve the Lord in one's eternal form, one re-enters the Lord's eternal pastimes in the spiritual world and serves the Lord according to one's natural desire and inclination. However, such a position is available only after one becomes completely perfect, free from all material desires.

This perfectional stage cannot be imitated by someone who is still under the influence of material desires. If the neophyte tries to jump artificially to this stage, he will be greatly hindered in his spiritual progress.

The method for attaining this state of pure desirelessness, in which one has no other desire except for serving the Lord, is to take complete shelter of a bona fide spiritual master and, under his guidance, strictly follow the rules and regulations of the *bhakti-yoga* system. Then one gradually becomes completely pure and qualified to be fully reinstated into one's original, eternal identity, in which one has full freedom to serve the Lord according to one's natural inclination. Even after attaining this perfectional stage, one still remains the humble servant of his spiritual master because the guru/disciple relationship is an eternal relationship.

Is Kṛṣṇa Consciousness Static?

No one can understand Kṛṣṇa completely, in all His manifestations. So does this mean that even in the spiritual world the *jīvas*, the spirit-souls, know only a part of the knowledge about God? And does everyone in the spiritual world simply know his own perspective of Kṛṣṇa, or do they all have a whole general vision of God?

No. It Is Ecstatic!

Because Kṛṣṇa's glories are expanding unlimitedly at every second, even Lord Kṛṣṇa - with His unlimited ability to know everything - has a hard time expanding His Kṛṣṇa consciousness fast enough to keep pace with His ever-expanding glories. So what to speak of the *jīvas*, who are His tiny parts and parcels? They are eternally engaged in expanding their Kṛṣṇa consciousness more and more and more for all of eternity. The conclusion is that Kṛṣṇa consciousness in never static. It is always ecstatic, expanding more and more for all of eternity.

Another aspect of this answer is that everyone perceives Kṛṣṇa in terms of their own particular relationship with Him. This feature of different *jīvas*, different spirit-souls, perceiving Kṛṣṇa in different ways was prominently manifested when Kṛṣṇa was in the wrestling arena of King Kaṁsa. This amazing pastime is described as follows in the *Kṛṣṇa* book:

> When Kṛṣṇa entered the wrestling arena with Balarāma and Their friends, He appeared differently to different people according to their different relationships (*rasas*) with Him. Kṛṣṇa is the reservoir of all pleasure and all kinds of *rasas*, both favorable and unfavorable. He appeared to the wrestlers exactly like a thunderbolt. To the people in general He appeared as the most beautiful personality. To the females He appeared to be the most attractive male, Cupid personified, and thus He increased their lust. The cowherd men who were present there looked upon Kṛṣṇa as their own kinsman, coming from the same village of Vṛndāvana. The impious kṣatriya kings who were present saw Him as the strongest ruler and their chastiser. To the parents of Kṛṣṇa, Nanda and Yaśodā, He appeared to be the most loving child. To Kaṁsa, the king of the Bhoja dynasty, He appeared to be death personified. To the unintelligent, He appeared to be an incapable personality. To the yogīs present, He appeared to be the Supersoul. To the members of the Vṛṣṇi dynasty He appeared to be the most celebrated descendant. Thus appreciated differently by different kinds of people present, Kṛṣṇa entered the wrestling arena with Balarāma and His cowherd boyfriends. Having heard that Kṛṣṇa had already killed the elephant Kuvalayāpīḍa, Kaṁsa knew beyond doubt that Kṛṣṇa was formidable. He thus became very much afraid of Him. Kṛṣṇa and Balarāma had long arms. They were beautifully dressed, and They were attractive to

all the people assembled there. They were dressed as if They were going to act on a dramatic stage, and They drew the attention of all people.

—end of quote from *Kṛṣṇa* book—

So Kṛṣṇa is so amazingly wonderful that everyone has their own personal, unique relationship with Him that continues to grow deeper and deeper, becoming sweeter and sweeter for all of eternity.

I remember in Kaliningrad when you expressed that you found this Kṛṣṇa consciousness to be interesting. I can assure you that there is nothing more interesting than this. It is so unlimitedly interesting that it continues to become more and more interesting for all of eternity. And what makes it even more interesting is that it is uniquely interesting for each and every devotee, and thus becomes even more interesting when the devotees share their realizations of Kṛṣṇa with each other. This point is confirmed in the *Bhagavad-gītā* as follows:

mac-cittā mad-gata-prāṇā
bodhayantah parasparam
kathayantaś ca māṁ nityaṁ
tuṣyanti ca ramanti ca

"The thoughts of My pure devotees dwell in Me, their lives are fully devoted to My service, and they derive great satisfaction and bliss from always enlightening one another and conversing about Me."

Bhagavad-gītā 10.9

So kindly fully dedicate yourself to an eternal life full of Kṛṣṇa consciousness. I can assure that you will find nothing more interesting in all the fourteen worlds.

Did Govardhana Have Potency Before?

Did Govardhana Hill have any potency before Lord Śrī Kṛṣṇa lifted it?

Potency Enhanced by Kṛṣṇa's Touch

Govardhana Hill certainly had great potency from the very beginning because he was originally in the spiritual world. He descended to the earth just for the purpose of participating in Śrī Śrī Rādhā-Kṛṣṇa's pastimes. He first appeared in Śālmali Dvīpa where he was accepted as king of the mountains. Later he was brought to Vraja-maṇḍala (Śrī Vṛndāvana Dhāma) by the sage Pulastya. So Govardhana's great spiritual potency was already there, even before being lifted by Kṛṣṇa. But after being lifted by Kṛṣṇa, Govardhana's spiritual potency was enhanced millions and billions of times.

Dispelling Myths – Misconceptions – The Vedic Version

Does This Saying Make Sense?

I came across the following saying: "Helping hands are better than praying lips." Does this make sense, or is it an excuse for escaping the mode of submission to the Almighty by prayers?

Lips Praying and Hands Helping

On the surface this statement may appear to be very nice to say that helping hands are better than praying lips. But if we delve into it a little deeper we see that it is incomplete. Why?

For our basic survival we depend upon rain both for drinking and for food production. Without rain the human society would die. What we can do with our hands for producing rain? Kṛṣṇa explains in the *Bhagavad-gītā* that rain comes as a result of *yajña* (sacrifice). What is the prescribed *yajña* for this age? The chanting of the Hare Kṛṣṇa *mahā-mantra*:

Hare Kṛṣṇa, Hare Kṛṣṇa, Kṛṣṇa Kṛṣṇa, Hare Hare
Hare Rāma, Hare Rāma, Rāma Rāma, Hare Hare

So the ideal formula for a healthy life is to first pray with the lips chanting Hare Kṛṣṇa at least 16 rounds daily on our *japa* beads in the early-morning, pre-dawn hours. This will bring the rain. Then we use our helping hands to milk the cows and to till the soil for producing food. We should not think that we can simply survive by the effort of our helping hands. We depend on God for the rain. Therefore we should always put first things first, by first praying with our lips and then engaging our helping hands in taking full advantage of the gifts of God.

Is God Formless?

You have tried to negate Śaṅkarācārya's interpretation of Veda as distortion. This is not right. After all, the ultimate form of worship is formless *nirguṇa* Brahman. It is all about awareness and consciousness. The means can be any method. The Guru's guidance is to be followed.

Simultaneously With and Without Form

You have nicely stated that the guru's guidance is to be followed. So why do then you argue with the Guru's guidance? You are contradicting your own words.

I am not negating Śaṅkarācārya's interpretation of the Vedas as distortion. Śaṅkarācārya is an incarnation of Śiva. It is he himself who negates his interpretation of the Vedas as distortion. I am simply repeating what Śaṅkarācārya has himself stated about his nirgunistic teachings.

Lord Śiva was ordered to incarnate as Śaṅkarācārya and introduced a misinterpretation of the Vedic literatures that was similar to Buddhism for the purpose of defeating Buddhism and reintroducing Vedic culture back into India. Then, in keeping with the Lord's plan, other *ācāryas* came who gradually presented the full and complete understanding of Vedic wisdom. That Śaṅkarācārya (Lord Śiva) knew that his nirgunistic presentation of Vedic wisdom was misleading and incomplete is confirmed by his own statement to goddess Durgā as is quoted below from the *Padma Purāṇa*:

māyāvādam asac-chāstraṁ
pracchannaṁ bauddham ucyate,
mayaiva kalpitaṁ devi
kalau brāhmaṇa-mūrtinā

> "[Lord Śiva informed goddess Durgā, the superintendent of the material world:] 'In the Age of Kali I take the form of a *brāhmaṇa* and explain the Vedas through false scriptures in an atheistic way, similar to Buddhist philosophy.'"

Therefore your statement - "this is not right" - is not right.

You are stating, "After all, the ultimate form of worship is formless *nirguṇa* Brahman." But this is half-hen logic. Brahman is both *saguṇa* and *nirguṇa* (with qualities and without qualities). Why do you only want to worship half of Brahman? This is incomplete.

When it is said that Brahman is *nirguṇa* (without qualities), this means that Brahman is completely devoid of any material qualities. And when it is said that Brahman is *saguṇa* (with qualities), this means that Brahman is full of unlimited varieties of spiritual qualities. These two concepts are not contradictory. Brahman is simultaneously overflowing with oceans of spiritual qualities, and at the same time is completely devoid of all material qualities.

How can we understand this? Isn't a saintly person full of all saintly qualities and at the same time devoid of all type of sinful qualities? If it is possible for a human being to be with and without qualities, certainly God can simultaneously be with and without qualities.

Perhaps you are unaware of the philosophical synthesis of Śrī Caitanya Mahāprabhu. The followers of the formless *nirguṇa* Brahman hold to the philosophy of *advaita* (oneness). And the followers of the *saguṇa* Brahman, the Supreme

Absolute Truth with form, hold to the philosophy of *dvaita* (twoness). Śrī Caitanya amalgamated both philosophies into what is the ultimate philosophical perfection, that the Supreme Absolute is simultaneously, inconceivably one and different. To take either half of Brahman only is incomplete. We should not be the like the farmer who only wanted the half of the hen that lays eggs and did not want the half of the hen which eats.

Half-hen logic kills the hen. Similarly, to perceive only oneness or only duality is also incomplete. It is trying to put a limit on God. Those who have achieved the highest stage of spiritual enlightenment perceive the Absolute as simultaneously with spiritual form and without material form.

What Must I Do to Become a Pure Devotee?

What must I do to become pure devotee quickly and surely, and to stay like that forever? How can I see if I am pure enough or not?

Here's How

To quickly become a pure devotee, chant 16 rounds of the Hare Kṛṣṇa *mahā-mantra* on *japa* beads every day, follow our regulative principles strictly, and fully dedicate your life's activity to the *saṅkīrtana* activities of spreading Kṛṣṇa consciousness all over the world.

The following verse from the *Śrīmad-Bhāgavatam* describes how you will know if you are becoming purified or not:

bhaktiḥ pareśānubhavo viraktir
anyatra caiṣa trika eka-kālaḥ
prapadyamānasya yathāśnataḥ syus
tuṣṭiḥ puṣṭiḥ kṣud-apāyo 'nu-ghāsam

> "Devotion, direct experience of the Supreme Lord, and detachment from other things — these three occur simultaneously for one who has taken shelter of the Supreme Personality of Godhead, in the same way that pleasure, nourishment and relief from hunger come simultaneously and increasingly, with each bite, for a person engaged in eating."
>
> *Śrīmad-Bhāgavatam* 11.2.42

In other words, just as by eating you will personally experience satisfaction, by advancing in Kṛṣṇa consciousness you will feel great peace and happiness, and you will begin to experience more and more that everything is within Kṛṣṇa and Kṛṣṇa is within everything.

Is Temple Worship Idol Worship?

The Bible says that we shouldn't bow down to any graven or molten image/idol of God. It says God thinks that worshipping an idol is bad. Wouldn't temple worship fall under this category of idol worship?

Kṛṣṇa Appears in a Visible Form

"Graven image" or "molten image" means something formed according to our own imagination. Such concocted forms of worship are also condemned in the Vedic literatures. The authorized Deity form of Lord Kṛṣṇa in the temple is not concocted according to imagination. It is strictly based on the scriptures and confirmed by the spiritual master. It is not an image of Kṛṣṇa. It is Kṛṣṇa Himself kindly appearing in a form that is visible to us. Just as God appears in the Old Testament in the form of burning bush, Lord Kṛṣṇa appears in the authorized Deity form within the temple.

Meaning of Dharma

I beg you to explain the meaning of the Sanskrit word *dharma*. Does it mean religion only?

Intrinsic Nature

Dharma means that which cannot be separated from a thing, i.e. its intrinsic nature. Just like the *dharma* of water is liquidity.

The *dharma* of the living being is to serve. He cannot avoid this nature. If he has no one else to serve, he will keep a dog for serving the dog. The perfection of *dharma* is to serve that person by whose serving we can automatically serve everyone. That person is God.

Caste System and Idol Worship

Does the caste system have any religious sanction in *sanātana-dharma*, the Vedic culture?

Why do the followers of *sanātana-dharma* worship idols? Can't we achieve the same goal without any idols? Which form of worship is superior - *nirguṇa* or *saguṇa*?

These two are the most trusted weapons of Christians and Muslims against Hindus.

Divine Varṇāśrama and Deity Worship

The original divine caste system, known as *daivī-varṇāśrama*, is prescribed in the Vedic literatures. That divine caste system is no longer being practiced. In the Kali-yuga it has become perverted into a different form, which is known as the demonic caste system (*āsurī-varṇāśrama*). The original, divine caste system meant that everybody in the society was nicely, happily engaged in earning their livelihood in a way that was just suitable to their nature. This system was degraded into a system in which one's social position was based upon one's birth, not one's natural qualities.

Nowadays people claim an exalted status as a *brāhmaṇa* when actually they do not possess any of the qualities of the *brāhmaṇa* as they are described in the *Bhagavad-gītā*. It is the caste-conscious *brāhmaṇas* of India who spoiled the caste system by insisting that they were *brāhmaṇas* simply on the basis of their birth. The actual quality of a *brāhmaṇa* is described as follows in the *Bhagavad-gītā*:

śamo damas tapaḥ śaucaṁ
kṣāntir ārjavam eva ca
jñānaṁ vijñānam āstikyaṁ
brahma-karma svabhāva-jam

"Peacefulness, self-control, austerity, purity, tolerance, honesty, knowledge, wisdom and religiousness — these are the natural qualities by which the *brāhmaṇas* work."

Bhagavad-gītā 18.42

The actual *brāhmaṇas* do not selfishly, proudly make an artificial show of these qualities. Rather they act as selfless teachers. Without accepting any salary, they dedicate their lives fully to teaching others how to develop these brahminical qualities for achieving the supreme perfection of going back to home, back to Godhead.

The Supreme Truth is both *saguṇa* (with qualities) and *nirguṇa* (without qualities). *Saguṇa* means that it is full of all transcendental qualities, and *nirguṇa* means that it is completely free from any mundane qualities. In other words, God is not without form. He undoubtedly possesses form. But His form is not like your form, that is subject to birth, death, old age, and disease. The Lord's form is eternally youthful, full of bliss, and full of knowledge. This is why Kṛṣṇa is described in the *Brahma-saṁhitā* as *nava-yauvanaṁ*, an ever-fresh youth.

Idol worship, worshipping a form that is not authorized in the scriptures, is condemned in the Vedic scriptures. Only the authorized Deity form of the Lord, in which the Lord has agreed to manifest His divine presence, should be worshipped. When the bona fide spiritual master invites the Lord to appear as the Deity in any one of his multifarious manifestations - such as Kṛṣṇa, Rāma, Nārāyaṇa, or Nṛsiṁhadeva - the Lord kindly appears at the request of His pure devotee. Such worship of the authorized Deity form of the Lord should never be considered to be idol worship, the worship of a false god. Rather, it is the present-day material civilization that is guilty of idol worship by building an entire so-called civilization based on the hedonistic principle of material sense gratification. They have made an idol out of their material bodies, and they spend their whole lives worshipping such false gods. It is therefore the so-called religionists who are guilty of idol worship, not the followers of *sanātana-dharma*, the Vedic culture.

In this age of Kali the Vedic scriptures prescribe that simply by chanting the holy names of God, one will achieve all perfection:

Hare Kṛṣṇa, Hare Kṛṣṇa, Kṛṣṇa Kṛṣṇa, Hare Hare
Hare Rāma, Hare Rāma, Rāma Rāma, Hare Hare

But the spiritual master also engages his disciples in the authorized Deity worship in the temple because this helps them to purely chant the holy names of God.

Is Mithra a God-Man?

I have recently heard of a Persian god-man named Mithra. His story and that of Jesus Christ are almost identical. Now I am confused.

All Incarnations Are Predicted in the Vedas

All the bona fide incarnations of God are predicted in the Vedic literatures. Nowadays it has become a fad to put forward some ordinary human being as God. But this cheating business is condemned in the Vedic literatures.

If you listen to anyone and everyone, you will always remain confused. This is why Lord Kṛṣṇa tells us to surrender at the lotus feet of the bona fide spiritual master. The bona fide guru is that person who only speaks according to the authoritative Vedic wisdom. He does not introduce any incarnations of God that are not predicted in the Vedic literatures for the purpose of misleading the innocent public.

Why Waste Time Chanting Hare Kṛṣṇa?

Do you know that Kalki Bhagavān is now available in India? He says that He is the Kalki Avatāra of Lord Kṛṣṇa incarnated on this earth along with his wife. He is performing miracles and giving initiation to aspirants. He removes all the *vāsanās* (desires) and enlightens people all over the world. When Lord Kṛṣṇa is within reach of everyone here, why chant the Hare Kṛṣṇa *mantra* 16 rounds every day and waste time? Why are you going on a world tour to spread Kṛṣṇa consciousness when Kṛṣṇa Himself is physically available here?

Don't Waste Time with Bogus Incarnations

The incarnation of God is understood according to the revealed scriptures, not according to the bogus claims of unscrupulous pretenders. According to the authorized revealed Vedic scriptures, Kalki Avatāra will not appear for another 427,000 years. His specific activities are clearly predicted in the *Śrīmad-Bhāgavatam*. He will wield a sword and ride on a horse named Devadatta. He will travel over the earth exhibiting eight mystic opulences. Displaying his unequalled effulgence and riding with great speed, he will kill the demons by the millions. If your so-called Kalki were the actual Kalki, this would be the topmost news story on planet earth. That I have only heard about him from you and not from the news media clearly indicates that this is not the real Kalki Avatāra.

Your so-called Kalki Avatāra may be healing the sick, but doctors do that also. Does that mean that the doctors are God?

We are following the authorized system of the most recent incarnation of God on this planet, Śrī Caitanya Mahāprabhu, as confirmed in the revealed Vedic scriptures. That you would criticize us for wasting time by executing the *yuga-dharma*, the prescribed duty for this age (chanting the Hare Krsna *mantra*), sadly indicates how much you have been misguided by this so-called Bhagavān (incarnation of God) and his followers.

I am sorry to have to speak such strong words to such a good and dear soul as yourself. But you have been very much misled, and I hope that my words may help to get you back on the proper path. Please do not take that my words are spoken in anger. They are clearly not. I am speaking to you with sincere love in my heart for helping you to become free from the cycle of birth and death.

Can't Kalki Be a Healer?

Is it not possible that when Kalki comes, He will be a healer instead? The Lord Kalki could come to make peace among all people and to help the lost souls find the right path rather than to destroy the false kings.

I'm not saying I believe that this man who claims to be Kalki Avatāra is the real thing. I am just saying when it was prophesied that Lord Jesus would be born, the Jews predicted a military leader, someone to bring a war and lead the Jews to a glorious age. Instead quite the opposite happened. Jesus was born and he brought a message of love and non-violence with his turn-the-cheek belief, and thus Judaism was reformed.

So would it not be possible that when Kalki finally does come, He will not be what we expected him to be - that He will instead be a passive man Who will not bring harm to any of His children, and Who loves us even more dearly than Jesus did?

Vedic Predictions Are Always Accurate

There cannot be any discrepancies in the Vedic predictions. Therefore, Kalki Avatāra will indeed appear at the end of the Kali-yuga 427,000 years from now and annihilate the demons. The predictions are so accurate that His father's name and His village name are also predicted. The planet earth will at that time be in a state of total chaos. The entire human population will be reduced to the size of pygmies and they will all be cannibals engaged in killing and eating each other. Kalki Avatāra's killing will be an expression of His unlimited love because anyone who is killed by Him receives immediate salvation. Because their brains will be too dull to comprehend transcendental knowledge, instead of preaching to them the Lord will mercifully deliver them by killing them. And then after they are annihilated a new Golden Age, the Satya-yuga, will begin.

Is God Nothing?

God is available to all those who seek him in the earnest way. It is immaterial whether we seek him as Lord Kṛṣṇa, Viṣṇu, God, Allah, Jesus or "Nothing." (Nothing also emanates from Him, if He is almighty.)

No, Because Nothing Does Not Exist

While you are right that God can be approached as Kṛṣṇa, Viṣṇu, God, or through His pure devotee, Lord Jesus Christ, your idea that we can seek God as nothing is incorrect.

Nothing cannot emanate from the Supreme because the substance nothing does not exist. Everything that emanates from the Supreme is substantial. It has substance. It is something. Otherwise it could not emanate from the Supreme.

In other words, there is no such thing as the substance nothing. It exists only as a concept. In that sense, on the conceptual level, nothing is not nothing; it is indeed something. So in conclusion we can understand that there is no such thing as nothing, since even nothing is something.

No Vegetarian Verses?

I have certain reservations about the non-usage of meat or eggs by Kṛṣṇa devotees. I did not find any verse banning the usage of meat, etc. in the *Bhagavad-gītā*. Your good self also did not mention it, but only mentioned about sacrificing food. The animals, birds, etc. are also the holy blessings of God, like vegetables and fruits, for mankind to take advantage of.

I have been a student of history. I read that when the Āryan tribe migrated to India after a snowstorm in Germany and were going through a period of starvation, the tribal elders feared that people might deplete their livestock by eating it. To save this from happening, the elders, by religious decree, declared the cow as Devimata to avoid its slaughter. They banned the use of meat as a food religiously, and to date this decree is being carried on.

Kṛṣṇa Clearly Instructs

In the *Bhagavad-gītā* Chapter Three, Text 13, Kṛṣṇa clearly states that devotees only eat foods which have first been offered in sacrifice. Then in Chapter Nine, Text 26 Kṛṣṇa lists which are the types of foods that He will accept. He only mentions foods from the vegetarian category. He does not mention meat, fish, or eggs.

The history you have read about the Āryan migration from Europe originates from the erroneous speculation of Western scholars who could not accept that such an advanced culture as the Āryan culture could have its origins outside of Europe. They have dated the Āryan migration thousands of years after the Āryan civilization was already flourishing in India as evidenced by the *Mahābhārata* and the *Rāmāyaṇa*.

Proof of Gītā's Legitimacy?

In most of the lectures of ISKCON, the writings of the *Gītā* are taken to be absolute truth. I would like to ask, "What is the proof of the *Gītā*'s legitimacy?"

There Are Many Proofs

There are many ways to understand the authenticity of the *Bhagavad-gītā*.

The first point is that it was directly spoken by the Supreme Lord Śrī Kṛṣṇa. This automatically makes it more authoritative than any other words that have ever been spoken in all eternity.

The fact that this most famous of all conversations was dictated by Vedavyāsa (the compiler of the Vedic wisdom), and written down by Gaṇeśa adds even more weight to its credibility.

Also the fact that the renowned *ācārya*, Sripad Śaṅkarācārya, who is an incarnation of Lord Śiva, has written a commentary on the *Bhagavad-gītā*, lends more weight to its credibility.

And then, the fact that Kṛṣṇa Himself appearing in the form of His own devotee, Śrī Caitanya Mahāprabhu, also accepted and promoted the teachings of the *Bhagavad-gītā*, gives it even more weight.

Further evidence is that the most empowered *ācārya* in history for spreading spiritual enlightenment all over the world, His Divine Grace A.C. Bhaktivedanta Swami Prabhupāda, has also reconfirmed the legitimacy of the *Gītā* and stressed its absolute importance.

And the reality that by carefully following the teachings of the *Bhagavad-gītā* one becomes qualified to directly meet God face-to-face, eye-to-eye, absolutely proves that it is not only bona fide, but also most highly effective.

There are many more ways to substantiate the authority of the *Bhagavad-gītā*. What I have given here is the mere tip of the iceberg. If you would like to delve more deeply into the topmost science of *Bhagavad-gītā*, I humbly request you to carefully study *Bhagavad-gītā As It Is* by His Divine Grace A.C. Bhaktivedanta Swami Prabhupāda.

Formlessness

It is generally believed that one progresses on the path of self-realization (with continuous blessings and guidance of a bona fide guru) from the Deity form of worship, toward non-form worship (meditation), and ultimately to a subconscious form of worship in a state devoid of any sound or form. What is your opinion on this school of thought?

Supreme Form Beyond Formlessness

You described the school of thought known as Impersonalism, in which one initially fixes the mind on the form of God as a temporary material crutch but then gradually gives up the idea of God with form and tries to merge into the formless Brahman. This system is based on the false premise that God has no form. Such a self-realization system may give one temporary relief from the suffering conditions of this material existence, but will ultimately fail to give the practitioner lasting relief because God ultimately has personality and form, and so do we in our liberated condition.

We may try to deny form and personality for some time, but we will eventually find this position to be very dry and unsatisfying. The pain of failed relationships may drive us into solitude, but because the nature of a human being is to associate with others, we will eventually try again to build meaningful relationships with others. So instead of denying God's form and personality, we should learn about Him from the spiritual master, from great saintly teachers, and from bona fide scriptures.

Does Kṛṣṇa Consciousness Decrease One's Self-Confidence?

It is said: whatever you do, do it for the Lord, and completely depend upon the Lord for its results. But my father says this will decrease your self-confidence. Is this correct?

Kṛṣṇa Consciousness Increases Self-Confidence Unlimitedly

I am very happy that you have been appreciating our distribution of transcendental knowledge.

You have presented an interesting question put forward by your father: Will doing everything for Kṛṣṇa and depending on Him for the results decrease one's self-confidence?

The answer is that doing everything for Kṛṣṇa and fully depending on Kṛṣṇa increases one's self-confidence unlimitedly.

In this material world everyone has a certain degree of self-confidence proportionate to their ability to judge things intelligently and act successfully. But because they are always acting and thinking under the constraints of the material modes of nature, there is always a limit to their self-confidence. In this material world, even the most highly successful man eventually meets with failure in the form of disease, old age, and death.

The Lord's devotee is an entirely different position. Because He has taken complete shelter of the Lord, he is no longer under the restrictive influence of the material nature. Therefore, he can act with unlimited self-confidence to accomplish what no ordinary mortal can accomplish. We see this practically in the examples of Arjuna, Hanumān, and all the great *ācāryas* (fully enlightened, divinely empowered, saintly teachers) in Vedic history. And if we will follow in the footsteps of these great *ācāryas*, we will also become unlimitedly empowered to accomplish what no ordinary mortal can accomplish.

Does God Desire?

I have heard many people say, "God wants this," or "God wants that." Does God actually have desires at all? I would rather hear from a Vedic authority, and I believe you are one of those. Please dispel my doubt.

God Desires Unlimitedly

Since everything originates in God, and since desire is one of the factors of existence, we can understand that desire must exist within God. And since He is the Supreme and surpasses all others, we can understand that His ability to desire is unlimited. He desires unlimitedly.

We can hear directly in the *Bhagavad-gītā* from Kṛṣṇa Himself where He describes clearly so many desires that He has for us to engage in His service. Of course, it is not that He needs our service. He desires for us to serve Him so that we become benefitted. Here is an example:

man-manā bhava mad-bhakto
mad-yājī māṁ namaskuru
mām evaiṣyasi yuktvaivam
ātmānaṁ mat-parāyaṇaḥ

"Engage your mind always in thinking of Me, become My devotee, offer obeisances to Me and worship Me. Being completely absorbed in Me, surely you will come to Me."

Bhagavad-gītā 9.34

And this is just one of the many, many verses in which Kṛṣṇa expresses His desires.

Social Divisions in the Bhagavad-gītā?

One's occupational duty is prescribed in *Bhagavad-gītā*, i.e., duties of *brāhmaṇa* (priestly-intellectual class), *kṣatriya* (warrior-administrator class), *vaiśya* (farmer-mercantile class) and *śūdra* (worker class). In the present-day scenario is it possible to allot duties like that? If not, how will the Vedic teachings be applicable? This is one side.

Also, at the present time everybody says that there should not be any caste or creed; yet at the same time violence breaks out because of caste conflicts. How does the *Bhagavad-gītā* explain this?

According to Natural Inclination

Occupational duties are understood in the *Bhagavad-gītā* according to one's natural qualities. It is not that one's occupational duties are dictated by one's birth. One who has the natural qualities of a *brāhmaṇa* (priestly-intellectual class) is meant to act in that capacity. And the same thing holds true for those who are inclined to act as military men, businessmen, farmers, or workers. There should be no caste/class distinction on the basis of birth. Such artificial caste consciousness is not in accordance with the Vedic scriptures. The Vedic wisdom analyzes one's social position according to his qualities and his activities, not according to his birth or a label placed on him by society.

When people artificially try to base social position on birth, there will naturally be so much fighting and class struggle. But if everyone is engaged according to their natural tendencies and talents, everyone will be happy with their position within the social structure. This is the real meaning the Vedic *varṇāśrama* system.

Status of a Mother

I do not know what is said about the status of a mother in the *Śrīmad-Bhāgavatam*, or *Bhagavad-gītā* or the Vedas. But I think I've heard it said somewhere that the status of a mother is even greater than that of God, and that even God does not care about one who does not respect and love his mother. Is this true?

My second question is: is it okay for someone to leave his mother and father because he thinks that the love of his parents might come in the way of his becoming Kṛṣṇa conscious? In other words, how would Kṛṣṇa look upon such devotees who are really devoted to him, but have deeply hurt the feelings of their parents in order to become Kṛṣṇa conscious?

She Is Meant to Liberate Us

According to the *Śrīmad-Bhāgavatam* no one should become a mother, a father, a guru or a leader unless they can deliver their dependents from the cycle of birth and death.

So although we always, as a matter of etiquette, offer our respectful obeisances to our parents, we must also see the difference between those parents who are properly guiding us in how to escape the cycle of birth and death and those parents who are misguiding us to try to enjoy this temporary material world.

If our parents are opposed to our becoming Kṛṣṇa conscious, and they forbid us to practice Kṛṣṇa consciousness, then we will have no choice but to respectfully neglect their instructions. We have had thousands of parents in thousands of lifetimes. If we do not take seriously to the pathway of self-realization, we will remain entangled in the miserable cycle of birth and death. Our first duty is to get out of this material world. Once we are situated solidly on the pathway of Kṛṣṇa-*bhakti*, we can then reach out and extend the mercy of Kṛṣṇa to everyone: our parents, our children, our friends, and society in general.

Everybody Is Confusing Me

There are many disciplic traditions claming authenticity for themselves. But many of them are rivaling each other. How do I find out which one is genuine and authentic?

In your answer to me you said that the *Śrīmad-Bhāgavatam* is the most important Vedic literature. Does that mean that the other Purāṇas are less important, or that they are not correct?

The Shivites claim that some other *Purāṇas* are more important. The Vedāntists claim that the *Upaniṣads* are more important than the *Purāṇas*. Oh! Everybody is confusing me.

Clear Understanding of Vedic Wisdom

In Vedic civilization there are four authentic, authorized *sampradāyas* (lines of disciplic succession) and they are all in agreement with each other. They do not dispute the authenticity of each other. Anyone who rivals these *sampradāyas* is not acting in accordance with Vedic authority.

There is no doubt that all of the Vedic wisdom is fully authentic and authoritative. Even though all medicines are genuine, if we take the wrong medicine it can make our disease worse. Therefore, medicine must be taken under the careful and expert guidance of the qualified physician. Similarly, the Vedic injunctions have to be understood and applied under the guidance of the expert spiritual master. It is not that if we take medicine without proper guidance we can become healthy. In the same way, we cannot become spiritually enlightened if we try to figure out the Vedic wisdom on our own.

If, in line with the teachings of the *Bhagavad-gītā*, we accept the authority of Lord Śrī Kṛṣṇa, and we also accept the authority of the great spiritual masters who have guided India's Vedic civilization since time immemorial, we will not be confused.

To an untrained student who is not yet initiated by a bona fide spiritual master, the *Vedas* can be confusing, as you are now experiencing. This is why it is enjoined that one not study the *Vedas* until one has taken shelter of a bona fide spiritual master. One reason for this is that the *Vedas* are full of many statements that appear on the surface to be contradictory.

For example, in addition to giving information to those on the highest platform of *sattva-guṇa*, the *Vedas* also provide guidance for those who are in the lower modes of material nature. For instance, there is one *Purāṇa* that guides those who want to eat meat as to how they can offer a goat to Goddess Kālī. They are required to whisper a *mantra* into the goat's ear: "Now I am killing you to eat you, but in the future you will kill me and eat me." Such Vedic injunctions are meant to encourage those who are addicted to meat-eating to give it up. Such Vedic injunctions are not meant to encourage meat-eating.

This is why we have to approach the *Vedas* under the guidance of the great *mahājanas*, not through our own mental speculation. If we take the guidance of the great *mahājanas*, those enlightened spiritual masters who have guided the Vedic society since time immemorial, we will properly understand the meaning and purpose of all the Vedic injunctions, and we will be able to see what is the inner purpose of all the Vedas, i.e. to become Kṛṣṇa conscious. This point is confirmed by Lord Śrī Kṛṣṇa Himself in the *Bhagavad-gītā* as follows:

"By all the Vedas, I am to be known."

Bhagavad-gītā 15.15

What Is Your State of Realization?

You have written: Regarding the state of pure mind/Buddha nature, please note that there are three stages:

- Pure mind (Brahman realization)
- Purer mind (Paramātmā realization)
- Purest mind (Bhagavān realization)

Which state of realization have you been able to achieve?

Consult Bhagavad-gītā

Those who are actually self-realized do not advertise themselves as such. To understand where someone stands spiritually requires that you must first become knowledgeable in the science of *bhakti* as described by Lord Śrī Kṛṣṇa in the *Bhagavad-gītā*. So my best advice to you is that you carefully study *Bhagavad-gītā*

As It Is by His Divine Grace A.C. Bhaktivedanta Swami Prabhupāda, the greatest of self-realized teachers. By doing so, you will then be able to discern who is spiritually realized and who is not and to what degree any person is spiritually realized.

Bhagavad-gītā—ABC's or King of Education?

It is said that the *Bhagavad-gītā* is the ABC level of spiritual life. It is also said that *Śrīmad-Bhāgavatam* is the Masters level and that *Śrī Caitanya-caritāmṛta* is the PhD level.

Lord Kṛṣṇa says in *Bhagavad-gītā* 9.2: "This knowledge is the king of education, the most secret of all secrets. It is the purest knowledge, and because it gives direct perception of the self by realization, it is the perfection of religion. It is everlasting, and it is joyfully performed."

If *Bhagavad-gītā* is *rāja-vidyā* - the king of knowledge - then why do we say that it is the ABC of spiritual life?

Both

You have raised a very interesting question. How can the *Bhagavad-gītā* be considered ABC knowledge, introductory knowledge, and at the same time the most advanced knowledge? Is this contradictory?

No. It is not contradictory. Since Kṛṣṇa declares the *Bhagavad-gītā* to be the king of knowledge, the highest level knowledge, we cannot doubt this. Then how can it be simultaneously ABC-level, introductory-level knowledge?

The answer is quite simple. The *Bhagavad-gītā* is the introduction to the highest level of knowledge. *Śrīmad-Bhāgavatam* and *Śrī Caitanya-caritāmṛta* also present the same highest level of knowledge. The difference is that they go more and more deeply into it.

We can understand a simple analogy in this connection. If you develop a relationship with the king, the first thing is that you are introduced to him. Then you develop a personal relationship with him, and later on, an even more personal relationship with him. At all three stages you are associating with the king: introductory level, personal level and more personal level. In a similar way, we associate with the king of knowledge in an introductory way in the *Bhagavad-gītā*, in an advanced way in the *Śrīmad-Bhāgavatam*, and in even a more advanced way in the *Śrī Caitanya-caritāmṛta*.

What Does "Tat" Mean?

Please explain the literal meaning of *tat*. I am conducting word studies, and I am not able to find the etymology or the literal meaning of this word. (I do understand *oṁ* and *sat*.)

Transcendental Absolute Truth

Śrīla Prabhupāda explains that *tat* means transcendental Absolute Truth. *Sat* means eternal and *oṁ* is a form of address. So the famous Vedic *mantra* "*oṁ tat sat*" means "O, eternal transcendental Absolute Truth."

Origin of India's Vedic Culture

I met one person who was claimed that it is a historical fact that there are cultures in India older than the Vedic culture. He said that Vedic culture came to India with nomads from the mountains, and that before that time, there was some traividya culture, with farmers, and that we can still see some remnants of that culture in South India, where the languages are not based on Sanskrit and the people look different. How am I supposed to understand this and explain to him that Vedic culture is the original one?

Historically Rooted in India

The concocted idea that Āryan culture came from outside of India has been tossed around by the mundane scholars for a long time. Because the original Indologists were European Christian missionaries - paid by their respective governments to establish the superiority of Christian European culture - they purposefully concocted the Āryan invasion myth to propagate the idea that the advanced Vedic culture originated in Europe. This is a blatant example of cultural chauvinism.

The Vedic histories confirm that the Vedic culture is eternal. It has no beginning point in the pages of history. Within this universe we see it going back to the very beginning of the universe, when Lord Brahmā was enlightened with Vedic wisdom while sitting atop a lotus flower.

In the recent history, there is conclusive evidence to prove that within the last 5,000 years the Vedic culture was thriving in India. It was not introduced into India by an invasion from Europe. The battlefield of Kurukṣetra, the place where Kṛṣṇa spoke the *Bhagavad-gītā* 5,000 years ago, is still there in India near Delhi. There is even a train station named Kurukṣetra. According to the Āryan invasion myth, the Vedic culture was not present in India 5,000 years ago. If that was so, how could Kṛṣṇa present the Vedic wisdom to Arjuna in India?

ISKCON

Śrīla Prabhupāda's Books & Mission - Spreading Kṛṣṇa Consciousness

Real Hindu Name for ISKCON

May I know the real Hindu name for the ISKCON sect as it is known among Bhāratīyas (followers of India's traditional Vedic culture) in India?

Brahma-Madhva-Gauḍīya-Śrīla Prabhupāda Sampradāya

According to the principles of the ancient culture based on the Vedic scriptures, ISKCON can be described as the Brahmā-Madhva-Gauḍīya-Śrīla Prabhupāda Sampradāya of Lord Brahmā. In the lineage of Lord Brahmā was the great *ācārya* named Madhvācārya. Then further along the lineage Kṛṣṇa reappeared to reconfirm the great potency of this lineage. He reappeared in this lineage 500 years ago as Śrī Caitanya Mahāprabhu, the great leader of the Gauḍīya Vaiṣṇavas. Then the 11th in the line from Śrī Caitanya is His Divine Grace A.C. Bhaktivedanta Swami Prabhupāda, the Founder-Ācārya of ISKCON. His followers are the 12th in the line from Śrī Caitanya Mahāprabhu. His followers and the followers of his followers constitute the present-day ISKCON. In the future there will be many more generations of followers. ISKCON will create millions of *ācāryas* to bring the happy days of Vedic *dharma* back to this planet for the next 9,500 years.

How Can We Have Ever-Exciting Spiritual Life?

How can I make spiritual life ever-interesting and ever-exciting, so that I can understand that actually there is nothing like it?

Be a Spiritual Revolutionary

To have an ever-exciting spiritual life you must fully embrace the mood of a spiritual revolutionary. This means that you must be determined to become a spotlessly pure devotee as soon as possible, as well as dedicating your every thought, word and deed to the respiritualization of the entire human society by injecting everyone you meet with the most sublime message of Kṛṣṇa consciousness.

Reading Only Bhagavad-gītā?

Śrīla Prabhupāda wrote so many books. Reading all of them is a waste of time. If we read only the *Bhagavad-gītā As It Is* and apply it to our life, can we get the essence of Vedic science and achieve spiritual perfection?

Please make a list of the most important authorized scriptures. I want to read only these in my life.

Fully Utilize Śrīla Prabhupāda's Ultimate Benediction

How can you say that reading all of Śrīla Prabhupāda's books is a waste of time? The best utilization of our life is to carefully read all of Śrīla Prabhupāda's books. Śrīla Prabhupāda instructed us to read all of his books. But he has mercifully put everything that we need to know into *Bhagavad-gītā As It Is*.

Rest assured that if you will spend your entire life reading that one book again and again, and if you will perfectly follow its teachings, there is no doubt that you will attain complete spiritual perfection.

In order to make it easier for you to fully comprehend and master the art of *bhakti* described in the *Bhagavad-gītā As It Is*, Śrīla Prabhupāda has also given us many other books as listed below. Kindly try to live your life in such a way that you can read all of these books. This will enable you to easily become fully enlightened and empowered - a perfect living embodiment of the teachings given by Lord Śrī Kṛṣṇa in the *Bhagavad-gītā*.

Here are the most wonderful and sublime books that Śrīla Prabhupāda has blessed us with. These books are truly the ultimate benediction for the suffering humanity:

Bhagavad-gītā As It Is
Śrīmad-Bhāgavatam
Śrī Caitanya-caritāmṛta
Kṛṣṇa, The Supreme Personality of Godhead
Śrī Īśopaniṣad
Nectar of Instruction
Teachings of Lord Caitanya
Easy Journey to Other Planets
Nectar of Devotion

How Can One Take Śrīla Prabhupāda's Instructions Seriously?

How can one take Śrīla Prabhupāda's instructions seriously, as one's heart and soul, and how can one get inspiration to do what Śrīla Prabhupāda wants in a practical way?

Remember Śrīla Prabhupāda's Dedication

You will never fully comprehend Śrīla Prabhupāda's devotional mood because there is no limit to the depth of his devotion. No matter how much you may understand his devotion, there will be still more which is beyond your comprehension, no matter how much you may advance in understanding his devotion. In short, his devotion is unfathomable.

The easiest way to become serious and inspired to do that which Śrīla Prabhupāda wants you to do is to always remember how dedicated he was to pleasing his spiritual master, Śrīla Bhaktisiddhānta Sarasvatī Ṭhākura. The life and soul of the disciple is to please his own guru and through him the predecessor *acāryas*. We saw this as the supreme quality of Śrīla Prabhupāda, and as his followers we must adopt this same mood.

Why Don't You Behave Ordinarily?

I'd like to know the need of enforcing one into spiritual realization by ISKCON devotees. If one wants spiritual realization, he will eventually come. So what is the need to dance on the streets like madmen shouting, "Hare Kṛṣṇa, Hare Kṛṣṇa"?

Love of God should be within heart. So why is it that ISKCON is making a show of spiritual realization by chanting on streets and what-not?

This is just an inquiry about your ideology. I am not questioning your legitimacy. I just want to know what is the need for enforcing *bhakti*.

Mercy Is Extraordinary, Not Ordinary

Some people argue, "When there is drought the people come to the well. The well does not go to the people." But the real fact is that in times of severe drought those who are very merciful dig irrigation ditches so that everyone can receive profuse water.

Proper or Improper Thrill?

When I spread the awareness of Kṛṣṇa consciousness amongst my friends and relatives, I get a thrill that wow, I have done such a nice thing. Is enjoying such a thrill correct or is it wrong?

All Credit Goes to Guru and Kṛṣṇa

It is natural to feel ecstatic when spreading Kṛṣṇa to others. There is nothing that pleases Kṛṣṇa more than when we broadcast His glories to those who have forgotten Him. And when Kṛṣṇa is greatly pleased, it is natural that the devotee will also feel great transcendental pleasure. There is nothing wrong in feeling this pleasure.

However, one should not allow such transcendental pleasure to become mundane pleasure by thinking oneself great for having attracted someone else to Kṛṣṇa. We should always remember that it is only by the undeserved grace of Guru and Kṛṣṇa that we can attract someone else to Kṛṣṇa consciousness. Therefore, we should always give all credit to Guru and Kṛṣṇa, and not take any credit for ourselves. If we foolishly try to take the credit, our ability to attract others to Kṛṣṇa will go away. And our happiness will go away also.

Why Disobey God's Orders?

Why must we spread Kṛṣṇa consciousness? Why preach the glories of the Gītā to the world? Did Kṛṣṇa not himself say:

idaṁ te nātapaskāya
nābhaktāya kadācana
na cāśuśrūṣave vācyaṁ
na ca māṁ yo 'bhyasūyati

"This confidential knowledge may not be explained to those who are not austere, or devoted, or engaged in devotional service, nor to one who is envious of Me."

Basically, only Kṛṣṇa's devotees may read from the *Gītā* and hear its infinite wisdom. Yet you travel the world telling every man and his dog about Kṛṣṇa.

I understand in the very next text it says:

ya idaṁ paramaṁ guhyaṁ
mad-bhakteṣv abhidhāsyati
bhaktiṁ mayi parāṁ kṛtvā
mām evaiṣyaty asaṁśayaḥ

"For one who explains the supreme secret to the devotees, devotional service is guaranteed, and at the end he will come back to Me."

This following text speaks highly of discussing the glories of God; however, it ONLY applies to discussing it with His devotees... only His devotees may hear or read the knowledge contained within the *Gītā*.

God would rather people come to Him on their own accord; this is His benevolent nature and His gift to us of free will and free choice. So why ignore this message which came directly from God Himself? Why do you preach?

Why Are You Disobeying God's Orders?

You are saying that it is an act of disobedience to the instructions of the Lord to preach the message of the *Bhagavad-gītā* all over the world. You have misunderstood the point that the Lord is making because you have taken it out of context. This statement must be understood in context with the Lord's other statement that all the ignorant people of the world should be engaged in devotional service. He makes this statement in the following verse of the *Bhagavad-gītā*:

na buddhi-bhedaṁ janayed
ajñānāṁ karma-saṅginām
joṣayet sarva-karmāṇi
vidvān yuktaḥ samācaran

"Let not the wise disrupt the minds of the ignorant who are attached to fruitive action. They should be encouraged not to refrain from work, but to work in the spirit of devotion."

Bhagavad-gītā 3.26

It is in the light of the above statement that we must understand what may appear to the uninformed observer to be the Lord's restriction of not explaining *Bhagavad-gītā* to the ignorant. If you read carefully the Lord's prohibition you will see that it is not a prohibition against the spreading of Kṛṣṇa consciousness. Rather it is prohibition against spreading the more confidential aspects of Kṛṣṇa consciousness to the general, ignorant population. Just as children are introduced to mathematics at the elementary level of "one plus one equals two" - not on the advanced level of calculus, which would merely confuse them - similarly the general population should introduced to Kṛṣṇa consciousness from the beginning point, not in its more confidential aspects, which would only confuse them.

In obedience to the Lord's instructions I always tailor my lectures to make them suitable for the particular audience. If the people are newcomers to Kṛṣṇa consciousness, I speak to them in an introductory non-confidential fashion, and if they are already devotees, I can go deeply into the amazingly sweet, confidential aspects of Kṛṣṇa consciousness. However, if according to the Lord's order we engage even the newcomers in acts of devotion, they can quickly become purified and become qualified to hear about the more confidential aspects of Kṛṣṇa consciousness. The easiest way to engage the ignorant in acts of devotion is to let them enjoy the sweet sound of Hare Kṛṣṇa *kīrtana*. Everyone enjoys some nice rhythmic and melodic musical sounds. So if we can satisfy their desire to hear nice, attractive music by making attractive *kīrtana*, they quickly become qualified to hear more advanced spiritual topics.

This is why we always precede our lectures with enlivened *kīrtana* to uplift the hearts of our audience before we begin speaking. I have even traveled to the Muslim world and introduced Hare Kṛṣṇa *kīrtana* in a public meeting. The people were so enlivened by the *kīrtana* that they became very eager to learn more about the transcendental process of Kṛṣṇa consciousness. When the people become attracted and eager to hear more and more about Kṛṣṇa, this means that they have been transformed into devotees by the magical power of the *kīrtana* and are now qualified for more confidential knowledge.

In the ultimate analysis, everyone is at heart a devotee of Kṛṣṇa because everyone was originally with the Lord in the spiritual world before falling into material existence. Therefore, explaining *Bhagavad-gītā* philosophy to the devotees ultimately means explaining *Bhagavad-gītā* to everyone. But because the generally ignorant population may become offensive or belligerent if explained the confidential aspects of spiritual knowledge, the preacher applies careful discretion regarding what he reveals and to whom he reveals it. He only gives them as much as they can accept in a joyful, positive way. He does not give them that which will cause them confusion. This is the real meaning of Kṛṣṇa's prohibition of not explaining confidential knowledge to the ignorant.

You have stated:

"God would rather people come to Him on their own accord; this is His benevolent nature and His gift to us of free will and free choice. So why ignore this message which came directly from God Himself? Why do you preach?"

You are saying that God would rather have the people come to Him, but you are ignoring the most basic and obvious fact that Kṛṣṇa Himself took the time and trouble to come to us by appearing within this material world to deliver the message of the *Bhagavad-gītā*. To reconfirm this principle of the absolute necessity of spreading Kṛṣṇa consciousness, Lord Kṛṣṇa reappeared 500 years ago as Śrī Caitanya Mahāprabhu.

Lord Kṛṣṇa is unlimitedly compassionate, and so are His devotees. This is why they do not remain silent while the ignorant masses are continually being smashed by the repetition of birth and death. When there is an epidemic, compassionate doctors rush to the scene to inoculate everyone to save their lives. Similarly, the Lord and His devotees manifest compassion upon the ignorant masses by broadcasting widely the transcendental teachings of the *Bhagavad-gītā*.

You are saying, "Why disobey God's orders?" One should not disobey God's orders. Lord Caitanya has ordered that everyone who has taken birth in the holy land of India should make their life perfect and spread Kṛṣṇa consciousness all over the world. If you were born in India and are not spreading Kṛṣṇa consciousness, I could thus ask you why you are disobeying God's orders.

Why Be Culturally Different?

Why is it necessary to have Indian names to join ISKCON? You also have an Indian-sounding name.

Is it not okay to assimilate ISKCON into the local culture? I see the same thing for dress. Why should somebody wear a *dhotī* or *sārī*? I feel the best thing to do is to change the mind, not the outer appearance. In India, where the Hindu way of life is more common, it is really very odd when we see a bearded Muslim man or veil-clad Muslim woman. I feel religion should not be shown by outer appearance but through the mind, thoughts and actions. It would be really fine to see the *sanātana-dharmī* clad in jeans and with a name like Jack, George or Jill instead of Indian names and wearing *sārī* and *dhotī*.

Totalitarianism or Freedom?

A person does not have to change his name or his dress to practice Kṛṣṇa consciousness. However, a person who is very serious about advancing in Kṛṣṇa consciousness will arrange every aspect of his life such a way to facilitate his Kṛṣṇa consciousness as much as possible. If some persons find that accepting Kṛṣṇa conscious names and Kṛṣṇa conscious clothing will facilitate their advancement in Kṛṣṇa consciousness, why should they be restricted from doing so? Why do you want to impose your cultural preferences upon others? If you can have your cultural rights, why others should be denied their cultural rights? A culture in which one is not allowed to accept what is favorable for their Kṛṣṇa consciousness is a totalitarian regime, whereas a culture which allows one to freely practice Kṛṣṇa consciousness is a culture of freedom. Why are you advocating totalitarianism?

Impossible for Everyone to Become Kṛṣṇa Conscious?

Do you agree with the fact that it is impossible to make everyone on this planet Kṛṣṇa conscious?

Everyone Will Become Kṛṣṇa Conscious

Lord Kṛṣṇa does state in the *Bhagavad-gītā*:

manuṣyāṇāṁ sahasreṣu
kaścid yatati siddhaye
yatatām api siddhānāṁ
kaścin māṁ vetti tattvataḥ

> "Out of many thousands among men, one may endeavor for perfection, and of those who have achieved perfection, hardly one knows Me in truth."
>
> *Bhagavad-gītā* 7.3

This tells us clearly that only a small handful of the world population will become Kṛṣṇa conscious. But then Kṛṣṇadāsa Kavirāja states in the *Caitanya-caritāmṛta*:

saj-jana, dur-jana, paṅgu, jaḍa, andha-gaṇa
prema-vanyāya ḍuvāila jagatera jana

> "The Kṛṣṇa consciousness movement will inundate the entire world and drown everyone, whether one be a gentleman, a rogue or even lame, invalid or blind."
>
> *Śrī Caitanya-caritāmṛta, Ādi-līlā* 7.26

He is saying that everyone will become Kṛṣṇa conscious. So is this a contradiction? From the mundane point of view it does certainly appear to be a contradiction. But then when we consider that Lord Caitanya is even more merciful than Lord Kṛṣṇa, we can begin to understand how it is possible that by the mercy of Lord Caitanya, that which is impossible can become completely possible.

There are rules, and there are exceptions to rules. The rule is that only a small percentage of the human population becomes spiritually awakened. But in this most amazing Caitanya Era, which began in 1486, it is possible and conceivable and predicted that the entire human population will become inundated in the tidal wave of Lord Caitanya's mercy by becoming Kṛṣṇa conscious.

When are you going to dive into this ocean? You have been sitting on the shore long enough.

Why Did Americans Take Kṛṣṇa Consciousness and Not the Indians?

You have previously written:

"He (Śrīla Prabhupāda) tried for years and years in India to attract people to join this movement but not one person came. But after arriving in America in 1965, within one year he was able to successfully launch ISKCON, the International Society for Kṛṣṇa Consciousness, which is now powerfully pushing forward a worldwide spiritual revolution."

Is there any specific reason for the Hare Kṛṣṇa movement getting firm grounds in the USA as compared to India? Please let me know, because I always marvel at this miracle.

Americans Were Materially Frustrated

The reason that the Hare Kṛṣṇa movement was able to take its original root in America instead of India was because at that time, in the 1960's, a large segment of the youth of America had become completely frustrated with the advanced materialism of the Western world and were looking for a spiritual alternative. At the same time in India, everyone was interested in how they could advance materially to become like the Western countries. Śrīla Prabhupāda's arrival in America could not have been timed better. This was the perfect arrangement of Kṛṣṇa. Śrīla Prabhupāda arrived just at the right time and in the right place to meet those persons who were the most enthusiastic to receive his message.

When Śrīla Prabhupāda took the American youths to India and the Indian people saw that the Americans were taking up Kṛṣṇa *bhakti*, they become inspired like anything and came forward with great enthusiasm to assist and join Śrīla Prabhupāda's movement. Now that ISKCON has become solidly established in India, the current generation of Indians is realizing how India's traditional Vedic culture is far, far more important than any advancement of material civilization.

In this connection there is *andha-paṅgu-nyāya*, the logic of the blind man and lame man. On their own, each of them is useless. But when the lame man with his good vision gets on the shoulders of the blind man who has strong legs, combined together as a team they become very effective. So India has spiritual vision, but is materially lame. And the Western world has material strength, but is blind in spiritual vision. If there is a combination of Western material advancement with India's Vedic wisdom, the entire world can live happily in a new era of peace and prosperity.

Perfection Before Preaching?

Must we become spiritually perfect before we engage in the supreme welfare activity of the spiritual enlightenment of all living beings?

If this is so, then how are we to share our Kṛṣṇa consciousness until reaching the state of perfection?

Share Whatever You Have Realized

Whatever you have realized about Kṛṣṇa you must share with others. Then Kṛṣṇa will give you more realization. And then when you share that, he will give you even more realization. In this way, your Kṛṣṇa consciousness and your spreading of Kṛṣṇa consciousness will go on increasing unlimitedly.

Does Kṛṣṇa Reward Us for Raising Our Children to Be Kind to Others?

I was wondering: if someone spends a lot of time teaching his children and caring for them and even being "proud" of their progress, is this a self-serving, materialistic goal, or does Kṛṣṇa look favorably upon this? I am a father of two small sons, and I try not to look upon them as accomplishments or trophies; but

I am happy to be their father and hope that I win Kṛṣṇa's favor by being good to them and teaching them how to be kind to others. Is there a reward for this?

The Ultimate Kindness

Raising children to be kind to others is an activity in the mode of goodness. Such a mood is a favorable mood for progressing further toward the transcendental platform, but it is not a substitute for it.

The duty of the father is to raise the children in such a way that they will not take birth again. Being kind to others is very nice, but it obliges us to take birth again to be repaid for the kindness that we gave to others in our previous lifetime. However, if we give to others the ultimate kindness of Kṛṣṇa consciousness, we will be delivered from the cycle of birth and death, and the people to whom we give Kṛṣṇa consciousness will also be delivered. Therefore, Kṛṣṇa consciousness is the ultimate kindness.

Will Kṛṣṇa Remove Obstacles?

I want to preach Kṛṣṇa consciousness, and because of your blessings and the infinite mercy of Kṛṣṇa, people are getting *japa* beads and they are starting their spiritual life.

Many appreciate me, but some try to stop me. Will Kṛṣṇa help me with these obstacles and allow my humble duty to proceed?

If You Strictly Follow

If you remain firm in your determination to be Kṛṣṇa conscious and spread it to others, Kṛṣṇa will remove all obstacles from your pathway. This is confirmed as follows in the *Bhagavad-gītā*:

yatra yogeśvaraḥ kṛṣṇo
yatra pārtho dhanur-dharaḥ
tatra śrīr vijayo bhūtir
dhruvā nītir matir mama

> "Wherever there is Kṛṣṇa, the master of all mystics, and wherever there is Arjuna, the supreme archer, there will also certainly be opulence, victory, extraordinary power, and morality. That is my opinion."
>
> *Bhagavad-gītā* 18.78

In other words, if you remain always strict in your practice of Kṛṣṇa consciousness by chanting at least 16 rounds of the Hare Kṛṣṇa mantra on *japa* beads daily and always avoid the four pillars of sinful life (illicit sex life, meat-eating, intoxication and gambling), you will be empowered by Kṛṣṇa to spread His sweet mercy to many, many souls who are currently drowning deep in the ocean of delusion.

Destruction of Criminal Tendencies

Is there any research institution to reduce and eventually achieve the destruction of all criminal tendencies in human beings?

ISKCON

Yes. There is an institution dedicated to the eradication of all criminal tendencies in human beings. That institution is known as ISKCON, the International Society for "Kṛṣṇa" Consciousness.

However, it should be noted that no research is required. Śrī Caitanya Mahāprabhu, the Supreme Personality of Godhead Lord Śrī Kṛṣṇa appearing as His own devotee, has already revealed the method. This is a verse composed by Him, which describes the cleansing effect of chanting the holy names of God:

ceto-darpana-mārjanaṁ bhava-mahā-dāvāgni-nirvāpanaṁ
śreyaḥ-kairava-candrikā-vitaraṇaṁ vidyā-vadhū-jīvanam
ānandāmbudhi-vardhanaṁ prati-padaṁ pūrṇāmṛtāsvādanaṁ
sarvātma-snapanaṁ paraṁ vijayate śrī-kṛṣṇa-saṅkīrtanam

> "Let there be all victory for the chanting of the holy name of Lord Kṛṣṇa, which can cleanse the mirror of the heart and stop the miseries of the blazing fire of material existence. That chanting is the waxing moon that spreads the white lotus of good fortune for all living entities. It is the life and soul of all education. The chanting of the holy name of Kṛṣṇa expands the blissful ocean of transcendental life. It gives a cooling effect to everyone and enables one to taste full nectar at every step."

Simply by spreading the chanting of the holy names of God all over the world we can put a complete stop to crime and terrorism.

Janmāṣṭamī Prayer

Shall we pray on Janmāṣṭamī for everyone to become a pure devotee of Kṛṣṇa?

First Save Ourselves, Then Others

Praying on Janmāṣṭamī for everyone to become a pure devote is very nice. But we must not forget that if we want such praying to be potent, we must first become fixed in pure devotional service ourselves. So our first business is to fully absorb ourselves in purely chanting the Hare Kṛṣṇa *mantra* regularly at least 16 rounds every day under the guidance of the bona fide spiritual master. After fixing our minds in this way in the mood of pure *bhakti*, we may then chant the following prayer for the benefit of all living beings throughout the universe:

svasty astu viśvasya khalaḥ prasīdatāṁ
dhyāyantu bhūtāni śivaṁ mitho dhiyā
manaś ca bhadraṁ bhajatād adhokṣaje
āveśyatāṁ no matir apy ahaitukī

"May there be good fortune throughout the universe, and may all envious persons be pacified. May all living entities become calm by practicing *bhakti-yoga*, for by accepting devotional service they will think of each other's welfare. Therefore, let us all engage in the service of the supreme transcendence, Lord Śrī Kṛṣṇa, and always remain absorbed in thought of Him."

Śrīmad-Bhāgavatam 5.18.9

Bhagavad-gītā in the UN?

Is it possible to raise the subject of the eternal religion given by Kṛṣṇa in the *Bhagavad-gītā* in the UN Assembly in the present world scenario for global peace, with the assistance of your esteemed organization? Both my friends, David (a Christian) and Mohammed (a Muslim), favor such a situation. Please express your views.

This Knowledge Can Save the World

We will be most happy to share this enlightened knowledge with the world leaders, if they will allow us the opportunity to do so. This knowledge of the Supreme Person and how we can perfectly harmonize with Him does not belong to a sectarian religion. It is the perfection of science and philosophy.

If the world leaders will simply open-mindedly hear from us, all the world's problems will easily be solved. All of humankind will be able to live in perfect harmony with each other and with the environment. There will be no more fear from terrorism, global warming, financial collapse, or any of the thousands of other problems that are presently plaguing the human society.

Is Śrīla Prabhupāda a Nitya-Siddha?

Sometimes a *nitya-siddha*, an ever-liberated personal associate of the Supreme Personality of Godhead, descends into this universe just as the Lord descends.

Is it true that Śrīla Prabhupāda is an ever-liberated, personal associate of Kṛṣṇa, and that he descends under arrangement of Kṛṣṇa for the deliverance of the general populace in Kali-yuga, or is it that he is a soul who achieves liberation through the purification process of *sādhana-bhakti*?

The Greatest of the Nitya-Siddhas

His Divine Grace Śrīla A.C. Bhaktivedanta Swami Prabhupāda is most definitely a *nitya-siddha*, an ever-liberated personal associate of the Supreme Lord. He is also known as a *śaktyāveśa avatāra* because he descended to this material world on the Lord's order for delivering the fallen, conditioned souls of this age. His mission was to write his most special books, the spiritual law books for the suffering humanity, and to launch ISKCON, the International Society for "Kṛṣṇa" Consciousness, that most auspicious spiritual movement which will go down in history for having saved the entire suffering humanity from chaos and despair.

Of all the great spiritual masters who have appeared throughout history, there is no one who is as empowered as Śrīla Prabhupāda for inundating the entire world in a tidal wave of Kṛṣṇa *bhakti*. These are not mere words. He has proven this by spreading the Kṛṣṇa consciousness movement all over the world in a mere eleven years, beginning from 1966 up to 1977. No other *ācārya* even comes close to what he has accomplished for counteracting this most dangerous age of Kali. Thus by comparative analysis we can see that Śrīla Prabhupāda is the greatest of the *nitya-siddhas*.

You Should Live in India, Not the USA

With pleasure I informed a friend of mine about your arrival in Vṛndāvana, India. He gave a strange reply as follows:

"He should always be in Vṛndāvana. Why does he live in the USA? If he advises others to stay away from materialism, why does he himself live in luxury in the USA? Why does he travel in luxurious, air-conditioned cars and live in posh bungalows? If he is true to his followers, he should live in India and not in the USA. He is a noble person, no doubt. But not living in Lord Kṛṣṇa's birthplace is a sin for someone who is head of ISKCON. Out of 365 days in a year, he has only 5-10 days for Indians. It is a matter of shame for him."

What would you say to such a person after reading his reply?

I Always Live in Vṛndāvana

Materialism and spiritualism have nothing to do with where we live. In fact it is a materialistic conception to think that by residing in one place as opposed to another that we will become more spiritual. The real determining factor is who we associate with. If we associate with great transcendentalists, we become great transcendentalists. And if we associate with mundaners, we become mundaners. Mostly all the inhabitants of both the USA and India are in material consciousness. But in both countries there are great transcendentalists to be found if one is very eager to seek them out.

Apparently your friend does not know the real meaning of staying away from materialism. Matter is the energy of God, and materialism means when we utilize that energy for our sense gratification. Conversely spiritualism means when we utilize that energy in God's service. Some people have the misconception that spiritualism means to have nothing to do with matter. But that is not a fact. We cannot avoid dealing with matter because we are surrounded by it on all sides. The key is that we have to engage whatever material facility we have in the service of the Lord; then we are spiritualists. The same principle applies both in the USA and in India.

You may tell your friend that I am constantly traveling and preaching all over the world because my Guru Mahārāja has ordered me to turn the entire world into the spiritual Vṛndāvana atmosphere. I am not staying in one place permanently to enjoy the material facilities there.

Kṛṣṇa's incarnation in this age, Lord Caitanya, has ordered that it is duty of all Indians to become spiritually perfect and do the highest welfare work of spreading Kṛṣṇa consciousness all over the world. But instead of going after Kṛṣṇa, the modern-day Indians are going after technology and money and are therefore neglecting their duty to become Kṛṣṇa conscious and make the whole world Kṛṣṇa conscious.

And now, when an American takes up the duty neglected by the Indians, your friend criticizes him for not spending more time in India. Apparently he is not aware that in the Vedic histories we have authoritative information that this entire planet was formerly India. Simply it is due to the influence of this materialistic age of Kali that India has been gradually shrinking more and more. Just like several decades ago Pakistan was chopped off as a separate country. Formerly the capital of the entire planet earth was Hastināpura, which is now known as Delhi, India. I have dedicated my entire existence to restoring the original Indian Vedic culture all over the world. What is your friend doing besides criticizing me?

So far no one has ever given me a posh bungalow for my residence or has driven me in a luxury car. I accept whatever meager transportation or place of residence is offered to me, even if is it very simple. But in this connection I ask your friend to kindly note:

Because the spiritual master is a representative of God, according to the authorized Vedic literatures, he is meant to be offered the same honor and respect that is given to God. When God is conveyed from one place to another, He is taken in a golden chariot. When He is offered a place of residence, the walls are bedecked with valuable jewels. So I think that even if my disciples were to offer me a Rolls Royce and a marble palace, it will still not be to the full standard.

I am not the head of ISKCON. I am simply one of the many spiritual masters who are working together within the ISKCON mission to bring about a spiritual revolution on this planet. I spend more or less time in a given place depending on how many lectures my students and disciples can arrange for me. If your friend can book for me an extensive lecture tour within India, I will be happy to spend more time in the wonderful, holy land of India.

The shame is not on me. I am doing my duty. The shame is on those Indians who are neglecting their duty. They have been ordered to make their lives spiritually perfect and spread Kṛṣṇa consciousness all over the world. It is these Indians who are neglecting their duty who should be ashamed, not me. I am properly situated in *dharma* (duty). It is they who have become *adharmīs*, neglectors of their duty.

Great Appreciation

I feel amazingly blessed by your encouraging words of wisdom! Your course is a life-changing blessing that has increased my thirst and desire for understanding Kṛṣṇa and for the sweet nectar that flows. I appreciate the pure insight you share with the world to spread Kṛṣṇa consciousness. It's created in me a deeper motivation and desire to devote my life to the service of spreading love and light to help enlighten the souls of individuals!

This Very Much Encourages Me

I appreciate very much your sweet loving sentiments. The exchange of love between devotees is described by Śrīla Rūpa Gosvāmī as one of the items of devotional service to Lord Kṛṣṇa. The more we can love Kṛṣṇa's representative, the spiritual master, the more our love for Kṛṣṇa will grow because he is the external manifestation of Kṛṣṇa within our hearts.

That you are so much inspired by my humble attempt to serve Śrīla Prabhupāda is his great kindness upon me. This very much encourages me to continue in my attempt to bring more and more lost souls throughout the world into the nectarean ocean of the Kṛṣṇa consciousness movement. I request that you take the regulative principles of Kṛṣṇa consciousness most seriously now and prepare yourself for initiation.

About the Author

His Grace Sriman Sankarshan Das Adhikari appeared in this world in St. Louis, Missouri, USA on 7 November 1947, the tenth day (daśamī) of the most holy month of Kartik according to the Vaiṣṇava calendar. He first met his spiritual master, His Divine Grace A.C. Bhaktivedanta Swami Prabhupada, in 1971 and was initiated by him on 12 August of the same year. Srila Prabhupada personally told this new young disciple that he was pleased with his sincerity and enthusiasm for spreading the Krishna consciousness movement. Sankarshan Das fully dedicated his life for serving the order of his spiritual master to become a guru and deliver the world. For the last 40+ years he has uninterruptedly served his spiritual master's movement, the International Society for Krishna Consciousness (ISKCON), in various capacities.

In the year 2000, in recognition for his full dedication to Srila Prabhupada's mission, ISKCON's Governing Body Commission (GBC) gave him their blessings to initiate disciples. Since that time he has been regularly traveling and lecturing extensively all over the world for reviving the dormant Krishna consciousness in the hearts of all living beings. Well known for his Internet-based training program, the Ultimate Self-Realization Course, he has attracted over 15,000 subscribers from over 100 different countries who receive a daily inspirational message and personal answers to their questions regarding how to become perfect in Krishna consciousness.

Those who are interested can join his course at: **www.backtohome.com**

Know Who You Are, Be Who You Are

The Ultimate Self-Realization Course™

Taught by His Grace Sankarshan Das Adhikari, disciple of His Divine Grace A. C. Bhaktivedanta Swami Prabhupāda, Founder-Acārya of the "International Society for Krishna Consciousness"

Expert instruction in the authentic art and science of spiritual self-realization

E-course

- Weekly lessons, reading guide and study questions with feedback

- Opportunity for personal inquiry and correspondence with His Grace Sankarshan Das Adhikari

- Learn at your own pace, on your own schedule, in your own home

"Thought for the Day"

- Daily inspirational messages, thoughtful questions and enlightening answers from Vedic authority

- Spiritual consciousness - ever-increasing and ever-fresh, delivered to straight to your inbox

No fee, no obligation, no hassle – confidentiality assured

The path of fulfillment is open for you.

Sign up today and begin your journey. . .

www.backtohome.com

Bibliography

Books by A. C. Bhaktivedanta Swami Prabhupāda:

___________. [1960] 1970. *Easy Journey to Other Planets*. Rev. ed. Los Angeles: Bhaktivedanta Book Trust. Original ed. Delhi: author.

___________. [1970] 1986. *KṚṢṆA: The Supreme Personality of Godhead*. Los Angeles: Bhaktivedanta Book Trust.

___________. [1974] 1988. *Teachings of Lord Caitanya, the Golden Avatāra*. Los Angeles: Bhaktivedanta Book Trust.

___________. 1974, 1975. *Śrī Caitanya-caritāmṛta of Kṛṣṇadāsa Kavirāja Gosvāmī*. 17 vols. Los Angeles: Bhaktivedanta Book Trust.

___________. [1975] 1993. *The Nectar of Instruction: An Authorized English Presentation of Śrīla Rūpa Gosvāmī's* Śrī Upadeśāmṛta. Los Angeles: Bhaktivedanta Book Trust.

___________. 1982. *Nectar of Devotion: A Summary Study of Śrīla Rūpa Gosvāmī's* Bhakti-rasāmṛta-sindhu, 2nd ed. Los Angeles: Bhaktivedanta Book Trust.

___________. 1983. *Bhagavad-gītā As It Is*, 2nd ed., rev. and enl. Los Angeles: Bhaktivedanta Book Trust.

___________. 1987. *Śrīmad-Bhāgavatam*. 12 cantos. Cantos 1-10, chapter 13 by Prabhupāda; canto 10, chapter 14 – canto 12 by his disciples. Los Angeles: Bhaktivedanta Book Trust.

___________. 1997. *Śrī Īśopaniṣad*, 3rd ed. Los Angeles: Bhaktivedanta Book Trust.

Additional reference:

Bhaktisiddhānta Sarasvatī. 1989. *Śrī Brahma-saṁhitā*. Los Angeles: Bhaktivedanta Book Trust.

Index of Verses Quoted

This index lists the verses quoted in each of the six topics of this book. Numerals in boldface type refer to the first and third lines of verses quoted in full. Numerals in ordinary-face type indicate partially quoted verses.

ā-brahma-bhuvanāl lokāḥ 33
ācāryaṁ māṁ vijānīyān 112
ādau śraddhā tataḥ sādhu- 164
ahaṁ sarvasya prabhavo 105, 206
antavat tu phalaṁ teṣāṁ 89
athāto brahma jijñāsā 108
ātmānaṁ rathinaṁ viddhi 33
bhaktiḥ pareśānubhavo viraktir 249
buddhiṁ tu sārathiṁ viddhi 34
ceto-darpaṇa-mārjanaṁ bhava
-mahā-dāvāgni-nirvāpaṇaṁ 134, 273
daivaṁ na tat syān na patiś
ca sa syān 180
daivī hy eṣā guṇa-mayī 85
dehino 'smin yathā dehe 13
dharmaṁ tu sākṣād
bhagavat-praṇītaṁ 51
etad vāṁ darśitaṁ rūpaṁ 106
ete cāṁśa-kalāḥ puṁsaḥ 105
guru-kṛṣṇa-prasāde pāya
bhakti-latā-bīja 217
gurur na sa syāt sva-jano
na sa syāt 193
īśvaraḥ paramaḥ kṛṣṇaḥ 100, 105, 206, 238
janma karma ca me divyam 213
jīvo jīvasya jīvanam 32
jñānaṁ te 'haṁ sa-vijñānam 50, 100
jñānena tu tad ajñānaṁ 128
kecit sva-dehāntar-hṛdayāvakāśe 82
kārpaṇya-doṣopahata-svabhāvaḥ 111
mac-cittā mad-gata-prāṇā 246
man-manā bhava mad-bhakto 6, 161, 257
manuṣyāṇāṁ sahasreṣu 10, 68, 269
mayā tatam idaṁ sarvaṁ 86
māyāvādam asac-chāstraṁ 248
na buddhi-bhedaṁ janayed 267
na jāyate mriyate vā kadācin 16
na tv evāhaṁ jātu nāsaṁ 71
nityo nityānāṁ cetanaś cetanānām 49
oṁ ajñāna-timirāndhasya 131
oṁ namo bhagavate
mukhyatamāya namaḥ sattvāya 92
oṁ pūrṇam adaḥ pūrṇam idaṁ 107
paraṁ brahma paraṁ dhāma 207
patraṁ puṣpaṁ phalaṁ toyaṁ 156, 170
pañca-tattvātmakaṁ kṛṣṇaṁ 96
pralayo payodhi-jale dhṛtavān
asi vedaṁ 93
premāñjana-cchurita
-bhakti-vilocanena 170, 211, 216
prāyeṇālpāyuṣaḥ sabhya 67
pūṣann ekarṣe yama sūrya
prājāpatya 234
rūpa-raghunātha-pade
hoibe ākuti 244
śābde pare ca niṣṇātaṁ 96, 104, 109, 206
sa cintayan dvy-akṣaram
ekadāmbhasy 99
saj-jana, dur-jana, paṅgu, jaḍa,
andha-gaṇa 270
samyaṅ-masṛṇita-svānto 168
samāśritā ye pada-pallava-plavaṁ 29
śamo damas tapaḥ śaucaṁ 251
sa niścayena yoktavyo 187
śarīra avidyā-jāl 152
śarīraṁ yad avāpnoti 18, 20
sarva-dharmān parityajya 21, 60, 216

sarva-yoniṣu kaunteya 42
satataṁ kīrtayanto māṁ 161
śravaṇaṁ kīrtanaṁ viṣṇoḥ 165
śrotraṁ cakṣuḥ sparśanaṁ ca 20
śuśrūṣoḥ śraddadhānasya 181
svasty astu viśvasya khalaḥ prasīdatāṁ 274
tad viddhi praṇipātena 5, 123, 160, 217
tad vijñānārthaṁ sa gurum eva abhigacchet 112, 217
tasmād guruṁ prapadyeta 112, 120, 125, 217
tat te 'nukampāṁ su-samīkṣamāṇo 213
tretā-yugādau ca tato 91
tribhir guṇa-mayair bhāvair 84
vadanti tat tattva-vidas 84, 87
vedāhaṁ samatītāni 82
veṇuṁ kvaṇantam aravinda-dalāyatākṣam- 231
vidyāṁ cāvidyāṁ ca yas 196
viṣayā vinivartante 220
vyavasāyātmikā buddhir 188
vāsudeve bhagavati 81
yajña-śiṣṭāśinaḥ santo 155
yasmin sarvāṇi bhūtāny 56
yas tu sarvāṇi bhūtāny 69, 227
yasya deve parā bhaktir 2
yasyaika-niśvasita-kālam athāvalambya 98
yasya prasādād bhagavat-prasādaḥ 217
yat karoṣi yad aśnāsi 161

Keyword Index

A

Abhayam. See: Fearlessness
Absolute Truth
accepting Kṛṣṇa's face as requirement for understanding, . 237
addressed in Vedic *mantra oṁ tat sat*, ... 262
Arjuna's description of Kṛṣṇa as, ... 207
as able to eat food & enjoy it,... 157
as *Brahman, Paramātmā & Bhagavān*, ... 84, 87
as devoid of contradiction,......... 72
as original energy of living entity, ... 8
as original underlying reality of all existence, ... 8
as pathway of escaping "grass is greener" syndrome, ... 224
as simultaneously one & different, ... 104, 249
beyond material designations, ... 49
Bhagavad-gītā as, ... 255
cannot be extinguished, ... 108
experience of elevates to absolute plane, ... 101
full realization of via practice, ... 44
ISKCON having most perfect & complete conception of, ... 51
ISKCON having most perfect & complete methodology of realizing, ... 51
Kṛṣṇa as, ... 101
logical necessity of, ... 43, 225
may be temporarily covered, ... 109
meaning of Kṛṣṇa's position as, ... 157
perception of does not relativize, ... 101
reaching the precincts of as the end of skepticism, ... 109
religion as means of connecting to, ... 43
simultaneously with spiritual form & without material form, ...248-249
spiritual master fully reveals, ... 109
Śrī Caitanya Mahāprabhu's citation of the Koran establishing the Lord as, ... 57
Śrī Caitanya Mahāprabhu's philosophical amalgam of *dvaita* & *advaita* conceptions of, ... 249
tat as, ... 262
understanding of as purpose of human life, ... 108
Ācārya(s)
after Śaṅkarācārya, ...210
as free from restrictive influence of material nature, ... 257
as givers of perfect knowledge, ... 137
as guides of Vedic civilization, ... 117
as one who teaches by example, .. 140
as present more than one at a time, ... 119
becoming disciple of required for knowing our eternal spiritual identity, ... 244
blessings of destroy irritation, ... 222
chanting on beads by, ... 140
disciple's life & soul dedicated to, ... 265
following in footsteps of, ... 167, 257, 263
ISKCON will create millions of, .. 263
mood of while chanting, ... 226
relishing direct association of the Supreme Lord, ... 226
Śrīla Bhaktivinoda Ṭhākura as, ... 196
Śrīla Prabhupāda as, ... 124
Śrīla Prabhupāda as most empowered among, ... 255, 275
Acintya-bhedābheda-tattva
defined, ... 104

Action(s) (activity)
as free will or bondage, ... 218
as sinful, ... 135
bhakti as, ... 156, 159
doer in, ... 80
in inaction, ... 171
in mode of goodness, ...272
not disrupting minds of those attached to, ...267
of Kalki, ...254
of *māyā*, ...203
of spreading Kṛṣṇa consciousness, ...61, 118, 249
of the sparrow, ...187
of those who've lost intelligence, ...95
spiritual master trains in different departments of, ...113
suffering through resultant, gaining liberation, ... 214
sunrise prompting, ... 137
to be used for Kṛṣṇa's pleasure, ... 4, 135, 154, 160, 166
topmost, ... 61
without attachment to results, ...37, 163
Advaitācārya
as devotional manifestation, ... 97
Ages, universal. *See: Yuga(s)*
Ahiṁsā (non-violence)
Lord Buddha's establishing, ... 45
Ajaṁ
Kṛṣṇa as, ... 207
Analogies
Absolute Truth & train, ... 83
arithmetic & basic spiritual knowledge, ...267
Arjuna & us, ... 111
belief & wind, ...103
body of water & Kṛṣṇa-conscious association, ...176
businessman & devotee, ... 166
candle & Kṛṣṇa, ... 236
change of bodies in this life & change of bodies after death, ... 12
devotees from pastimes 5,000 years ago & devotees in spiritual world, ... 241
desire & fire, ...114
eating & taking shelter of Kṛṣṇa, ... 249
experience of the Lord & experience of any great person, ... 31
fish out of water & us, ... 225
flying in an airplane & life in the material world, ... 210
foreign country & spiritual world, ... 235
Ganges River & devoted mind, ...181
God's form & ours, ... 238
heart & courtyard, ...146
heart & garden, ...139
heart & hotel, ...168
hen & Vedic literature, ...248
herbivores & human body, ...183
India & Western countries, ...271
intelligence & driver, ... 34
Ivy-league school entrance requirements & regulative principles, ...121-122
Kṛṣṇa & India, ... 70
Kṛṣṇa & root of tree, ... 126
Kṛṣṇa & thunderbolt, ... 245
medicine & Vedic injunction, ...259
medics & devotees, ... 268
meeting a king & learning spiritual knowledge, ...261
modern-day culture & Vedic culture, ...128
modes of material nature & spiritual energies, ... 236
Oṁ & saying "Hey, you", ... 230
Pakistan & whole world divided from Vedic culture, ... 276
physician & spiritual master, ... 130, 138
playing *mṛdaṅga* with two hands & coordinating spiritual life with material responsibilities, ... 195

prison & material world, ...37
puddle & ocean of birth & death, ... 224
rock & hard heart, ... 208
snowflakes & *jīva* souls, ...67
soil & soft heart, ...208
spiritual master & father, ...193
sunlight & soul, ... 75
water & soul, ...203, 250
Ancestors
worship of, ...89
Anger how to conquer, ... 171
Animal(s)
as children of God, ... 124
as loved by devotee, ...227
eating like, ...154
giving up eating of, ... 124, 151, 191
how to become, ...191
humans who behave like, ... 151, 154
killing of under restriction, ...124, 183, 191
meat-eating allowed for, ...183
no more sacred than microbe or carrot, ...153
not to blame for environmental disruption, ...183
progressing toward human form, .150
result of slaughtering, ... 47, 124, 151, 153, 181, 191
taking birth as for proof of *karma*, ...191
Annihilation of universe(s),
Fish incarnation delivering earth from, ... 92
spiritual particles unharmed by, ..239
Arcanam
defined, ...165
Arjuna
as co-guarantor of opulence, victory, extraordinary power, & morality, ...272
as possessed of complete self-confidence, ...257
as renouncer of the fruits of action, not action itself, ... 197
as serving by his ability, ...113, 197
doubts of, ...171
focused on Kṛṣṇa amid hellish conditions, ... 198
following in footsteps of, ... 111, 113, 198, 257, 272
Kṛṣṇa's statements to, ... 74, 82, 178, 210, 213
as evidence of Vedic civilization's existence 5,000 years ago, ...262
Kṛṣṇa accepted as Lord by,....206-207
mood of during inquiry, ...111
surrender of, ... 111, 257
Āryan(s)
European Indologists' invasion theory of, refuted, ...255, 262
Association
bad rejected in favor of solitude, . 177
giving love to inspire others via, . 195
God also wants, ...71
method of with a great man, ...31
of devotees, ...19, 24, 31, 160, 176, 177, 185, 207-208, 225,229
better than solitude, ... 177
intense hankering for, ...201
Kṛṣṇa will give more and more if sincere, ...185
of Kṛṣṇa,.............................21, 41, 81, 109, 185, 219, 226
of materialism disguised as religiosity, ...177
of mind & senses, ...34
of spiritual master, ... 126, 132, 160
through Śrīla Prabhupāda's books, ... 185
Atheists
art of debating with, ... 205
as unaware of their connection with God, ...76
Buddhists as,........................... 45
destination of, ... 73

equation of demigods with the Supreme Lord by, ... 145
material world, made for, ...73
Śaṅkarācārya's teaching for, ...248
Ātmā
defined,................................ 68
Attachment
destination of person bound by, ... 21
how to overcome, ... 4, 164, 176, 204
not disrupting the minds of the ignorant, who have fruitive, ...267
offense of maintaining material, .. 145
pretending to be God conscious while exhibiting, ...30
to Absolute Truth, ... 51, 164
to happiness, ... 163
to intoxication, ...186
to meat-eating, ... 46
to not doing one's duty, ...74
Austerity (austerities)
as brahminical quality, ... 251
as nectar for the Kṛṣṇa-conscious person, ...166
as wealth of the renounced, ... 166
in tandem with joy in *bhakti,* 166
Kṛṣṇa as beneficiary of, ... 135
of preaching, ... 85
on Ekādasī, ...178
performed as an offering to Kṛṣṇa, ... 161
Authorities. *See:* Government, Human being(s), Spiritual master(s)
Avatāras. See: Incarnations

B

Balarāma, Lord
along with Kṛṣṇa entering wrestling arena, ...245
as having long arms, ...245
as integrated expansion, ...94, 224
as Kṛṣṇa Himself in role of brother, ...94
Rāma as name of, ...137
Banyan tree,
worship of as limb of *bhakti*, ... 167
Bathing,
as activity in *bhakti,* 147, 153, 200
Battle of Kurukṣetra. *See:* Kurukṣetra, battle of
Beauty,
as epitomized by lotus,............. 230
as opulence of the Lord, ...207
of devotees' smiles, ... 192
of Kṛṣṇa,
as one of the reasons the author loves Kṛṣṇa, ... 166
evident to the people in general, ..245
telling others about, ...208
of peacock feather, ...239
God has the most, ...53
of Lord's figure, ... 192, 231, 234, 238
Begging
for blessings of demigods to surrender to Kṛṣṇa, ...95
for help from Guru & Kṛṣṇa, ...218
for Kṛṣṇa's forgiveness when offense is inevitable,............... 158
for spiritual rather than material benedictions, ...144
Hare Kṛṣṇa *mahā-mantra* as,...... 50
of Kṛṣṇa, ... 114
to chant purely, ...134
Beings. *See:*
Living entities; Souls
Benediction
of Lord to allow devotees to act even more powerfully than the Lord alone, ...208
of pure consciousness, ...144
saṇkīrtana movement as, ...135
Śrīla Prabhupāda's books as, ... 264
the best, ...144, 264
Bhagavad-gītā
age of, ...91, 100
Arjuna's glorification of Kṛṣṇa in, ...207
Arjuna's surrender in, ...111

as advanced among scriptures of the world, ... 1
as introduction to highest knowledge, ... 261
as non-sectarian scripture, . 12, 54, 60
as possessing everything you need to know, ... 50, 95, 128, 264
as reference for determining authority of guru, ... 117, 129
as supplemented by other books,. 264
authenticity of, ...255
becomes more interesting in association of devotees, ... 246
four verses for perfection, ... 160-161
heard by Manu, ...91
Kṛṣṇa came to deliver, ... 268
mankind strayed from, ... 63
most authoritative & popular edition of, ...1
on animal-killing, ... 46-47
on brahminical qualities, ...251
on consciousness at time of death, ... 13-14, 18
on demigod worship, ... 89
on eternality of soul, ... 1,6, 67, 71
on extent of its authority, ... 51, 95, 96, 128
on freedom from birth & death, .. 33, 213
on highly focused intelligence, ... 188
on how to show love & devotion, .. 6, 65, 95, 170
on Kṛṣṇa's instruction to chant,.... 65, 143, 149, 161
on Kṛṣṇa's omnipotence, ... 91
on Kṛṣṇa's omnipresence, ... 85, 86
on Kṛṣṇa's omniscience, ... 82
on Kṛṣṇa's origination of everything, ... 91, 96, 101, 206, 207
on Kṛṣṇa's reciprocation with devotees, ... 85, 104, 211, 219
on meaning of conventional proposition,........................... 66
on means of self-realization, ... 5, 113
on means of transmigration, ... 13, 18, 20
on mind, ... 140, 187, 188
on natural qualification for occupational duties,................ 258
on *prasādam*, ... 157, 255
on rain, ... 247
on rarity of Kṛṣṇa consciousness, ... 68, 269-270
on realm of pure mind, ...87
on responsibility for action, ... 74
on seeing Kṛṣṇa everywhere, ... 85
on sense control, ... 169, 178-179, 187, 220
on serving according to one's ability, ... 113-114
on spiritual master, ... 123, 129, 160, 161, 217
on surrender to Kṛṣṇa, ... 2,1, 60, 95, 216
on the Vedas, ... 260
on transcendence of the illusory energy, ... 85, 89, 213
on understanding self & body, ... 13
on universal family, ... 42
preaching about, ... 125, 268
applying discretion while, ... 268
Kṛṣṇa removes obstacles for those engaged in, ... 272
reveals Kṛṣṇa as the heavenly father, ... 52
study of, ... 1, 2, 4, 6, 38, 95, 96, 178, 180, 182, 215, 256, 260
as item for enhance observance of Ekādasī, ... 178
as required item for disciple, ... 182
how to engage in, ... 38
lets you feel Kṛṣṇa's presence, ... 215
lets you know how to surrender to Kṛṣṇa, ... 251
to know Kṛṣṇa's desire, ... 182, 256
to understand where someone stands spiritually, ...260

without accepting authority of, ... 38
surrendering to follow, ...210
the author simply presents, ... 113, 117, 215
Śrīla Prabhupāda purely presents, . 51
Śrīla Viśvanātha Cakravartī Ṭhākura on, ... 114
Bhagavān
imitators of, ...252
Kṛṣṇa as *svayaṁ-*, ... 105
percentages of, ... 90
with *brahman & paramātmā*, ...84, 87, 260
Bhāgavatam. See: Śrīmad-Bhāgavatam
Bhāgavata Purāṇa. See: Śrīmad-Bhāgavatam
Bhakta
Lord appearing as, ... 97
Bhakti-rasāmṛta-sindhu
on nine processes of *bhakti*, ... 164
Bhaktisiddhānta Sarasvatī Ṭhākura
as spiritual master of our Śrīla Prabhupāda, ... 118, 265
Bhaktivedānta Swami Prabhupāda, His Divine Grace A.C., *See:* Prabhupāda
Bhaktivinoda Ṭhākura
as ideal example of householder, .196
prayer for honoring *prasādam* by,.152
Bhakti-yoga. See: Devotional service
Bhāva
as stage of devotion preceding *prema*, ...164, 168
as worship of Kṛṣṇa, ...206
Bible
as younger than *Bhagavad-gītā*, ...100
on animal-killing, ...124, 182
on creating man in the image of God, ...238
on idolatry, ...250
Bird
encaged (analogy of soul in body), ...197, 200
sister of Garuḍa, ...187
Birth
according to consciousness at time of death, ...13
all species of life made possible by, ...42
among the demigods, ghosts, spirits, ancestors, ... 89
as false qualification for *varṇa*, ... 251, 258
as ghost, ... 26, 89
defects, ... 15
ducks taking next as humans, ...150
human, ... 14, 15, 21
in India means one must preach as per Lord Caitanya's order, ...268
never take again, ...33, 213
of Jesus, ... 52
of Kṛṣṇa, ...106
second from spiritual master, ... 130
with death old age & disease, .23, 27, 30, 37, 38, 80, 176, 184, 21, 232, 251
everyone will get tired of, ... 27
Birth & death cycle
choosing path of, ... 221
devotees advise everyone to escape, ...36, 253
the reason that, ...268
eating non-offered food forces one into, ... 155
entanglement in via false sense of "I", ... 73, 184, 214
entanglement in via lack of seriousness, ...259
entanglement in via prayers for material things, ...223
external to living entity, ... 17
forced to enter due to envy, ... 127
hellish planets stopping-off point in, ...21
imitation God-consciousness keeps one within, ...30
liberation from
choosing path of, ... 221
concocted religious systems won't help with, ... 51

devotional love for the Supreme as a matter of, ... 106
Ekādasī's role in, ... 178
everyone will eventually receive, ...27
great determination for, ... 176
guardians must provide access to for dependents, ... 194, 259, 272
impossible if you run away from the truth, ... 38
not possible by remembering past lives, ...18
requires testing, ... 24
Śrī Īśopaniṣad Mantra 11 on, ... 196
those in pure goodness achieve, ... 68
those serious about become Kṛṣnatarian, ... 155
those serious about surrender to spiritual master through initiation, ...201
via a liberated soul only, ... 112,
via chanting, ... 9, 28, 30, 102, 135, 147
via going back to Godhead, .. 33, 213
via human birth, ... 16, 21
via preaching, ...272
via surrender to Kṛṣṇa, ... 12, 21, 27, 36, 64, 85, 148
via *sādhana-bhakti,* 178
with the author, ... 11
words of the author/ Kṛṣṇa fully potent for, ...215
meant for atheists, ...73
ocean of shrunk to the size of hoof-print of a calf, ...224
parents who keep children within, ...193
save spouse from, ...208
those who are in goodness remain in, ...68
we have been in for millions of lifetimes, ... 163-164
Yamarāja's role in, ...21
Blasphemy. *See:* Offenses
Blessings. *See:* Benedictions, Mercy
Bodily concept of life
as cause of pain, ...70
as ghost, ...26
begins from childhood, ...15
cause of overeating, oversleeping, ...159
cheating oneself via, ...214
compared to aromas in the air, ... 18
conventional proposition on, ...66
freedom from,
by prayer, ...38
by seeing the changeless self, ..13, 78
for centering, ...182
in various bodies, ...12, 16
keeping us entangled in birth & death, ... 12, 73, 184
known as false ego, ...73
Kṛṣṇa's form liberates from, ...234
limited to one's own body, ...107
overcoming via *bhakti*, ... 159
sex as ultimate reinforcement of, . 214
Body (material)
acting only for pleasure of distracts from *bhakti*, ... 135
animating principle within, ... 78
any sexual inclination based on identification with, ...184, 214, 215
as birdcage,.......................... 197, 200
as lump of ignorance, ...152
caring for along with focusing on the Lord, ... 197, 210
changing from one to another within this lifetime, ...13
as evidence that I am separate, ... 17
child overpowered by *māyā* identifies with, ... 15
compared to chariot, ...34
decays when soul leaves, ... 20
determined by mentality, ... 17, 20
dualities due to possessing, ...35
false ego as identification with, ...71, 73, 184

freedom from, ...20, 184, 213
fully Kṛṣṇa conscious even within, ... 242
gross composed of earth, water, fire, air, & ether,...............19
leaving, ... 161
leaving when young, ...19
material life comes with birth & demise of, ... 200
near-death experiences due to soul temporarily leaving, ... 19-20
no better medicine for healing than Kṛṣṇa consciousness, ... 37
offering to Kṛṣṇa, ... 37, 134, 165
of ghost, ... 26
of human designed for vegetarian diet, ... 175, 183
of tiger designed for flesh-eating,.175
pain due to identification with, ... 70
paleness of as ecstatic symptom, ..168
Paramātmā within, ...83
prāṇa within, ...68
purification of, ... 157
soul aware of pains & pleasures only within his own, ... 107
soul carried into gross by subtle, ... 19
soul enters another at death, ...18, 20, 22
soul immovable within, ... 77
soul is not slain with slaying of, ... 17
subtle composed of mind, intelligence, & false ego, ... 19
you are not your, ... 13, 182, 215, 233

Body (spiritual)
as bird in a cage, ... 200
as original ego, ...9
as passenger in car of material body, ... 34
free from old age & disease, ... 231
fulfills spiritual desires, ... 209
regained after discarding subtle material desires, ... 19
revived via Kṛṣṇa consciousness, ... 17, 213,
similar to Kṛṣṇa's body, ... 238
suppressed by the material world, ... 9

Brahmā, Lord
as original created person, ... 100
as possessing his own planet, . 99-100
as *sampradāyācārya*, ... 263
Brahma-saṁhitā of, quoted,.............98, 99, 105, 206, 216
enlightened with Vedic wisdom, ..262
name of not equal to name of Lord Viṣṇu, ... 145
quoted in *Kali-santaraṇa Upaniṣad* on Hare Kṛṣṇa *mantra*, ... 138
receiving the Sanskrit syllables "*ta pa*", ... 99
time of, ... 137

Brahman
Arjuna declares Kṛṣṇa to be, ... 207
compared to *paramātmā* & *bhagavān* 84, 87, 260
half-hen logic applied to, ... 249
identification with, ...73
mentioned in *Bhagavad-gītā*, ... 42
mentioned in *Śrīmad-Bhāgavatam*, ... 112, 120, 125, 217
misunderstood by Māyāvādi philosophers, ... 71, 256
purpose of human life to inquire about, ... 108

Brāhmaṇa(s)
being cannot induce Kṛṣṇa to accept an offering, ... 156
Lord Śiva appears as a, ... 248
occupational duties of, ... 258
qualities/qualifications of, ... 251

Buddha
as name of the Supreme, ... 1, 45
Buddhists worship of, ... 45
nature of, ... 87, 260
mission of, ... 44, 95

Buddhi-yoga, recommended in *Bhagavad-gītā*, ... 267

Business & *vaiśyas*
as occupational duty, ... 258

burden of wealth on, ... 133
compared to devotee, ... 166
in Kṛṣṇa consciousness, ... 197

C

Caitanya, Lord
advice of, ... 217
as *bhakta-rūpa*,........................ 97
as Supreme Personality of Godhead, ... 253, 255, 270, 273, 276
as *ācārya*, ... 255, 263
call out for the help of, ... 152-153
golden era of, ... 36
in conversation with Muslim scholar, ... 57
Kṛṣṇa consciousness movement of, ... 39, 119
way paved for by Buddhism, ... 45
Lord Nityānanda as first expansion of, ... 97
mission of, ... 118-119
order of, ... 202
philosophical synthesis of, .. 248-249
Śrī Advaita Ācārya as incarnation of, ... 97
verse one of *Śikṣāṣṭakam* by, ... 134-135
Caitanya-caritāmṛta cited
on chanting fixed rounds, ... 143
on inundation of world with Kṛṣṇa consciousness, ... 39, 270
Caste system, Vedic. *See: Varṇāśrama-dharma* system
Chanting
as first priority, ... 139
as hearing, ... 179
as intoxication, ... 186
benefits of, ...9, 50, 61, 136, 146, 147,216, 235, 247, 252,273
best method of, ... 139, 140, 142, 147, 180-181
Bhagavad-gītā on, ...161
by Christians, ... 55
by Lord Caitanya, ...149, 253, 273
by Muslims, ...58
constantly, 5, 30, 38, 143, 184-185
defined, ...143
deity worship meant to empower, ...142
japa, ...4, 121, 138, 139, 143, 148, 180-181, 199, 228, 247,273
Kṛṣṇa's reciprocation with, ... 166
mood of Vaiṣṇava *ācāryas* while, . 226
prayer for, ...38
specifically Hare Kṛṣṇa, ...138, 141-142
stages of, ...144
verse one of *Śikṣāṣṭakam* on,.134-135
while offering food, ... 152
wide scale introduction of, ... 39, 171
within nine processes of devotional service, ...165
with offenses, ...35, 137, 155
Cheaters & cheated
so-called gurus as, ...125
so-called religionists as, ...206
Children, duty toward, ...193, 196, 259, 272
Civilization. *See:* Society
Cleanliness
as one of 26 qualities of a devotee, ...226
when cooking for Kṛṣṇa, ...153
Comparisons. *See:* Analogies
Compassion
as blessing from *ācāryas*, ...222
as non-sectarian, ...181
of devotees, ... 26, 85, 202
of Garuḍa, ... 187
preaching, ... 222
Conditioned souls
as eternal servants of Kṛṣṇa, ... 79
delivered by pure devotees, ... 36-37, 112, 275
delivered devotional service, ... 58-59, 106, 112
floating in *prāṇa*, ...68

habituated to *māyā*, ... 93
pastimes of the Lord amazing to, .174
Confidential knowledge. *See:*
Devotional service;
Knowledge
Consciousness
artificial caste, ... 258
at the time of death, ... 13, 17, 19
change of, ... 19
conditioned, ...68, 79, 148, 174, 275
perceives things as
contradictory,............................ 228
defined, ... 78
effect of intoxication on, ... 175, 189
fixed in by higher taste, ... 220
individual compared with
Supreme, ... 8, 34, 50
of non-humans, ... 33, 183
original nature of, ...8, 16, 19,
56, 65, 77, 148, 184
perfected/purified, ...31, 56, 95,
128, 143, 154, 172, 199
uncovered by mercy of Guru &
Kṛṣṇa, ... 228
while chanting, ... 136, 145
See also: Kṛṣṇa consciousness;
Living entities
Constitutional position,
understanding, ... 115
Cow(s)
economy based on, ... 39
killing of, as punishable, ... 191
milking as work, ... 247
no overpopulation of, ... 191
Cowherd boys/girls, as
friends of Kṛṣṇa, ... 228, 232, 245
Creation
age of the, ... 99
Kṛṣṇa aloof from, ... 86
of a new world, ... 42, 55
of fine brain tissue, ... 157
of God by Himself, ... 101
of man in image of God, ... 238
of millions of *ācāryas* by
ISKCON, ... 263
of sects, ... 56
of us as eternal, ... 229
perfection of Kṛṣṇa's, ... 27, 192
with maintenance & destruction, .57,
239
without love, ... 27
Creator, Kṛṣṇa as, ... 229
Criminal activities
freeing the world from, ... 68
free to choose, ... 80
ISKCON dedicated to eradication
of, ... 273
met with prisons, ... 37
running rampant, ... 35, 184

D

Darkness, mode of. *See:*
Ignorance, mode of
Death
as one of fourfold
miseries,........................23,27, 30,
37,38, 80,176,184,221,232, 251, 257
bondage to, ... 73, 80,
193, 201, 215, 259
by cannibals, ... 36
chemicals not afraid of, ... 78
conditional consciousness arises
with, ... 106
consciousness at time of
purified, ... 27, 69, 223, 235, 241
conditioned, ... 69, 224
liberation from, ... 33,51,
64, 68, 73, 80, 102, 134-135,146,148,
178, 198, 207, 253
via *bhakti*, ... 178, 201
via Krishnatarian diet, ... 155
via liberated soul, ... 112, 201,
216, 223, 268
of fish on land, ... 225
personified, Kṛṣṇa as, ... 245

senses as network of paths leading to, ...152
suffering due to envy, ...127
Deity form(s) of Supreme Lord
Bhagavad-gītā purport on offering food to, ... 157
not an idol, ... 47-48, 250, 251, 252
Śrīmad-Bhāgavatam purport on worship of, ... 240
worship of augments chanting, ...142
Delusion. *See:* Illusion/delusion
Demigods
ācārya as representative of,...112-113
are not God, ... 95
authorized worship of, ... 95
satisfied by service to God, ... 95
considering name of equal to Kṛṣṇa's as offensive, ...145
held responsible for liberation of their dependents, ... 193-194
Kṛṣṇa as Supreme Lord of, ... 135
worshipers of, ... 89, 95
Demon(s)
annhilation of by Kalki, ...254
caste system of, ... 251
Kaṁsa as, ...120
struggling to be happy in dungeon of, ... 67
Departed ancestors, taking birth among, ...89
Designations, bodily
in garb of religion, ... 12, 68
Kṛṣṇa consciousness open to all regardless of, ...61
Lord transcendental to, ... 41
Desire(s)
adau śraddhā as, ... 164
at time of death, ... 13, 69
basic, ... 79
fire of, ... 114
for immortality being innate indicates eternality of self, ... 69
for many mouths, ears, ...146
for opposite sex, ... 214, 218
for real happiness, ...217
fulfilled by Kṛṣṇa, ... 209, 219
material, ...12, 14, 18, 37, 135, 143, 171, 187, 197, 221, 226, 244
mind as channel for, ... 71
need not be renounced, ... 162
of atheists, ...73
of ghosts, ...26
of Lord, ... 101, 157, 215, 233, 257
pure, ...1, 16, 19, 98, 112, 121, 129, 135, 157, 168, 186, 225, 243
spiritualized, ... 27, 162, 267
unfulfilled, ... 171
varieties of material bodies meant to fulfill, ... 14, 19, 20, 37
Detachment
from material sense gratification, ...68, 249
Determination
in *bhakti,* 150, 161, 176, 182, 187
Kṛṣṇa's response to, ... 187-188, 272
required for initiation, ...121
required from mental control, ... 139-140
Devotee(s) of Supreme Lord
ability to see Lord, ... 216, 237, 242
& *prasādam,* 155, 158, 255
as part of spiritual authority structure, ... 118-119, 135
as performers of inaction in action, ...171
as spiritual-revolutionary, ... 263
as *śaktyāveśa avatāra,* 95
attitude of, ... 179, 186-187, 198, 213, 223, 227
bereavement of association with, ... 185, 201
canvassing others to become,.222,268
celebration of Janmāṣṭamī by, ... 52
compared to worshipers of demigods, ...89
Dāruka as example of, ... 172

Deity form manifested for
sake of, ... 49
demigods as, ...95
desire of, ...163, 186-187, 253
difficulties in life of, ...30
effects of association with, ... 24
enthusiasm for becoming, ...48, 90, 187, 203
guidance of, ... 27, 110, 120, 170, 179, 207, 217 219
in beginning stages, ... 174
inclination of for a particular
service, ...77
in mood of *sakhyam*, ... 240
in spiritual world, ...210, 232, 241
ISKCON centers house, ... 4, 177
Kṛṣṇa's reciprocation with, ... 136
lifestyle options for, ...162, 244
looked down on by so-called
Christians, ...46
Lord's feature as, ...97, 140, 255, 273
Lord's instructions for, ...131, 202
naming of, ...235
Nārada Muni's appearance to, ...94
never feel helpless, ...30
never wants to merge, ... 31, 248
nurture love of Kṛṣṇa, ... 75-76
observance of Ekādasī by, ... 178
oneness of,............................. 64
pastimes of Kṛṣṇa for pleasure
of, ...241
patience of, ... 163-164
pleasure of, ...275
position of, ...257
relating with, ... 78, 111, 126, 135, 198, 246, 277
self-love of, ...183
set proper example, ... 26, 196
smiling face of, ...192
standards for being a serious, . 6, 125, 135-136, 150, 155, 178 190, 231
symptoms of advancement for, ...226
use of beads by, ...140
use of free will by, ... 75, 80, 218
worshipping/ serving, ...59, 180, 209, 214
Devotional service to Supreme Lord
as only means to approach
Kṛṣṇa, ... 156
as platform of free will, ... 218
beginning with tongue, ... 185
brings relief from material life, .57,80
desiring that everyone should
engage in, ...267, 274
engaged in by wise persons, ...206
exchange of love in, ...277
four verses for perfection of, .160-161
frees one of karmic reactions, ...31, 81, 153
glorification of in Koran, ...58
gradual purification of, ... 160, 161, 167, 244
happiness resulting from, ...163
in *sakhyam*, ... 240
paramount importance of
attitude in, ... 179
practiced under proper guidance, .14, 70, 164, 216
revives one's transcendental
vision, ...120
while working a job, ...196
Disciple(s).
See: Disciplic succession(s); Spiritual master(s)
Disciplic succession(s)
four authentic lines of, ...259
knowledge transmitted via, ...38, 118, 190
placement in as qualification
for bona fidelity, ... 129
pleasing Kṛṣṇa through, ... 126
Disease
& medicine,........... 36, 37, 138, 259
as part of fourfold miseries, ... .23, 27,30, 37, 38, 80, 176, 184, 221, 232, 251, 257
of body, ... 171
of mind, ...24, 37

spiritual master suffering from, ... 126
Distress. *See:* Suffering
Dualities
escaping material condition of, .21,35
perception of without oneness incomplete, ... 248-249
Duplicity
as result of greed for wealth, ... 190
guarding against via skepticism, .. 108
Duty (duties)
Arjuna's confusion about, ... 111
of father, ... 272
of guru, ... 124, 130
of Indians, ... 276
of Śrīmatī Māyādevī, ... 10
prime, ...1, 30, 37, 65, 114, 129, 162, 197, 200, 253, 258
pursuance of granting authority, .. 48, 130
right to perform, ... 74
secondary, ...30, 37, 195, 197, 200, 210, 259

E

Earth element. *See:* Element(s)
Earth planet
at end of Kali-yuga, ... 253
Hastināpura as former capital of, .276
Kṛṣṇa's descent to, ... 53-54, 241, 246, 253
living in harmony with, ... 39, 55, 174, 183
Lord Brahmā residing outside of, .. 99
Mahārāja Ikṣvāku as king of, ... 91
Eating
appetite for, ...233
enough to keep body & soul together, ...226
Mādhavendra Purī uninterested in, ...143
of fellow human beings, ...254
of food offered in sacrifice, . 159, 160, 171, 255
of meat, ... 6, 15, 46, 121, 129, 133, 191, 194, 199, 208, 227,260,272
of too much grain by hen, ... 248-249
of vegetables, ...155
Economic development.
See: Occupation(s); Wealth
Ecstatic symptoms
cause of, ... 77
in stage of *bhāva*, ...168
of Dāruka, ... 172
via preaching, ...265
Education
Bhagavad-gītā as, ...261
in subject of Kṛṣṇa consciousness, ...202
saṅkīrtana as, ... 263
Ego
defined, ... 73
false. *See:* False ego
Ekādasī, 167
simplest form of, ... 178
Element(s), material
as less tangible than spirit, ...238
Kṛṣṇa's body transcendental to,.... 238
listed, ...19
Energy (energies)
focusing on Kṛṣṇa, ...61, 142, 163, 172, 192, 197
material, ... 14, 19, 28, 84, 80, 147, 242, 276
attraction to, ... 133
declaring war on, ...93, 176, 198
devotee not influenced by, ... 226
purpose of, ...37, 79
skepticism of, ...34
origin of,.................. 81, 94, 101, 222
spiritual, 8, 17, 20, 49, 69, 95, 146, 150, 166
Enjoyment. *See:* Happiness; Sense gratification
Enlightenment. *See:* Devotional service
Envy
as sixth enemy, ... 147

of devotees, ... 112, 135
of Kṛṣṇa, ... 127, 229
pacification of, ... 274
resulting from intoxication, ... 190
Equanimity
of devotee, ... 226
of *karma*, ... 191
of Kṛṣṇa, ... 42, 208
Evolution
of consciousness, ... 19, 33
of species, ... 14, 16, 151
Example, necessity of, ... 26, 57, 196
Existence, Kṛṣṇa as
cause of, ... 57, 101, 105, 205, 207, 238
Expansions of Lord. *See:*
Kṛṣṇa, expansions of;
Supreme Lord, incarnations of

F

Faith
as non-sectarian, ... 59
as not blind, ... 44, 106
in the Holy Name, ... 135, 146
in spiritual life, ... 30, 113, 118, 167, 187, 226
result of, ... 2
lack of, ... 25, 190
observance of Ekādasī with, ... 178
preliminary form of, ... 164
processes of strengthening, ... 25, 130, 177
Falldown
caused by imitation of great
transcendentalists, ... 179
of disciple, affecting spiritual
master, ... 125
of soul from spiritual world, ... 152
picking yourself up after, ... 182
False ego
as cause of criticism, ... 135
as constituent of material
body, ... 19, 22, 71
when being corrected, ... 171
Fame
as opulence of Kṛṣṇa, ... 29, 38, 207
as weapon of Māyādevī, ... 10
used in Kṛṣṇa consciousness, ... 162
Family (family life)
in agrarian economy, ... 39
Kṛṣṇa consciousness
in, ... 196, 198, 200, 208
name Kṛṣṇa implying
intimate mood as in, ... 109
Faultfinding
avoided by honest disciple, ... 122
impossible toward a devotee, ... 226
Fear
freedom from, 21, 60, 216, 224, 274
of global warming, ... 184
of one's true identity, ... 164
Field of activities, conception
of doer in, ... 80
Fighter(s). *See: Kṣatriyas*
Fire
as element, ... 19
compared to *sādhana*, ... 175
of love, ... 75
of material existence, ... 31, 39, 114, 135, 173, 273
Fish
eating, forbidden, ... 6, 151, 153, 155, 157, 159, 170, 178, 180, 225, 255
out of water, ... 29, 225
incarnation of Lord as, ... 91
Food
appetite for, ... 232-233
dependency on rain for, ... 247
living entities as, ... 32, 151, 155
meat as, ... 46, 175, 191
offered to idols, ... 48
offered to Kṛṣṇa, ... 6, 139, 160, 166, 170, 178, 191, 208, 255
quota of, ... 183
reflection of, ... 133
symbolized as poison, ... 179
thanking God for, ... 150

Foolishness
application of skepticism to direct experience of Supreme as, ... 34, 109
considering oneself God as, ...78-79
desire to be center as, ...79, 241
faultfinding as, ... 127
identification with body as, ... 71
pursuit of material happiness as, ... 67
sticking hand in fire as, ...31
suicide as, ...26
trying to extinguish individual existance as, ... 66
trying to make God sectarian as, ... 41
Forefathers. *See:* Ancestor(s)
Forgetfulness. *See:* Illusion; *Māyā*
Forgiveness
blocked by pride, ... 30
originating in Kṛṣṇa, ... 53
asking Kṛṣṇa for, ... 158
See also: Compassion, Mercy, Offenses
Fortune of human birth, ... 15
Freedom from material world & desires. *See:* Detachment; Liberation
Free will & independence
& doer, ... 80
& *karma*, ...218
& Kṛṣṇa's plan, ... 23, 27, 74
as basis of love, ... 26, 31
misuse of, ...32
Friendship
as relationship with Kṛṣṇa, ... 67, 109, 165, 230, 241
comparison of material & spiritual, ...75
conditional, ...186
as characteristic of devotee, ... 226
Fruitive activity (activities)
being unaffected by, ...119, 198, 213
child-rearing as, ... 272
condemned, ... 95
day as time for, ...138
described in Koran, ...57
differentiated from chanting the holy names, ...145
from past as cause of present situation, ...15-16, 38, 144
inclinations according to, ... 184
in inaction, ...171
offering result of to Lord Kṛṣṇa, ... 199
renouncing, ...135
self as non-doer of, ...74
social position partially determined by, ...258

G

Gambling, disadvantages of,.............................. 6, 121, 129, 133, 139, 178, 180,190, 199, 228, 272
Ganges River, devoted mind compared to, ...181
Garuḍa & sparrow, ... 187
Ghost(s)
Birth as, ...26
Desires of, ... 26
Kṛṣṇa consciousness frees from influence of, ... 194
Worship of, ... 89
Gītā. See: Bhagavad-gītā
Goal of life as pure devotional service, ...29, 57, 70, 158
God. *See:* Absolute Truth; Kṛṣṇa
God consciousness. *See:* Kṛṣṇa consciousness
Godhead, returning to
choosing path of, ... 221
concocted religious systems won't help with, ...51
devotional love for the Supreme as a matter of, ...106
Ekādasī's role in, ... 178
everyone will sooner or later earn, ... 27
fixed determination for, ...176
guardians must provide access

to for dependents, ...259, 272
impossible if you run away
from the truth, ... 38
not possible by remembering
past lives, ... 18
requires testing, ... 24
Śrī Īśopaniṣad Mantra 11 on, ...196
those in pure goodness are prepared
for, ...68
those serious about becoming
Krishnatarian, ... 155
those serious about surrender
to spiritual master, ...201
via a liberated soul only, ... 110, 231
via chanting, ... 9, 30, 102, 135, 146
via human birth, ... 16, 21
via preaching, ...272
via surrender to Kṛṣṇa, ... 13, 17,
22, 27, 36, 64, 80, 148
via *sādhana-bhakti*, ...178, 187, 188
with the author, ... 11
words of Kṛṣṇa fully potent
for, ...216
Gods. *See:* Demigods
Goodness, mode of
early morning as time of, ... 138
freed from passion & ignorance, ... 68
chanting leading to, ... 146
raising children as activity in, ...272
along with passion & ignorance, ..85,
236
Gopīs,
beads representative of, ...143
Gosvāmī(s)
chanting by, ... 143
Rūpa, ...146, 167, 179, 277
six, ...244
Govardhana
expanded in Australia, ...243
potency of, ... 246
Government(s)
blind, ...68
funding of Christianity, ... 262
lawful citizens & criminals
both dependent on, ...74
police officer as good as, ...48, 130
weak, ...63
Gravity as quality of a devotee, ... 226
Gṛhasthas. See: Family life,
Varṇāśrama-dharma system
Guṇas. See: Modes of material nature
Guru. See: Spiritual master(s)

H

Hanumān
example of, ...257
as great personality, ... 135
Happiness
& austerity in Kṛṣṇa
consciousness, ... 166
bewildering of Māyāvādīs by, ... 232
detachment from, ...35, 163
enabled by Kṛṣṇa, ...242
in *varṇāśrama-dharma* system, ... 251,
258
loss of, ... 37, 67, 214
of Lord, as purpose of living
entities' existence, ...75
of mother sparrow, ... 187
of the author, ... 2, 3, 4, 56,
57, 87, 90, 98, 107, 145,148,166,169,
172, 180, 181, 193, 214,215,233,256,
274, 276
realization of, ... 3, 20, 27, 52,
58, 75, 87, 98, 122, 126,160,173,198,
204, 208, 211, 217, 249
for whole world, ...174, 194, 263, 254
Hare Kṛṣṇa *mantra* quoted, ... 4, 5, 28,
50, 54, 73, 109, 133, 140, 146
Haridāsa Ṭhākura, ...57, 143, 179, 181
Hate indicative of state of
illusion, ... 69, 227
Health
& sickness, ...35
meat &, ...191
spiritual & material, ... 37, 95, 200,
233, 253, 259

Hearing
  & chanting,.6, 30, 136, 168, 186, 231
  as one of nine processes of *bhakti*, ... 165
  as part of *ekādasī-vrata*, ... 178
  by Lord of His devotees words, ...157
  learning by, ... 191
  of Arjuna, ... 197
  prayer for, ... 38
  reading as, ... 179
  submissively, ... 43, 212
  taste for, ... 164, 165, 180
Heart
  anarthas in, ... 39, 62, 147, 173
  compared to courtyard, ... 146
  compared to garden, ... 139
  compared to hotel, ... 168
  compassion in, ... 26, 202, 208
  dedication of as meaning purpose & value of life, ... 10
  devotees in, ... 201
  effect of instructions on, ... 116
  feeling spiritual world to be home in, ... 147
  Lord present in, ... 44, 83, 102, 201, 212
  love of God within, ... 4, 27, 110, 115, 134, 168, 170, 181
  purification of, ... 197-198
  rectification of, ... 127, 144, 151, 197-198
  self within, ... 73
  softening of by *bhāva*, ... 168
  Vedic knowledge within, ... 6
  worshiping Lord with, ... 37, 206, 214, 215
Heavenly planets
  as within material world, ... 89
  of Lord Brahmā, ... 100
  process of going to, ... 89
Hellish planets as within material world, ... 21
Heroic mood, ... 186
Historical literature. *See: Bhagavad-gītā, Purānas, Śrīmad-Bhāgavatam*
History
  challenges for spiritual revolutionaries in, ... 204
  existence beyond limits of, .. 237, 262
  erroneous doctrines of propagated, ... 255
  highlight for all of, ... 275
  incarnations in, ... 95
  most empowered *ācārya* in, . 190, 255
  spiritual masters in, ... 43, 54, 55, 95, 117, 206, 243, 257, 275
Holy day(s)
  Ekādasī as, ... 167, 178
  similarity of, ... 52
Holy place(s)
  residence in as item for *bhakti*, ... 167
Honesty
  as insufficient for accessing Absolute Truth, ... 84
  in the author's presentation of Kṛṣṇa consciousness, ... 131, 222
Honor
  felt by the author, ... 131
  given to everyone, ... 42
  given to the four regulative principles, ... 186
  given to *guru*, ... 130, 276
  given to photographs of God, ... 237
  given to *prasādam*, ... 52, 154, 159
  given to scriptures, ... 135
  given to viceroy, ... 48
Householder life. *See:* Family life
Human being(s)
  among various forms of life, ... 12, 16
  ascending to form of, ... 12, 16, 33, 150, 151
  connecting with, ... 60
  decency of, ... 151
  dependency on rain, ... 247
  dietary needs of, ... 156, 157, 175, 183, 191
  form in spiritual world, ... 237

law books for, ... 275
most important question in
life of, ... 1, 49, 108
perfecting existence of, ... 39, 62
personal/social nature of, ...256
prime duty of, ... 18, 129
problems in society of, ...62, 63, 64, 149, 173, 227, 252, 254
relationship with animals, ... 124
serving demands of, ...64
spiritual life as highest service to, . 49
transforming society
of, ...39, 55, 135, 174, 197,202, 203, 263, 264, 270, 273,274
Humility
& chanting, ...146, 183
& self-esteem, ... 183
as qualification of offering
to Kṛṣṇa, ...157
as qualification of *guru*, ...129
development of as evidence of
advancement, ... 176
development of as purpose of
material world, ...27
of the author, ... 49, 56, 59, 113, 117

I

Ignorance
Absolute Truth transcendental
to, ...109
& free will, ...21
& concept of different religions, ...42
& depression, ...93
as bliss, ...21
as characteristic of material
life, ...56, 74, 79, 84, 132, 236
as disqualification for confidential
aspects of devotional service, 267, 268
body as lump of, ... 152
chanting Hare Kṛṣṇa &, ... 268
deliverance from, ... 61, 151, 268
feelings of helplessness as, ...30
Illicit sex. *See:* Sex, illicit
Illusion
as one of six enemies, ... 147
bondage to, ... 190, 227
concept of different religions
as, ...43, 55
freedom from as characteristic of
devotee, ...226
mixed with spiritual realization, 69
purpose of, ...37, 71
society influenced by, ... 68, 202
Śrīmatī Māyādevī, personification
of, ...15, 28, 78, 79, 93, 242
transcending, ... 11, 28, 56, 106, 202, 219
Immortality
qualification for, ...196
soul's attribution of, ...55, 64, 193
universal desire for as evidence of,. 69
Impersonalism
& imaginary liberation, ... 66
defined, ... 4
delineated in Koran, ...58
in action, ...166
limitations of, ...157, 171, 256
Incarnations. *See:*
Kṛṣṇa, incarnation(s) of
Income. *See:* Wealth
India
analogy using first trains in history
of, ...84
& Americans, ...271, 276
& caste system, ...251
& myth of Āryan invasion, .. 255, 262
Buddhism in, ...45, 248
compared to Kṛṣṇa, ... 70
duty of persons from, ...268, 277
false identification with, ... 73
misconception in, ... 105
position of British viceroy in
history of, ...48
spiritual masters throughout
history of, ...117, 260

the author's early aspiration
to go to, ...10
the author's preaching in, ... 192
Vedic civilization of,. 44, 55, 235, 248
Vṛndāvana in & beyond, ...241
Individuality
as eternal nature of
consciousness, . 64, 66, 67, 77, 78, 94
denied by Māyāvādīs, ...66
fear of, ...164
perfected by dovetailing with
Supreme, ...8, 9, 197
valued in *bhakti*, ...31, 131, 162
Infamy of Indians who neglect
their duty, ... 277
Inquiry
appreciated by the author, ...44, 49,
107, 118, 129, 145, 146
appropriate method of, . 85, 111, 118,
133, 161, 167, 217
from spiritual master for those
far from devotees, ... 185
joined with service, ...123
Intelligence
allowing for realization of miserable
conditions, ... 63
as part of subtle body, ...19, 22
as car driver, ... 33-34
as qualification of *brāhmaṇas*, ...258
as safeguard from *māyā*, ... 114, 190
contradistinct from mind, ...33-34
characteristics of one possessing,. 47,
169, 170, 188
dovetailing of in preaching, ... 36, 61,
222
highly focused, ...188
in prayer, ...144
judged epistemologically, ... 191
Kṛṣṇa as seen by those
who lack, ...245
lacking in demigod-
worshipers, ... 89, 95
lacking in leadership, ...63
lacking in sinners, ...216
material variety of, ...257
of student appreciated by
the author, ... 44, 223
requirement of Kṛṣṇa
consciousness for, ...156
skepticism &, ...109
satisfaction of in Kṛṣṇa
consciousness, ... 11
International Society for Krishna
Consciousness. *See:*
Kṛṣṇa consciousness movement
Intoxication
& four regulative principles, .. 6, 121,
129, 133, 178, 180, 194, 199,228,272
condemned in scripture, ...190
not an excuse for breaking law, ... 74
not recommended for
meditation, ...175
of the soul, ... 186, 190, 202
ISKCON. *See:*
Kṛṣṇa consciousness movement
Īśopaniṣad cited, ... 56, 69, 107,
196, 227, 234, 264

J

Janmāṣṭamī, ...52, 273
Japa
as hearing, ...179
as requirement for
initiation, ... 121, 129, 141, 142
before sunrise, ...119, 137, 138, 199
benefit of, ...141, 143, 194,
199, 228, 247, 249, 272
defined, ... 143
performed by pure
devotees, ... 143, 197
rounds of defined, ...148
techniques for,............. 137, 142, 144

Jesus Christ
as spiritual master,............. 44, 55, 59
compassion of, ... 52
obedience to, ...41, 42, 58, 115, 254

prayer of, ... 53
Jīva
defined, ... 68
fallen nature of, ... 67
in material world, ... 32, 155
in spiritual world, ... 245
originating from Kṛṣṇa, ... 70, 75
purpose of existence for, ... 75
relationships with Kṛṣṇa, ... 68, 245
See also: Conditioned soul(s); Living entity (entities)

K

Kali-Santaraṇa Upaniṣad cited, ... 50, 137, 138, 147
Kali-yuga, *yuga-dharma* in age of, ... 142
Kalki, Lord
activities of, ... 254
scheduled appearance of, ... 254
Kāma. *See:* Attachment; Desire, material
Kaṁsa, King, ... 106, 120, 245
Kandarpa (Cupid), Kṛṣṇa compared to, ... 231, 245
Karma
& chanting, ... 144, 145
& impersonalists, ... 171
& predestination, ... 218
applicable beyond material designations, ... 12
accepted on principle by Buddha, . 45
as cause of environmental disruption, ... 39
as determinate for financial situation, ... 24
as determinate for next body, ... 19
as determinate for sexual inclination, ... 184
as determinate for time of death, ... 19
as determinate for time spent in hellish planets, ... 21
concept of in Bible, ... 46-47
dedication to, ... 221
for killing, ... 33, 191
freedom from, ... 110, 171
as manifestation of God's love, ... 219
not to disrupt the minds of those attached to, ... 267
obedience to spiritual master not determined by, ... 110
of a *brāhmaṇa*, ... 251
of children, ... 15
of disciples taken by spiritual master, ... 125
of Kṛṣṇa, ... 213
of ghost, ... 26
of wealthy person, ... 38
Karmī(s). *See:* Materialist(s)
Kaṭha Upaniṣad cited, ... 33-34, 49
Keśava, Kṛṣṇa glorified as, ... 93
Killing
advocated by sectarian minds, ... 62
allowed under regulation, ... 155
of animals. *See:* Animals, killing under restriction
of demons by Kalki, ... 254
of everyone as inevitability, ... 33
of Kuvalayāpīḍa by Kṛṣṇa, ... 245
punishment for, ... 47, 151, 153, 155, 191
Kindness
of devotees, ... 95, 218, 272, 277
of Kṛṣṇa, ... 75, 85, 251
King(s)*See:*
Government(s); Kṣatriya(s);
Kingdom of God. *See:* Spiritual world
Kīrtana. *See:* Chanting
Knowledge
about Kṛṣṇa, ... 49, 274
advancement of, ... 128
& darkness, ... 132
& Paramātmā realization, ... 84
& skepticism, ... 108
as quality of *brāhmaṇas*, ... 251
assessment of, ... 260-261

Bhagavad-gītā as topmost, ... 50-51, 100, 261
experience of pain by those possessing, ... 25
fortitude of, ... 103
from Kṛṣṇa, ... 2, 4
from spiritual master, ... 5, 87, 117, 118, 123, 129, 135
Kṛṣṇa full of, ... 100, 240, 251
lacking at end of Kali-yuga, ... 254
of self, ...98
pure devotee full of, ... 17, 21, 27, 65, 72, 77, 80, 241
saṅkīrtana as life of, ... 134-135
speculative variety of, ... 57, 73

Kṛṣṇa abode of, ... 33, 67, 102, 147, 156, 164, 207, 213, 221, 226, 227, 230, 231, 241
acting for, ... 136, 171, 194, 199, 209
activities of. *See:* Kṛṣṇa, pastimes of
Arjuna's testament about, ... 207
as absolute truth, ... 101
as all-knowing, ...81, 116
as all-pervading, ... 48, 57, 86
as all-powerful, ... 74, 81
as beginning of everything, ...238
as beginningless, ... 238
as beyond the modes of nature, ... 75
as Bhagavān, ...105
as cause of all causes, ...99, 105, 135, 238
as controller, ... 23, 212, 232
as cowherd boy, ... 245
as creator, ...229
as deliverer of His devotee, . 8, 60, 85, 95, 103, 146, 216
as enjoyer, ... 27, 75, 78, 91, 94, 101, 106, 137, 150, 152, 154, 157, 228, 232, 242
as eternal, ... 1, 50, 56, 57, 70, 75, 78, 83, 101, 105, 229, 262
as everywhere. *See:* Kṛṣṇa, as all-pervading
as father, ...11, 30, 41, 48, 53, 55, 58, 59, 63, 144, 151, 193
as friend, ... 165
as goal of life, ... 58, 69
as Govinda, ... 98, 99, 105, 206, 216
as identical with Viṣṇu, ...109
as inconceivable, ... 53, 65, 72, 104, 136, 174, 211, 216, 249
as inexhaustible, ... 84
as Keśava, ...93
as life's origin. *See:* Kṛṣṇa, as origin
as limitless, ...17, 64, 72, 94, 103, 203, 207, 219, 231, 242, 245, 248, 254, 257, 268
as Lord, ... 10, 14, 54, 69, 83, 94, 96, 115, 126, 135, 142, 156, 164, 168, 216, 227, 250, 255, 275
as Lord in the heart. *See:* Supersoul
as Mahā-Viṣṇu, ...98
as maintainer, ...49, 234
as master, ... 80, 272
as most perfect name, ... 102
as Nārāyaṇa, ... 93, 224, 251
as *oṁ (oṁ-kāra)*, ... 230
as omnipotent, ... 86
as omnipresent, ... 48, 86, 151
as omniscient, ... 57, 81, 116
as one with & yet different from everything, ... 66, 104
as only person we can trust, ... 204
as origin of all, ... 57, 91, 98, 101, 102, 104, 205, 207
as orgin of Viṣṇu, ...95
as owner of all. *See:* Kṛṣṇa, as proprietor
as *paraṁ dhāma*, ... 207
as person, ... 41, 49, 62, 94, 102, 106
as Yogeśvara, ...272
attachment to, ... 164, 176

authority of, ... 14, 48, 71, 80, 260
beauty of, ... 207, 231
begging to, ... 134
Bhagavad-gītā spoken by, ... 5, 6, 10, 12, 13, 38, 42, 43, 46, 50, 71, 74, 82, 84, 85, 96, 104, 105, 113, 114, 123, 129, 140, 143, 149, 155, 159, 160, 169, 170, 179, 187, 188, 206, 207, 211, 213, 220, 247, 251, 255, 258, 260, 267, 269
blessings of, ...132, 178, 194, 204
body of. *See:* Kṛṣṇa, form(s) of
Brahman &, ... 84, 87
chanting names of, ...9, 121, 144, 148, 180, 197, 228, 247, 273
compared to India, ...70
compared to root of tree, ... 126
compared to thunderbolt, ...245
compassion of. *See:* Kṛṣṇa, mercy of
consciousness about. *See:* Kṛṣṇa consciousness
conscience directs one to, ...115
Dāruka's service to, ...172
Deity forms of. *See:* Deity form(s) of Supreme Lord
Demigod(s) &, ...89, 94, 95, 112, 135, 145, 194
Demon(s) &, ...67, 120, 251, 254
devotional service to, .. 12, 31, 57, 58, 69, 81, 120,135,153,156,164,167, 180, 185, 196, 206, 216,218,240,244, 267, 274, 276
disciple of, Vivasvān as, ... 91
disciplic succession &. *See:* Disciplic succession; Spiritual master(s)
dissolution by, ... 57
divinity of. *See:* Kṛṣṇa, as Supreme Lord
duality &, ...66, 106
earthly pastimes of. *See:* Kṛṣṇa, pastimes of effulgence of, ...231, 233, 234, 253
See also: Brahman
energies of. *See:* Energy, of Lord
envy of, ... 112, 127, 229
equality with
none have quantitative, ... 31, 27, 104, 106
qualitative, ... 17, 27, 57, 104, 248
equal disposition of, ...208
everything within, ...104, 249, 257
expanded as Supersoul. *See:* Supersoul
expansion(s) of, ... 27, 81, 90, 91, 94, 97, 98, 102, 106, 224, 236
See also: Kṛṣṇa, form(s) of; Kṛṣṇa, incarnation(s) of; Supersoul
faith in, ... 2, 25, 30, 42, 59, 62, 106, 112, 118,129, 135, 146, 167, 177, 188, 226
features of three, ... 84, 87, 260
flute of, ...53, 229, 231
food offered to. *See:* Kṛṣṇa, prasādam of
forgiveness of, ... 53, 158
form(s) of, ...49, 85, 97, 105,109,140,165, 192, 203, 224, 231, 234, 238, 251, 256
friends & playmates of, 228, 232, 245
glories of, ... 37, 52, 74, 91, 96, 135, 146, 153, 160, 170, 174, 178, 186, 230, 245, 265
Govardhana Hill &, ... 243, 246
human beings in image of, ...238
illusory energy of. *See:* Energy; *māyā*
imitation of, compared with obedience to, ...78
incarnation(s) of, ... 45, 91, 95, 97, 105, 251, 276
independence of, ...72
intelligence given by, ... 44
internal energy of, ...70, 97
in *Brahma-saṁhitā*, ... 100, 105, 206, 211, 216
in *Śrīmad-Bhāgavatam*, ... 105, 212
Kaṁsa &, ... 106, 120, 245

killing by, ... 245, 253
knowledge about, ... 127
literature about, ... 106
living entities &. *See:*
Living entities, Kṛṣṇa &
lotus feet of, ... 14, 24,57, 65,88, 115,121,148,150,162,165,198,227
reason for designation as, ... 29, 224
lotus mouth of, ... 231
love of, ... 176, 211
Mādhavendra Purī &, ... 143
meditation on, ... 234
memory of, ... 6, 25, 30, 38, 165, 168, 194, 223, 231, 243
mercy of, ... 8, 23, 28, 36, 37, 48, 59, 92, 123,146, 155,158,163,173, 194,197,203,208, 213, 217, 228, 230, 254, 259, 272.
See also: Kṛṣṇa, *prasādam* of
name(s) of, ... 1, 16, 29, 35, 38, 42, 42, 45, 55, 57, 60, 63, 65, 105, 109, 121, 133, 150, 165, 183, 184, 185, 197, 207, 215, 226, 230, 235, 252, 273.
See also: Chanting
obedience to, ... 38, 46, 267
obeisances to, ... 6, 92, 97, 161, 214, 257
offerings accepted by. *See:*
Kṛṣṇa, *prasādam* of
oneness of a pure devotee with, ...64
opulence(s) of, ... 57, 157, 240
parents of, ... 106, 228, 245
pastimes of, ... 17, 38, 94, 127, 165, 228, 232, 241, 246
perceivable only
spiritually, ... 84, 127, 249
pervading everywhere. *See:*
Kṛṣṇa, as omnipresent
planet(s) of, ... 67, 73, 81, 226, 227, 230, 231, 235, 241
prasādam of, ... 158, 170, 178, 185, 255
Rāma as name of, ... 137
reciprocation policy of, ... 104, 110, 219
remembrance of at time
of death, ... 223
representative of, ... 120, 123, 125, 129,130,162, 163, 166, 214, 216, 217
submission to, ... 121, 123
weapons of, ... 232
worship of, ... 45, 57,58, 95, 135, 160,162, 165, 206, 212, 216, 229, 231, 240, 257
in deity form, ... 142, 250, 251
Kṛṣṇa consciousness, ...7, 9, 17, 43, 28, 36, 41, 57, 69, 131, 140, 174, 177, 186, 196, 202, 220, 228, 246,267, 272
Kṛṣṇa consciousness
movement, ... 6, 7, 51, 121, 124, 129, 148, 177, 180, 194, 199, 259, 263
Kṛṣṇaloka. *See:*
Spiritual world
Kṣatriya, ... 186, 245
Kurukṣetra, ... 117, 262

L

Law. *See:*
Government(s); Vedas,
regulations of
Laziness, ... 67
Leader(s). *See:*
Government(s); *Kṣatriyas,*
Spiritual master(s)
Learning. *See:*
Education; Intelligence;
Knowledge
Liberation, ... 57, 64, 66, 112, 197, 232
Living entity (entities), ... 12, 14, 18, 26, 31, 57, 68, 70, 72, 81, 94, 114, 133, 135, 157, 191, 212, 227, 228, 273, 274
Living force. *See:*
Consciousness; Living

entity (entities)
Logical argument, ...42, 106, 151, 237, 249, 254
Lord, Supreme. *See:* Kṛṣṇa, Supreme Lord
Love for Lord, ...3, 23, 39, 41, 54, 76, 124, 134, 146, 163, 164, 170, 176, 207, 213, 215, 218, 226, 238
Lust, ...147, 168, 173, 184, 190, 214, 218, 245

M

Mādhavendra Purī, ...143
Mahā-Viṣṇu, ... 98, 224
Mammonism. *See:* Materialism
Mankind. *See:* Human being(s)
Marginal energy. *See:* Living entity (entities)
Marijuana, ... 175
Marriage, ... 201
Material desires. *See:* Attachment; Desires, material
Material energy. *See:* Energy, material
Materialism, ...59, 196, 271, 276
Materialists, ... 39, 205
Material world
  bodies produced to enjoy in, ... 12
  Durgā devī as superintendent of, . 248
  escape from, ... 16, 259
  fall into, ...241
  lotus flower in, ...230
  miseries of, ...23, 27, 38, 80, 176, 184, 221, 232, 251
  misunderstandings imposed by, ... 8
  no innocence in, ... 15
  original ego suppressed by, ...9
  purpose of, ... 23, 24, 27, 30, 32
  reality beyond, ... 11
  repeated birth in, ... 18, 19
  self-confidence in, ...257
  spiritual culture within, ...235
  Śrī Caitanya Mahāprabhu within, ...268
  Śrīla Prabhupāda's descent within, ...265
  trying to exploit, ... 259
Matter. *See:* Energy, material
Māyā, ...71, 74, 78, 85, 93, 228
Māyāvāda philosophy. *See:* Impersonalism
Māyāvādī(s). *See:* Impersonalist(s)
Meditation, ...3, 140, 142, 146, 243
Mercy. *See:* Kṛṣṇa, mercy of
Mind
  absorption of at time of death, ...13
  & chanting, ...134, 146, 197
    with beads, ...140
  & conscience, ... 115
  & faith, ...188
  & intelligence, ... 34
  as cause of suffering, ...37
  as covering of self, ...71
  as imperfect, ...128
  attracted to Kṛṣṇa, ...180
  engaged in thinking of Kṛṣṇa, ...109
    result of, ...6, 160, 257
  humble state of, ... 146, 183
  ineffective for going beyond itself, ...9
  in *brāhma-muhūrta,* 119, 137, 138
  in trance, ...87
  liberated, ...9
  of Dāruka, ... 172
  of impersonalists, ...256
  offering food in, ... 152
  pure, purer and purest, ...87, 260
  surrender of, ... 165, 209
Miscreant(s). *See:* Demon(s)
Miseries of life, ... 24, 27, 38, 80, 176, 184, 221, 232, 251
  See also: Suffering

Missionary work. *See:* Preaching
Mode(s) of nature, ... 84, 85, 93, 164, 228, 236, 259, 260
Modesty. *See:* Humility
Mokṣa. *See:* Liberation
Money. *See:* Wealth
Monism. *See:* Impersonalism
Moon, ... 135, 273
Morality, ... 45, 148, 272
Mother(s), ... 15, 17, 106, 130, 132, 134, 190, 194, 228, 259
Mountains, ... 77, 246
Mukti, ... 214
Murder, ... 15, 124, 151,153
Mystic Yoga. *See:* Yoga

N

Nārada Muni, ... 94,207
Nārāyaṇa, ... 91, 224, 251
Narottama Dāsa Ṭhākura, ... 243-244
Nature. *See:* Material nature
Nirguṇa worship, ... 248, 251
Nityānanda, Lord, ... 97, 153
Nondevotees. *See:*
Atheist(s); Demon(s);
Impersonalist(s); Materialist(s)
Nonviolence, ... 45
Nṛsiṁhadeva, Lord, ...203, 251

O

Obeisances, ...6, 92, 97, 130, 132, 161, 214, 257, 259
Objects of senses. *See:*
Sense objects
Obligation. *See:* Duty
Occupation(s), ... 162, 195, 200, 258
Ocean, ... 72, 101, 104, 187, 224, 233
Offense(s), ...146, 180
Old age, ... 23, 27, 38, 80, 176, 184, 221, 232, 251
Oṁ(kāra), ...230
Oṁ tat sat, ... 262
Opulence. *See:* Wealth
of Kṛṣṇa. *See:*
Kṛṣṇa, opulence(s) of
Origin of life. *See:*
Life, origin of

P

Pāda-sevanam, ... 165
Pain. *See:* Suffering
Pañca-tattva, ...97, 195
Paramātmā. *See:* Supersoul
Paramparā. See:
Disciplic succession
Passion, mode of, ... 84, 93, 137, 164, 236
Patience, ... 139, 182
Peace, ...4, 11, 25, 27, 30, 32, 37, 42, 107, 138, 146, 152, 174, 204, 209, 226, 249, 251
Perfection
devotees striving to achieve, ... 240
devotees who have achieved, ... 240
in all respects, ... 6, 118, 237, 252, 261, 264, 276
of *acintya-bhedābheda* philosophy, ... 248
of all paths, ... 3, 42
of comprehension that we are not this body, ...6
of *dharma,* 124, 252
of going back to Godhead, ... 235, 251
of ISKCON, ...51, 122
of knowledge, ...98, 117, 241
of Kṛṣṇa, ...107
of Kṛṣṇa's actions, ... 27, 271
of life, ... 31, 67, 102, 268
of loving affection, ... 4
of *samādhi,* 87
of science and philosophy, ...274
of seeing the Lord, ... 244, 245
of understanding, ...5, 90
of your dreams, ... 3

prayer for, ... 11
rarity of, ... 9, 68, 269
realization of Absolute
Truth, ... 8, 84, 87
relationship with spiritual
master continuing after, ...244
via chanting, ... 42, 50, 61, 73, 102
via spiritual master's guidance, ...6, 9, 13, 61, 83, 113, 114, 124
via surrender, ...14, 41, 64, 83, 113
Philosopher(s), ...66, 156, 157, 232
Lord as, ... 234
Philosophy, ...4, 24, 44, 54, 66, 106, 109, 164, 202, 225, 237, 248, 268, 274
Physical nature. *See:* Nature, material
Physician, spiritual master compared to, ... 130, 138
Piety, ...14, 39, 136, 145, 213
Pilgrimage sites, ...167
Planet(s), ...15, 67, 89, 135, 253
Pleasure. *See:* Happiness; Sense gratification
Poetry, ... 114
Possessiveness. *See:* Attachment
Power,.........................10,24,28,58,62, 85, 92, 141, 146, 186, 187, 214, 222, 268
Prabhupāda, Śrīla
as spiritual master, ... 10, 57, 113, 117, 122, 131, 133, 177, 190, 230, 275
as *ācārya* 124, 255
books of, ... 51, 185, 264
Prahlāda Mahārāja cited, ... 165, 203
Prāṇa, ... 68
Prasādam. See: Kṛṣṇa, *prasādam* of
Prayer(s), ...49
& action, ...247
as process of devotional service, .. 165
empowerment of, ...273
for effective preaching, ... 202
for honoring prasādam, ... 152, 157
for universal well-being, ... 274
from *Śrī Īśopaniṣad,* 234
in mood of surrender, ... 11, 49, 223
of child in womb, ...15
of Christ Jesus, ... 49, 53
of the author, ... 11, 38, 133
"oṁ ajñāna-timirāndhasya", ... 132
purpose of, ...75
to go back to Godhead, ...242
Preachers of Kṛṣṇa consciousness. *See:* Devotee(s)
Preaching, ...6, 113, 162, 191, 196, 228, 254, 268, 276
Prema. See: Love for God
Present age. *See:* Kali-yuga
Pride, ... 30, 171, 190
Priest(s). *See:* Sage(s)
Procreation, ...6, 178, 180
Punishment, ... 22
Purāṇa(s), ... 232, 248, 260
Pure devotee(s), ...24, 26, 31, 48, 58, 59, 90, 95, 97, 112, 130, 156, 163, 170, 180, 183, 186, 187, 202, 203, 210, 212, 216, 217, 227, 234, 237, 241, 244, 246, 249, 251, 254, 263
Pure devotional service, ... 12, 28, 160, 244, 274
Pure goodness, ... 68, 146
Purification, ...127, 157, 171, 241, 249, 267
Purity, ...9, 117, 129, 197, 251

R

Rādhārāṇī, ... 96, 153, 166, 244, 246
Rain, ... 208, 247
Rakṣa(s). See: Demon(s)
Rāmacandra, Lord, ... 91, 94
Rasas,............................... 67, 244, 245
Realization of God. *See:* Kṛṣṇa consciousness
Reflection, ... 76, 133, 214, 233

Regulative principles, ... 121, 167, 180, 186, 199, 220, 228, 249, 277
Reincarnation. *See:* Birth & death cycle; Transmigration of souls
Religion(s), ... 12, 35, 60, 216
birth in a particular, ... 12
principles of, ... 252
separated conceptions of,
manmade, ... 14, 42, 54, 60, 63, 206
spiritual platform of, ...13-14, 41, 42, 52, 62, 75, 124, 274
Religious principles. *See:* Religion, principles of
Remembrance, ...165, 168, 194, 223, 231, 235, 237, 243, 266
Renunciation, ... 10, 100, 166, 198, 200, 207,
Repetition, ... 116, 117, 120, 170, 176, 191, 221, 248
Residence, significance of, ...65, 67, 89, 231, 276
Respect, ... 42, 46, 49, 92, 112, 130, 132, 135, 146, 165, 171, 186, 214, 219, 226, 259, 276
Responsibility. *See:* Duty
Retirement. *See:* Renunciation
River(s), ...54, 139, 181, 184
Rounds, chanting of, ... 6, 30, 47, 119, 121, 129, 148, 178, 180, 195, 197, 220, 228, 249, 272, 273
Rūpa Gosvāmī, ... 179, 277

S

Sacrifice(s), ...135, 151, 155, 157, 247, 255
Sādhaka, ... 240
Sādhu(s), ... 64, 164
Sage(s), ...58, 181, 207, 246
Saguṇa worship, ... 248, 251
Saintly persons, ... 42, 58, 60, 64, 76, 119, 136, 182, 248, 257
Sakhyam, ... 165
Samādhi, ... 87
See also: Remembrance; Meditation
Saṁsāra. See: Birth & death cycle
Sankarshan, meaning of, ... 133
Saṅkīrtana, ... 173, 215, 249, 273
Sannyāsa. See:
Renunciation;
Varṇāśrama-dharma system
Sanskrit language, ... 6, 77, 99, 102, 128, 138, 154
Sat defined, ...262
Satisfaction, ... 5, 26, 133, 147, 152, 159, 167, 209, 215, 246, 249
Satya-yuga, ... 254
Schooling. *See:* Education
Science(s), ...42, 57, 61, 85, 91, 98, 103, 112, 131, 169, 181, 217, 219, 221, 235, 256, 260, 274
Scientist(s), ...42, 103, 108
Scriptural injunction(s). *See:* Regulative principles
Scripture(s), ... 58, 64, 112, 119, 123, 125, 135, 136, 146, 174, 180, 217, 232, 256
Vedic. *See:* Vedic literature
Seclusion, ... 198
Seed, ... 42, 46, 110, 217
Seeing, actually, ...56
Self. *See:* Living entities
Self-control, ...251
Self-realization, ...5, 19, 34, 41, 42, 62, 83, 129, 142, 164, 184, 207, 221, 235, 257, 259
Self-realized soul(s). *See:* Devotee(s); Liberated soul(s)
Sense gratification, ...60, 62, 68, 114, 135, 144, 168, 200, 204, 215, 218, 221, 232, 252, 276
Sense object(s), ... 20, 214, 220
Senses, ...26, 27, 34, 47, 62, 74, 87, 114, 128, 135, 146, 152, 157, 168, 176, 187, 214, 215, 226, 232
Service to Lord. *See:*

Sex, ... 6, 121, 129, 133, 178, 180, 182, 184, 194, 199, 215, 228, 272
Siddhas, ... 10, 68, 240, 269, 275
Silence, ... 179, 226, 268
Simplicity, ... 157, 182, 276
Sinful reactions, ...14, 60, 145, 216
Sinner(s). *See:* Demon(s); Materialist(s)
Śiva 90, 135, 145, 212, 248, 255
Slaughter of animals. *See:* Animals, killing under restriction
Sleep, ...9, 73, 143, 159, 178, 181
Society, ...128, 149, 162, 173, 174, 183, 191, 193, 247, 251, 258-260, 263, 274
  of devotees. *See:* Kṛṣṇa consciousness movement
Soldiers. *See: Kṣatriyas*
Souls. *See:* Living entities; Conditioned souls
Species of life, ...42, 151, 175, 183, 221
Speculation, ...38, 57, 87, 118, 128, 187, 255, 260
Speech, ... 35, 42, 95, 115, 117, 129, 170, 175, 215, 253, 268
Spirit, ...135, 168, 241
Spiritual body. *See:* Body (Spiritual)
Spiritualism. *See:* Religion
Spiritualists. *See:* Devotees; Sages
Spiritual knowledge. *See:* Knowledge
Spiritual life, ... 6, 42, 52, 111, 113, 116, 118, 121, 124, 178, 197, 199, 263
Spiritual master(s)
  acceptance of, ...114, 216
  & deity worship, ...251, 252
  & *dīkṣā,* 113, 114, 121, 125, 129, 148, 164, 167, 231, 235, 277
    purpose of requirements for, ... 121
  & *śikṣā,* 113
  as father, ...193
  as giver of spiritual name, ...235, 243
  as most confidential servant of Kṛṣṇa, ...48
  as physician, ...130, 138
  association with, ... 2
  eternal connection with, ... 223, 244
  faith in, ...2
  following in footsteps of, ...6, 140, 167, 198
  guidance of, ...12, 13, 24, 27, 34,36,61,87, 113, 114, 120, 130, 165, 197, 201, 221, 259, 260
  Haridāsa Ṭhākura as, ... 57
  honoring of, ... 48, 131, 132, 135, 276
  humility of, ... 130
  imitation of, ... 193
  importance of, ...42, 56, 113, 115, 129, 180
  Jesus Christ as, ...55
  karma taken by, ... 125
  knowledge presented by, ... 5, 6, 10, 37, 64, 125, 250, 256
    as scientific, ... 42, 130
    handed down, ...85, 117
    how to receive, ... 85, 118, 123, 130, 132, 160, 167, 207, 216, 217
  love of, ... 124, 277
  mercy of, ...86, 112, 125, 134, 217
  obedience to, ...69, 110, 114, 118, 121,126,125,134, 163, 164, 167, 201, 227, 259
    lack of, ... 145
  power of, ..25, 39, 110, 115, 116, 126
  putting trust in, ...204
  qualification of, ...112, 116, 119, 120, 124, 129, 194, 217
  sent by Lord, ...8, 109, 110, 123, 223
  separation from, ...132
  service to, ...123, 198, 265
  shelter of, ...37, 115, 116, 117, 121,125,129,130, 178, 194, 201, 216, 244, 259
    purpose of taking, ... 253

the author as, ... 130, 276
Śrīla Prabhupāda as, ...10, 57, 113, 117, 122, 131, 133, 177, 190, 230, 275
surrender to, ... 49, 110, 116, 121, 124, 209
Śvetāśvatara Upaniṣad &, ... 190
Spiritual sky. See: Spiritual world
Spiritual world, ...17, 18, 27, 29, 31, 32, 36, 59, 67, 78, 79, 127, 131, 147, 148, 161, 162, 192, 193, 201, 210, 213, 225, 228, 232, 235, 235, 237, 245, 246, 268
Splendor, ... 231
Śraddhā. See: Faith
Śravaṇam. See: Hearing
Śrīdhara Svāmī quoted, ... 229, 240
Śrī Īśopaniṣad. See: Īśopaniṣad
Śrīmad-Bhāgavatam cited, ... 6, 15, 22, 29, 32, 51, 67, 84, 87, 92, 99, 105, 114, 120, 125, 165, 178, 180, 189, 193, 194, 212, 214, 217, 232, 240, 241, 249, 253, 259, 274
Śruti. See: Hearing, Vedic literatures
Stars. *See:* Planets
Steadiness, ... 124, 125, 140, 157, 164, 226
Strength, ...46, 92, 148, 176, 221, 253
Subtle body. *See:* Body, subtle
Śūdras, ...258
Suffering(s), ...12, 16, 17, 20, 38, 37, 54, 68, 76, 80, 85, 98, 106, 110, 126, 125, 151, 153, 162, 184, 196, 197, 202, 203, 208, 213, 225, 257, 275
Sun, ... 42, 60, 75, 101, 128, 138, 139, 180, 228
Sun-god. *See:* Vivasvān
Supersoul, ...44, 84, 86, 245
Supreme Being. *See:* Kṛṣṇa
Supreme Brahman. *See: Brahman*
Supreme destination. *See:* Godhead, returning to; Spiritual world
Supreme Lord. *See:* Kṛṣṇa; Viṣṇu, Lord; Supersoul
Supreme Personality of Godhead. *See:* Kṛṣṇa
Surrender to Lord, ...1, 14, 21, 28, 41, 48, 49, 55, 59, 60, 69, 78, 85, 95, 104, 111, 117,121, 125, 129, 148, 150, 162, 165, 195, 198, 203, 204, 206, 227, 241
See also: Devotional service,
Surrender to pure devotees, .. 111, 114, 115, 120, 124, 129, 198, 220, 223, 252
Svāmī(s). See: Gosvāmī(s)
Śvetāśvatara Upaniṣad quoted, ... 2, 190
Śyāmasundara, Lord, ... 170, 211, 216
See also: Kṛṣṇa

T

Tapasya. See: Austerity; Renunciation
Teacher(s). *See:* Spiritual master(s)
Temple(s), ... 115, 143, 159, 178, 179, 192, 198, 207, 218, 224, 240, 250, 252
Ṭhākura, Haridāsa, ...143, 179
Thinkers, great. *See:* Sages
Threefold miseries. *See:* Suffering
Time, ... 17, 21, 49, 67, 71, 139, 146, 163, 197, 198
Time & place, ...59, 271
Tolerance, 146, ... 171, 251
Trance. *See:* Samādhi
Transcendence. *See:* Kṛṣṇa consciousness; Liberation
Transcendentalism. *See:* Devotional service; Kṛṣṇa consciousness; Self-realization; Yoga
Transcendentalist(s), ...84, 87, 143, 179, 215, 276
See also: Devotees; Sages; Yogīs
Transcendental knowledge. *See:* Knowledge, spiritual

Transmigration of soul(s), ...12, 17, 22, 86, 89
Trustworthiness, ...30, 204
Truth
absolute. *See:* Absolute Truth
relative, ... 225
Tyāga. See: Renunciation

U

Understanding. *See:* Knowledge
Universe(s), ... 4, 24, 190, 205, 215, 234, 243, 262, 274
Upaniṣads quoted, ...2, 34, 49, 56, 69, 107, 111, 137, 138, 190, 216, 227, 234, 264

V

Vaikuṇṭha, ...29, 67
Vaiṣṇava-aparādha. See: Offenses
Vaiṣṇava philosophy. *See:* Devotional service; Kṛṣṇa consciousness
Vaiṣṇavas. *See:* Devotee(s)
Vaiśya(s), ...258
See also: Business & *Vaiśyas*
Vandanam in Kṛṣṇa consciousness, ...165
Varṇāśrama-dharma system, ...258
Vāsudeva, ... 81, 181, 212
Veda(s), ... 20, 45, 92, 96, 115, 124, 145, 182, 216, 248, 259
Vedānta-sūtra quoted, ... 108
Vedic civilization. *See:* Āryan(s); Varṇāśrama-dharma system
Vedic injunction(s), ...111, 161, 216, 259, 260,
Vedic knowledge, ... 4, 10, 39, 86, 117, 118, 123, 127, 129, 135, 274
See also: Veda(s)
Vedic literature, ...2, 30, 46, 54, 95, 98, 106, 116, 120, 128, 138, 145, 151, 196, 248, 253, 259, 263, 276
Violence, ...32, 190, 193
See also: Eating, of meat
Virtue(s)
austerity as. *See:* Austerity
of *brāhmaṇa(s)*, ... 251
of charity. *See:* Charity
cleanliness as. *See:* Cleanliness
of compassion, ... 26, 85, 181, 187, 202, 222
of detachment. *See:* Detachment
determination as, ... 121, 139, 150, 161, 176, 182, 187
of equanimity. *See:* Equanimity
of faith. *See:* Faith
of fearlessness. *See:* Fearlessness
of forgiveness, ...30, 37, 158
of freedom
from anger, ... 171
from envy, ...274
from false ego, ... 73, 135, 171
of honesty, 84, 131, 222, 251
of humility. *See:* Humility
of intelligence. *See:* Intelligence
of kindness. *See:* Kindness
of memory. *See:* Memory
of mental discipline. *See:* Mind, discipline of
of nonviolence. See: Nonviolence
of patience. *See:* Patience
of peacefulness. *See:* Peacefulness
of purity. *See:* Purity
of religiousness. *See:* Religion
of renunciation. *See:* Renunciation
of resolution, ...188, 195
of respect, ...226, 259
of sacrifice. *See:* Sacrifice
of self-control. *See:* Self-control
of silence. *See:* Silence
of simplicity. *See:* Simplicity
of tolerance. *See:* Tolerance
of trustworthiness, ...204
of truthfulness. *See:* Truthfulness
of Vedic study. *See: Vedas*
of wisdom. *See:* Wisdom

Viṣṇu, Lord, ...50, 90, 91, 94, 99, 105, 109, 141, 145, 165, 187, 224, 254
Viṣṇu-tattva, ... 224
Viśvanātha Cakravartī Ṭhākura, ...114, 132, 217
Viśva-rūpa. See: Universal form.
Vivasvān, ... 91
Voidism. *See:* Impersonalism.
Vṛndāvana, ... 67, 73, 167, 192, 230, 235, 240, 241, 244, 245, 246, 276
vyavasāyātmikā intelligence, .. 114, 188

W

War, ...35, 43, 93, 176
Warriors. *See: Kṣatriyas*
Water, ...95, 122, 156, 170, 203
Wealth, ... 35, 86, 100, 133, 166, 190, 197, 207
Weapons, ...232
Weather, ... 186
Welfare work, ... 202, 286
  See also: Charity,
Western world, ... 10, 255, 271
Wife, ... 57, 132, 196, 229
Wind, ...103
Wisdom, ... 6, 26, 36, 56, 90, 107, 124, 130, 141, 248, 251, 252, 255, 258, 259, 262, 266
Wise men, ...47, 79, 206, 267
Women, ... 15, 17, 31, 34, 63, 177, 190, 260
  See also: Family life
Work, ...113, 119, 146, 152, 154, 162, 178, 187, 192, 194, 196, 200, 202, 203, 226, 251, 258, 267, 276
  See also: Fruitive activities; *karma*
Worker(s). *See:* Fruitive worker(s); *Śūdras*
Worship
  of Buddha, ...45
  of demigods, ...89, 94, 194
  of ghosts/spirits, ...89
  of Kṛṣṇa, ... 45, 57, 58, 95, 135, 160, 162, 165, 206, 212, 216, 229, 231, 240, 257
  Deity of, ... 142, 251, 252
  of *nirguṇa* Brahman, ... 248
Wrath. *See:* Anger

Y

Yamadūtas, ... 22
Yamarāja, ...21-22,
Yaśodā, ...228, 245
Yoga, ...128, 187,
  bhakti, ... 10, 128, 163, 164, 187, 233, 244, 274.
  See also: Devotional service
Yogeśvara, ...272
Yogī(s), ... 84, 142, 178, 245
Yuga, ...63

Guide to Sanskrit Pronunciation

Throughout the centuries, the Sanskrit language has been written in a variety of alphabets. The mode of writing most widely used throughout India, however, is called *devanāgarī*, which literally means "the city writing of the devas, or gods." The *devanāgarī* alphabet consists of forty-eight characters, including thirteen vowels and thirty-five consonants. The ancient Sanskrit grammarians arranged the alphabet according to concise linguistic principles, and this arrangement has been accepted by all Western scholars. The system of transliteration used in this book conforms to a system that scholars in the last fifty years have almost universally accepted to indicate the pronunciation of each Sanskrit sound.

The short vowel **a** is pronounced like the **u** in b**u**t, long **a** like the **a** in f**a**r, and short **i** like the **i** in p**i**n. Long **ī** is pronounced as in p**i**que, short **u** as in p**u**ll, and long **u** as in r**u**le. The vowel **ṛ** is pronounced like the **ri** in **ri**m. The vowel **e** is pronounced as in th**ey**, **ai** as in **ai**sle, **o** as in g**o**, and **au** as in h**ow**. The **anusvāra** (**ṁ**), which is a pure nasal, is pronounced like the **n** in the French word *bon*, and **visarga** (**ḥ**), which is a strong aspirate, is pronounced as a final **h** sound. Thus **aḥ** is pronounced like **aha**, and **iḥ** like **ihi**.

The guttural consonants - **k**, **kh**, **g**, **gh**, and **ṅ** - are pronounced from the throat in much the same manner as in English. **K** is pronounced as in **k**ite, **kh** as in Ec**kh**art, **g** as in **g**ive, **gh** as in di**g h**ard, and **ṅ** as in si**n**g.

The palatal consonants - **c**, **ch**, **j**, **jh**, and **ṇ** - are pronounced from the palate with the middle of the tongue. **C** is pronounced as in **ch**air, **ch** as in staun**ch h**eart, **j** as in **j**oy, **jh** as in he**dgeh**og, and **ñ** as in ca**ny**on.

The cerebral consonants - **ṭ**, **ṭh**, **ḍ**, **ḍh**, and **ṇ** - are pronounced with the tip of the tongue turned up and drawn back against the dome of the palate. **Ṭ** is pronounced as in **t**ub, **ṭh** as in ligh**t h**eart, **ḍ** as in **d**ove, **ḍh** as in re**d-h**ot, and **ṇ** as in **n**ut.

The dental consonants - **t**, **th**, **d**, **dh**, and **n** - are pronounced in the same manner as the cerebrals but with the forepart of the tongue against the teeth.

The labial consonants - **p**, **ph**, **b**, **bh**, and **m** - are pronounced with the lips. **P** is pronounced as in **p**ine, **ph** as in u**ph**ill, **b** as in **b**ird, **bh** as in ru**b h**ard, and **m** as in **m**other.

The semivowels - **y**, **r**, **l**, and **v** - are pronounced as in **y**es, **r**un, **l**ight, and **v**ine respectively. The sibilants - **ś**, **ṣ**, and **s** - are pronounced, respectively, as in the German word *sprechen* and the English words **sh**ine and **s**un. The letter **h** is pronounced as in **h**ome.